WOMEN
OF THE
FAR RIGHT

Glen Jeansonne

WOMEN OF THE FAR RIGHT

The Mothers' Movement and World War II

THE UNIVERSITY OF CHICAGO PRESS

Chicago and London

GLEN JEANSONNE is professor of history at the University of Wisconsin—Milwaukee. He is the author of *Race, Religion, and Politics: The Louisiana Gubernatorial Elections of 1959–60* (1977); *Leander Perez: Boss of the Delta* (1977); *Gerald L. K. Smith: Minister of Hate* (1988); *Messiah of the Masses: Huey P. Long and the Great Depression* (1993); and *Transformation and Reaction: America, 1921–1945* (1994).

The University of Chicago Press, Chicago 60637
The University of Chicago Press, Ltd., London

©1996 by The University of Chicago
All rights reserved. Published 1996
Printed in the United States of America

05 04 03 02 01 00 99 98 97 96   1 2 3 4 5

ISBN: 0-226-39587-1 (cloth)

Library of Congress Cataloging-in-Publication Data

Jeansonne, Glen, 1946–
    Women of the far right: the mothers' movement and World War II/
Glen Jeansonne.
        p.   cm.
    Includes bibliographical references and index.
        1. Women—United States—Societies and clubs—History—20th
century.   2. Neutrality—United States—Societies, etc.
3. Neutrality—United States—History—20th century.   4. Women
radicals—United States—History—20th century.   5. Right-wing
extremists—United States—History—20th century.   6. United States—
Politics and government—1933–1945.   I. Title.
HQ1904.J4   1996
305.4′06′073—dc20   95-35974
                                                                    CIP

⊚ The paper used in this publication meets the minimum requirements of the American National Standard for Information Sciences—Permanence of Paper for Printed Library Materials, ANSI Z39.48–1984.

To Michael Gauger

═ CONTENTS ═

ILLUSTRATIONS

═══ PREFACE ═══

W*omen of the Far Right* is an outgrowth of two decades of research on twentieth-century American politics, work that began with my Ph.D. dissertation. Reared in Louisiana, an idiosyncratic state where politics is a more popular spectator sport than football, I wrote my dissertation on the life of Leander H. Perez, one of the state's leading bosses. That study, subsequently published, led to biographies of Gerald L. K. Smith and Huey P. Long, other Louisiana political figures with national influence. Like Perez, Smith was a reactionary of the right. Long had traits of the right and the left, yet he shared some traits with Perez and Smith, two of his lieutenants.

All three biographies, and this book, are critical of their subjects. When asked, "Why write about people you dislike?" I can simply answer that the far right fascinates me. Often, however, I respond that one's intellectual diet is enhanced by variety, which includes digesting some ideas that one dislikes. Balanced history requires studies of villains, heroes, and those who combine heroic attributes with tragic flaws. Further, individuals who are heroes to some are villains to others. Nonetheless, it is not essential for one to agree with one's subjects to understand them. Sharing an identity with one's subject—gender, race, or nationality—might enhance empathy, but it is not a prerequisite to writing a fair book (indeed, it might prejudice one in favor of the subject). One of the more penetrating studies of American democracy, for example, was written by the Frenchman Alexis de Tocqueville.

At first, I intended to trace far-right women from the 1930s to the 1980s. I found little evidence of such women after World War II, however, at least not on the scale of the 1930s movement. Yet people who had not done research on the far-right women of the 1930s wanted a book more like the one I had planned originally. This reminded me of the problem Rick Nelson described in his song "Garden Party." His audience at the party wanted to hear the songs that evoked memories of when he had been Ricky Nelson in the happy family of the *Ozzie and Harriet* television show. But Rick Nelson had matured and changed; he wanted to sing other songs. Nelson concluded that since he could not please everyone, he might as well please himself.

I do not agree entirely with Nelson—after all, a historian hoping to be widely read must write for more than personal gratification—although I can understand his feelings, for I could not accommodate those who wanted me to put the 1930s movement into the context of contemporary women conservatives, or of feminism. *Women of the Far Right* is not a study of conservatives. These women had only limited relevance to mainstream conservatism, in their times or now. Such terms as "extremists," "bigots," and "reactionaries" properly describe them. They contradict those feminist scholars who consider right-wing women insincere or mere pawns of men. Nor does the movement fit within the parameters of feminism, as I will show.

Some might object to the use of the word "mothers" and the phrase "mothers' movement" in referring to the isolationist women and their groups. I do not intend to imply that these women were typical mothers. Yet "mother" is appropriate because many of the women were mothers who based their agitation upon maternal arguments against war. The participants themselves used "mother" to define the movement. Those who monitored and opposed the movement, including journalists, commentators, the Federal Bureau of Investigation (FBI), politicians, and Jewish organizations, likewise used this description.[1]

Women of the Far Right posed organizational problems because I knew a little about various leaders of the movement but not a great deal about any individual. I could not write detailed biographical profiles, so I decided to integrate the stories of the leaders with their organizations. My introduction and conclusion establish a context for the mothers and analyze the movement. The middle chapters combine a narrative of one or more groups with

---

1. See Sonya Michel, "American Women and the Discourse of the Democratic Family in World War II," in *Behind the Lines: Gender and the Two World Wars*, ed. by Margaret Randolph Higgonet et al. (New Haven, Conn.: Yale University Press, 1987), 154–67.

On the subject of terms, I think Laura McEnaney's otherwise excellent M.A. thesis creates confusion by using "America First" to describe the mothers. This blurs the distinctions between the mothers' movement, the America First Committee and Gerald L. K. Smith's America First Party. First, the mothers' membership overlapped with that of the two male-dominated organizations, yet the mothers' movement was female-dominated. Second, the committee dissolved after Pearl Harbor, unlike the mothers' groups. Third, the party was not organized until 1943, well after the mothers peaked. In addition, McEnaney employs "family altar," which Smith used to describe the religious life of his family, as a metaphor for the mothers. But Smith never used the term to describe activities outside his family and none of the mothers used such a term. See McEnaney, "Defending the Family Altar: Gender, Race, and Family Politics in the America First Movement, 1940–45" (M.A. thesis, University of Wisconsin—Madison, 1990), and "He-Men and Christian Mothers," *Diplomatic History* 18:1 (winter 1994), 47–57. On Smith's activities during World War II and his relationships with the mothers' leaders, see Glen Jeansonne, *Gerald L. K. Smith: Minister of Hate* (New Haven: Yale University Press, 1988), chapters 4 and 5.

an interpretation of the principal figures. I compare and contrast the groups and leaders, examine regional variations, and discuss the ideology and activities of the movement. The epilogue is an analysis of prejudice, especially anti-Semitism, emphasizing anxiety as a contributing factor. I try to show the implications of my ideas for combating bigotry.

An additional problem in writing this book was a paucity of information, in primary as well as secondary sources. Only Elizabeth Dilling and Cathrine Curtis left papers, which reveal nothing about their private lives. Oral history proved infeasible. No membership lists existed in the public domain to guide me to living participants, and because most of these would have been in their nineties, their recollections would likely have been vague, limited, and of dubious credibility. I contacted relatives of the participants, to no avail. Most were children during World War II, dimly aware of their mothers' activities, and they consider the movement an embarrassment that should not be publicized. Kirkpatrick Dilling, for instance, refused to cooperate with me, fearing that an academician's book would be hostile to his mother's views (an understandable concern).

The chief sources were investigative reports compiled by the federal government and organizations such as the American Jewish Committee, the Anti-Defamation League of B'nai B'rith, and the American Jewish Congress, but these contain nothing about the mothers before or after their isolationist crusades. The transcript of the 1944 mass sedition trial, in which Dilling was a defendant, was consulted, yet like FBI records, it had to be used carefully because of questions about its reliability. Other papers and reports were found in the Minnesota Historical Society.

Newspaper articles provided facts, although the accounts were repetitious and included little analysis. The books of investigative journalists such as Avedis Derounian were used prudently.[2] Sometimes written in a hyperbolic style, these works contained only brief accounts of various women and few details about individuals.

Still, problems of organization, source limitations, and the stress of writ-

---

2. Leo P. Ribuffo suggests that historians should use the works of journalists cautiously because these writers often exaggerated the threat of the far right and made factual errors. Ribuffo's advice is well taken, although it is possible to use such works by verifying their reliability with other sources. In almost every case in which I cite a book such as *Under Cover* (or government investigative reports, of which one also should be skeptical), the information is corroborated by several sources. Most of the material in this book is corroborated by a variety of sources.

On Ribuffo's point about sources, see Ribuffo, *The Old Christian Right: The Protestant Far Right from the Great Depression to the Cold War* (Philadelphia: Temple University Press, 1983), 189–93.

ing were less worrisome than my conclusions. Particularly troubling were my reflections on the scope of anti-Semitism and my pessimism, expressed in the epilogue, about efforts to fight prejudice.

After twenty years as an academic historian, several religious metamorphoses, and almost a decade of marriage to a theologian, I have concluded that God created the world to confound humanity and that historians are his or her accomplices after the fact. With this book, I might have made a modest contribution toward that end.

$\equiv$ ACKNOWLEDGMENTS $\equiv$

My principal intellectual and personal debts for this book are owed to Michael Gauger, a former student of mine at the University of Wisconsin—Milwaukee, who combined the best qualities of an editor, a historian, and a friend. There are few persons who combine Michael's knowledge of American history with his sense of how to organize a manuscript, and his keen eye for factual and logical errors. During a busy and stressful time in his life, he devoted much of his energy to helping me research, polish, and revise the manuscript. Like his unflagging encouragement, his editorial and academic skills were crucial to the development of the book.

I owe intellectual and personal debts to Sharon Pace Jeansonne, my partner in this book as well as in my life. A sympathetic and astute critic of my work, Sharon offered advice for revisions. During a hectic time in her academic career, she spent two weeks helping me conduct primary research at the Blaustein Library of the American Jewish Committee in New York City, identifying and photocopying important material. Sharon also assisted my study of feminism and helped educate me in the history of nuances of Judaism.

I am grateful to Leo P. Ribuffo, one of the referees of this manuscript for the University of Chicago Press. I met Leo more than twenty years ago, while each of us was working on a study of Gerald L. K. Smith and other figures of the far right. Since then, we had many intellectual and personal exchanges, and I have profited from Leo's advice, scholarship, generosity, and friendship.

My friendship with Herbert M. Levine dates from the fall of 1964, when he was my political science professor in my freshman year at the University of Southwestern Louisiana. Later, I was a colleague of his for two years at Southwestern Louisiana. Herb has written hundreds of letters of recommendation for my applications for fellowships, grants, and jobs, and has helped me develop contacts with publishers, agents, and scholars. Also, Herb is responsible for locating most of the photographs for this book at the Library of Congress. He is a talented scholar and a mensch.

I have borrowed liberally from the work and ideas of Kari Frederickson and Stasia Von Zwisler, two of my former graduate students at the University of Wisconsin—Milwaukee. Frederickson's M.A. thesis on the Ku Klux Klan, which required her to research the role of women in the Klan, contributed to my knowledge about the relationship of women to the right. Her paper on Cathrine Curtis was a major source for my chapter on Curtis. Frederickson also suggested books and articles on feminism and women's history. A scholar who has a rare combination of intelligence, diligence, common sense, and open-mindedness, she will succeed in academia, given the opportunity, and she will certainly succeed in life. Zwisler wrote an astute analysis of Elizabeth Dilling for her M.A. thesis, found a collection of Dilling's papers at the School of Christian Liberty in Arlington Heights, Illinois, and obtained permission to use the collection. I appreciate the cooperation of the library staff at the school. The staff permitted me to use the papers, answered my questions, and facilitated my research.

Laura McEnaney, a graduate student at the University of Wisconsin—Madison, permitted me to use her M.A. thesis on women isolationists, particularly those involved in Smith's America First Party. Also, I benefited from her article on the movement, published in *Diplomatic History*. Although our analyses differ, our intellectual collaboration has been cordial and enlightening.

Juanita Terry, a former reference librarian at Williams College, planted the seed that germinated into this book. While researching Smith for me, Terry discovered information about Dilling and the mothers' movement. She researched it on her own, turned the material over to me, and suggested I write a book about the movement.

The staff of the Blaustein Library, especially Cyma Horowitz and Michelle Anish, found dusty file folders dealing with my subjects, gave me permission to photocopy them, and made my research at the American Jewish Committee enjoyable and fruitful. Horowitz, Helen Ritter, and Ruth Rausch introduced me to the staff of the YIVO Institute for Jewish Research in New York City and obtained permission for me to use the YIVO Trends Analysis Files. Morris Fine of the American Jewish Committee helped me locate information about my project and shared his knowledge of the far right. The material at the committee, intended for internal use in the 1930s and 1940s, is not integrated into the materials available to researchers at the Blaustein Library. Without the materials made available by the committee and the YIVO Institute, writing this book would have been impossible. Also, in New York City, the Anti-Defamation League of B'nai B'rith, especially Gail Gans, provided information. Marcy and Michael Holdowsky let me stay at their home in

Connecticut for several weeks, allowing me to commute to New York to complete my research there.

I discovered further resources while working in the Smith papers at the Bentley Historical Library at the University of Michigan. Director Francis X. Blouin arranged for me to teach at the university for a year, which enabled me to remain in Ann Arbor to examine the papers. From that research came my biography of Smith and some of the material for *Women of the Far Right*. The Bentley staff, especially Nancy R. Bartlett, William K. Wallach, Kenneth P. Scheffel, and Thomas E. Powers, as well as the history department at the university, made the year enjoyable and productive.

Flori Whyte did extensive research for me at the Library of Congress, the National Archives, and other libraries and newspaper files in the Washington, D.C. area. A skilled researcher, she found sources I might have overlooked, including photographs and rare personal information about Agnes Waters and other women. Whyte and Alan Kovan provided notes and photocopies from the transcripts of the 1944 sedition trial, stored at the National Archives repository at Suitland, Maryland. Kovan, an archivist with the National Archives, encouraged and aided my initial research while he served as director of archives at the University of Wisconsin—Milwaukee.

Henry Lawton photocopied materials for me from the then-unprocessed Curtis collection at the New York Public Library and conducted research on Curtis. In addition, Lawton, the secretary-treasurer of the International Psychohistorical Association, and Paul Elovitz, a past president of the organization, introduced me to psychohistorical research.

The Minnesota Historical Society, St. Paul–Minneapolis, provided me with a grant to use the unprocessed Mothers of Minnesota papers in the Jewish Community Relations Council of Minnesota collection. The library staff at the society photocopied hundreds of pages of documents for me. The staffs at the Pennsylvania Historical Society in Philadelphia and at the New York Public Library also deserve my thanks for photocopying and microfilming documents for me.

Benjamin Harris, professor of psychology at the University of Wisconsin—Parkside, helped locate photographs at the Hoover Institution Archives. Sondra Bierre of the Hoover Institution found the photographs suggested by Harris in the National Republic Collection and discovered photographs in other collections. I am grateful to Bierre and the Hoover Institution for reproducing the photographs.

Several people and organizations associated with the University of Wisconsin—Milwaukee assisted me. I want to thank the staff of the Golda

Meir Library, particularly former director William Roselle; his successor, Peter Watson-Boone; the interlibrary loan department; and the reference department. Kenneth D. Buelow, assistant director of research at the Graduate School, and Robert A. Jones, associate dean of the Graduate School, helped locate sources of funding, and I received research grants from the Graduate School. I would also like to thank the University of Wisconsin Institute on Race and Ethnicity, particularly Thomas V. Tonnesen and Winston A. Van Horne. The institute provided me with a grant to purchase research materials. Janice D. Yoder, former director of the Center for Women's Studies on my campus, wrote letters of recommendation and made available the center's resources. William F. Halloran, then dean of the College of Letters and Science, and Richard D. Meadows, associate dean, helped provide the time and resources to complete this study, as did Frank Cassell, then chair of the history department. Ruth Schwertfeger of the German department helped identify sources of funding and encouraged my study of anti-Semitism. I profited from discussing the history of anti-Semitism with Tom August, one of my colleagues in the history department. Other colleagues, Helena Pycior, Bruce Fetter, and David Buck, wrote letters of recommendation for grants and fellowships. Gail M. Jacobsen aided my work in many ways. Keith Brown served as my summer research assistant as a participant in the Ronald T. McNair program for minority students.

Daniel C. Maguire, professor of theology at Marquette University, has helped me obtain several grants over the past decade. Susan Ware, Blanche Wiesen Cook, Vaughn Baker Simpson, Vickie Hennessey Cummins, Light T. Cummins, Mathé Allain, Thomas C. Reeves, and Benjamin Hubbard also supported my grant applications, as did the late William Ivy Hair, who served as my dissertation adviser at Florida State University and set high standards with his scholarship.

A grant from the John D. and Catharine T. MacArthur Foundation enabled me to devote eighteen months solely to research. The American Council of Learned Societies, the American Philosophical Society, and the Earhart Foundation provided other grants. I especially want to acknowledge Antony Sullivan of the Earhart Foundation, who sent me reading materials relevant to my study, an Albert J. Beveridge Award from the American Historical Association, and a Travel-to-Collections grant from the National Endowment for the Humanities.

I wish to acknowledge the comments of the second referee of my manuscript for the University of Chicago Press. Although the limitations of my sources prevented me from following some of her suggestions, her comments helped me sharpen my focus, improve my analysis, and develop a consistent theme.

I especially want to thank Douglas Mitchell, my editor at the University of Chicago Press. I am grateful for his support of the project at every stage, his faith in my ability to complete it, and his sound sense of the assets and liabilities of the manuscript. Any writer would appreciate an editor who combines the wisdom of Solomon, the patience of Job, and the promptness of the United Parcel Service. Matt Howard of the University of Chicago Press worked with me in many ways and answered my numerous questions.

Others contributed in ways more personal than academic, yet these were equally crucial. Rabbis Jay Brickman, Terry Bookman, Yosef S. Samuels, and Yisroel Shmotkin taught me about Judaism. Stephen A. Webre, who has helped me in many ways since we met as college freshmen, helped me remember the world does not end when the sun sets, and that it is more important to do things right than to do them tomorrow. I wish to thank my mother, who taught me that one can profit from doing things one dislikes (such as eating vegetables and revising manuscripts). I would like to thank my late father, whose example taught me more about tolerance than I absorbed, and who taught me that quitting is the only failure. My young daughters Leah and Hannah helped make this book relevant. I hope they will be able to pursue their destinies and to live secure against the scourge of anti-Semitism.

Although many unselfish individuals contributed to the research and writing of this book, any flaws in fact and conclusions are my contributions.

═══ ONE ═══

The Context of the World War II
Mothers' Movement

To the Allied victory in World War II, American women made an indispensable contribution. Loyally they supported the war effort even though it entailed sacrifices and inequities, including employment discrimination, separation from loved ones, and the burden of combining work and family responsibilities. Women took jobs in war plants, volunteered for military service, staffed the government bureaucracy, planted victory gardens, saved important material such as scrap metal and rubber, provided medical treatment for soldiers as doctors and nurses, and covered the war as journalists. They symbolized national solidarity and democracy in action.[1]

But a minority of women, motivated by a complex, ironic mixture of maternal love and fanatical prejudice, opposed American participation in the war. Right-wing antiwar movements have been rare in the United States, and the mothers' movement was rarer still because it involved women as members and as leaders to an unprecedented degree.[2] The mothers' story has elements of paradox and tragedy. It also raises questions about isolationism, gender and morality, and women's history, questions whose answers are far from definitive and often unsettling. It is a disturbing tale, which nevertheless must be told if we are to be honest about our history.

The movement originated in California shortly after the German invasion of Poland in September 1939 started the war. It gradually became a decentralized confederation of some fifty to one hundred groups that sprang up on both coasts and in the Midwest. (Only the large organizations and those that left some record can be described here.) The absence of membership lists or other decisive evidence makes it impossible to certify the total membership; yet there may have been as many as five million to six million members. The *Chicago Tribune,* one of the newspapers that promoted the mothers, attributed ten million members to a single organization—the Los Angeles–based National Legion of Mothers of America. Groups that monitored the movement were impressed by the enlistments, and their estimates are only slightly lower than those of the movement's supporters. Further, the ability of the mothers' groups to mobilize thousands of women on short notice for demonstrations indicates a sizable membership. Admittedly, some women joined innocently, unaware of the leaders' bigotry, and dropped out upon discovering the direction of the crusade.[3]

A dearth of evidence also makes it difficult to describe the members, although there is enough to indicate they were disproportionately white, middle-class, and middle-aged. Christianity was dominant, with denominational diversity. The ranks in the Midwest included mostly Protestants, and the East had more Catholics than did any other region. The leaders, exclusively white Christians near or at middle age, differed from the membership in being mainly college-educated and in belonging to the upper middle class. Of those who were mothers, a few had young children, but in many cases their families were small and their children were grown or independent. Their relative lack of household responsibilities and their financial security permitted them freedom to crusade. It is likely that many had gained organizing experience in women's clubs, political parties, or far-right movements led by men.[4]

Operating on small budgets and modest funding—nominal dues, subscriptions and contributions from individuals and businesses—the mothers published books, pamphlets, and newsletters, propaganda whose presentation and content ranged from the slick and sophisticated to the crude and barely legible. They testified before Congress, picketed the White House, collected petitions, and participated in political campaigns. They made up an autonomous channel in the broad isolationist river. With each step that brought the United States closer to intervention, the current grew swifter.[5]

In influence and power, the mothers peaked during the debate over Lend-Lease. They lost that fight, however, and the isolationist coalition won few battles. The isolationists' chief achievement was to hinder President Franklin Roosevelt's ability to move as expeditiously as he would have liked in aiding the Allies. Those on the far right helped create in the minds of some Americans an exaggerated fear of native fascism, a "Brown Scare" (in Leo P. Ribuffo's words) that fed a government campaign against subversion. If the fear and the response were exaggerated, the potential of the far right was far from inconsequential, and the right's infusion of masses into the isolationist movement was startling.[6]

After the Japanese attack on Pearl Harbor catapulted the United States into the war, most of the mothers' allies, such as the America First Committee, disbanded and supported the government. But the mothers' movement remained active, resisted the war effort, and campaigned for a negotiated peace that would have left the German and Japanese militarists in power and permitted them to retain some of their conquests. Never did the mothers' leaders believe the war against the Axis was justified, even after the Allied victory and the revelation of the Holocaust.[7]

The mothers' movement was a singular example of the long involvement of women in movements that challenged the status quo, usually out of motives nobler than those of the mothers. Often animated by religion, humanitarian women have organized to promote social reforms including peace, abolition, temperance, education, and improved living and working conditions.[8] In the nineteenth century, this ferment was manifested in what Nancy F. Cott terms the woman movement, a rubric that indicated women's efforts to improve their status and usefulness to society.[9]

Working in reform groups, women became conscious of their capacity to lead movements, of the special interests of their gender, and of their identity as a group oppressed by many of the political and cultural roles that the male-led society expected them to fulfill. Women and men attributed to women (particularly to mothers) sensitivity and compassion that made them effective agents of change. This imagined aura of purity, however, was limiting as well as flattering. If women became active in the sordid male world of business, politics, and diplomacy, it was feared, they might become tainted. Women's activities, then, had to be confined to a sphere in which women were guardians of morality, with an emphasis on issues that involved children, the family, the poor, and the uneducated.[10]

Women also have been limited by men within many social movements. These groups need women to serve as followers, recruiters, and fund-raisers, and to add their perceived moral credibility. But women have been expected to subordinate their desire for liberation to the organizations' major objectives, lest they be dismissed as selfish and divisive. Some social movements that espouse equality for women and men, moreover, do not emancipate women. Socialists, for instance, argue that capitalism enslaves women, and that when capitalism is overthrown, they will be free. In most successful socialist revolutions, though, women were not liberated; they became equal with men in suffering from destitution and government repression.[11]

Patriarchy was identified as the root of restrictions on the status, power, and flexibility of women. Under a patriarchal system, males dominated the family and political and social institutions. Ultimately, women realized that the only way to transcend these constraints was to act according to their own identity and interests. But it was difficult for them to agree on a common identity without confirming the basis of patriarchy, which held that because women differed physically from men, they were inferior. "How were women to be understood as a gender group vis-à-vis men without suppressing women's differences from one another and without fixing women into a definitional straitjacket of sex-typing?" Cott asks.[12] A related problem was that women were unclustered and lived with the men who tyrannized them. "Precisely because most women cannot avoid contact with men," William H. Chafe explains, "they lack the clear-cut sense of group identification which comes from living apart as a nation, a religious group, or a neighborhood."[13]

Feminism, the successor to the woman movement in the 1910s, was an attempt to overcome these obstacles.[14] There is general, if not total, agreement about the philosophy behind feminism. Cott writes that feminism includes opposition to a sex hierarchy, the belief that gender restrictions are created by society, and a sense of group identity. "It [feminism] requires gender consciousness for its basis yet calls for the elimination of prescribed gender roles."[15] Linda Gordon suggests that "feminism is a critique of male supremacy, formed and offered in the light of a will to change it, which in turn assumes a conviction that it is changeable."[16] Sara Ruddick believes a feminist is a person who thinks "gender divisions of work, pleasure, power, and sensibility are socially created, detrimental to women . . . and therefore can and should be changed. Most important . . . feminists are partisans of women."[17]

Feminism represented a recognition that women wanted far more than the nurturant service and moral uplift that the woman movement emphasized—far more than just the vote, for which they had been campaigning for decades. Women sought to tear down the barriers that separated them from economic independence, sexual freedom, and full participation in public life. Severing the ties the woman movement had to Christianity and conventional respectability, Cott writes, "Feminism partook of the free-ranging spirit of rebellion of the time, which exploded in many forms, from the Ash Can school of painting to the 'one big union' idea of the Industrial Workers of the World."[18]

Feminists realistically worried that if they conceded the existence of gender differences, they would buttress the idea that women were inferior to men. Some drew parallels to racial discrimination based on alleged innate differences between whites and blacks. (A number of feminists agreed there were gender differences yet disagreed over whether they were products of conditioning or of nature.) Nor would feminists accept the argument that women, as the weaker sex, benefited from laws passed to protect them. The implication that women needed this protection was condescending.[19]

Because the right reinforces traditional roles for women, conservatism seems antipathetic to feminism. Whether feminism is compatible with conservatism in a theoretical sense is debatable, although historically it has been allied with the left.[20] "Feminism was born ideologically on the left of the political spectrum, first espoused by women who were familiar with advocacy of socialism and who, advantaged by bourgeois backgrounds, nonetheless identified more with labor than with capital and hoped for the elimination of exploitation by capital and the intervention of a democratically controlled state," Cott writes. "They considered themselves socialists or progressives leaning toward socialism and had, unlike most of the American population, a tolerance for 'isms.'"[21]

The early feminist movement was unified in pursuit of its chief goal, the right to vote, but once the goal was achieved, women's politics never enjoyed comparable unity. There was little agreement about the next step, Susan Ware observes.[22] The National Woman's Party wanted to work for passage of an Equal Rights Amendment to the Constitution, whereas other women leaders argued the measure would eliminate protective legislation and do more harm than good. Strategies diverged over whether women should strive to be an independent political force or work within the two major parties; over whether women should seek incremental reform or radical change. Leaders such as Carrie Chapman Catt and Jane Addams, who had cooperated in working for suffrage, found it impossible to reconcile their differences, Catt objecting to sex segregation and Addams believing a female identity was essential for reform.[23]

The problem was compounded when women failed to vote in a bloc for social change, confounding a key suffragist prediction. When male politicians realized they could not orchestrate the women's vote, the influence of the feminist movement declined after 1925, Ware notes.[24] Thus in the first decade after winning the vote, women worked at cross-purposes instead of working toward a few ends important to females as a group. The experience, Cott writes, "ironically proved the absence rather than the substance of gender solidarity. The 1920s shattered any confidence that women should or would act predictably together on candidates of either sex, on legislative protection of working women or children, on peace, or on Prohibition."[25]

On the issue of peace in the 1920s, there were in fact divisions among women, showing that activist women had not been attracted exclusively to the left and foreshadowing the mothers' movement. Conservative groups, among them the Daughters of the American Revolution (DAR) and the American Legion Auxiliary, joined the right-wing National Patriotic Council in attacking feminists and pacifists, including Catt, Addams, and members of the leftist International Council of Women. The Ku Klux Klan (KKK) was able to attract women.[26] (Ironically, in the 1930s it was liberals who called for strengthening the American military and intervening in the war, and it was right-wing extremists who demanded that the United States stay out of war.)

"The superpatriotic attacks not only beat the drum to the right and revealed that women spanned the spectrum from the reactionary to the progressive," Cott explains. "Their agitations about Bolshevism and subversion affected the meaning and practice of feminism, by association and by analogy. They inculcated the very notion of women as a political group or class as un-American, a 'Bolshevik' notion."[27] Recriminations ensued, further polarizing left and right. In the 1930s some women turned to the far right, making up a large proportion of the movements of extremists Gerald L. K. Smith and Father Charles E. Coughlin.[28]

Some of these women, who would become leaders of mothers' organizations, had embarked upon a path similar to the one followed by feminists, only to take a fork in the road that reached a dead end in reactionary politics. As mothers, they believed they possessed assets that made them different from men—indeed, far superior to men. But they also argued that they were significantly similar to men and therefore deserved a voice equal to men's in politics and diplomacy. Like feminists, the mothers combined the ideal of equality with the argument that women could create societies more just and compassionate than the ones men had made.[29]

Still, the mothers were not feminists. There are important distinctions between the groups, beyond the obvious point that they originated on opposite ends of the political spectrum. For one thing, the mothers did not meet generally accepted feminist criteria. Janet Saltzman Chafetz and Gary Dworkin, for instance, remark, "Feminists have everywhere manifested substantial antipathy to authoritatively structured organizations."[30] The mothers' organizations, we will see, were autonomous fiefdoms dominated by a single autocratic leader or an oligarchy.

The mothers fell short of more crucial characteristics identified by Chafetz and Dworkin: feminist movements focus on problems specific to women, seek permanent solutions to women's oppression, and build enduring organizations.[31] The mothers did not concentrate exclusively on women's issues, did not challenge patriarchy, and did not create lasting organizations.

The mothers' solutions to social ills bespoke a gender consciousness, although the mothers owed their primary allegiance to their ideology, not to their gender. They accepted motherhood as the essence of women and male primacy as the essence of national strength. The problem was not that men were in charge but that the wrong men were in charge: men who had ignored the interests of women, even of women who shared their views; men who had demeaned motherhood by subordinating it to male activities; men who worked in the despised Roosevelt administration and schemed to embroil the

United States in war. Adopting a value by which women peace activists had lived for some time, far-right women employed a maternal justification for their cause. They maintained that mothers, especially interested in protecting their sons, had to clean out government and bring the proper men to power.[32]

It is appropriate to think of the mothers' movement as ameliorative rather than as feminist. An ameliorative women's movement, Chafetz and Dworkin explain, "does not challenge the privileged status of males in the society, but only seeks to make more effective the female's pivotal roles as wife and mother. . . . such a movement might work to enhance the legal, educational, or even political status of women, but preserve as paramount the women's obligations as wife and mother." By contrast, feminist movements "have sought to ensure total social and economic equality for women, thereby altering both the sex stratification and gender role systems."[33]

The ideological incompatibility of the mothers and feminists is further evidenced by the hostility of far-right women to Eleanor Roosevelt, a favorite of liberal women. Far more visible publicly than other first ladies, Roosevelt inspired many women who hoped for freedom from gender stereotypes. Her interests were wide-ranging. She supported civil rights, among a number of liberal causes, and resigned from the DAR after it denied the black singer Marian Anderson the opportunity to perform in Constitution Hall. (Roosevelt then helped arrange an Anderson performance in front of the Lincoln Memorial.) We will see that to far-right women, Roosevelt was a villain, an inept mother who sacrificed her family to satisfy selfish ambitions, a traitor to womanhood. That some of the more sophisticated mothers shared qualities with Roosevelt yet parted company with her ideologically and politically made them hate her all the more. Flexible, pragmatic, and reflecting qualities that were coming to dominate national opinion, she was a moral relativist (as were her husband and liberal internationalists). She was bound to clash with the mothers, who were moral absolutists.[34]

Understanding that the mothers were not feminists is as important as understanding that the mothers were not political conservatives. To attempt to label them as such would be misleading and an injustice to principled, tolerant conservatives. It is true that conservatives, as well as the far right, felt threatened by the world of the 1930s, in which values, politics, and diplomacy were in flux. But the mothers, perceiving their adversaries as evil, were so paranoid as to propagate preposterous ideas. Conservatives did not proclaim that Hitler was really a cat's paw of a centuries-old global Jewish-communist conspiracy (a complaint that a few disillusioned mothers were to make after the war), or advocate the persecution of American Jews, for example. In the political mainstream, reality was not distorted as the mothers distorted it.[35]

Movements such as the mothers', Chafetz and Dworkin write, often arise during periods of social stress. Women feel they are alienated and marginalized, that their interests are in peril; their group consciousness crystallizes. They reason that their problems can be effectively addressed by mass action. Although most women's rebellions have attacked a conservative establishment, right-wing groups can form in response to a political order based on liberal values. Ambitious women who have apprenticed in previous movements take the lead. Urbanization facilitates organization by creating a critical mass to generate action.[36] For the mothers' movement, all of these conditions existed.

There had been discontent among right-wing women before the 1930s. Tension began in the 1920s, a decade of cultural rebellion, permissiveness, and change that disturbed Americans who believed in premarital sexual abstinence, clearly circumscribed gender roles, and nuclear families as models for the nation. Yet it took the dramatic political and diplomatic developments of the 1930s—the New Deal and the war—to provide catalysts for the mothers' movement. The economic emergency gave rise to the welfare state. Worse, federal encroachment in daily life would grow if the United States entered the war. Women would face the rupture of families, the loss of husbands and sons, race mixing, new work responsibilities, and threats to Christian solidarity.[37]

Christianity played a prominent role in shaping the mothers' commitment to capitalism, country, and traditional families. The mothers were more militant in their faith than were the women reformers within the Quakers, the Unitarians, and the more egalitarian sects. The less stable their personalities, the more the far-right women relied on conformity and tradition for protection. Religious verities were the bedrock of their psychological security and identities. They were charged with passing their religious faith on to successive generations. They believed Christianity defined Americanism and was essential to the nation's destiny. Amid all of the social shocks, it had to triumph.[38]

Fear of an uncertain future is natural—even healthy—and not confined to the far right. Self-deception and blaming others for troubling developments are common defense mechanisms that do not inevitably degenerate into pathologies. With the mothers, however, scapegoating became a way of life, and in their time, liberals, communists, and especially Jews were the scapegoats. They found plausible Hitler's canard that Jews were behind communism, believed he was a protector against communism, even a good Christian, and ignored the führer's depravity. The mothers thus drew upon, and contributed to, the history of anti-Semitism in America.[39]

Jews had planned the Civil War, the assassination of Abraham Lincoln, and the Great Depression, according to the mothers. By feeding Americans a diet of booze, lewd movies, night clubs, jazz, and glamorized sex, they would weaken the moral fiber of the United States, leaving it defenseless against communism. Then Jews and their allies would conspire to draw the nation into war against Hitler. The young men whom the mothers raised from birth would be slaughtered in a fruitless war, leaving the conspirators to destroy Christianity and control the world, with FDR as dictator. Only the mothers could save their sons and country. They stood ready to fight, believing the Lord would help them prevail.[40]

═ TWO ═

Elizabeth Dilling and the Genesis of a Movement

Elizabeth Dilling once joked that she had an even disposition: she was mad all the time. The militant crusader, who called herself "little poison ivy" because she irritated people, was the most important woman to emerge on the far right in the 1930s. Dilling was so notorious that Sinclair Lewis based a character on her in *It Can't Happen Here,* his novel about fascism coming to America.[1] Her campaign against communism and Judaism, animated by enmity toward Roosevelt, marked the genesis of the fifth-column women's movement.[2]

Dilling was driven by furies. Her husband conceded that she was "a little queer."[3] The muscular, six-foot, 200-pound Albert, who punched a man who made fun of Elizabeth, was mild compared to his spouse. Like most women of her time, she used her husband's name and was conventional in her certainty that "no communist revolution will cause women enthusiastically to prefer brick laying to feminine pursuits."[4] Her activism, however, was not traditional. A self-styled "professional patriot"—a "Tory, super patriot, 100 per center or patrioteer"[5]—she vowed, "I'd die in a good cause and not shrivel up like a watery old turnip that's frostbitten in the fall."[6]

Dilling imagined conspiracies against the United States, Christianity and patriots such as she; even groups that appeared benign were scheming. Compromise with the plotters was anathema.[7] "I love all that the cross and the flag of this country stand for and I shall not pussyfoot with those who do not," she said.[8] Fearing the New Deal threatened her position as a member of the privileged class, she rebelled against the Democratic coalition of liberals, Jews and Blacks. Accepting the Bible literally, she was disturbed by social trends such as free love and racial mixing. It was her wish to give her life for Jesus. She would be rewarded in heaven.[9]

Dilling was born in Chicago on April 19, 1894, the second child and only daughter of Lafayette Kirkpatrick and Elizabeth Harding. A surgeon, her father sprang from Scotch-Irish stock. Her mother's family was English and French. Dr. Kirkpatrick, who died when she was six weeks old, would not have liked his daughter's career because he felt women should lead sheltered lives. He left his family wealthy and his widow, who raised Elizabeth and her brother Kirkpatrick alone, added to the family's wealth by selling real estate. Kirkpatrick, born seven years before Elizabeth, also was a realtor and was wealthy by twenty-three, having developed properties in Hawaii.[10]

Elizabeth was a "highly emotional, eager girl with a dramatically sculptured face, enormous brown eyes and a quick, giddy laugh, somewhat lonely," a relative said.[11] She was raised an Episcopalian but attended the Academy of Our Lady, a Catholic girls school, and the Starrett School for Girls, where she was a self-motivated student. The nuns inspired her to read the Bible from cover to cover. In her teens, she wrote forty-page letters to girlfriends about scripture. They thought she would be an evangelist. Her moods were mercurial, however; she was tense and morose. Her mother sent her on a three-month vacation to the Southwest to help her recover from depression, and they traveled together in the United States, Canada, and Europe.[12]

In 1912 Dilling enrolled at the University of Chicago to study music and languages. Her goal was to play in a symphony orchestra. She became fluent in French and learned to play the harp, studying with Walfried Singer, the Chicago Symphony's harpist, and with Alberto Salvi, an internationally known musician.[13] Dilling showed little interest in history, politics, or public speaking. Politics was rarely discussed at home because her mother and brother preferred to talk about music, drama, business, and travel. Dilling studied for three years but left the university without a degree because she was lonely. She became bitter about her college experience, and for the rest of her life, she harbored grudges against professors.[14]

A beautiful woman, Dilling was nervous in mixed company. Nevertheless, in 1917 she began to date an Army officer whom she had met on a pleasure trip to Tucson, Arizona. She was intrigued by his romantic notes in French and their long horseback rides. Then he told her he liked the philosophers Kant, Hegel, and Nietzsche. He gave her philosophy books with underlined passages stating that women were to be dominated and that they respected men who beat them. Women, he said, did not really count as human beings. Dilling spurned his marriage proposal, reciting a poem she wrote to ridicule his ideas. No man would dominate her.[15]

Soon afterward Elizabeth met Albert Wallwick Dilling, an engineer who was studying law. Like her, he was religious and enjoyed music; his political views also were similar to hers. Albert, born in Salt Lake City of Norwegian parents, was raised a Methodist but joined the Episcopalian church that Elizabeth attended. The couple dated for nine months and were married in the summer of 1918, a few months before Albert was admitted to the bar. They bought an comfortable house in Wilmette, a Chicago suburb. For the next thirteen years, Elizabeth was a housewife who entertained, raised a family, and did charitable work.[16]

During most of their marriage, money was not a major problem for the Dillings. Elizabeth inherited wealth from her mother and aunts, enabling her to buy the couple a house and a 237-acre farm. In addition, the Dillings could afford a cook and housekeeper once Albert became chief engineer for the Chicago Sewerage District. An entrepreneur with few scruples, Albert parlayed that job into a small fortune. In 1920 he convinced the district to install a sewage treatment process in three plants without paying royalties to the British patent holders. Albert then resigned, acquired a secret interest in the patent rights, and instigated a suit against Chicago for patent infringement. The city settled out of court for $818,000, of which Albert received a portion.[17]

Elizabeth and Albert had two children: Kirkpatrick, born in 1920, and Elizabeth Jane ("Babe"), born in 1925. (Unlike Babe, Kirk, who became a lawyer and entered practice with his father, was active in Dilling's career as an anticommunist.) But the marriage was turbulent. Less than three years after the couple married, Albert began an affair with a woman he met at a Sanitation Department picnic. Elizabeth learned of their involvement and drove her mother, who carried a revolver, to the woman's house. They shattered the front window with a bullet, forced their way in at gunpoint, warned the woman to stop seeing Albert, and took back Elizabeth's jewelry, which he had given to his mistress. Elizabeth made Albert promise never to see the woman again, and he gave Elizabeth $100,000 not to divorce him. Yet Albert could not remain faithful. He soon acquired two new mistresses, and the Dillings separated twice before divorcing in 1943.[18]

Before Dilling took up anticommunism, her avocation was travel. She told a friend that if she were free of responsibilities, she would spend all her time traveling. Dilling's family went abroad ten times between 1923 and 1939. The more she traveled, the more she appreciated the United States.[19]

In 1923 the Dillings traveled in Britain, France, and Italy, and had an audience with the Pope. Dilling was frustrated by the anti-American attitudes she found among the British and the French. The former Allies gave Americans no credit for helping win World War I and complained because the United States had not entered the war sooner. On her steamship trip back home, an Englishman saw Kirk wearing a sailor suit with "U. S. Navy" on it, and commented that the Navy was a joke. "Oh, I don't know that it is such a joke," Dilling retorted. "It has been able to lick Great Britain twice and I think it could do it again." She vowed that if there were another war in Europe, she would work to keep her country out.[20]

Germany was another destination that made an impression. The family toured there in 1931, and Dilling returned in 1938. In 1938 she noticed "great improvement of conditions there over 1931. Personally I thank God for the opposition Germany is making against communism."[21] On her next visit, the government paid her expenses and she attended Nazi party meetings. The people, she wrote, were healthy, well fed. "There is no question about it. The German people under Hitler are contented and happy. . . . don't believe the stories you hear that this man has not done a great good for this country."[22]

Dilling's travels in 1938 also took her to Palestine, where, she said, she filmed Jewish immigrants ruining the Holy Land. England had betrayed the Arabs by permitting Jewish immigrants to steal Arab land, she added, but the Arabs blamed the American government, which they said was Jew-controlled. On her way back to the United States, Dilling toured Spain, a country in the throes of civil war. She considered the Spanish Loyalists atheistic communists and the rebel leader, Francisco Franco, a brave Christian. The Loyalists butchered priests and nuns, said Dilling, who filmed what she claimed were Red torture chambers and churches razed by communists. Later, she showed the film during her anticommunist talks.[23]

No trip made more of an impact on Dilling than her month-long tour of the Soviet Union with her husband in 1931. The Soviet experiment with communism appalled her. She found ill-clothed, impoverished people decimated by disease and genocide. Six-year-old children, naked to the waist, begged for cigarettes. Shelves in stores were half-empty and goods were "for display only." About the only groceries for sale were bread and cucumbers. "The food made you sick at your stomach. It did me."[24] Roads were rutted and her buses broke down. (There were Rolls Royces for communist officials in Moscow, however.) The houses were dingy and smelly. Women did heavy work, such as carrying stones to build a subway.[25] Dilling particularly objected to the "sex equality with men," state-run orphanages and child-care centers, collective kitchens, contraception, and abortion in the Soviet Union.[26] Her fears were exacerbated by Russian guides, whom Dilling claimed were Jews. One guide told her communism would conquer the world, beginning with a revolution in China and culminating in the takeover of United States. The guides also showed her a map on which American cities had been renamed for Soviet heroes.[27]

Dilling's anxieties about communism arose mainly because of the Soviet rejection of Christianity. After viewing Lenin's preserved body in Red Square, she wrote, "He's god in Russia. Pickled in alcohol under glass. A little sandy-whiskered thing. A poor substitute for Jesus Christ. I thought to myself—

pooh, you don't amount to much."[28] In truth, "There was no God, no conscience, a rule of force, might and brutality, and no mercy."[29] The government
aggressively attempted to eradicate religion and convert cathedrals and mon-
asteries into atheist museums. Moscow's Church of the Redeemer and
Leningrad's St. Isaac's Cathedral were "filled with displays ridiculing Jesus
Christ as a bootlegger, Christian Holy Communion as cannibalism, and
Christianity as rubbish, impeding the Five Year Plan."[30] When Dilling saw
plans to tear down Russian churches to build a Palace of Soviets, she thought
of Jesus. "You may hate HIM all you like. I LOVE HIM. I cannot talk here but
if I ever get out of here I WILL TALK." And she did.[31]

At first, Dilling's crusades against communism were motivated by religion, not politics. Dilling sympathized with Protestantism, fundamentalism,
and conservative Catholicism. She was an admirer of Coughlin and of such
Protestant ministers as Smith, Gerald B. Winrod, and W. B. Riley. Her writing
praised only those who favored her views. She quit her church's sewing guild
because she said a Red had provided sewing materials, and she resigned from
her church because the pastor was a liberal. Dilling switched to a church
where Kirk was to be confirmed, but she grew disgusted when the minister
told her he did not have time to read her anticommunist diatribes. She said
she was nauseated by her church's attitude toward communism, had to restrain herself to avoid being thrown out, and had no time to waste in church
activities. Albert also stopped attending church and contributing money.[32]

Pacifism was not for Dilling, whose Christianity was a fighting faith. She
could not confine herself to praising God; she had to denounce God's enemies. She believed Jesus had commanded Christians to fight infidels, quoting
Matt. 10:34: "Think not that I am come to send peace on earth, I come not to
send peace, but a sword."[33] Christianity was the only force that could defeat
communism, yet even Christians were vulnerable. "It is great to convert
people but it is also important to keep them from walking into Satan's Red
pits of Bolshevism disguised as humanitarianism—and the greatest suckers
in the world for doing this are Christians," Dilling wrote.[34]

Nor did Dilling want the peace of religious tolerance. She was shocked to
learn of an interfaith dinner at a synagogue in her area, addressed by a rabbi
who was a board member of the National Conference of Christians and Jews.
His attendance and speech, she thought, were contrary to the injunction to
Christians in 2 Cor. 6:14: "Be ye not unequally yoked with unbelievers." To
Dilling's dismay, she noted that at the close of the gathering, the diners sang
"Irving Berlin's substitute for 'The Star-Spangled Banner,' 'God Bless Amer-
ica.'"[35]

Other targets were the Young Men's Christian Association (YMCA) and

Young Women's Christian Association (YWCA). Dilling set out to expose these Red-infested organizations lest gullible Christians contribute money to them. Not only was Jesus not mentioned in the YWCA industrial song sheet distributed from national headquarters, "but it includes such well-known Red revolutionary songs as the 'Internationale.'" The associations cooperated with communist fronts such as the National Association for the Advancement of Colored People (NAACP) and the American Civil Liberties Union (ACLU). They were attempting to break down families and facilitate a communist takeover by distributing birth control information to children. Furthermore, the YMCA and YWCA permitted Whites and Blacks to swim together in their pools; supported antilynching legislation, a ruse to prevent good Americans from lynching communists; supported the Scottsboro boys, Black teenagers who allegedly had raped a white woman; and gave money to Loyalist Spain. The "C" in "YMCA" should have been changed to "Communist."[36]

In 1931 Dilling adopted anticommunist crusading as therapy, after her doctor told her she was close to a nervous breakdown and that travel and activities would help her nerves.[37] Upon her return from the Soviet Union she began to study communism intensively and to seek explanations for it in the Bible. She became a student of Iris McCord, who taught at the Moody Bible Institute and broadcast a radio program over Chicago station WMBJ. McCord arranged for her to address church groups that listened to WMBJ and expressed an interest in anticommunism. Dilling began to show her home movies of Russia to organizations such as DAR and the American Legion. Originally she had no intention of becoming a professional anticommunist; her speaking was a hobby. Nonetheless, word spread about the woman who was an expert on communism and a captivating speaker.[38]

Demand for Dilling grew, her audiences increased, and speaking and writing began to consume her time. She expanded her schedule to include women's clubs, chambers of commerce, veterans' organizations, and Kiwanis and Rotary clubs. Within a year, she was speaking as many as five times a week. She lectured throughout the Midwest, in the Northeast, and occasionally on the West Coast. She typically received money for railroad fare, meals, and hotel expenses, plus fifty percent of the collections taken at her talks, where she sold pamphlets and tracts. Sometimes she was paid an honorarium, usually less than a hundred dollars.[39]

Dilling made the same talk to each group, spitting words with the rapidity of machine-gun fire. As props, she used Red banners and flags, the YWCA songbook, magazines, pamphlets, and newspapers. She sang the "Internationale" and songs she had composed about the Red menace. From time to time Albert, who accompanied her, led the audience in song while she distributed song sheets and literature. Dilling mimicked Eleanor Roosevelt and faked a Yiddish accent that her audiences found hilarious. She normally spoke for at least two hours. The audience sat raptly, fearing it might miss a good story or important reference. No one seemed to question her expertise as an anticommunist, even though she modestly called herself "just a woman with a mouth."[40] She never filled football stadiums, as did Smith, or had a national radio program such as Coughlin's. Still, she could draw crowds—most numbered in the hundreds of people, but by 1939 she addressed thousands—and electrify audiences. After one lecture, about fifty people from the audience arose to pledge their lives to Jesus as the antidote to communism.[41]

Dilling received substantial research aid from Col. Edwin Marshall Hadley of Chicago. In 1932, they organized the Paul Reveres, an organization to promote Americanism and combat communism. Headquartered in Chicago, it spawned chapters in other cities. There were no dues and anyone over eighteen who adhered to republican principles was eligible to join. Each chapter financed its operations through donations. Dilling served as national secretary until 1934, when she resigned over a dispute with Hadley, and a few months later the organization expired due to apathy. The Paul Reveres, Dilling's first anticommunist organization, marked her emergence as a serious crusader. Like Paul Revere, Dilling sounded an alarm: "The communists are coming!" She warned, "One need not go to Russia, nor to the slums, to find communism." And she told an audience in suburban Chicago that communist influence "flourished in our own North Shore society." Indeed, some clergymen in her community were on the payroll of the Communist Party.[42]

While resting for a week due to illness, Dilling read the autobiography of Emma Goldman, a Jewish atheist who had "foul sex ideas." The anarchist's shocking book convinced Dilling it would take a mother like her to spur the men of the country to fight communism. "Have women like me who believe in beautiful Christian ideals the right to sit in their rose-shaded living rooms while a fire burns in the nation's basement and the Emma Goldmans fill the platforms with their dirt and anti-American ideas?" she said.[43]

Dilling learned she could reach more people by writing. In 1932 McCord encouraged her to summarize her lectures in a series of articles for a weekly newspaper in Wilmette. After the articles were published, Dilling collected and published them as a pamphlet entitled *Red Revolution: Do We Want It Here?* The DAR bought 10,000 copies for distribution to local chapters.[44]

From a part-time agitator, Dilling evolved into a fanatic, working until midnight seven days a week, then rising early the next morning to resume her work. She dropped other activities and limited her friends to anticommunists. But her feverish activity alternated with despair over public indifference about communism and over her wealthy friends' reluctance to contribute money to her cause. Communists prospered, she complained, while she labored in poverty and obscurity. Dilling wished she could build a concentration camp for businessmen who ignored the communist threat. Sometimes she felt like letting the revolution come to the United States; then she would fight to her death on the barricades.[45]

Cataloguing every communist and pro-communist organization in America became an obsession. Ultimately Dilling collected more than one hundred thousand file cards, each containing the name of a person or organization with pro-communist affiliations. To gather her information, Dilling read and clipped articles in newspapers and magazines for nearly thirty years. She mined the publications of fellow anticommunists as well as those of Reds. Her voracious appetite for reading also led her to accumulate a large library of books about politics, history, law, philosophy, Jews, communism, organized labor, economics, revolution, and foreign policy. Yet she found it difficult to keep current because she was so busy. Snippets of what she read, or heard on the radio or in conversation, turned up in her writing.[46]

Reading literature she detested, Dilling grew nervous and irritable. Nevertheless, she slaved away at her research, fearing that communist organizations would arise more quickly than she could catalogue them. She operated on the principles that someone who was once a communist was always a communist and that "all Reds are liars. If a Red denied being Red, that is part of the Red camouflage and makes him Redder than ever."[47] She misunderstood much of what she read, especially material written by liberals.

Dilling's office was always a mess, filled with uncompleted work. She wrote that "every drawer in our office is filled with unindexed material" and "we are as swamped as a person trying to shovel a mountain of sand with a teaspoon."[48] Dilling was inundated with requests for information. One man sent her a list of twenty-seven people he wanted her to look up; another wanted several documents. Some days she did nothing except make photostatic copies of material and search for information to mail. She complained that most people did not offer to pay for the information, did not send stamps, and did not thank her. But Dilling read and answered as much of her mail as she could, working even when exhausted or ill.[49]

In contrast with Smith, Winrod, and Coughlin, Dilling had a meager budget and employed few helpers. She was funded primarily by her husband, who assisted her research so conscientiously that he neglected his law practice. Unlike Smith, she never became wealthy through her crusades; in fact, she operated at a loss. Because she could not afford a large staff, Dilling relied on volunteers or friends. Once she

> nabbed everyone to help who came into the office Saturday after-noon and by night we were twelve. Albert went out and brought in a sandwich, pie and coffee supper for all and we ate at our nine-foot office table and even sang some songs. . . . Helping we had a dear woman with a husband and son, Episcopalians, several Moodyites, a Methodist, two Roman Catholics, and a member of the Anglo-Saxon Federation. Our office is strictly *pro*-Christian and only *anti*-Red. Theological hairsplitting is taboo.[50]

Dilling never wrote a periodical that brought in paid subscriptions or headed an organization that charged dues. In 1938 she founded the Patriotic Research Bureau, whose monthly bulletin was sent free to those on her mailing list. She obtained names from people who signed up at her lectures. Dilling accepted contributions from readers, yet most were five dollars or less. Sometimes her followers made sacrifices to send money. One woman whose income was $40 a month and who was going blind sold a $100 bond for $77 and sent $75 to Dilling. An elderly man who worked as a cement mixer sent her $100 and left everything he owned to Dilling in his will. "The very poor people out of work or on WPA relief who have sent in their precious mites with sincere prayers for the cause, are what touch and keep me going to slave daily and to take more kicks!" Dilling said.[51]

Dilling did have a few wealthy supporters. Henry B. Joy, a retired Detroit industrialist, sent her several thousand dollars. Dean Solenberger of Cleveland, whose company manufactured piston rings for automobiles, sustained her for about five years. Four other businessmen in Cleveland and one in Boston sent her money monthly. Henry Ford bought her office furniture and typewriters and, in 1939, put her on his payroll at $200 a month for six months. Her only consistent support, however, came from Albert and her inheritances. Payments for her lectures, she complained, were not commensurate with her stature. "If the nation's acknowledged leading expert on subversive activities is not worth $50 and expenses while ordinary forum radicals are paid $150 to Mrs. Roosevelt's $1500 per lecture, then my efforts are entirely wasted," she wrote.[52]

In 1935 Dilling tried unsuccessfully to obtain money from drugstore tycoon Charles R. Walgreen by aiding him in a purge of alleged communists at the University of Chicago. Walgreen had withdrawn his niece from the university after she told him she was being taught by communist professors. He demanded a public hearing and enlisted Dilling's help. When university President Robert Maynard Hutchins refused to conduct a witch-hunt, Dilling charged, "He's afraid to hold a hearing because he's the Reddest kind of Red."[53] Hutchins might have been unaccommodating, but Dilling and Walgreen persuaded a committee of the Illinois Legislature to convene a hearing on her demand that the university be closed for violating state sedition laws.[54]

The last witness to testify, Dilling pulled reams of documents from a bulging briefcase, then launched into a tirade as her supporters screamed, "They ought to kill every communist!"[55] Flapping her arms, rolling her eyes, shouting, she held forth for thirty minutes and threatened to make a radio broadcast, if necessary, to continue. Dilling accused four professors of being communists and claimed the university chaplain had said "Russia is the hope of the world."[56] The Red tide extended to Harold Swift, a member of the famous meat-packing company family and president of the university's board of trustees. A "cream puff type of Red," Swift was one of the "second-generation millionaires who likes to play around with radicals. Some rich men turn to booze, some to chorus girls, and others to communism." When the revolution came, his throat would be slit.[57] The invective did not persuade the committee, which concluded the charges by Dilling and Walgreen's niece were unfounded. No action was taken.[58]

Dilling found Red infestation at her children's schools. While Kirk was in high school, she complained that his teacher forced him to bring home and read communist literature such as the *Daily Worker.* Kirk later enrolled at Cornell University to study engineering and attended a lecture by Communist Party official Robert Minor. Kirk asked Minor what he thought of Elizabeth Dilling. When Minor said Dilling belonged in an asylum, Kirk identified himself and denounced Minor. A few weeks later, the school put him on probation. Cornell said he was punished for burning a sulfur candle that filled a dormitory with smoke and for filling a light fixture with water. Kirk admitted to the pranks, yet his mother said he was persecuted for his anticommunist views.[59]

Cornell was dominated by communist professors who invited subversive speakers such as Minor to campus, Dilling said. "This is the slickest, slimiest way of winning students' sympathies for communism."[60] Professors undermined students' morals by encouraging free love and by using books written by Jewish communists to teach about sex. One of the books had chapters on masturbation, homosexuality, and premarital sex; the author, who encouraged students to use prophylactics, wrote that morality was changeable, not immutable. In the campus library, Dilling found 110 Marxist books and 47 books by Sigmund Freud, a "Red Jew" who "probably did more than any single man to break down moral decency and spread sex filth in the guise of 'science.'" There were 15 books by John Dewey, "the atheistic 'Progressive Education' head and idol of the Reds," and 53 books by philosopher Bertrand Russell, including *Why I Am Not a Christian.* Dilling said a man had gone to visit Russell's school and a nude nine-year-old girl answered the door. "My God!" the man exclaimed. The girl coldly replied, "There is no God," and slammed the door.[61]

Northwestern University, where Elizabeth Jane enrolled, was worse than Cornell. A professor had tried to teach Elizabeth Jane sex education until Dilling stopped him. Atheist professors encouraged students to stay out all night drinking at honky-tonks. One of Elizabeth Jane's male friends dropped out of school so he could have more time for sex.[62]

Dilling investigated other colleges tainted by Reds. Ford paid her $5,000 to look into the University of Michigan, where she found eighty-one Freudian books in the library and interviewed a mental health counselor whose office was lined with volumes by Freud. The Los Angeles Chamber of Commerce paid Dilling to investigate the University of California at Los Angeles, and she concluded the campus reeked with communism.[63]

If Dilling did not match the prominence of Coughlin or Winrod in the far-right movement, her influence outlasted theirs because she wrote books. Long after their fulminations had faded, her books were sold, read, and quoted by right-wing groups.

Early in 1933 Dilling thought about compiling a list of communists, anarchists, socialists, and pacifists, whom she identified indiscriminately as Reds. She worked on the project twelve to fourteen hours a day for eighteen months. What had started as a pamphlet grew into a book that she published herself in 1934, *The Red Network: A Who's Who and Handbook of Radicalism for Patriots.* The strident 352-page book was divided into three sections: articles describing communism, information on more than four hundred sixty "subversive" organizations, and a compilation of more than thirteen hundred "Reds" with their affiliations. Poorly written, the text lacked professional editing. It was filled with long, unwieldy quotations from ultraright writers, and typographical, spelling, and grammatical errors. More important, the book was a mass of innuendo and inaccuracy, relying on guilt by association and fraudulent sources.[64]

Dilling's paranoia about communism in the United States showed in her attacks on women's organizations and female reformers. She labeled as subversive such groups as the Women's Trade Union League, the League of Women Voters, and the American Birth Control League. Among the women singled out as Reds were Addams, Florence Kelley, Eleanor Roosevelt, Edna

St. Vincent Millay, and Montana Congresswoman Jeannette Rankin. "In many ways, it is ironic that Dilling tagged major women's organizations as radical, because the women's movement as a whole had lost most of its radical associations by the 1930s," Ware observes.[65]

Dilling wrote about communist influence among politicians, clergymen, rabbis, authors, broadcasters, journalists, scientists, lecturers, and ordinary citizens. In the ranks of Red politicians were Senators George W. Norris of Nebraska and Gerald P. Nye of North Dakota, and the late Sen. Robert M. La Follette Sr. of Wisconsin. Red writers and journalists included Lewis, Theodore Drieser, H. L. Mencken, and William Allen White. Foreign leaders Mahatma Gandhi and Chiang Kai-shek were Red, as were John Dewey, theologian Reinhold Neibuhr, and lawyer Clarence Darrow. It required forty lines of small type to explain Albert Einstein's role in the communist conspiracy. Einstein had entered the country illegally and his theory of relativity was overrated because nobody but Einstein understood it. Some of his sins were that he was a Jew, he purchased paintings by communists, and he had been a guest in the Roosevelt White House.[66]

Readers learned that hundreds of communist organizations operated in the United States and around the world. Examples were the Federal Council of Churches, the World Court, the League of Nations, and the American Federation of Labor (AFL). The chief devil in the communist conspiracy, however, was the New Deal. Dilling warned that the congressional elections of 1934 might be the last opportunity "to vote Karl Marx [Roosevelt] out of office," before he organized "a united front General Strike culminating in Red seizure of power."[67]

The Red Network, priced at fifty cents wholesale and $1.15 retail, sold 2,000 copies within ten days. By 1941 it had gone through eight printings, and 16,000 copies had been sold in addition to the thousands given away.[68] Dilling advertised the book, placed it in Chicago bookstores, and sold it by mail, with Albert handling the packing. Also helping with sales and distribution were the KKK, the Knights of the White Camellia, the German-American Bund, and the Aryan Bookstore. Winrod offered free copies of The Red Network to new subscribers to his journal, The Revealer. Roy Zachary, national field marshal of the Silver Shirts, recommended the book. George Robnett, executive secretary of the Church League of America, used it extensively. Riley, president of the Northwestern Bible Training School and pastor of the First Baptist Church of Minneapolis, said he had distributed hundreds of copies. Officials of the DAR and the American Legion endorsed the book. The Federal Bureau of Investigation (FBI), the New York and Chicago police departments, and the Pinkerton Detective Agency purchased copies.[69]

The Erie Chemical Company, which manufactured tear gas, bought and distributed more than fifteen hundred copies on the premise that its tear gas could be used to control crowds of communists and labor agitators. The company sent copies to all of its salesmen, to the National Guard in each state, and to hundreds of police departments. Ten copies were sent to the San Francisco office of the Standard Oil Company, a potential customer. A munitions company in Los Angeles distributed 150 copies, hoping it could sell ammunition for use against communists. Other detective agencies and industrialists distributed the book, the former hoping to provide services against communist agitators, the latter seeking to discredit labor unions. In addition to earning money from such sales, Dilling became a more popular lecturer and increased her speaking fees. Anti-Semites praised her. One magazine in Germany described her as the "female führer" of the United States.[70]

Not everyone considered *The Red Network* a masterpiece of research, however. Methodist Bishop G. Bromley Oxnam said, "If there be any book anywhere that contains more robust and athletic falsifiers than that volume, I do not know it. It is not taken seriously by anyone who is worthy of the name 'student.'"[71] Miles M. Goldberg, of the Chicago chapter of the Anti-Defamation League of B'nai B'rith, remarked, "Practically everybody in America who does not agree with her is listed as communist in her *Red Network*."[72] Eminent psychologist Gordon Allport, who used *The Red Network* as an example of prejudice, quipped, "Apparently, if you step off the sidewalk with your left foot you're a communist."[73] Journalist Heywood Broun complained that Dilling accused him of being a member of the W. I. R., but he did not know what the initials stood for and could not find anyone who did.[74]

Dilling insisted she never made a mistake in her research, claiming that "the book is more accurate down to the pettiest detail than Ivory Soap is pure."[75] When *The New Republic* published an essay discrediting her book, Dilling replied that the article was "piffle and full of piffling inaccuracies."[76] In fact, the book was a gross exaggeration of communism's threat. Few of the people she listed were dangerous, and those who belonged to communist organizations were exercising their rights of free speech and association.

Two weeks before the presidential election of 1936, Dilling published her second book, *The Roosevelt Red Record and Its Background*. She described the 439-page tome as "a comprehensive study of the radical movement, in which President Roosevelt now plays a leading role—a startling narrative of the forces maneuvering America toward Red dictatorship."[77] Dilling had 6,000 copies printed by the Geographical Publishing Company of Chicago. Again Albert packed and shipped the book, which sold for one dollar.[78]

Dilling hoped the undigested compendium of news reports, clippings, and rumors would help defeat the Democratic presidential ticket and congressional candidates. But the Republican National Committee advised Republicans not to use it. The GOP decision was a setback for Dilling, who had worked intensely to complete the book—she was so busy she had not answered her letters in months—and confessed that the labor had exhausted her. Documenting the Red activities of the New Deal required more effort than one person could make. No one might ever know how many Reds served under Roosevelt.[79] Fighting communism was lonely work, and sometimes Dilling felt her labor reaped few results. She might be better off in Germany, where she was appreciated, she told Joy.[80]

The Roosevelt Red Record expanded on the lists of *The Red Network,* and the writing was even sloppier. Dilling quoted entire articles from newspapers and magazines; one quotation ran for six pages. Of course, the scissors-and-paste compilation did not stop figures on the far right from hailing the book. Among those recommending it were prominent anti-Semites Smith, Pelley, Charles B. Hudson, E. J. Garner, Joseph Kamp, and Lawrence Dennis. Pelley called it a "devastating array of facts and figures" and termed Dilling "one of the outstanding heroines of this hectic national period." Hudson wrote, "*The Roosevelt Red Record and Its Background* and *The Red Network* are the only reference books of their kind; are recommended by patriotic experts everywhere; are packed with accurate, irrefutable data."[81] But Sinclair, after reading in *The Roosevelt Red Record* that he was a communist, called Dilling a "pitiful, terror-stricken, hate-consumed candidate for an asylum."[82]

To those who said *The Roosevelt Red Record* was biased against the Roosevelts, Dilling replied, "I ought to be in jail for what I have not said about and Mr. and Mrs. Roosevelt."[83] Dilling preferred Hitler to the president, considering Roosevelt more dictatorial. "In my opinion, Benedict Arnold's treasonable act against the United States, by comparison with Roosevelt's aid to Communists and Communism, should rank as a petty misdemeanor."[84] FDR was a devious, manipulative, and power-mad communist.[85] To disarm resistance to his dictatorship, he planned to enact legislation limiting the private possession of firearms. Thus Dilling advised Joy to build a fortress refuge, stocked with guns and ammunition, to escape the Reds.[86]

Roosevelt's "Jew Deal," Dilling wrote, was taken from the *Communist Manifesto.* Roosevelt was implementing Marx's measures for communizing a nation, such as the abolition of private property, a progressive income tax, restriction of inheritances and the confiscation of dissidents' property. Also ominous were the centralization of banking, collectivization of industry and agriculture, welfare programs, business regulation, and relocation of the population for political purposes. Illustrating the varieties of subversion under the New Deal, Dilling described Red inroads among Blacks, the youth movement, churches, labor organizations, trade unions, and agricultural cooperatives.[87] Sadly, wealthy men sponsored this subversion. "It is rich men like Roosevelt, [Harold] Ickes, [Henry] Morgenthau, Vincent Astor, and the clique who seem to play best the socialist game of raving and ranting against the rich in their race for personal power," Dilling proclaimed.[88]

Other Reds in the New Deal were Frances Perkins, Harry Hopkins, Rexford Tugwell, Leon Henderson, James A. Farley, Hugh S. Johnson, and Justice Louis D. Brandeis. Communists were "in every key spot in the government," Dilling stated.[89] The New Dealer she most detested, though, was not an elected or appointed official but Eleanor Roosevelt, "a disgrace to the nation." Eleanor was an unfit mother whose children smoked, drank, divorced, and wrecked cars. Dilling made up satirical songs and stories about the Roosevelts and circulated rumors, such as the tale that FDR caught gonorrhea from Eleanor, who caught it from a Black man. If there was anyone worse than a male liberal, it was a female liberal such as Eleanor. Dilling might have felt threatened because Eleanor symbolized a changing identity for women. FDR, she complained, was too weak to control his wife.[90]

Dilling believed that if FDR were reelected in 1936, there would be no more free elections in the nation, so she worked to nominate a viable "nationalist" Republican alternative. Her first priority was to defeat the candidacy of Idaho Sen. William E. Borah. If Borah were nominated, the voters would have a choice between two communists, she feared. Borah had supported diplomatic recognition of the Soviet Union, Social Security, the Agricultural Adjustment Act, and the ACLU; the *Chicago Tribune* had called him an "Idol of Moscow." Dilling wrote a pamphlet entitled *Borah: "Borer from Within" the G.O.P.* and distributed 5,000 copies at the Republican National Convention in Cleveland. She took credit for denying Borah the nomination.[91]

Gratified by Borah's defeat, Dilling was disappointed by the nomination of Kansas Gov. Alfred M. Landon. Landon looked like a night clerk trying to appear serious, she wrote. He was a poor speaker and Dilling feared Roosevelt would outtalk him. Moreover, Dilling considered Landon stupid; the Dillings gave the middle name "Landon" to their stupid little cocker spaniel. Landon's associates also concerned Dilling. His running mate, Chicago publisher Frank Knox, was a liberal who printed Red propaganda in his newspaper and employed a Red book reviewer to praise FDR. Jews ran Landon's campaign. After deciding that the Dillings had no alternative but to support Landon, the lesser evil, Albert went to Republican campaign headquarters in Chicago to volunteer, only to be told he must work under two Jews.[92]

Dilling was angered by the ineptitude of the Landon campaign and by the overconfidence of businessmen who supported Landon. She and Albert dined with six businessmen who boasted they need not campaign because Landon would win easily. On the way home, Dilling told Albert she wished communists would start shooting at businessmen to arouse them from lethargy. She complained that neither Landon nor Roosevelt discussed the real issue, which was "Marx versus Washington." After Roosevelt won and Landon carried only two states, Dilling's solace was to say "I told you so" to the industrialists who had predicted Landon would win. They got what they deserved, she said.[93]

In 1940 Dilling was involved in the presidential campaign again. As in 1936 she wanted the GOP to nominate a "nationalist." Alas, all of the prominent Republicans were as Red as Roosevelt and were manipulated by Jews. Thomas E. Dewey had prosecuted Fritz Kuhn, the patriotic leader of the German-American Bund, and had helped sponsor an ACLU conference. Sen. Robert A. Taft of Ohio had been an attorney for the Red AFL. Even Sen. Arthur H. Vandenberg of Michigan, whom Dilling had once admired, had become a New Dealer. Depressed by her fear that Dewey, Taft, Vandenberg, or Wendell L. Willkie might win the nomination, she wrote a scathing essay condemning the major contenders, Wanted—A Presidential "Man on a White Horse."[94] Dilling eventually supported Willkie, albeit without enthusiasm. When Roosevelt won, she sneered, saying the country would get what it deserved.[95]

Dilling timed the publication of her third book, The Octopus, to influence the campaign and was disappointed because it seemed to have little effect. More than her previous books, this work was directed at Jews. It was so anti-Semitic that she published it under a pseudonym, the Rev. Frank Woodruff Johnson. She feared being called anti-Semitic and Albert thought the charge might hurt his law practice. When people wrote to Dilling with questions about Jews, she often referred them to Johnson's fine book. "The Jews can never prove that I'm anti-Semitic," she said. "I'm too clever for them." Dilling arranged for Hudson, a Jew-baiting pamphleteer in Omaha, Nebraska, to distribute the book.[96]

The "octopus" was the Anti-Defamation League of B'nai B'rith, which tried to undermine Christianity and engineer a communist coup in the United States. The book marked a new phase in Dilling's career, in which she would emphasize that Jews were behind communism. Marxism was a Jewish invention and Marx "was a descendant of a long line of rabbis."[97] The Bolshevik leaders were Jewish, financed by the Jewish banking house of Kuhn,

Loeb, and Company. Hundreds of thousands of Jewish communists had fled Czarist Russia to come to the United States, where they congregated in New York City and practiced communism, making the metropolis the "Jew-communist" capital of the world.[98]

In her later writing, Dilling expanded upon the theme that Jews were responsible for communism. "The person who does not know that Marxism and Jewry are synonomous is uninformed," she wrote. When "Marxist Jew" Bela Kun took over in Hungary in 1919, "sex filth was introduced along with atheist teachings in the public schools, homes were robbed and bodies thrown into the Danube daily. I met a Hungarian official who offered to get me pictures of ovens in which nuns were baked alive."[99]

Dilling claimed she had not set out to slander Jews, but once she began investigating communism, she inevitably traced Marxism to its source. "Sound Jews deplore the fact that no one with open eyes can observe a Red parade, a communist, anarchist, socialist, or radical meeting anywhere in the world without noting the prominence of Jewry." If followed that "the majority of the Jews in the U. S. A. are under Marxist leadership."[100] Racial libel laws were attempts to eliminate patriots who exposed Jews. "The first thing a Communist government does is to pass laws to imprison and kill anti-communists for anti-Semitism, for anyone who studies communism learns it is but the political vehicle and tool of Judaism."[101]

The Octopus and Dilling's other anti-Semitic writings, including tracts also written under the pseudonym of Johnson, established Dilling as a star in the galaxy of anti-Semites. Hudson and Winrod devoted several issues of their magazines to praising *The Octopus*. Hudson mailed copies of the book to every member of Congress. Winrod wrote that the book, a "thunderbolt," was "smashing all records for sales and circulation." He recommended it to ministers: "Every pastor who would know the unpleasant truth about the underhanded methods used to weaken, confuse and devitalize the Christ-forces of our nation should have a copy of *Octopus* in his study." He compared *The Octopus* to Martin Luther's Ninety-five Theses and said Dilling's book exposed Jewish attempts to enslave Gentiles just as *Uncle Tom's Cabin* exposed the cruelties of slavery.[102]

Other anti-Semites praised *The Octopus*. Edward James Smythe suggested, "Millions of Christians should be reading *The Octopus*—it is the greatest indictment of the Mongolian Jews I have ever read." Garner, a reactionary publisher and author later indicted for sedition, wrote, "Every phase of Jewish control, in every field of American life, is exposed in the pages of this book." Protestant minister William Kullgren advertised *The Octopus* in his monthly *Beacon Light,* terming it "one of the most revealing documents ever written on the Jewish question." It was a bargain: "Just imagine getting a book of 256 pages for 50 cents."[103]

Dilling needed only to add Blacks to the conspiracy of Jews and communists to complete her triangle of hate. Communists used Blacks to do their dirty work for them, she found; communists put Blacks in the vanguard of revolution, then enslaved them. "The interracial idea is one of the strongest dogmas of Socialism-Communism," she wrote. "It remained for Karl Marx to insist that agitation must not cease until the races and sexes be poured into one melting pot to be moulded into one mass, as planned by Marx, not by God." Dilling was infuriated by communist fostering of interracial sex. "I have never attended a Communist party mass meeting without observing the public petting of Negroes and whites," she wrote. "At one meeting three burly Negroes were pawing their white girl companion, a college-type blonde wearing a squirrel coat."[104]

Dilling was scandalized to hear that several Blacks were advisers to Roosevelt and other New Dealers: "James Pryor, a Negro, is confidential secretary to President Roosevelt. Robert H. Weaver, a Negro politician, has been appointed Special Assistant to Secretary Ickes, salary $6,000 per annum."[105] The Roosevelts, wanting Black votes, pandered to Blacks. "The studied, insincere and obsequious flattery by the Roosevelts and their radical supporters of the Negro people is without precedent in any American political party. However, it is not by accident but follows, as closely as other parts of the Roosevelt Socialist program, the old well-laid, well-thought-out plan of the Marxists to enlist and use the Negro to change the American system of government and the entire social order."[106] Particularly galling were the efforts of Eleanor Roosevelt, who spoke to Black organizations, invited Black leaders to the White House, and posed for photographs with Blacks. "At Detroit, Mrs. Roosevelt posed for a winning vote-getting interracial picture, showing herself grinning broadly into the face of a Negro girl and clasping one of the girl's hands which held a flower for Mrs. Roosevelt."[107]

Dilling made common cause with some of the more infamous racists in the country. "For me," she wrote, "there is no treat equal to gabfesting and exchanging data with fellow crusaders."[108] She was the first woman to be admitted to the inner circle of anti-Semitic and racist crusaders, and to be treated as an equal by such established bigots as Smith, Winrod, Pelley, and Coughlin. She obtained access to huge files about Jews, communists, Blacks, and New Dealers maintained by zealots like Harry Jung of Chicago, head of the American Vigilant Intelligent Federation, and Nelson E. Hewitt, a "super-patriot" who edited an anticommunist weekly. She received aid from Francis Ralston Welsh, a lawyer who used his wealth to research "subversive" organizations. (After his death in 1938, Welsh's files were bequeathed to Dilling.) In addition, William Randolph Hearst and Robert McCormick used their newspapers to promote Dilling's crusades.[109]

Dilling became increasingly conscious of her role as a woman in far-right movements that had been monopolized by men. Knowing she stood little chance of taking over a male-led movement, she enlisted women allies, including Lyrl Clark Van Hyning of Chicago, Agnes Waters of Washington, D. C., and Marguerite Morrison of New York. Dilling viewed women as an untapped resource for the far right and saw herself as their leader. Anticommunism by itself was not enough to galvanize women into a distinct movement, although the threat of war was sufficient, particularly because mothers feared the loss of sons and spouses.

Meanwhile, Dilling cultivated contacts among male and female isolationists, some of whom did not share her antipathy to Jews and Blacks and perhaps did not know of it. Still, they all opposed Roosevelt and forged a network that included congressmen, businessmen, publishers, and celebrities such as Charles A. Lindbergh. Alone, Dilling posed little threat to American democracy, but in alliance with powerful men and legions of zealous women, she could become a potent force in the movement to fight Roosevelt as the American ship of state headed on a collision course with Hitler's Reich.

☰ THREE ☰
The Fifth Column

The anticommunist and anti-Semitic movement that Dilling launched in the 1930s was kept alive by pro-fascist propaganda, some of it imported from Germany, before merging with the isolationist movement in 1939. Many leaders in the former movement were not outright fascists, but they subscribed to fascist tenets, including extreme nationalism, a master race, the power of will, the supremacy of emotion over intellect, and the obligation to follow a führer. Inadvertently or deliberately they served the fascist cause, and the Nazi government, aware of their value in fomenting defeatism and dividing Americans with anti-Semitism, helped coordinate their activities.

National socialism was introduced to the United States shortly after becoming a factor in German politics. In 1924 the National Socialist Teutonia Association was organized in Detroit by the brothers Fritz and Peter Gissibl to proselytize recent German immigrants. By 1932 the association, headquarterted in New York, had branches in Chicago, Los Angeles and Cincinnati, and it grew as the Great Depression worsened.[1]

After Hitler became chancellor in January 1933, the Nazi Propaganda Ministry instructed its Psychological Laboratory to devise strategy to undermine the American government. The laboratory determined that the key was to exploit dissatisfaction with the New Deal among conservatives and channel this alienation. Nazi agents in the United States were to set Gentile against Jew and to promote the idea that the government had fallen into the hands of Jews and communists. "It's child's play to make good anti-Semites of the Americans," a Nazi agent wrote to his superiors. Two German organizations kept the psychological saboteurs in the United States supplied with anti-Semitic propaganda: World Service, headquartered in Erfurt, and the German Fighters' Society, located in Hamburg. These sources sent millions of pamphlets and bulletins to inspire race hatred. The material found its way into the publications of Nazi sympathizers such as Dilling, Coughlin, Smith, Pelley, Winrod, and the mothers' organizations.[2]

Germany realized it would be more successful by working through American puppets than by permitting its hand to appear behind propaganda. Therefore, it fostered the development of German American organizations as successors to the heavy-handed Teutonia, which had been dominated by

German-speaking immigrants. The first of these groups, the Friends of the New Germany, was created in July 1933. Headquartered in New York City, it was led by Heinz Spanknoebel, who obtained a charter from Hitler's deputy, Rudolf Hess. Spanknoebel's organization included a uniformed contingent that corresponded to Hitler's SS, drilled, carried nightsticks, and kept order at rallies. Its members reportedly attacked Jewish merchants and painted swastikas on synagogues. The Friends also opposed communists and Blacks and urged all right-thinking Whites to unite against non-Whites. The organization gained about six thousand members by 1935, but its excesses led to an investigation by the House Un-American Activities Committee (HUAC), and Spanknoebel fled to Germany just ahead of deportation proceedings. With the group discredited, Germany dissolved the Friends in 1935.[3]

Into the breach stepped the German-American Bund, whose führer, Kuhn, sought to integrate Americanism with Nazism. "Our task over here is to fight Jewish Marxism and communism," said Kuhn, a naturalized American citizen who had fought in the German Army in World War I. "So long as there's a swastika, there'll be no hammer and sickle in this country."[4] The Bund became the largest of the pro-Nazi organizations, with an estimated ten thousand members in 1937, including five thousand uniformed storm troopers. The group set up camps for paramilitary training, established a youth organization modeled after the Hitler Youth, and staged yearly rallies to celebate Hitler's birthday. Members proclaimed loyalty to Germany and to the United States, although they condemned the New Deal.[5] Kuhn, who referred to a "Jewish dictatorship" under FDR, disliked the president's appointment of Jews to office and attempted to create an anti-Roosevelt voting bloc of German Americans. He advocated that Jews be fingerprinted, photographed, and ordered to carry identification cards "so we would know who is walking around us in this country."[6]

Women were integral to the Bund's work, organizing into cells and infiltrating social clubs and school groups in which they could exploit prejudice against Jews and Britain. They boycotted Jewish merchants, swelled the ranks at pro-Nazi rallies, and insulted people who looked Jewish. Many of these women belonged to the mothers' movement. Dilling was a Bund favorite: her books were praised in its publications and promoted by Germany, and she spoke at Bund gatherings.[7]

Bund notoriety peaked with a rally on Washington's Birthday in 1939 in New York. Some twenty thousand Nazi sympathizers packed Madison Square Garden, and ten thousand people demonstrated against the Bund outside as two thousand police officers maintained order.[8] Already, however, Bund membership had begun to decline due to bad publicity, stemming from the group's support for atrocities on Kristallnacht in 1938, when Jewish stores in Germany were destroyed, synagogues were burned, and innocents were arrested. In 1938 HUAC investigated the Bund, and in 1939 Kuhn was sentenced to prison for embezzling from the Bund treasury. His successor, Gerhard Wilhelm Kunze, attempted to revive the organization, declaring, "A Jew is supposed to be a living being, but so is a flea. But the flea is not going to live on me, and neither is the Jew." Nevertheless, the Bund declined after Kuhn's conviction. Germany, fearing that Washington might be provoked into severing diplomatic relations with Berlin, ordered its citizens to resign from the Bund.[9]

A few Americans were employed to collaborate with the German propaganda program, most notably George Sylvester Viereck, a poet, novelist, and journalist who had been a paid propagandist for Germany in World War I. Through diplomat Hans Thomsen, Germany gave Viereck more than five hundred thousand dollars to influence Congress and distribute propaganda. He edited a magazine published by the German Library of Information in New York, contributed articles to Coughlin's monthly, *Social Justice,* wrote pro-German, anti-Semitic books, and bought a small publishing company that he converted into a propaganda mill. Further, he recruited allies in the House and Senate and paid federal officials to deliver speeches and write books. The books were distributed via a network of Axis collaborators, including Smith and Dilling.[10]

Viereck's closest ally was isolationist Sen. Ernest Lundeen of Minnesota. Lundeen headed a figurehead group organized by Viereck and funded by the German government, the Make Europe Pay War Debts Committee, whose chief objective was to discredit interventionists. Viereck had another friend in Congressman Hamilton Fish of New York. Fish introduced Viereck to George Hill, Fish's assistant secretary, who was put on the Nazi payroll. Viereck wrote isolationist speeches that were delivered by sympathetic members of Congress and inserted in the *Congressional Record.* Hill ordered reprints and mailed them under congressional franks. When the scheme was discovered, Hill and Viereck were convicted of serving as unregistered agents of a foreign government and sentenced to prison.[11]

After 1938 the Nazi government relied less on paid agents and more on American sympathizers to promote its cause. By 1939 there were more than eight hundred organizations that were pro-fascist or pro-Nazi. Most were small and local in focus, but cumulatively their impact was significant.[12]

Crudely written publications and cartoons that used fabricated quotations emphasized the fifth columnists' themes. The Jew-dominated American government, directed by the dictator in the White House, intended to eradicate Christianity and create a world communist state. Jews controlled the

British Empire and primed Europe for communism by creating the Soviet Union, where thirty million Gentiles had been slaughtered. In the United States, Jewish control encompassed the press, radio, and movies as well as the government. A constant menace, Jews were evil and unpatriotic, corrupting everything they touched. Instead of following the Constitution, most followed the Talmud, which taught them to rape, enslave, torture, and crucify Christians. Jews had even kidnapped Lindbergh's baby in 1932 for use in a ritual sacrifice.[13]

The closest thing the American pro-Nazis had to a *Mein Kampf* was Lawrence Dennis's *The Coming American Fascism,* written to "rationalize fascism before it became an accomplished fact in the United States." Dennis had served in the Army and Foreign Service and worked as a Wall Street broker. He edited an ultraright magazine, *The Awakener,* with the notorious anti-Semite Joseph P. Kamp; found friends in Dilling and in more moderate isolationists such as Lindbergh, Nye, and Wheeler; and boasted that Smith "listens to me." From 1936 until the attack on Pearl Harbor, Dennis condemned democracy, extolled the dictatorships of Germany and Italy, and argued that fascism was the only cure for American economic ills. A defendant in the 1944 mass sedition trial, Dennis served time in prison on other charges.[14]

Henry Ford was the inspiration and financial godfather to dozens of anti-Semitic propagandists. In 1922 the automobile manufacturer was nearly elected to the United States Senate, and in 1923 he was a serious contender for the 1924 presidential nomination of both major parties. In 1920 his newspaper, the *Dearborn Independent,* started a series of anti-Semitic articles entitled "The International Jew," which ran for almost two years. Based largely on *The Protocols of the Learned Elders of Zion,* a forged account of a Jewish plot to conquer the world by undermining Christian civilization, the articles were later issued as a book. Ford's backing lent a veneer of respectability to anti-Semitism.[15]

Ford gave money to the Nazi Party in Germany in the 1920s and employed Nazi sympathizers in Detroit, including Spanknoebel and Kuhn. In addition, Ford gave thousands of dollars to such Nazi sympathizers as Dilling, Smith, and the authors of the anti-Semitic journal *Scribner's Commentator.* He opposed American participation in World War II until Pearl Harbor and refused to manufacture airplane engines for the British. Hitler admired him: the führer hung a portrait of the industrialist in his office and awarded him a medal, the highest honor the Reich could bestow upon a foreigner. Ford never renounced or returned the medal.[16]

No leader of the anti-Semitic isolationists was more controversial than

Coughlin, founder of a Catholic church in Royal Oak, Michigan that grew to attract a large congregation due partly to his network radio broadcasts. A gifted orator with a mellifluous voice, Coughlin made complex problems seem simple. He turned from religion to politics as the Great Depression worsened. Originally a supporter of President Herbert Hoover, he grew impatient with Hoover's limited approach to the financial crisis. Coughlin advocated inflated, silver-backed currency; an end to the Federal Reserve System; and the creation of a national bank.[17]

Coughlin supported FDR for president in 1932, but after the election they clashed, broke over monetary policy, and became foes. The priest joined Smith and Francis E. Townsend in 1936 to found the Union Party and to run a candidate, North Dakota Congressman William Lemke, against Roosevelt. After FDR won overwhelmingly, Coughlin grew bitter. Arguing that Nazism was a "political defense mechanism" against Jewish communism, he predicted, "Someday the Jews will get what's coming to them. Just wait and see." He attacked Roosevelt's Jewish advisers in *Social Justice* and drew praise from the likes of Dilling.[18]

Coughlin's isolationism intensified. Claiming that international bankers and New Dealers were pushing the United States toward war, he opposed every step toward intervention: repeal of the arms embargo, conscription, and Lend-Lease. Far from being an enemy of the United States, Germany was the only nation preventing a communist takeover of Europe, Coughlin maintained. Anyway, American intervention would be futile because Britain and the USSR were doomed to defeat, and because the fate of France—a country controlled by Marxists, atheists, and Jews before Nazi conquest—should not concern Americans. If American boys had to fight in Europe, was democracy worth saving? "Never forget, Mr. and Mrs. America, that your boy is being counted today. The international warmongers, footing up the man-strength of the United States, are figuring on your boy for the guns." The Jews were not worth saving either, since they had declared war on Christians first. "Must the entire world go to war for 600,000 Jews in Germany?" Coughlin asked. The best course, he concluded, would be to let Germany conquer Britain and the Soviet Union.[19]

Coughlin attracted thousands of female supporters, and women joined the Coughlin-influenced Christian Front, which harassed Jews on the East Coast. Dilling and her secretary, Mary Leach, made pilgrimages to Royal Oak, where they had cordial visits with the priest. Moreover, admirers of Coughlin carved out leadership roles in mothers' groups, among them Rosa Farber and Mary Decker of the Mothers of the U. S. A. (based in Detroit), Frieda Stanley of the United Mothers of America (based in Cleveland), Edith Scott of the

Philadelphia branch of the National Legion of Mothers of America, and Mynnie Fischer of Mothers Mobilizing Against War (based in Milwaukee). Coughlin appreciated the backing of these organizations. When the mothers from Detroit and Cleveland staged a "death watch" in the Senate lobby during a debate over conscription, he praised them in *Social Justice.*[20]

The preeminent leader of the far right, unique in his ability to unite the respectable and the lunatic fringes, was Smith. A onetime preacher born in Wisconsin, Smith entered politics as the organizer of the Share Our Wealth Society for Louisiana Sen. Huey P. Long. After Long's death, Smith fraternized with segregationist Georgia Gov. Eugene Talmadge and joined with Coughlin and Townsend in the Union Party. He then settled in Detroit, befriended Ford and Dilling, and fought Roosevelt, unions, communists, Jews, and internationalists. Funded by contributions from businessmen and patrons on his mailing list, he founded nationalist organizations: the Committee of One Million in 1937, the Christian Nationalist Crusade in 1942, and the America First Party in 1943. Also, Smith ran for the United States Senate in 1942 and for president in 1944.[21]

After the 1936 presidential election, Smith focused on fighting Roosevelt's foreign policies. He argued the European war was started by Jews who attacked German Christians and desired a world communist state ruled by Joseph Stalin and Roosevelt. In 1940 Smith initiated an antiwar petition. The effort yielded a list of one million signatures that Vandenberg submitted to Congress. And at Fish's request, Smith appeared before the House Foreign Affairs Committee and the Senate Foreign Relations Committee to testify against the Lend-Lease bill. Lend-Lease would tempt Britain's enemies to fight the United States, violate neutrality, undermine the Monroe Doctrine, and make FDR a dictator, Smith asserted. He condemned Britain and the Soviet Union and demanded an end to immigration.[22]

Smith believed he, like Hitler, was persecuted by the Jews and maligned by the Jew-dominated media. The Jews hated Hitler, Smith said, because the führer was a Christian who believed in the Bible. Reprinting an address in which Hitler used biblical references to justify his anti-Jewish policy, Smith asked, "What good Christian American can find any fault with the above quotations? Could it be that the same Jew-controlled newspapers that lied to us about Father Coughlin and Gerald Smith failed to tell us the truth about Hitler?"[23]

Smith knew Fish and wrote him flattering letters, but Fish's replies were perfunctory. Smith told the congressman that Fish deserved to be president and praised his stand against Lend-Lease. Still, after Pearl Harbor, Fish distanced himself from Smith.[24]

Smith's closest friend in the House was Clare E. Hoffman of Michigan, who spoke at meetings of the America First Party, subscribed to Smith's magazine, *The Cross and the Flag*, and inserted Smith's propaganda into the *Congressional Record*. Smith called Hoffman "one of the most courageous men in the United States Congress" and circulated thousands of copies of Hoffman's "Roosevelt is a Judas" speech. Smith's racism troubled Hoffman, however, and they broke after the war, when Hoffman introduced legislation prohibiting racial discrimination in employment.[25]

Another Roosevelt-hating congressman from Michigan, Roy O. Woodruff, was close to Smith. In August 1942 Woodruff inserted a letter from Smith into the *Congressional Record*, terming Smith a "great leader." The next year Woodruff inserted the featured editorial from the first issue of *The Cross and the Flag* into the journal. During the war, Woodruff opposed the rationing of rubber, an issue that Smith borrowed for the centerpiece of his 1942 Senate campaign.[26]

Smith was an ally and, he said, a personal friend, of the isolationist Vandenberg, who praised Smith's "inspiring chairmanship" of the Committee of One Million and called him "the voice of America." Vandenberg said, "It certainly is comforting and helpful to have you 'in my corner' when the bell rings for these big battles."[27] The correspondence continued after Pearl Harbor, and Smith's fawning flattered the senator. When Michigan residents having trouble with the federal bureaucracy wrote to Smith, he referred them to Vandenberg, who obtained results.[28]

Sen. Robert R. Reynolds of North Carolina shared Smith's bigotry. In 1938 Reynolds organized the isolationist, anti-Semitic Vindicators Association, Inc., and founded a newspaper, the *American Vindicator,* which would claim 30,000 subscribers. Reynolds advocated the registration and fingerprinting of aliens and deportation of "undesirables." In a Senate speech in 1938, he said, "Hitler and Mussolini have a date with destiny. It's foolish to oppose them, so why not play ball with them?" Reynolds furnished anti-immigrant speeches in franked envelopes to the ultrarightist George Deatherage, who addressed and mailed them. Also, Coughlin and Dilling reprinted and distributed Reynolds's speeches. Smith was Reynolds's closest friend on the far right, however. Reynolds wrote a letter to Smith, praising the first issue of *The Cross and the Flag,* and Smith published it as an endorsement. "Mr. Smith, insofar as I know, is a real, genuine American who loves his country better than any other country in the world, and I do not believe I could pay a man a higher compliment than that," Reynolds wrote to a constituent.[29]

Nye, who claimed that "those of the Jewish faith are contributing to the cause of intervention," collaborated with Smith. He spoke at a Smith rally in

Detroit on March 2, 1941, and permitted his name to be used for Smith's cause. Nye corresponded with Smith and did not object when Smith boasted, "The best man in the United States Senate is Gerald Nye. I love Nye. We have exchanged many long, personal letters."[30]

To some degree, Smith's movement was an incubator for the mothers' movement. His ideology appealed to ultraconservative women. Smith told women they had an honored place in his crusade. His emphasis on motherhood was a way to offer them recognition. Editorials in *The Cross and the Flag* praised mothers and urged them to form associations. "If you are a Christian mother, organize a little mothers' group in your community," Smith wrote. And late in the war, he asked, "Who is better qualified to cooperate with us in our America First movement than the mothers of our heroic sons?"[31]

At his rallies, Smith sold thousands of copies of Dilling's books as well as *Women's Voice,* the chief Midwestern newspaper of the mothers' movement. Dilling spoke often at Smith's meetings, although the ideological soul mates clashed personally because neither liked strong, competing personalities.[32] Smith had no such problem with Norma Lundeen, widow of the senator who died in a plane crash in 1940. The female speaker who most frequently accompanied Smith, she toured the Midwest with Smith, claiming he represented the ideals of her husband. Smith even sponsored her as a candidate for Congress from Minnesota. "Some day, Mrs. Lundeen will be one of the most influential women in American politics," he said, a prediction that failed to materialize.[33] Other partners on the podium were Catherine Brown, a leader of the National Blue Star Mothers of America, and Stanley. Brown and Stanley spoke at the 1944 nominating convention of the America First Party.[34]

Smith's followers were disproportionately female, white, middle-class, middle-aged, and Protestant, judging from the mail Smith received and from photographs and written accounts of his meetings. Many of his followers joined the mothers' movement. Too, women furnished much of Smith's voluntary labor force, answering and sorting mail, keeping accounts of donations, getting speakers, renting halls, securing permits, and lining up publicity for rallies. His salaried office workers, Renata Legant Martz and Opal Tanner White, were women.[35]

But there was no room for women in leadership positions. Smith had a domineering attitude toward women. His marriage was a tyranny and he never permitted his wife to express publicly an opinion of her own. His view was not based exclusively on sex stereotypes, for he would not share power with men or tolerate allies who did not agree with him. Nonetheless, he did demand conformity to rigid gender roles, male supremacy among them. Like many of the women who spun off isolationist, anti-Semitic organizations from movements such as his, Smith attacked Eleanor Roosevelt for violating gender roles. For the First Lady's activism he blamed FDR, complaining that a man who was too weak to control his wife was too weak to run the country— an odd charge in light of his argument that Roosevelt was a dictator.[36]

The most bizarre figure on the American far right during the 1930s and early 1940s was Pelley, a writer, religious mystic, and organizer of the para-military Silver Shirts. Raised by a family of religious zealots, Pelley had a vivid imagination that enabled him to become a successful writer of novels, short stories, and screenplays. Wealthy but depressed and unstable, he turned to religious mysticism, perhaps motivated by guilt for straying from his parents' teachings. In 1928, on the verge of a nervous breakdown, his creativity lost, he retreated to a California mountain cabin for rest. On the night of May 28–29 he had a hallucination in which he died and went to heaven. Oracles instructed him about his mission, then returned him to earth. When he re-gained his senses, Pelley was a changed man: he gave up alcohol and tobacco, his insomnia disappeared, and his creativity returned—although it was di-verted into spiritualistic channels. For the rest of his life, Pelley claimed to receive instruction from the spirit world.[37]

Pelley's mysticism might have been innocent enough had it not been com-bined with rabid anti-Semitism and admiration for Hitler. After publishing spiritualist magazines in the late 1920s and early 1930s, he turned to militant anti-Semitism when Hitler was appointed German chancellor. Pelley consid-ered Hitler's rise a signal to mobilize forces in the United States against de-monic Jews. Consequently, he modeled the Silver Shirts on Hitler's Black Shirts.[38]

The Silver Shirts were meant to help Pelley establish a Christian common-wealth and to thwart Jewish attempts to install a communist dictatorship in the United States. "The adroit thing to do," Pelley wrote to a Nazi agent in New York, "is to let a spontaneous American movement be born here that has exactly similar principles and precepts to Hitler's that shall be American in character and personnel, and that shall work shoulder to shoulder with Ger-man aims and purposes."[39] To those Jews who complained about the Silver Shirts, Pelley warned, "Any kike who thinks he can tell me what kind of shirt I can wear, or that I can't wear a grey one with a scarlet 'L' on it, will get a punch in his nose that he'll remember till he lands in Abraham's bosom."[40]

Silver Shirts pledged to follow Pelley and obey the Bible. They wore para-military uniforms resembling those of German storm troopers, drilled, and carried arms. Membership peaked at about fifteen thousand in 1933 but de-clined to five thousand by 1938.[41] Pelley said that when he took over the country, his Silver Shirts would be the elite of the Army, police force, and government. Every resident would belong to a vast civil service, hold shares in a national corporation, and be rewarded with honorary titles rather than money. Pelley would ban banks, unions, and lawyers, as well as disenfranchise Jews and confine them to one city per state.[42]

Pelley and many of his disciples were paranoid, seeing evil Jews everywhere. The aspiring führer claimed that all communists were Jews, and if someone pointed out a Nordic communist, Pelley would respond that the communist must have a Jewish mind. One Minneapolis follower said the static on her radio was broadcast by Jews so she could not hear the news. In addition, Silver Shirts circulated rumors that Treasury Secretary Henry Morgenthau, a Jew, had silver quarters manufactured in the Soviet Union and bought them for five cents each. Others said the symbol of Roosevelt's National Recovery Administration (NRA), which included an American eagle, was the biblical Mark of the Beast.[43]

According to Pelley, symbols on the walls of a pyramid at Gizah prophesied a Jewish takeover of the United States on September 16, 1936—Rosh Hashanah, the Jewish New Year. When the Jews tried to take over, FDR would proclaim martial law and cancel the November presidential election, in which Pelley was a candidate. Pelley did little campaigning, except in the pages of *Pelley's Weekly,* and was on the ballot only in Washington state, where he polled fewer than sixteen hundred votes. His credibility was eroded further when no Jewish takeover was attempted. Pelley blamed his defeat on the Jews and said FDR's victory hastened the conflict between the forces of light and those of darkness.[44]

Beginning in 1935 Pelley encountered legal troubles due to the tangled finances of his many enterprises, problems that occupied most of his time until he began to turn his attention to foreign affairs in 1938. He applauded the Kristallnacht violence against German Jews, wrote that Germany was an ideal country, and called Japan a paper tiger that could be defeated by "one lone Yankee's fists." In 1939 Pelley advocated American neutrality because he considered Hitler's cause just and because he knew war would enhance FDR's power. He predicted Britain's defeat and warned that if the United States entered the war, democracy would be destroyed at home. After Pearl Harbor, he continued to praise Hitler and condemn Jews, saying the United States was fighting on the wrong side and that the war was waged to protect "Mongolic Judaists." In 1942 Pelley was convicted of circulating seditious propaganda and sentenced to fifteen years in prison. While languishing in jail, he became a defendant in the mass sedition trial of 1944.[45]

Pelley pioneered the use of women in the pro-Nazi movement, creating Petticoat Platoons in Southern California. In addition, the Silver Shirts used women to distribute literature because women evoked less hostility than did males. The idea of using women, which helped recruiting, originated with Henry D. Allen, whose wife, Pearl, became a leader of Silver Shirt women on the West Coast. The German Propaganda Ministry, mobilizing women for the Nazi cause and bringing some American women to Germany for training, inspired Allen's idea.[46]

Winrod, a fundamentalist minister from Kansas, was less complex than Pelley but equally militant as an anti-Semite. Winrod started his ministry at seventeen and developed a regional reputation, creating an organization to combat the teaching of evolution and to uphold Prohibition. In the 1920s he began to study communism and decided Jews were responsible. He approved of Hitler's suppression of Jews, accepted *The Protocols,* and claimed the anti-Christ was a Jew. According to Winrod, Christianity flourished in Germany, whose führer was the only leader bold enough to defy Jews. (Winrod hated Catholics as well as Jews; he opposed Democratic presidential nominee Al Smith, a Catholic, in 1928.)[47]

Winrod embraced anti-Semitism at the same time he became a harsh critic of the New Deal. He loathed Roosevelt's fiscal policy, considered the New Deal communistic, and condemned the president for extending diplomatic recognition to the Soviet Union. FDR was also faulted for the repeal of Prohibition. After a drunken driver damaged Winrod's car, Winrod sent a telegram to the White House, saying he was holding FDR personally responsible and was demanding $100 for repairs. He was disappointed when FDR ignored the demand.[48]

In 1938 Winrod ran for the Republican nomination for United States Senator from Kansas. The high point of his notoriety, the campaign frightened liberals, one of whom said the "Jayhawk Nazi" was on Hitler's payroll. Winrod finished a distant third, running well in counties where the KKK had been strong in the 1920s. Then came a personal setback: in 1940 his wife Frances, filed for divorce on grounds that he wanted to be führer of the United States. A few years after divorcing, however, they remarried.[49]

Like others who sympathized with Hitler, Winrod turned to foreign policy in the late 1930s, and much of his work from 1939 to 1941 involved keeping the United States out of war. Winrod viewed the outbreak of World War II as the coming of the apocalypse. Capitalist profiteers and journalists had pushed the United States into World War I and were now rehashing their propaganda. These traders in the tools of death were allied with New Dealers who wanted to save German Jews from Nazism. Winrod denounced the war even after Pearl Harbor and was the first individual named in the mass sedition indictment handed down in 1942.[50]

Winrod had close relations with agitators who preached defeatism, especially Dilling and Smith. In 1938 an informant saw stacks of Dilling's pamphlet *Dare We Oppose Red Treason?* at Winrod's office in Wichita.[51] Dilling described Winrod as a "sound Christian fundamentalist" who published an "excellent monthly."[52] She gave away subscriptions to Winrod's magazine, *The Defender,* to persons on her mailing list and described Winrod in glowing terms. "Dr. Winrod issues a fearless Christian magazine with much material not found elsewhere. . . . If you do not already subscribe, you need the *Defender.* If you do subscribe, send in the names of one or more Christian friends who do not." Of Smith, Winrod said, "We've often had prayers together; he's one of my closest friends." Winrod considered Smith a protégé and advised him on fund-raising by mail and on publishing.[53]

Deatherage, who tried to unite the far right during the late 1930s, was likewise a friend of Smith. Leader of a neo-Klan white supremacist group, the Knights of the White Camellia, Deatherage created a pro-fascist party called the American Nationalist Confederation in 1937. Pelley, Fry, and Donald Shea, director of the National Gentile League, were among those associated with the confederation. In 1937 Deatherage also called an American Christian Front Conference attended by about seventy ultra-right groups. He had a führer for the United States: George Van Horn Moseley, a retired Army general.[54]

Moseley had been a general during World War I and became Army deputy chief of staff under Gen. Douglas MacArthur. But after he was bypassed for chief of staff, he retired with a grudge against Roosevelt. Tall, erect, and handsome, with forty-three years of Army service, Moseley seemed the perfect vehicle for a right-wing military coup. He appealed to the far right because he was authoritarian, anti-Semitic, and a Klan sympathizer. "Democracy, hell!" he said in 1940. "It's nothing but communism. We don't want the mob rule of democracy."[55] An advocate of sterilizing Jews, he believed that "the whole tribe should be eliminated from the human race."[56]

Unfortunately for Moseley, he damaged his cause in May 1939, when HUAC, believing it had uncovered a fascist plan to make him führer, called him to testify. His lengthy opening statement, covered by the press, was so racist it was expunged from the record. Moseley warned of a Jewish-led communist conspiracy that threatened the country. He refused to drink water during the hearing, for fear that Jews had poisoned it. Soon it became clear that the aging ex-general lacked the judgment, magnetism, and stamina to lead a rebellion. A far-right plot to bring him to power was never carried out.[57]

By 1940 those working to create a hospitable climate for Hitlerism in the United States and a distaste for fighting it overseas had evolved into a collaborative isolationist network. Prominent in this coalition was the America First Committee, the brainchild of Douglas Stewart Jr., a student at Yale University Law School. Stewart organized a chapter at Yale in consultation with his friend Lindbergh, who suggested he approach Gen. Robert E. Wood, chair of Sears, Roebuck, and Company, for help in expanding the movement. Wood agreed to become national director and on September 4, 1940, the committee was introduced to the public.[58]

Several eminent Americans served on the committee board or on subcommittees, including Lindbergh, Ford, Hugh S. Johnson, former director of the NRA, Mrs. Burton K. Wheeler, Mrs. Bennett Clark, and Katheryn Lewis, daughter of labor leader John L. Lewis. The membership swelled to about 850,000—most living within three hundred miles of headquarters in Chicago—and included Democrats, Republicans, and a few liberals hostile to FDR. Financing came from a few businessmen, who contributed $8,000 to $100,000 each. Followers were encouraged to write letters to newspapers, circulate petitions, organize meetings, and spread propaganda. The committee sponsored speeches by Johnson and Senators Wheeler, Robert M. La Follette Jr., Henry Cabot Lodge, David Walsh, and Arthur Capper. Some speeches were reprinted as pamphlets and given to local committees to distribute.[59]

Although the committee repudiated the support of fascist sympathizers, its membership included partisans of far-right organizations such as Coughlin's, Smith's, and the mothers' groups. The mothers' movement and the committee recruited members from each other. In January 1941, for example, ten thousand members of the Roll Call of American Women, based in Chicago, voted to merge with the committee because their aims were similar. In addition, Dilling spoke to America First chapters.[60]

A meeting of the Philadelphia chapter of the committee on August 20, 1941 illustrated the influence of mothers' groups and ultrarightists. The gathering was packed with members of the National Legion of Mothers of America and adherents of the Mothers and Daughters of Pennsylvania; the majority of those present were women, chiefly of German, Irish, and Italian descent. A man arose from the audience to say that what Hitler had done in Germany should be admired and that the real menace was the United States. Fish, the featured speaker, said Roosevelt was trying to frighten people and the nation would be at war if not for the committee. "The most precious thing in the world is a mother's son; help protect him by fighting for his rights,"

Fish said. The meeting ended with members vowing to work against Roosevelt's reelection.[61]

By far the biggest drawing card of the America First Committee was Lindbergh. The first pilot to fly solo across the Atlantic Ocean, he had been the greatest American hero of the 1920s. A shy man, Lindbergh initially enjoyed acclaim but disliked crowds. Fame soured his life; his privacy was violated, especially in 1932, after his infant son was kidnaped and murdered. Seeking relief, Lindbergh and his family moved to England, yet they were unhappy. The country that made them feel most at home was Germany, where Lindbergh was revered as an expert on aviation, not as a curiosity, and protected from crowds. In 1938 he accepted the Service Cross of the German Eagle, a high medal, from the government. Urged to return the medal after German aggression was exposed, he refused.[62]

Returning to the United States in 1939, Lindbergh tried to prevent American entry into the war. In his first national radio speech, about two weeks after the German invasion of Poland, he argued that intervention was contrary to American interests because the surrounding oceans made the United States invulnerable to attack. (The German Air Force was an additional concern, as he believed it was invincible, an impression fostered by Nazi leaders.) He urged the country to build a strong Air Force and Navy but to confine them to the Western Hemisphere and to deny credit to Britain.[63]

Lindbergh made many more speeches and the content varied little. He maintained that a British defeat was imminent and of almost no consequence to Americans, and that Roosevelt's war aims were equivalent to Hitler's. He saw no moral differences between the leaders of the German Nazis and the leaders of the American and European democracies. Lindbergh did not consider himself anti-Semitic, even though he was insensitive to the plight of European Jews and tended to believe conspiracy theories.[64] Not surprisingly, he and FDR hated each other. The president considered Lindbergh a Nazi sympathizer.[65]

On September 11, 1941, Lindbergh jeopardized his respectability with a speech at an America First Committee rally in Des Moines, Iowa. He blamed the British, the Jewish, and the Roosevelt administration for changing American policy from neutrality to involvement in European affairs, a course that, he said, was actually inimical to Jewish interests. "Instead of agitating for war the Jewish groups in this country should be opposing it in every possible way, for they will be among the first to feel its consequences." Lindbergh concluded by warning that Jews posed the greatest danger to the United States "in their large ownership and influence in our motion pictures, our press, our radio, and our government."[66]

The speech delighted Dilling, Coughlin, and Smith. Lindbergh and Smith dined together, at the latter's invitation, and Smith urged him to run for the presidency.[67] Lindbergh declined to run, yet they stayed in touch and Smith later told his sister that he and Lindbergh "have become fast friends."[68] Most Americans, however, were not so friendly, pouring complaints into committee headquarters after the speech. Lindbergh rejected protests over his criticism of Jews, saying, "I would rather say what I believe when I want to say it than to measure every statement I make by its probable popularity." He continued to speak in the next few months, but his credibility was damaged. On December 7 it was blown to bits at Pearl Harbor.[69]

Lindbergh also had been instrumental in organizing a second antiwar organization, the No Foreign War Committee, launched in December 1940. Financed by Midwestern businessmen and industrialists, some of whom owned properties in Germany, the group was led by Verne Marshall, an Iowa journalist who had won a Pulitzer Prize in 1936. The America First Committee and ultraright groups sent literature for Marshall's group to distribute. Many Bund members joined. Ida Mae Cooper, Dilling's New York representative, worked as a volunteer at the New York headquarters, where Jews were not permitted. Marshall planned to organize a hundred local chapters and supply each with speakers and propaganda. He spent $70,000 on full-page advertisements in newspapers in a few months; each ad asked for contributions so more ads could be purchased. Marshall claimed he received ten thousand letters a day with donations averaging ten cents each.[70] Many of the letters were anti-Semitic. One condemned the "Jew bankers of New York who are trying to get this country to save their fellow Jews in London."[71]

Women, including many who had campaigned for Willkie, filled volunteer positions for the No Foreign War Committee. Maude DeLand, a vigorous woman of seventy, was one of the distributors of propaganda for the committee. DeLand, who had close ties with ultraright women, filled her hotel room in New York with trunks packed with pamphlets.[72]

The excesses of the No Foreign War Committee consigned it to oblivion. Lindbergh cancelled a speech under committee auspices because it included participation by the Christian Front. Later, he resigned from the committee. The organization was embarrassed when journalists revealed its ties with pro-Nazi German Americans and pro-fascist Italian Americans, and when a German shortwave radio transmission mentioned the committee as useful to the Nazi cause. With financial support declining in the spring of 1941, Marshall suspended the organization and returned to Iowa to practice journalism.[73]

The fifth column was not so solid as it appeared. Led by men and women who had more venom than reason, it was a series of petty empires that never fit together snugly. Despite its weaknesses, though, the movement grew quickly from a flicker to a flame that threatened to set the nation ablaze. The National Legion of Mothers of America, which towered above the early mothers' groups in size and influence, offered a preview of what was to come—and a chilling hint of what might have been.

$=$ FOUR $=$
The National Legion of Mothers of America

Less than a month after Hitler invaded Poland, three California mothers of draft-age sons, Frances Sherrill, Mary M. Sheldon, and Mary Ireland, founded the first mothers' organization. The National Legion of Mothers of America was inspired by Hearst, who opposed Roosevelt and believed he could promote isolationism by publicizing the opposition of mothers to war. In cities where Hearst newspapers were published, NLMA chapters were formed, beginning in Los Angeles and expanding eastward. The newspapers carried stories about the growth of the organization and included membership forms (although the journals' precise relationship to the organization was kept vague). Mrs. N. F. Munson, chair of the San Francisco branch, thanked Hearst for showing "the same foresight that his mother showed when she sponsored the Child Welfare movement in 1897."[1]

Hearst's Los Angeles *Herald-Express* declared that the NLMA, the only major mothers' group headquartered in the West, was "motivated solely by patriotism," and composed of "the commonplace mothers, the type familiar in story and song . . . but grimly determined to fight any attempt to send their sons to fight on foreign soil."[2] The newspaper claimed that the first woman to sign up when the Los Angeles office opened on October 12 skipped breakfast to enroll. "I feel it is a great honor to be the first mother to sign up to fight for my boy," she said. "I have a 21-year-old son and I'm going to fight for him. It was too much trouble to bring him into the world and bring him up all these years to have him fight the battles of foreign nations."[3] The mother of a 17-year-old son said, "It is imperative that we organize to keep our boys out of Europe's struggles. We can do it, because women can always do what they set out to do."[4]

The demand for membership forms was so great the founders exhausted their supply and called for volunteers to bring typewriters to headquarters to register applicants. Some ten thousand women in Los Angeles joined in the first six days of registration and letters flooded in from other states. The NLMA concentrated on signing up as many members as possible to impress Congress, which was considering repeal of the Neutrality Act provisions requiring an embargo on arms sales to belligerents. All women were welcome regardless of race, religion, or political party; American citizenship was the only requirement for membership. No dues were charged. Most women who joined had draft-age sons.[5]

The NLMA wanted to serve as a medium through which women could express mass opposition to war. It urged women to vote but did not tell them how to vote, and it prohibited participation in partisan politics.[6] Members were expected to keep informed on current affairs. "We found that a great many women do not read the newspapers as carefully as they should," a Los Angeles organizer said. "So we are urging all the members to read the newspapers every day and keep abreast of the important things that are happening. We have suggested that they clip and keep important news stories and speeches so that they can compare them and judge wisely."[7]

The founders intended to support an adequate national defense, to resist subversive groups, and to oppose the use of American troops for any purpose except defending the United States against attack. The country should tend to its own affairs, and if it sought to fight, it should fight internal foes who were trying to take over. "[If] we must fight, we have our enemies right at hand and there is no need to travel 3,000 miles to find them,"[8] the NLMA executive council stated.

The NLMA emphasized grass roots enlistments more than rallies, broadcasts, or marches. Its structure resembled a pyramid, starting with small local groups and culminating in a nationwide organization. Seven women could join together to create a sentry post. Each post elected a leader and seven leaders constituted a patrol. Patrol representatives created community councils that elected state councils. The state councils elected a national executive committee. Sentry posts were created for Blacks, Italian Americans, German Americans and high school girls. The organization was meant to be democratic, with members having input into decisions to foster a feeling of participation. Nonetheless, the pyramid structure established a chain of command.[9]

Members, whose meetings were held in schools and churches, took part in activities that included study groups and discussions. Volunteers were sought for a speakers bureau that would provide orators to women's organizations. Recruiters went door to door to solicit new members, and newspaper advertisements were placed to attract support. Most of the NLMA funding came from businessmen such as Hearst, but there were other donations, revenue from subscriptions to the legion newspaper, and from sales of pins featuring an American flag and a white dove of peace.[10]

The NLMA newspaper, the *American Mothers National Weekly,* was capably written, without the vicious Jew-baiting of Dilling's publication, although it was stridently anticommunist. Among the newspaper's claims were that American money and brains had subsidized the Bolshevik Revolution, that

Senator Burton K. Wheeler, Charles Lindbergh, Kathleen Norris, and Socialist leader Norman Thomas share the platform at an America First Committee rally on May 23, 1941, at Madison Square Garden in New York. Associated Press photo.

most European refugees were communists, and that Mexicans might invade the United States and join with southern Blacks to end White supremacy. An editorial condemned "atheism in our churches" and warned that only Christianity could save the country. The newspaper made no estimate of its circulation, yet it probably had several million readers.[11]

The credibility of the NLMA was enhanced in January 1940, when popular novelist Kathleen Norris accepted its presidency. Norris had worked as a teacher, journalist, and secretary to support five siblings after her parents died suddenly in 1899, when she was nineteen. In 1909 she married writer Charles G. Norris and moved to New York, where he became editor of *American* magazine and she began publishing short stories and novels. Norris attracted a readership of millions and became the highest-paid writer of her time, publishing eighty-five novels and selling ten million copies between 1911 and 1959. A traditional moralist, she wrote sentimental novels upholding family values; she was accused of writing by formula. Norris also was an activist for pacifism, Prohibition, and opposition to capital punishment.[12]

She believed war was cruel and should be avoided at all costs, and that the Axis danger was not so great as the danger of going to war.[13]

After taking office, Norris began a schedule that included conferences, speeches in California, and a national tour. "No woman, not even if she were a queen, has ever been heard when men talked of making war," she said. "In all the twenty years since the last European war, no man has risen to stop this tide." Still, she took heart in the NLMA. "In this organization, after twenty years of work with peace movements, I see for the first time a gleam of hope."[14] The organization was "catching on like a prairie fire with the women of America" and would enlist twenty million of the twenty-eight million women of voting age.[15] Women should not fear an attack on the United States because "we have two good watchdogs, the Atlantic and the Pacific."[16] Norris scolded those who wanted to lead the country to go to war: "Shame on you people who for money, trade expansion, and territorial gains would destroy the peace of the world!"[17] Anglophobia crept into her language. "There is no democracy in England," she said. "There hasn't been since the war started. And there will be none here if we get into war."[18]

Belying the organization's profession of nonpartisanship, Norris and many of the NLMA leaders were Republican opponents of the New Deal. Norris denounced Roosevelt for failing to end unemployment despite wasting billions of dollars, and for trying to dupe the United States into war. She condemned him for saying that the country's first line of defense was in Europe and that all Americans would be prisoners if Hitler won the war. The president had not promised to keep American boys at home until he began his campaign in 1940, and after he won reelection Americans would die on foreign battlefields, Norris warned. Thus she endorsed Willkie and campaigned vigorously for him.[19]

Norris spent the summer working for Willkie and trying to defeat the Burke-Wadsworth Selective Service bill before Congress. She argued that because no invasion was imminent, a volunteer military force was sufficient. If conscription were a necessity, Congress should support a plan proposed by Hearst to draft young men for three months of military training. This type of conscription, modeled on the Swiss example, would create a citizen army adequate to repel any invaders, Norris concluded.[20]

In July 1940 Hannah M. Conners of Milton, Massachusetts, carried the battle in testimony before the House Military Affairs Committee. Connors represented the New England district of the NLMA, which claimed 14,000 members in her state. American boys, she said, wanted the opportunity to volunteer; they were not slackers who must be drafted. They would not want to fight for a foreign country even if drafted, however, and conscripts sent abroad would not be good fighters because their hearts would not be in the battle. And American hearts were broken when the United States fought for England and France in World War I, Connors added.[21] Other NLMA representatives took a more activist role in opposing the draft. In September, when the Senate debated conscription, they gathered outside the chamber, wearing black dresses and veils and keeping a "death vigil."[22]

Meanwhile, in 1940 California became the first state to establish a state-wide NLMA unit when it held a convention in San Francisco in June. Each community council had the right to send an unlimited number of delegates and some one thousand attended. A plan of action was developed for all California chapters and Sherrill was elected state president. "We must work fast, for at the rate the war's going, our sons will soon be in Europe," Sherrill said. "That's one of the reasons for this conference."[23]

Chicago was another area of growth for the legion. Within two weeks of the founding of the NLMA, a unit had been established in the city, with Mrs. Henry W. Hartough as chair. "Mothers have not been allowed to say what they think in the councils of government," Hartough said. "Women must wake up to the fact that this is not a fight for any one women's club, professional, literary, or social club. It is a fight of all mothers, all women, to keep our loved ones at home."[24] In the first few weeks, women sent in slogans and songs for the organization. One submitted a song entitled "Let's Stay Home" and suggested it become the NLMA theme song. A few Black mothers inquired about joining and were segregated into separate sentry posts, as NLMA rules dictated, but little effort was made to recruit Blacks.[25]

Hartough soon expanded her recruiting to a number of Midwestern states and became regional director. Sometimes she lured entire organizations into the fold. The Child Conservation Club of Huntington, Indiana voted to affiliate with the NLMA, and Hartough won a major coup when a Milwaukee women's club with 50,000 members joined. Also urging women to join were the *Chicago Tribune* and Hearst's Chicago *Herald-American*. The latter kept a running count of membership and printed letters from women praising the organization. "It is not right to take our own good boys and leave the penitentiaries full of men who are no credit to society," one mother wrote.[26]

By December 1939 the NLMA had been organized in thirty-nine states and claimed to be the largest women's organization in the nation. Hartough predicted that membership would reach one million in the Midwest within a year, and at the end of 1939, she claimed to have met her goal. By February 1940 the NLMA boasted seventy-five thousand members in Los Angeles, more than a hundred thousand in New York City, about eight thousand in Atlanta, and even about six thousand in South America. In June 1940 some two million women voted by mail on three resolutions and approved them overwhelmingly. The resolutions called for requiring a national plebiscite to send soldiers overseas; a strong defense; and a permanent committee to investigate un-American activities. The vote inspired Congresswoman Jessie Sumner of Illinois to introduce a bill preventing the use of American troops in conflicts outside the Western Hemisphere without congressional consent. Although the mothers worked hard for the bill, it was defeated. Finally, by January 1941, the NLMA claimed four million members nationwide, and during the debate over Lend-Lease that winter, membership soared.[27]

While Norris led the NLMA, Dilling remained aloof. When a woman wrote to ask her what she thought of the NLMA, Dilling responded she would not join because Norris was soft on communism.[28] Other leaders on the far right did not share Dilling's view. In the December 11, 1939 issue of *Social Justice,* Coughlin endorsed the NLMA and invited women to write to him and "be put in touch with responsible leaders and regional organizers as well as honestly and wisely counselled on their problems by their beloved Radio Priest." Coughlin announced the creation of the NLMA on national radio, urged women to join, advised local leaders, to whom he gave extensive publicity, and helped launch chapters.[29] Endorsements from Pelley, Smith, and Viereck followed.[30]

Norris did not want such backers. She tried to repudiate anti-Semitism and asked Coughlin to withdraw his endorsement, but he refused. Extremists began to infiltrate, and take over, local units. Los Angeles Bundists gained influence over Sherrill, the national secretary, and Bundists and Coughlinites dominated the Philadelphia chapter. The Philadelphia leader, Edith M. Scott, fraternized with Joseph Gallagher and Bessie Burchett, leaders of the Coughlinite Anti-Communist Society. Scott warned that "if the President puts us in war, we certainly will show him what we can do. He made a promise and if he lets us down we certainly will fix him."[31] Anti-Semitism was rife in the chapter. One member said Hitler was no danger to Americans, but she wished he would come over to clean up the "damn Jews." Eventually the chapter seceded from the NLMA.[32]

The New York chapter also raged out of control and left the NLMA. Christian Front elements sympathetic to Coughlin and pro-Nazi women led by Mrs. Livingston Rowe Schuyler, a vicious anti-Semite, gained sway. Schuyler belonged to several pro-German organizations, was a friend of anti-Semite Allan Zoll, and participated in the plot to make Moseley military dictator of the United States. She and her partisans objected to working with the founders of the NLMA because one of them was a Catholic and one was a Jew.[33]

Norris was displeased when mothers affiliated with the New York chapter planned to create a women's rifle corps to shoot invading paratroopers. This was too much even for such a supporter of home defense as she.[34] Despite her protests, the mothers created the Molly Pitcher Rifle Legion, named for the woman who was said to have armed herself in the American Revolution. The Molly Pitchers collected rifles and ammunition and found two Army sharpshooters who promised to train them in the use of weapons. To justify the corps, Edna Johnson, the corps leader, said that if the housewives of Europe had been armed, France would not have fallen; all the men were at the front and there were no means of defeating aerial invaders.[35]

The Molly Pitchers, who severed their connection with the NLMA in May 1940, urged women to "Buy Christian, Vote Christian, Employ Christian" and to "Boycott all Sponsors on the English Jew Controlled Radio!" In addition, the Molly Pitchers claimed "no Jew is a true American," that a Jewish draft board member in New York sold deferments, that "Jew Communist Stooges" were corrupting the American Legion, and that New York District Attorney Thomas E. Dewey was a "Communist stooge" whose office "stinks with Jew Communist lawyers." Roosevelt, though he was a fellow stooge, was called upon to deport Jewish refugees to open sixteen million jobs for Christian Americans.[36]

Another flyer charged that Roosevelt's secretary of state, Cordell Hull, planned to give two million destitute farmers one-way tickets to Brazil to make room for Jewish refugees. The administration would then give the Jews jobs, and it would take twenty-five million Christian workers to subsidize them in lives of comfort. The flyer demanded the impeachment of the president and his cabinet and ended with a song to the tune of the "Battle Hymn of the Republic": "Americans have nothing in common with the greedy Jew Bolshevik parasite / Who would lash us into serfdom and crush us with his might. / Is there anything left for us but to organize and fight?"[37]

After the New York chapter quit the NLMA, Norris expelled the Boston and Cleveland chapters, in which fascist sympathizers had won control. Increasingly she viewed her attempts to control chapters as hopeless and resigned as president at the first annual legion convention in April 1941. She remained active in antiwar work, though. She became honorary vice president of Women United, a New York–based organization that sent women to Washington to insist that Roosevelt keep his campaign promise of peace. Norris also was a charter member of the America First Committee and gave talks with Lindbergh, whom she defended in newspaper columns. She was one of the featured speakers at a mass rally in Madison Square Garden that included Lindbergh, Socialist Party leader Norman Thomas, and Senator

Wheeler. Lindbergh's wife, Anne, who was on the platform, was disappointed with Norris's speech, "which upset me because it was almost pure sob stuff (mothers losing their boys) when she can be so much more positive. But the crowd likes her." After the Pearl Harbor attack, however, Norris supported the American war effort and advised others to do the same.[38]

The 1941 convention marked the splintering of the legion as well as Norris's exit from the organization. Delegates voted to establish an executive committee to coordinate three groups: the National Legion, the Mothers of the U. S. A., and the Women's National Committee to Keep the U. S. Out of War. Sherrill, who had accepted the cooperation of anti-Semites, was to lead the first group. The second was a Coughlinite group in Detroit with ties to Dilling, and the third was founded by Cathrine Curtis, a lobbyist and friend of Dilling and other anti-Semites. Curtis was elected chair of the coordinating committee. The coalition held a conference in Chicago in September 1941, endorsing resolutions calling for neutrality, repeal of the Lend-Lease Act, impeachment of Roosevelt, and the release of all draftees from the Army.[39]

Meanwhile, the Philadelphia mothers under Scott grew more anti-Semitic, xenophobic, and vitriolic. Their speakers included anti-Semites, Roosevelt-haters, and Nazi sympathizers. The pro-Nazi *Scribner's Commentator* was sold at meetings. Members complained that beer was served at Army camps, and that conditions for draftees were so bad that boys were committing suicide.[40] One woman said she had been to the Soviet Union, which was much worse than Germany because everyone in the USSR was dirty and ragged and no one could attend church. Another mother said Germany was better than England or the United States because the Germans had more churches and churchgoers.[41] Elizabeth Baker complained that Roosevelt had doubled taxes "so we could give it all to Britain," and that politicians were feted in the United States when Americans were hungry and destitute.[42] Scott said the British had paid agents, usually rabbis, working for American intervention. The mothers, who booed every time Jews were mentioned, voted to send letters to Hull and Congress, demanding that all the British citizens in the United States interested in involving the nation in a war with Germany be sent back to England.[43]

A Black man invited to speak to the mothers, Dr. Adolphus W. Anderson, advised them to support the work of the America First Committee. Frances V. Gowen added that she welcomed Black mothers as members, and other women said they would prefer Blacks to Jews. On another occasion, Scott appealed for the admission of Blacks and told Catholic members that three of their popes, as well as St. Augustine, had been Black. It shamed her that Whites were hasty with Blacks. "So in the future try to be a little more sympathetic toward them as they are harmless," said Scott, who had attended a meeting of Black mothers. "I, for one, would rather have the friendship of a colored person than a communist." This led to discussion about the superiority of Blacks to Jews. A Mrs. Campbell said Jews were responsible for epidemics in Army camps and that nine out of every ten Jews had syphilis. She knew this was true because a doctor had written a book about it. Jews removed the book from public libraries.[44]

Agnes Waters, invited to speak, denounced Blacks and Jews. Scott had asked her not to speak on religion, Waters said, but Jewish treachery was the issue of the day. She had supported FDR in 1936, then changed her mind when he began to surround himself with Jews. "The Jews have every key position in Washington, and if you mothers come down to Washington when you want something done, you will have to talk to some kike in order to have it done," she said. Moreover, Jews incited "niggers" in the south to revolt against white supremacy. Many mothers appeared bored near the end of Waters's two-hour diatribe.[45]

Another rabble-rouser, Dr. Joseph Vansant, told the group Hitler wanted peace but Roosevelt and Churchill wanted war. Vansant, who said his brother-in-law had attended Harvard with FDR, claimed that Roosevelt was always broke and borrowing money, and that the president's father had left FDR's money in a trust fund because he knew his son would squander it. How could the president manage the nation's finances when he could not handle his own?[46]

Sherrill told the mothers of deplorable conditions at Army camps: draftees were forced to sleep on bare, damp ground and some froze to death; on maneuvers, trucks drove without lights, resulting in wrecks that constituted mass murder; and at one camp, there had been forty suicides. Sherrill condemned Eleanor Roosevelt for dominating her husband and pushing him toward war. "The further East you come, the more you get to hear of fear that Hitler is going to invade us," she said. "In other words, the closer you come to Roosevelt the more you fear Hitler."[47]

Things became most unruly in September 1941, when Fish spoke to the Philadelphia women. A consistent supporter of isolationism and the America First Committee, he had praised Norris for her peace work. Now Fish said Congress should decide whether the nation should go to war, and if Roosevelt led the United States into war without the consent of Congress, he would be guilty of treason. After Fish completed his talk, William Rigney, who often attended the group's meetings, asked how the president could be impeached. Fish replied that a two-thirds vote of Congress would be needed. He did not think it would be possible because of the Democratic majority, but the majority could be overturned at the next election. Rigney mumbled that people would not wait that long.[48]

Burchett then arose and asked what could be done if that congressional majority declared war. Fish answered, "I want to go on record that if Congress by virtue of the power vested in it by the Constitution declared war, I would go to the people and urge them to support the war." The audience began to boo and shout "No war and no fighting by the American people against Germany!" Burchett leaped out of her seat and said, "I would be willing to be shot for treason rather than fight on the side of Soviet Russia." Fish asked the members if they would refuse to support the government in a constitutional war and the audience shouted "Yes!" He threw up his arms in disgust and said, "I shall stop talking right now. I cannot and will not address any audience which refuses to support its government in a legal and constitutional act."[49]

Like many local groups, the Philadelphia group ignored Norris's advice to disband after the Pearl Harbor attack and join her in supporting the war effort. The chapter met the day after the attack and vowed to continue its work. Members blamed the war on Roosevelt and complained that their sons would do the fighting while Roosevelt's sons had desk jobs. "I think it was the English ships flying the Japanese flag that attacked us," a Mrs. Kunkel said. "We should use horsewhips on the congressmen." A Mrs. Lavell noted that she had written to the Japanese Embassy to say American mothers wanted peace, and the embassy had replied that Japanese mothers wanted peace, too. One woman lamented that Christian sons were going to die for Jews. A Miss Hickman said the American alliance with the Soviet Union meant the end of Christianity and priests would no longer be allowed to say Mass. She suggested that the Philadelphia mothers compel Congress to stop sending money to England and the Soviet Union; mothers should surround the Capitol and keep Congress inside until it acted on their demands. The talk, however, was not translated into effective action, a failure that plagued the chapter and other units that broke from the NLMA.[50]

The last relatively moderate woman to direct the unified NLMA was atypical of the prominent mothers' leaders. Only Norris had a national reputation long before the war, as a writer and a reformer. She had devoted her energies to a variety of humanitarian causes, in the progressive movement of the first two decades of the century, and in the women's peace movement of the 1920s.[51] She was not a bitter, frustrated failure who needed to participate in the antiwar movement of the late 1930s and 1940s to gain power and influence. The sole mothers' leader whom the contemporary press termed a feminist, Norris resembled Dilling in some respects, yet she more closely resembled nineteenth-century and early twentieth-century female reformers. Like Dilling, she reflected the early feminists' beliefs that women were morally superior to men and could influence politics by setting a moral example. Unlike Dilling, she thought women should influence politics by exerting pressure as a bloc.[52]

Norris had opposed all wars in principle, not only World War II, although she came to support the American war effort and had no sympathy for Hitler.[53] She thus stood in contrast to most of her counterparts in the mothers' movement, who emphasized not that all war was wrong but that war against Hitler was wrong. She was neither an anti-Semite nor a demagogue who attributed evil intentions to political foes, searched for scapegoats, or interpreted the war as a master conspiracy—even though she was an Anglophobe who believed the British wanted to spill American blood to save themselves.[54] Unwilling to win at all costs, Norris did not match other mothers' leaders in authoritarianism, compulsion, or competitiveness.

Still, Norris was conservative in temperament and politics. A wealthy woman with a stake in the economic status quo, she vigorously defended capitalism against New Deal reforms, consistently voted Republican, and campaigned against Roosevelt, whom she considered a dictator. She believed in conventional morality and patriarchy, yet she was less likely than were some mothers to equate immorality with liberal lifestyles, even Eleanor Roosevelt's. When Norris opposed the first lady, it was for political reasons.[55]

Norris's moderation made the NLMA potentially more inclusive than the later mothers' groups, but her moderation proved a handicap within the movement. Almost unique among the leaders, she was less rabid than her followers, and her tolerance of diversity forced her to resign in frustration when inflexible right-wingers became dominant. In fact, Norris was more of a figurehead than a hands-on leader. She might have been chosen to head the NLMA largely because her name and reputation lent credibility to the organization. Apparently that was Hearst's intention: to use women such as Norris to legitimize his vendetta against FDR. The NLMA flourished partly because of his financial support and the publicity in his newspapers. Hearst seems to have worked behind the scenes and there is no evidence to indicate his exact role, which he wanted to obscure.[56]

The NLMA was significant because it suggested the potential of mobilizing conservative women who opposed American involvement in the war. It was the first major organization to use maternal arguments effectively against the war and Roosevelt's foreign policy. In women, the group helped arouse a sense of gender solidarity based on the belief that they might suffer from a conflagration beyond their control. Although it was conservative in orientation, the NLMA was less interested in maintaining principles than in the specific issue of avoiding war. Religious themes, which animated the work of Dilling and like-minded women, were subordinate as well, yet religion was a factor. The membership was larger and more diverse than that of the extremist groups that succeeded the NLMA. Nevertheless, the NLMA was predominantly White, middle class, and Republican.[57]

Without the example of the NLMA, the mothers' movement likely would not have developed so rapidly. The organization was a victim of its success, however. It grew so quickly that moderates lost command and the NLMA lost direction. In its later stages, recruitment seems to have been undertaken merely to inflate membership. More important, other than writing letters to Congress, the leaders never developed tactics to keep the United States out of war.

The experience of the NLMA illustrated how difficult it was for a large national organization—the first and last mothers' organization that succeeded, if temporarily, in organizing women on a national scale—to rein in its affiliates and prevent hate groups from taking them over. Further, the NLMA demonstrated that the beliefs that brought women together against war—including religion, morality, family cohesion, gender interests, and resistance to liberal change—could not offset significant centrifugal forces that pulled organizations apart. No matter how quickly the mothers' movement grew, the threat of war also grew and moderate protest could not avert it. The more setbacks the movement encountered, the more extreme it became. The militance of the Philadelphia mothers, fervor that Norris and Fish could not contain, was symptomatic of a movement that degenerated from relative moderation into a loose coalition dominated by Coughlinites, anti-Semites, and Nazi sympathizers.

In a limited sense, the NLMA was a bridge between the 1920s women's peace organizations that opposed all war to the larger, bigoted organization of ultraconservatives. Norris, who had roots in the earlier movement, eventually concluded the latter movement was flawed by its excesses and withdrew to other isolationist channels. She recognized that the NLMA began with idealism, only to open Pandora's box and let loose reaction that spread like a plague of hate.

FIVE

Cathrine Curtis and the Women's National Committee to Keep the U.S. out of War

An isolationist who fused fascist propaganda with maternalism, feminism, and rabid nationalism, Cathrine Curtis was distinguished by her shrewdness, energy, charisma, combativeness, and talent for organizing. Not only did she become a leader in the coalition that included the National Legion of Mothers of America, but she created and dominated other groups, the most prominent being the Women's National Committee to Keep the U.S. Out of War. She was perhaps the most effective female organizer on the extreme right.[1]

Although her organizations attracted publicity, Curtis never told interviewers about her background and her personal life is shrouded in secrecy. Married and divorced three times, childless, she refused to discuss her marriages and used her birth name, leading some people to believe she had always been single. Born in Albany, New York, she was the only child of rich parents, George M. Curtis and Flora Taylor Curtis. Intelligent, Curtis studied under private tutors, then graduated from St. Agnes High School in Albany, and attended New York University but did not complete a degree. Her father, a speculator in stocks and bonds, was the first in his neighborhood to buy an automobile. Speculation came easily to Curtis: at fifteen she invested several hundred dollars in railroad stock; her stock rose nine points within two days.[2]

In her twenties she moved to the Southwest, where she operated a citrus ranch near Phoenix and met the best-selling novelist Harold Bell Wright. Impressed by the slim, six-foot, confident woman, Wright told her she resembled a character in one of his novels and invited her to Hollywood to star in the movie *The Shepherd of the Hills*. Curtis moved there, joined the cast, and became an actress and producer, one of the few women filmmakers in the early days of motion pictures. Her most successful film was *The Sky Pilot*.[3]

In Hollywood, Curtis continued to invest and became rich, able to survive the stock market crash of 1929. In the 1930s she moved to New York City, where radio station WMCA hired her to host a twice-weekly program, *Women and Money*, in 1934. Using her program to promote her concept of feminism, she espoused women's financial independence and legal equality. For women, knowledge of finance "is as important as a knowledge of home economics," Curtis said.[4] She condemned the policies of the New Deal, particularly its regulation of Wall Street, and praised the Supreme Court's nullification of the National Industrial Recovery Act. Her strident anti–New Deal rhetoric convinced her sponsors to terminate the program abruptly after she denounced the New Deal as a betrayal of George Washington's policies on February 22, 1935. Criticizing the cancellation as discriminatory, complaining that the Communist Party was free to broadcast, she claimed her right to free speech had been violated.[5]

Curtis's listeners, angered by the cancellation of her program, sent her hundreds of letters that included contributions to her cause and invitations to speak. In March 1935 she accepted an invitation to speak in Utica, New York, to five hundred women, who received her enthusiastically and urged Curtis to create a financial organization for women. As a result, she founded Women Investors in America in May 1935 and, later, the Women Investors Research Institute. A nonprofit, educational organization with a commodious headquarters in a Fifth Avenue building Curtis owned, Women Investors in America combined anti–New Deal economic conservatism and advocacy of women's rights. By 1939, membership in Women Investors in America had grown to three hundred thousand women in twenty-eight states. And the members of the Women Investors National Committee, women who advised Curtis, were mostly wealthy and belonged to organizations such as the National Society of New England Women, the DAR, and the National Society of the Daughters of 1812.[6]

Curtis's organization, operating through local clubs, gave financial seminars for women, sponsored talks and lectures by Curtis and other financial experts, and issued pamphlets and books, including *Women and Money, Women and Taxes,* and *Women and Utilities.* Curtis lectured in twenty-five states within three years after incorporation and distributed more than one million pieces of literature. She also provided an information service for women, published a weekly newspaper, *Woman Courageous,* disseminated financial statistics, and helped large corporations break down their lists of stockholders to determine how much stock was owned by women. Funding for the organization came from dues ranging from fifty dollars per year for founding members to one dollar for affiliates, and from contributions. Curtis accepted no salary.[7]

Women's economic independence was the citadel against communism, Curtis said. "It is the women who guard the family pocketbook and the women have decided to guard the nation's pocketbook."[8] That decision led her to lobby against legislation she considered unsound. For instance, Curtis testified against the Wealth Tax bill of 1935, claiming it would mean a lower standard of living for the wives and children of deceased men; that taxation of inheritances discriminated against women, the beneficiaries of most inherited assets; and that funds generated by the life insurance policies of deceased spouses and parents should not be taxed. Increased federal taxing and spending in general found no favor with Curtis, who also opposed strikes, particularly sit-down strikes.[9]

In 1936 Women Investors in America held its first Financial Congress in Chicago, gathering some four thousand women capitalists to defend their investments and attack the New Deal. "Capitalism is not a devouring monster," Curtis said in her keynote address, "and all the bitter denunciations emanating from ignorant and prejudiced sources cannot alter the fact that America owes her supremacy to capitalism. Woman, of course, through her great ownership of insurance, trust funds, stocks, savings accounts, and homes, is the greatest capitalist in the world. We must mobilize to save this capitalism!" A Hearst newspaper columnist who spoke told the women that the enemy, the New Deal, was "motivated by repression and tends to stratify our society." Grace Brosseau, a member of the executive committee, attributed the New Deal to a conspiracy inspired by Adam Weishaupt, founder of the Society of the Illuminati (actually an innocent philosophical debating society) in Bavaria in 1776; Weishaupt begat Marx and Marx begat Roosevelt. Another speaker called the New Deal revolutionary and said Roosevelt intended to confiscate property. At the concluding banquet, speakers urged women to defeat FDR in the next election.[10]

In 1937 Curtis borrowed the organizational apparatus of Women Investors in America to spin off the Women's National Committee for Hands Off the Supreme Court, which opposed FDR's court-packing plan. Members of Women Investors automatically became members of the new committee, which claimed three hundred fifty thousand women and nineteen national organizations. In October, at Borah's invitation, Curtis testified before a Senate subcommittee against FDR's plan. Accompanied by fifty women wearing silk badges to symbolize opposition to the proposal, Curtis said the measure encouraged contempt for the judiciary. She then filed a petition against the plan, containing twenty five thousand signatures from throughout the country. Later, Borah congratulated Curtis for helping defeat the plan.[11]

Curtis's confederate in Women Investors was her lover, Michael Ahearn, who served as publicity agent and director of the research institute. A vicious anti-Semite, Ahearn had a long history of involvement in the ultraright movement. He had served as publicity agent for James True, inventor of a weapon resembling an axe handle that he called the "Kike killer." ("For a first-class massacre, more than a truncheon is needed," True said.) Ahearn collaborated with True in creating the anti-Semitic newsletter *Industrial Control Reports,* to which Curtis subscribed, and was affiliated with Deatherage, Pelley, and Kamp.[12]

Curtis's taste in Jew-hating literature did not stop with the True–Ahearn sheets. She kept a "Jewry" file full of anti-Semitic pamphlets and clippings, including tracts by Hudson, Francis Ralston Welsh, E. N. Sanctuary, and Robert E. Edmondson. One such tract claimed the Lindbergh baby kidnapping was a Jewish plot, and another blamed Jews for communism, World War II, and conspiring to destroy Christian civilization. Curtis had a complete run of Edmondson's *American Vigilante Bulletins* for 1939–41, which included such titles as "New Deal Last Stronghold of Jewry," "Segregate the Jews!" "Fear of Roosevelt and His Jews Overshadows Hitler," and "Roosevelt's Jewish Ancestry." After World War II began, she subscribed to *World Service,* published by the German government to justify its military aggression and persecution of Jews. For her part, Curtis compiled a list of prominent Jews from various states, recording their occupation, country of birth, and whether they were Masons. She also compiled a list of Jews appointed to offices under the New Deal.[13]

Curtis's first foray into foreign policy came in 1939, with FDR's decision to seek repeal of the arms embargo. Testifying before the Senate Foreign Relations Committee on May 6, she said Roosevelt was using foreign affairs to conceal economic problems at home. Curtis wanted Congress to remain in session during the European crisis and rescind all foreign policy powers delegated to the president. A senator, she said, had told her members of Congress were receiving about five thousand letters a day about the embargo, and only ten of every thousand supported Roosevelt's position. Curtis sent a copy of her testimony to Coughlin and wrote that many of her supporters were his followers.[14]

Privately, Curtis expressed dismay that Congress was like a flock of sheep led by the president. British propaganda and internationalists, too, were giving Americans an erroneous interpretation of world events, aimed at embroiling the United States in Europe. Even women's organizations were being fooled. Nonetheless, she said, "I am more convinced than ever that the women are the only ones who can accomplish anything." Indeed, women would have to bring about a miracle to keep their country from war.[15]

After polling hundreds of women, many of whom, she found, were ignorant of the issues, Curtis decided to act, announcing the creation of the Women's National Committee to Keep the U.S. Out of War on September 20, 1939. Her purpose was to stimulate women to think about, and discuss, foreign policy. Curtis said she had never registered as a Republican or a Democrat and that her movement was likewise nonpartisan, although she added, "The New Deal party, of course, is un-American in its philosophy." Curtis sent telegrams to women's groups asking them to join, and all members of Women Investors were made charter members of the new organization; thus, the membership would be composed largely of wealthy women. She was gratified by telegrams and letters that she received, mostly from affluent women affiliated with her other organizations. One of the first to volunteer to help was a friend of Curtis, the aviator Laura Ingalls, who offered her time and two airplanes if the committee would pay for gasoline and upkeep. The committee's budget provided five thousand dollars for Ingalls to make a promotional flight over the eastern states and give speeches.[16]

Ingalls, a pioneer in women's aviation, had been a concert pianist, vaudeville dancer, and nurse. Born in New York in 1902, educated at elite private schools in Vienna, Paris, and New York, she spoke seven languages. At twenty-five, Ingalls became the fifteenth woman in the United States to receive her pilot's license and the first to graduate from a government-approved flying school. She embarked upon a career in stunt flying and by the 1930s had become the chief rival to Amelia Earhart as premier woman flier in the United States. In 1930 she set records in aerial acrobatics, performing 980 consecutive loops and, a few days later, 714 barrel rolls. In 1931 she considered flying the Atlantic solo but abandoned the idea. In March 1934 she became the first woman to fly over the Andes Mountains, and in the next month became the first person to fly around the perimeter of South America. In 1935 she set a speed record for a woman flying from the West Coast to the East Coast of the United States.[17]

Undeterred by numerous crashes, Ingalls subordinated everything to her flying, had no time for humor or domestic chores, and lived in hotels or rooming houses near airports. She yearned passionately to become the most famous woman flier. "I'd rather fly than eat, drink, or run around, and I mean it," she said.[18] Ingalls also was interested in politics. Enamored of German efficiency, Hitler's ideology, and Aryan supremacy, she believed it would be wrong for the United States to oppose the Third Reich. In 1936 Ingalls sent a message to Roosevelt advocating peace and friendship with Germany.[19]

On September 26, 1939 Ingalls made a two-hour flight over Washington, violating the White House air space to drop peace pamphlets addressed to Congress. The flight came when special precautions were being taken to protect the White House and other public buildings. Written by Curtis, the pamphlets stated that women would not tolerate the sending of their husbands and sons to fight in a foreign war. In an echo of Curtis's testimony that May, the pamphlets urged Congress to stay in session throughout the war emergency and to resist the president's request to repeal the arms embargo. When Ingalls landed, she was arrested and told she had violated the law by flying over the White House and dropping flyers over a populated area. At a hearing of the Civil Aeronautics Board, Ingalls pleaded for leniency on the grounds of her safety record, said she had not intended to disobey the law, and added that the air space around the White House was not defined clearly. The board suspended her license for one week and made her study air safety.[20]

If Ingalls felt remorse for her escapade, it was not evident the day after her landing. She and Curtis tried to force their way into a closed session of the Senate Foreign Relations Committee, which was considering an amendment to the Neutrality Act to permit arms sales to the Allies. "And this is the government of the United States!" Ingalls exclaimed. "I can't understand it. Imagine! Holding hearings behind closed doors! This is a dictatorship already."[21] Barred from the committee room, Curtis wrote a note to Key Pittman, chair of the committee. When he did not answer, she wrote a note to Vandenberg, but he did not answer either. (Finally, Borah, who spoke with the women as he left the room, gave them an audience in his office.)[22] Brought together by their frustration with official Washington, Ingalls and Curtis forged an alliance to preserve American neutrality that was to grow stronger and survive until Pearl Harbor.

Not all of Capitol Hill was hostile, however. Curtis cultivated relations with Senators Reynolds, Wheeler, Nye, and Hiram Johnson, and Representatives Hoffman and Sumner. Hoffman and Nye inserted her speeches and pamphlets in the *Congressional Record,* and Wheeler helped arrange her appearances before the Senate Foreign Relations Committee. Sumner, a feminist, was a friend who met Curtis for dinner in New York and Washington. Off the hill, Curtis's allies included Coughlin, to whom she sent copies of her antiwar pamphlets, as well as Edmondson and True.[23]

Naturally, Curtis developed ties with women from various organizations, including Rosa Farber of the Mothers of the U. S. A., Beatrice Knowles of the United Mothers of America, Marguerite Morrison of the American Women Against Communism, and Marie Smith of the women's division of the No Foreign War Committee. Moreover, Curtis worked with Dilling until they broke over tactical differences in fighting Lend-Lease. Elizabeth and Albert Dilling lunched in New York with Curtis and Ahearn, who were "doing a fine work fighting for the American system of private property," Elizabeth Dilling wrote. Curtis returned the admiration, writing to Dilling to say she appreciated her efforts and requesting a copy of *The Protocols.*[24]

Throughout 1940 Curtis campaigned against Roosevelt's program to send military and economic aid to Britain. She argued that aid short of war allocated too much power to the president and created a dictatorship. Mothers joined Curtis in objecting to the plan. A Wisconsinite complained that "the present government is more concerned with the fate of the British Empire than with the fate of millions of American boys who will have to do the fighting and the dying." The women disagreed with the administration's decision to trade destroyers for naval bases; if the destroyers were essential to the British, they must be valuable to the Americans.[25] Another mother feared the United States was sacrificing its defense to rescue Britain. "I proudly gave a son, only 16 years old, in the 1st World War," she wrote. "Have four sons now and would rather see them dead at my feet than again fight to preserve the British Empire."[26]

For such women, maternal arguments had a prominent role in the case against war. When a nation put itself on a wartime footing, Curtis maintained, the interests of women were sacrificed to the needs of the state. In the Soviet Union, "children became the property of the state," and in Germany, "women were urged to bear more and more children for the protection of the state."[27] The Women's National Committee emphasized that war would negate the work of mothers: homemaking and nurturing sons from cradle to manhood. Many women, then, thought they should take it upon themselves to save the nation from warmongers. "If women could put over the deadly Prohibition and could achieve also the uphill task of securing the vote for women, it is a disgrace to women if the women, who each one as a mother is nailed in agony to the cross to give life, cannot *do* not, as an army of *mothers*, keep this country out of war by their efforts alone," wrote Mrs. H. Ernestine Bulger Ripley, a recipient of one of Curtis's pamphlets.[28]

Women's concerns about safeguarding sons from danger were invoked in pamphlets Curtis wrote in 1940 and 1941. She mailed the tracts with the aid of Nye and Hoffman, both of whom provided franked envelopes that her volunteers addressed. In *Undermining America,* Curtis claimed that the Rhodes, Carnegie and Rockefeller foundations had conspired to return the United States to the British Empire.[29] London's imperialism was exposed in *Britain's War Aims,* as Curtis tried to prove that Britain started the war to control world trade and to conquer Germany, the United States, and the Soviet Union. The British had no scruples about exploiting other nations to enrich themselves; for example, so many rifles had been sent to Britain that 10,000 soldiers at Fort Dix, New Jersey had only sixty rifles.[30] In *The March of Democracy,* Roosevelt was called a demagogue who was a consequence of mob rule. Only under a republican form of government could liberty survive.[31] Hoffman inserted *The March of Democracy* into the *Congressional Record,* and Curtis called upon women to contribute money to send one million copies to influential persons.[32]

Curtis's belief that women were the protectors of productive capitalism was the thesis of *Military Capitalism vs. Industrial Capitalism.* Male-inspired, military capitalism "is founded upon force and destruction."[33] Her most popular pamphlet, however, was *Your Answers to the War Dancers,* a counterattack on proponents of war who fired "word shrapnel" from propaganda guns. War was needless because Germany posed no threat, militarily, economically, or ideologically, Curtis wrote. The United States had only to remain self-sufficient, so the country would not be undermined by products of Nazi slave labor and possible cutoffs of raw materials, and to maintain a republican form of government to avoid the degradations of democracy.[34]

Besides propaganda, politics was a concern of Curtis throughout 1940 and 1941. She spent October 1940 campaigning for Willkie, only to be bitterly disappointed by Roosevelt's re-election in November. To lead the Republicans to victory in the next presidential election, she wrote a platform to solve domestic problems before intervening abroad. She called for the GOP to draft a comprehensive alternative to the New Deal, including repeal of laws impeding industrial recovery and expansion, elimination of wasteful spending, and an end to the farm surplus. Furthermore, the United States should take territories in the Western Hemisphere in payment of World War I debts, establish a Bureau of National Defense independent of the president, and build highways for national defense.[35]

No act of the Roosevelt administration infuriated Curtis more than the Lend-Lease proposal. On February 10, 1941, she denounced the plan at a session of the Senate Foreign Relations Committee, in what she called her most important appearance before a congressional panel. She said Europe detested the American form of government and was attempting to draw the United States into war to destroy it. Partisans of the bill, which had passed in the House, were using the technique that had led to totalitarian governments in Europe: whipping the public into hysteria over fear of invasion.[36]

Lend-Lease, Curtis said, would "wipe out our Constitution and form of government and deprive us of all our liberties" by authorizing Roosevelt to give away assets without congressional consent. Planning not only to suspend the Constitution but also to suppress the two-party system and establish a dictatorship, FDR was confident the legislation would pass—so confident that he was ordering coffins and casualty tags for American soldiers. If the measure passed, the nation would be totally dependent upon Britain for national defense. Passage also would mean war that would slaugh-

ter 1.5 million American boys, wreck industry, throw millions into unemployment, and pave the way for world communism.[37]

Curtis coordinated women's groups opposing Lend-Lease, including the
Mothers of the U.S.A., the women's division of the No Foreign War Committee, the American Women Against Communism, and the DAR. "I regard Mrs.
Curtis as the most capable woman in the country today," an appreciative Rosa
Farber said. "She not only knows politics but she knows Washington."[38]
Curtis worked behind the scenes, directing groups of two or three women
who met with senators privately; the women then followed up their meetings
with letters. Yet she clashed with Dilling, who believed confrontations and
demonstrations should be employed to defeat the bill. "She's giving the
movement a black eye," Curtis lamented.[39] Moreover, "Mrs. Dilling's esca-
pades on the Hill and her third arrest on Friday has done considerable damage in that it has practically closed the doors of Senators to calls by women. I
have been hoping daily that she would quiet down and go home, but publicity seems to have made her a bit 'heady.'"[40] Once she told Dilling, "You simply must call off that parade, Betsy! I have done more than anyone for the
women's movement and it will ruin everything."[41]

After waging a crusade that kept her awake for all save a few hours each
day, Curtis was crushed when Lend-Lease passed. She said she was surprised
that opponents would end the Senate debate without a filibuster, disappointed that Vandenberg, perhaps influenced by friends in the British Embassy, had betrayed the cause without a fight. At least those who voted against
Lend-Lease would go down in history "as some of the country's greatest patriots and statesmen."[42]

As Curtis found sinister implications in Lend-Lease, so she saw omens
even in a small cosmetic change in the masthead of the *Congressional Record*:
"With the *Great Seal* reduced in size, with the Great Circle of *United Strength*
removed, with that unprotected seal moved to the LEFT and with the words
'UNITED STATES OF AMERICA' entirely dropped, just what Nation is it
whose Congressional proceedings and debates are so published?" she demanded. "Is this the first step toward making the *Congressional Record* the
record of proceedings of a Congress of some NEW NATION—a 'WORLD
DEMOCRACY', or perhaps 'UNION NOW???'" Hudson reprinted her accu-
sations in his monthly publication, *America in Danger!*, and the Bund repeated them.[43]

In April 1941 Curtis composed and began circulating a "Mothers' Day Petition" against involvement in war, aimed at members of Congress. The petition asserted men had no right to destroy life without the consent of women,

and that the war resulted from the failure to include mothers in the peace process. "We are confident that the presence of mothers at the conference table will soothe temperaments, heal wounds now minor, prevent destruction of life, and bring a lasting peace to the entire world," it stated.[44]

While the petition was circulating, the Women's National Committee released the results of a mail poll of several thousand women. Curtis said she had commissioned the poll to provide sound data about women's attitudes toward the war. The poll showed that 94.9 percent opposed participation in the war and the same percentage opposed joint citizenship with Britain. Only 5.1 percent favored war. Antiwar sentiment was especially strong west of the Allegheny Mountains, but 77 percent of the prowar vote came from the eastern seaboard and 41 percent from New York City alone. The objectivity of the poll is dubious, yet even reputable polls taken after Pearl Harbor showed women to be less enthusiastic about the war than were men.[45]

Eleanor Roosevelt's plan to conscript women for a year, which she proposed in an article in the May 1941 *Ladies Home Journal,* also drew Curtis's ire. In June, Curtis—who detested Eleanor even more than she detested FDR—attended the Conference of Young Women in New York to oppose drafting women. Speakers claimed such a draft would be undemocratic, would break up homes, and would undermine the morals of young women. (The First Lady's proposal was never implemented.)[46]

Curtis took action again, when the administration began to consider using warships to convoy vessels delivering aid to Britain. She circulated a petition against convoying and, in late May, presented a 5,000-foot-long document, bearing the signatures of two hundred thousand women, to Senator Charles W. Tobey of New Hampshire, in support of his anticonvoying resolution. Curtis said the petition was the largest she had ever presented to Congress, exceeding the one against packing the Supreme Court. She also presented Tobey with a silk American flag. "I hope we will not sin against this flag by carrying it into a foreign war," he said. Still, the opposition of Curtis, the mothers, and Tobey was not enough to prevent convoying from going forward.[47]

Curtis was particularly busy during the preceding month. She inherited the leadership of the National Legion of Mothers of American from Norris after the NLMA splintered. Curtis then embarked on a speaking tour of the Midwest and West. Sometimes sponsored by the America First Committee, she shared platforms with Nye, Mrs. Wheeler, Mrs. Champ Clark, and other America First leaders. But the truncated NLMA was not sufficiently militant for her. Curtis privately complained that it included leftists and former New Dealers, and that many businessmen who were members were greedy for war profits.[48]

On May 11, before Curtis spoke to a meeting of the Mothers of Sons Forum in Cincinnati, Dr. L. M. Birkhead, director of the anti-Nazi Friends of Democracy, warned area residents that Curtis was a Nazi sympathizer. "Although Miss Curtis denies any sympathy for Nazism, she has won the approval of Nazis in the United States for publicizing some of their doctrines and repeating their propaganda," he wrote to the *Cincinnati Post.* Birkhead pointed out that many of the ideas advocated by the Women Investors in America and the Women's National Committee to Keep the U.S. Out of War bore a striking resemblance to Nazi propaganda. True, who distributed Nazi propaganda, had put one of Curtis's pamphlets on his "must" reading list and Hudson, another Nazi sympathizer, had publicly approved her work. Furthermore, the official Bund newspaper had reprinted one of her leaflets.[49]

Curtis's speech justified Birkhead's alarm. When she cited her poll and said only people on the East Coast favored war, the audience mumbled, "You know it's the Jews." She complained that "Washington is filled with British agents" and that the United States was giving up too much to defend Britain: 800,000 rounds of ammunition (leaving just a three-day supply for American soldiers) and 800 planes (all but 18 were in storage in Britain). The British expected America to pay for the war, which would last ten years and cost $100 million a day. Curtis did not blame Hitler for the war, yet she said Germany and Britain were secretly negotiating for peace, hoping to involve the United States in a war against Japan, before dividing the world. The women in the audience nodded in agreement and crowded around Curtis to congratulate her after her talk.[50]

Even with her schedule of speaking engagements and her correspondence, Curtis found time to return to Washington to testify before congressional committees. In July 1941 she appeared before a Senate panel to oppose a bill that would authorize the president to conscript private property during a military emergency. Curtis argued that the bill would authorize the president to rob investors of profits, ruin small businesses, and lead to a dictatorship. The senators did not seem impressed with her testimony, but the bill was never enacted. Later that month, the House Military Affairs Committee heard her condemn a plan to remove limits on the number of men drafted and their length of service. Roosevelt was following the path of all dictators in manipulating the military as a prelude to seizing power, she said. If he continued to defy the majority of Americans, they would rise in armed revolt against the New Deal. Despite opposition from Curtis and others, Congress passed the measure by one vote.[51]

The isolationist movement declined rapidly after passage of Lend-Lease; its failures drained the movement's appeal. After the Pearl Harbor attack, the

Women's National Committee to Keep the U.S. Out of War disbanded. Still, Curtis continued to denounce administration policies. Increasingly, Women Investors focused on combating restrictions on the domestic economy, such as rationing and price controls.[52]

Like isolationism, Ingalls's influence waned, although her downfall, rooted in a speaking tour that she started in July 1941 for the America First Committee and the Women's National Committee, was more dramatic. National America First officers had been told to be wary of Ingalls because she was an extremist, yet reports from local chapters were so enthusiastic that she was allowed to continue. Her tour was notable for her vehement addresses and straight-armed Nazi salutes. Convinced Hitler would win the war, she hoped he would unite Europe and "take care of the situation" in the United States, which had a "lousy democracy."[53]

If Ingalls's sound and fury unsettled some America First members, they were just what Germany wanted to hear, for the Third Reich had secretly employed her from the beginning of her association with the America First Committee. She had initiated her collaboration by approaching Baron Ulrich von Gienanth, the second secretary of the German Embassy in Washington and the covert head of the Gestapo in the United States. Paid a monthly stipend, she was worth the expense, according to the baron, who was overjoyed with Ingalls's work. Ingalls read *Mein Kampf* carefully, underlining passages in red ink, and studied material recommended by the Nazis in preparation for her speeches. She consulted *The Roosevelt Red Record* and *The Octopus,* in addition to pamphlets such as Hitler's *My New Order,* and *Germany and the Jewish Question.* Also, Ingalls carried briefcases bulging with anti-Semitic tracts provided by the German Library of Information.[54]

On tour, Ingalls corresponded with von Gienanth and Thomsen, the German charge d'affairs in Washington. After the British lost Crete and the battlecruiser *Hood* in combat with Germany, she wrote to Thomsen, "I could tear the skies in triumph. Heil Hitler!" Another time, she wrote to him, "Some day I will shout my triumph to a great leader and a great people. . . . I have a telegram already written 'Sieg Heil' to send you." After the fall of France, she suggested to von Gienanth that she fly to Europe to promote "another Munich" peace; von Gienanth, however, replied that the best thing she could do for Germany was to promote the America First Committee. And to Curtis, Ingalls explained, "I have always known the best way to keep the United States out of war was to pray for, or aid, a swift German victory. . . . Visit me in my little chalet near Berchtesgaden [Hitler's retreat in Germany]."[55]

When Germany and Italy declared war on the United States on December 11, 1941, Ingalls rushed to Washington to ask von Gienanth for the names of persons "who can continue our work in this country."[56] A week later, she was arrested and charged with being an unregistered agent of the German government. At her trial, a New York plastic surgeon who had treated Ingalls testified that while she was in the hospital, she wore a swastika pendant and called Hitler "a marvelous man." Ingalls's correspondence with Curtis and von Gienanth was introduced into evidence, and FBI agents testified they had had Ingalls under surveillance for several months. Ingalls, the only defense witness to testify, claimed she had initiated contacts with the Germans to spy on them for the United States, but she admitted she had passed no information to the American government. The jury deliberated for only an hour before convicting Ingalls, who was sentenced to serve from eight months to two years in a federal prison. She was released twenty months later, having been transferred for fighting with another inmate and adjusting poorly to prison.[57]

The ordeal of arrest, trial, and incarceration did not rid Ingalls of Nazi sympathies. In 1944 she denounced the Allied invasion of Normandy: "This whole invasion is a power lust, blood drunk orgy in a war which is unholy and for which the U.S. will be called to terrible accounting. . . . They [the Nazis] fight the common enemy. They fight for independence of Europe—independence from the Jews. Bravo!" In July of that year, after her probation ended, Ingalls tried to enter Mexico. Her luggage was inspected in El Paso, and government agents found clippings about Nazi activities and notes on German and Japanese shortwave radio broadcasts to which she had been listening. She praised the Japanese broadcasts as "lucid, logical, and realistic" and commented, "They make all the war exaltation and breast-beating in the U. S. not only ridiculous but stupid. . . ." By this stage of the war, the United States was confident of victory and less worried about Ingalls. The government prevented her from entering Mexico but did not prosecute her for the seditious material she was carrying.[58]

The woman who attracted followers such as Ingalls is an enigma. Curtis was a very private woman, and our knowledge of her parents, upbringing, education, spouses, and personal life is fragmentary. Perhaps it was her wish to remain a mystery; she removed most of the personal material from her papers before donating them to the New York Public Library. An analysis of her personality and motives is therefore largely speculative.[59]

Curtis might have learned to compete through her father's influence. Her upbringing appears to have emphasized making money, and much of what she knew about investing she learned at home. To succeed in finance, she had to pry open doors that were open to men, a necessity she resented.[60] She took pride in her ability to excel in a male-dominated field and came to believe the fate of the nation was linked to economic equality for women. Prosperity was

impossible without protecting the rights of women in business and investment, argued Curtis, who devoted her career to bringing women financial
knowledge.[61]

Curtis hated FDR because the New Deal required increased governmental
control over the economy, business regulation, higher taxes, deficit spending,
and an alliance with organized labor. She equated the New Deal program with
socialism, communism, and labor radicalism. World War II required federal
intervention in the economy and a deadly alliance with the British and the
Jews. Her antipathy toward the British and her anti-Semitism were animated
largely by economic concerns. The British, she believed, wanted to dominate
the world and force the United States to rejoin the British Empire. The Jews
dominated banking, politics, movies, and radio. Worse, the British and the
Jews were part of a worldwide anti-American conspiracy that included communists and international bankers. American resources were too valuable to
be given away to communist-oriented interests abroad that posed a greater
menace than fascism.[62]

On economic issues, Curtis was closer to mainstream conservatism than
were most of the prominent mothers. She maintained that the economic
changes brought about by the New Deal and World War II meant intolerable
sacrifices for women, just as the war would mean the loss of relatives, the
disruption of families.[63] But financial values, to her way of thinking, were
more important than religious values for the stability of the individual, the
family, the country. Religion did not play a key role in her life or propaganda,
as it did for those of other mothers' leaders. She rarely talked about God or
spiritual matters, and there is no record of her belonging to a church or reading extensively about religious topics. Her personal life, including her di-
vorces and her living with a man to whom she was not married, were
inconsistent with the mothers' religious principles.[64]

One of the more intelligent mothers' leaders, Curtis excelled in business,
investment, acting, producing, and broadcasting, whereas many of her peers
in the movement were not employed outside the home. Her antiwar crusades
reflected her diversity. She was interested in the prerogatives of single women
as well as the interests of wives and mothers; she wrote and spoke about subjects besides anti-Semitism and anticommunism; and she communicated
with people on an intellectual level rather than on a purely emotional level, as
seen in her disputes with Dilling. She attracted a broader, more varied following than Dilling but inspired less intense loyalty.[65]

Curtis seems to have mirrored the split personality of the 1920s, a period
of political conservatism and cultural rebellion, the time when her views
were fixed. Although she sympathized with change in culture, she resisted

change in politics and economics because she had a stake in the status quo. Her wealth was derived primarily from risky speculation, so she could never be sure of its permanence. What she won one day could be gone the next, a danger that was magnified by the upheaval of the times. She stood to lose control of her fortune. Like some of her colleagues in the mothers' movement, she was one of millions of people who were anguished during a period of great flux, torn by forces they could neither understand nor master, and ready to personalize their fears by holding Jewish bankers or other scapegoats responsible for the upheaval.[66]

There were other similarities between Curtis and her peers among the mothers' leadership. Curtis was authoritarian, compulsively active, easily angered, and she had no friends who were not ideological sympathizers. She had many male acquaintances and most seem to have been anti-Semites. She demanded that friends accept her views and directions, equating dissent with disloyalty and purging from her organizations those who insisted on thinking for themselves. Believing she was superior to the women she led, Curtis found it difficult to cooperate with women of comparable ability, who threatened her—an ironic insecurity, given her considerable talents—and with women of lesser acumen. Also, she criticized others for faults she shared with them, a trait of many prejudiced people. To take but one case, one of her frequent criticisms of FDR was that he wanted to be a dictator, yet she was a dictator in her realm.[67]

Despite her desire to see women succeed, Curtis had views on gender questions that were fraught with paradoxes, as were those of others in the mothers' movement. First, she was highly critical of Eleanor Roosevelt. Complaints about Eleanor's alleged loose morals did not resonate with Curtis. She wanted women to surpass traditional social roles and must have admired Eleanor for her achievements in that direction. But Curtis must have considered Eleanor a traitor to the upper class in embracing liberal economics, and she felt the First Lady's success was undeserved. Eleanor had married into affluence and power instead of working for them, as Curtis had worked. Too, she probably resented Eleanor for being a strong personality who could rival her. Second, Curtis fought for women's rights even though she stopped short of calling herself a feminist or of attacking the patriarchy directly. Third, she found it possible to be feminist in orientation yet reactionary in economics and politics. She was an anti-Semite who sympathized with Nazism, an extreme anticommunist who resorted to demagogic appeals to win followers, a woman who appropriated the maternal arguments of pacifists and turned them into pro-Hitler propaganda.

Curtis's influence was substantial because she seems to have represented hundreds of thousands of women who agreed with her sufficiently to join her organizations and subscribe to her publications. Her partisans suffered from discrimination and the patriarchal system, but they belonged less to the class of the oppressed and the needy than to the economic elite.[68] With Curtis and the mothers, the contradictions were many.

=== SIX ===

Dilling and the Crusade against Lend-Lease

From the earliest indications that Europe might go to war, Dilling's sympathies lay with the fascist nations. In 1936 Dilling was thrilled at the news that Franco had launched a rebellion against the Spanish Republic, and she hoped the right-wing Catholic would defeat the leftist Loyalists. Two years later, Dilling traveled to Spain to see the war firsthand. Knowing of her anticommunist books, Franco's officers gave her permission to visit the front, where she took still and motion pictures, and made notes for articles. Claiming that Franco's troops respected churches and civilians, she said the Loyalists, backed by the Soviets, looted churches and raped nuns. Dilling photographed "churches ruined by the Reds with the same satanic Jewish glee shown in Russia" and "the bones of the gentle nuns ripped out of their coffins" by Loyalist troops. Her photos proved Franco's troops had not bombed Guernica, but houses had been "devastated by the fires set by Reds."[1]

Dilling returned to Spain in 1939, with Franco on the verge of victory, and found the situation encouraging. Franco was "fighting with Spain's decent element for Christianity and against typical Bolshevist atheistic murder and chaos."[2] Americans did not know this, however, because their Jew-controlled press smeared the general and withheld the truth about the Loyalists. "Did Americans get a truthful impression from the press about the Communist-Socialist-Anarchist church-burning Spanish government strongly favored by Jewry?" Dilling asked.[3]

After returning to the United States, Dilling addressed mothers' groups about Franco, including a slide show with her presentations. Later she produced a film based on her footage and showed it to reactionary audiences. Franco's soldiers were shown rebuilding bombed buildings and doing other good works; Spanish children were shown greeting Dilling with the fascist salute. During a closeup of buildings in ruins, she shouted, "It was all done by the Reds! They bombed the churches and blew up all the houses when they retreated!"[4] Despite the Loyalist violence, she knew Franco's Spain was "a paradise of order and decency compared to dirty Red Russia which wants Franco overthrown."[5]

Dilling also had kind words about Nazi Germany. She traveled there in 1938 and was able to report that Germans were happy, industrious, and efficient under Hitler, who had done a great deal of good for his people and helped Christianity flourish. After he came to power, the Bible outsold *Mein Kampf,* atheist societies were disbanded, the government subsidized the construction of 200 churches, and children were given time off from school for religious education. In return, all Hitler required was that ministers confine themselves to religion and refrain from discussing politics.[6] As for Jews, if they were loyal to Germany, they were safe; they were persecuted only if they were communists. Nazism was a legitimate response to their perfidy, and considering that German Reds were Jewish, it was no accident that Nazism became anti-Semitic.[7]

Dilling found the fascist philosophy attractive for its defense of property rights, support of religion, advocacy of class harmony, and battle against communism. The only foe feared by communists, fascism had come to Germany and Italy because democracy was too weak to carry the fight. "I don't care what these countries are doing to their own people," she said. "They at least have stopped Communism from running rampant over Europe."[8] Fascists and fascist sympathizers were good friends of Dilling. She knew the British fascist leader Gen. Oswald Moseley, and the fascist George Van Horn Moseley was one of her favorite Americans.[9]

By 1939 Dilling had moved far beyond anticommunism to become a rabid anti-Semite and Nazi sympathizer. Favoring appeasement of Germany, she denounced criticism of fascists and blamed the war on communists and Jews, never on the Axis. Just as in World War I, Americans were asked to "fight the Jews' battles all over again." Jewish journals were "trumpeting for a war and dictatorship war regime against Hitler at any cost." But there was a risk. "If the Jews succeed in hollering America into war, what happened to Jews in Germany might seem like a kindergarten compared to what they might get in America when the dead bodies start coming home, as Americans are a much hotter-tempered a people."[10] In addition, there was a risk for the United States. The nation had spread its defense thin by devoting so much to protecting the British Empire, and its untrained and poorly equipped troops would be slaughtered by the Germans.[11]

Roosevelt, of course, deserved a great deal of blame. His Democratic Party and administration were communist-controlled; for proof that he was controlled by Jewish communists, one had to look no further than the Torah on display at his library in Hyde Park, New York.[12] Trying to drag the nation into war illegally, he made the Constitution a "rag" in his hands, an offense for which he deserved to be in prison.[13] His aim was to get the United States drunk on a New Deal cocktail, whose recipe read, "Take a dash of sentimental altruism and blend with hypocrisy bitters; fill with urge-to-rule-others; season with graft until palatable; serve with half-cracked ice, tinted Red."[14] There was more dictatorship in the New Deal than in Hitler's Germany, and "There is no aggressor who has equalled the FDR-Churchill declaration that they intend to control the entire world even if it bleeds America white."[15] Still, Germany had been patient in the face of provocations. "Nor has Germany yet committed a single hostile act against America in reprisal for seven years of American boycotts, spite tariffs against German goods, and the insults and hysterical cries for war of New Deal officials," Dilling wrote in 1940.[16]

The Nazis cheered for Dilling. *World Service* advertised her books and urged Americans to contribute money to her cause.[17] Officials used her writings as sources in their reports about the United States. Johannes Klapproth, head of the American section for *World Service,* prepared a report for Hitler in which he praised Dilling. "Would God there were more Elizabeth Dillings!" Viereck remarked to the German ambassador.[18]

For Dilling's views, there were many forums. One of them was a 1938 "pro-American" rally attended by about two thousand people at the Hotel Commodore in New York. Promoted by the German-American Bund and the American Women Against Communism, the anti-Semitic gathering had speakers such as Fritz Kuhn and New York Congressman John J. O'Connor, but Dilling was the featured attraction. She received all the money collected from spectators and from the sale of her books in the lobby. Speakers denounced Jews and Roosevelt, and there were rounds of applause when Hitler and Mussolini appeared in a film shown at the close of the rally.[19] In October and November of 1938, Dilling was in attendance at conferences of leading anti-Semites in Chicago. Participants included Winrod, Sanctuary, and Smythe; among those who planned to attend but could not were Pelley, Deatherage, Dennis, and George Van Horn Moseley. The conspirators agreed on objectives, and the wife of a prominent merchant promised to subsidize a fascist movement in the United States.[20]

Cooperation with the America First Committee would have seemed natural for Dilling, although she was wary at first. She said wealthy Jews belonged to the organization and the leaders were of questionable character. For example, Wood was a trustee of the Rosenwald Fund, a Black communist group to which Eleanor Roosevelt belonged. Dilling also pointed out that many of the professors who belonged to the committee were members of the ACLU. These qualms aside, she began to identify with the committee because its aims paralleled hers, and she was gratified to learn that Jewish newspapers attacked the organization.[21]

The mothers' movement peaked early in 1941, in the fight to defeat the

Lend-Lease bill that would allow Britain to purchase arms on credit or borrow them for the duration of the war. The battle had its origins in September 1940, when Hudson, writing in *America in Danger!*, called for a mothers' march to impeach Roosevelt. "Some time ago we suggested the only effective protest against 'sellout' by Congress would be a determined 'March on Washington' by aroused MOTHERS from all over the nation. . . . Who will be the Joan of Arc in this crisis?" The answer, he believed, was Dilling.[22] In October, Hudson met with Dilling and Winrod in Chicago to plan such a march, then returned to Wichita and issued calls for women to rally behind Dilling and send her money. He acted as a clearinghouse for information on the enterprise and publicized it. Coughlin, too, joined the clamor for the march and promoted it in *Social Justice*.[23]

After Lend-Lease passed the House in February 1941, Dilling decided to act, viewing opposition to the measure as an issue to galvanize mothers. Collaborating with antiwar organizations, she spoke at rallies in Chicago and other Midwestern cities to solicit volunteers and created a group, the Mothers' Crusade to Defeat H.R. 1776, to coordinate the effort. Joining Dilling were Curtis, Stanley, Farber, Fischer, and Sherrill. Their work was complemented by the America First Committee, the Friends of Social Justice, and some DAR units.[24]

Elizabeth Dilling's crusaders from the Chicago area, en route to Washington to demonstrate against Lend-Lease in February 1941, pose at Grand Central Station in New York. Chicago Tribune photo.

When the bill went to the Senate, Dilling said, it would be time for women from throughout the nation to converge on Washington. "We want to start a cavalcade to Washington that will flood the Capitol with petticoats and cause all Congressmen who are supporting this bill to reconsider," she said. "If necessary, we will lie on our faces on the Senate steps. Praying women exert a strong influence."[25] Even if the bill passed, Dilling was unwilling to quit. "If this bill becomes law, the only thing we can do is to start subterranean organizations in an effort to win back the Republic." Dilling told women to write to Congress to protest Lend-Lease, and as a result, the two houses received more mail than they had on any issue since the fight over the Versailles Treaty.[26]

One young woman took a more dramatic approach. On February 5 Margaret Russell, sitting in the Senate gallery in a black dress, put on white gloves and a skull mask, rose during a debate on the floor, and chanted "Death is the final victor!" Russell, not affiliated with any organization, had dressed in Senator Wheeler's office and had been taken to the gallery by Rankin's secretary. Capitol police ejected her from the gallery, detained her briefly, and sent her home to New York.[27]

Meanwhile, Dilling and her mothers solicited marchers and prepared to descend on Washington. She arranged round-trip fare from Chicago and booked rooms at the Plaza Hotel. Women were urged to give money to those who could not afford the trip; those receiving subsidies had to agree to participate in demonstrations and stay at least a week.[28] On February 11, Dilling and one hundred women left on the Capitol Limited train and were joined in Washington by five hundred women from Wisconsin, Iowa, Michigan, Ohio, New York, and Maryland. Many of the women did not realize the implications of their activities, but they became a mob when Dilling stirred them. On their first night in the city, the mothers rallied in the hotel dining room and sang "Our boys' bodies shall not rot in foreign graves" to the tune of the "Battle Hymn of the Republic." After the closing verse—"Down With King Franklin's Bill, we'll never be his slaves/While mothers carry on!"—some of the women cried.[29]

The mothers put in long days at the Capitol. Curtis encouraged them to visit senators from 9 A.M. to 6 P.M. in groups of two and three to seek commitments to oppose Lend-Lease. Sometimes they had to wait two or three hours for a five-minute audience. Some senators would not see them at all. The women tried several times to see Illinois's Scott Lucas, a supporter of the bill, who took his name off his door and locked it. On February 11 Fischer and forty other women were ejected from the hall outside the office. (Fischer complained police handled her so roughly that she had to seek treatment at a hospital.)[30]

Dilling, who participated in visits and demonstrations, persisted and got into Lucas's office, leading a group inside through an open door. The senator offered to meet the women one at a time, yet Dilling screamed, "I don't trust him! We'll all go in!" He offered to shake hands with each caller, a gesture that Dilling spurned. One woman shouted "You dirty dog!" Another yelled, "We're laying for you and we'll get you in Illinois!" Still another seized Lucas by the ankle and knelt to pray. Lucas, who was not persuaded to change his mind about the bill, said he never had encountered anyone like the mothers. "Somehow, I don't believe Senator Lucas enjoyed our little call," Dilling said.[31]

Another Lend-Lease supporter, Florida's Claude Pepper, frustrated Dilling by eluding her for days. Finally, she and others went to his office and demanded to be let in. Told that he was on the Senate floor, they began to chant "We want Pepper!" When they refused to stop, police arrested Dilling and her secretary, Jean Lundgreen, for disorderly conduct, and they were released on five dollars' bail each. Dilling was convicted the next day, although the judge suspended her sentence and returned the bail.[32] Unrepentant, Dilling said, "Pepper is a coward. He's just an old scaredy-cat and won't talk to us. How much is he getting to sell this republic out?"[33]

On February 15 and February 26 Dilling led parades down Pennsylvania Avenue, which culminated in mass meetings. The women marched in twos, playing kazoos, singing—they were unable to hire a band—and carrying American flags, placards, chest protectors, and umbrellas with slogans such as "Kill Bill 1776, Not Our Boys." One pair of women bore a black coffin with a skeleton labeled "Fruits of Bill 1776."[34]

Dilling had heard, erroneously, that Virginia Sen. Carter Glass wanted war so badly that he had put British flags on the corners of his desk. On February 27, when she and other women demonstrated outside his office, Dilling suggested they confront Glass, eighty-four, and give him an American flag. A policeman blocked the door and told them Glass would see them one at a time. Some twenty-five women sat down and refused to leave the corridor even though police ordered them to do so. Dilling was arrested and the others were ejected; when Clara Nibberich, one of the demonstrators, shouted that they all might as well be arrested, police obliged her by arresting her. Dilling and Nibberich were booked for disorderly conduct and required to post bond.[35]

This time, the authorities were not so lenient with Dilling, who went on trial for six days, with her mothers packing the courtroom and picketing outside. The arresting officer testified that Dilling and her women blocked the entrance to Glass's office, chanting "Down with the Union Jack!" In a demonstration that looked like "a kindergarten," women crawled on the floor, and

Capper "had to hopscotch over the women's legs to get by."[36] Dilling testified she had only exercised her right of free speech and her right to petition representatives. The judge recognized these rights but said their exercise should not be disorderly. Pointing out that this was Dilling's second conviction, he fined her twenty-five dollars and Nibberich fifteen dollars. A tearful Dilling said it was the kind of justice she had expected from a Roosevelt judge.[37]

Nor was Dilling finished with Glass. During a recess in the trial, she wrote him a note calling him a warmonger who should register as a British agent: "You will be known to millions as a traitor to the republic, another Benedict Arnold, an overaged destroyer of American youth."[38] Glass asked the FBI to investigate the mothers for links to foreign governments. "I likewise believe it would be pertinent to inquire into whether they are mothers. For the sake of the race, I devoutedly hope not." An infuriated Dilling responded, "That is the most insulting thing I have ever read. If Carter Glass is interested in how many children these women have, why doesn't he come down and count heads?" Dilling offered to produce photos of her son and daughter and said one of her followers at the demonstration had thirteen children, five of them draft-age males.[39]

The day after Dilling's conviction, Missouri's Bennett Clark defended her on the Senate floor and condemned Glass for requesting the investigation. Lucas came to Glass's defense, saying, "A man eighty years old is entitled to protection from people of this type." Clark said he received all callers courteously. That might be true, Lucas replied, but Clark had never met anyone like Dilling.[40]

By the time Dilling's trial ended, the Senate debate was near its completion. Desperate, the mothers tried to win over the upper house on March 8. Fifty women picketed the White House and tried to deliver letters to Roosevelt. Elsie Canef was ejected from the Senate gallery when she unrolled and hung over the balcony a banner reading, "H.R. 1776 means war—vote no."[41] That day, Lend-Lease passed with minor amendments, 60–31. On March 11, the House avoided a conference committee by passing a resolution concurring in the Senate amendments, 317–71. Later that day, Roosevelt signed Lend-Lease into law.[42] The mothers had changed only one vote, that of New Mexico Sen. Dennis Chavez, and Dilling and her disciples had damaged their cause, drawing ridicule from the press—even from the *Chicago Tribune*—and alienating congressmen whom they confronted.[43]

Most of the mothers, including Dilling, left Washington after the Senate passed the bill. Still, the groups Americans United, United Mothers of America, and the Roll Call of American Women met in the city to plan an antiwar third party. They agreed to support the requirement of a popular referendum to declare war and to call for mediation of the European war by nations of the Western Hemisphere. The party intended to enter candidates in the 1942 congressional elections, but the coalition was destroyed with the attack at Pearl Harbor.[44]

Dilling opposed the war even after the attack, although family difficulties distracted her. Her marriage, always rocky, began to fall apart. At the heart of the trouble were Albert's infidelities, a decline in the family finances, and Dilling's single-minded crusade, which forced her to neglect her family. Over the years, Albert bought presents for his mistresses and spent large sums to support them. When Albert's tax returns were audited in 1941, Dilling discovered financial discrepancies, became convinced he would not give up other women, and filed for divorce in Chicago on February 24, 1942.[45] Albert filed a countersuit accusing her of drunkenness, drug addiction, profanity, and abuse. Ignoring his support of her activities, he charged she was a fanatic who formed the Patriotic Research Bureau to incite "class and religious hatred." Albert also claimed his wife's reputation as a bigot had driven away his clients and made it impossible for him to earn a living as a lawyer.[46]

The case became national news; Walter Winchell broadcast the charges that Dilling was a drunkard and an addict. Dilling filed a million-dollar libel suit against Albert, his attorney, Maurice Weinshenk, Winchell, and Winchell's assistant, Howard Mayer.[47] Dilling's children and housekeeper testified for Dilling, and Albert turned to his wife's enemies for support. Shouts and fistfights punctuated the court sessions, and the judge, Rudolph Desort, said he came to court each day expecting turmoil. At one session, Dilling admitted for the first time that she had written *The Octopus*. Claiming the book was an answer to B'nai B'rith, she said, "It airs their dirty lying attempts to shut every Christian mouth and prevent any one from getting a fair trial in this country." Spectators gasped and Desort held Dilling in contempt. Kirk lunged at spectators who said his mother must be demented, and four fights erupted in the corridor. The court adjourned in disarray.[48]

At the next session, four policemen and eight bailiffs preserved order but Dilling was held in contempt twice. Albert withdrew the charges of drunkenness and drug addiction, explaining that Dilling drank wine and took sleeping pills. On cross-examination by Thomas W. Miller, Dilling's attorney, Albert admitted he had paid $18,590 to mistresses, yet he charged that his wife hid $5,500 in a closet in their home. The hearing broke up in a fight between Kirk and Weinshenk. Elizabeth Jane, who joined the fight, was struck in the head, and Kirk's fiancée, Betty Bronson, burst into tears.[49]

There was another spectacular session on April 21, when Weinshenk filed a motion to make Dilling produce the files of the Patriotic Research Bureau.

Weinshenk also demanded a list of contributors, including foreign governments; a list of correspondents registered as Axis agents; her income tax records since 1935; and correspondence with thirty-five pro-fascist figures, including Coughlin, Smith, Kuhn, Ingalls, Pelley, Viereck, Winrod, and others whom he named. The list read like a "Who's Who" of the far right. The next day, however, Albert fired Weinshenk for not consulting him before filing the motion that, Albert said, implied his wife was a Nazi. Weinshenk claimed Albert really fired him because an investigation of the bureau would implicate Albert. Weinshenk vowed he would come to court until Albert paid him.[50]

In May, Desort dismissed Weinshenk and the couple agreed to an uncontested divorce. Dilling paid her four fines for contempt and dropped the libel suit. But in June, the Dillings decided they did not want to divorce after all. Albert praised Dilling as "a wonderful woman and one of the smartest and bravest I have ever met." He signed a statement recanting his charges and attributing them to Weinshenk and B'nai B'rith. Both parties dropped their divorce suits and Dilling apologized for the conduct that led to contempt charges. The attorneys remained unpaid and Albert tried to disbar Weinshenk. Desort dismissed the divorce suits in August.[51]

Albert moved in with Dilling, and when she was indicted for sedition in 1942, he defended her. Nevertheless, the reconciliation did not last. Albert began seeing his mistress and, in September 1943, moved to Reno, Nevada, to establish temporary residence for the purpose of seeking a quick divorce. On September 17 he filed a suit against his wife, charging cruelty. Dilling did not contest the divorce and on October 18, 1943 the twenty-five-year marriage ended. Dilling complained she had enjoyed a happy home until "organized Jewry" planted a "bleached gold digger" to ruin her household "through my weak husband."[52] Although she remarried, Albert remained her real love, they reconciled as friends, and he continued to serve as her attorney.[53]

After the Pearl Harbor attack, Dilling resisted rationing, denounced the Allies, and refused to say anything critical of Hitler. In 1944 she campaigned without enthusiasm for Dewey, complaining he had been a cantor in a synagogue. When Roosevelt was reelected, she was philosophical, writing that if the country was to go to hell, it might as well go there under an expert. She rejoiced at Roosevelt's death and attempted to prevent American membership in the United Nations.[54]

To the question of what made Dilling a fanatical anti-Semitic, anticommunist crusader, there are no simple or definitive answers, yet she must have been influenced by her upbringing, family, and private life. As she grew into adulthood, there was nothing in her temperament that foreshadowed her activism. Until she found a cause, however, she seems to have drifted through life rudderless, neither happy nor fulfilled.

Although Dilling was stubborn and mercurial, she was not crude or insensitive until her hatred for Jews overwhelmed her common sense. Her spiritual side, her study of foreign languages and music, and her travels abroad, show she was humanistically oriented. She wanted to understand other peoples and cultures, as she wanted others to understand her. Dilling required deeper emotional commitments than did most people. But she found no contentment from her family or friends, despite a home life that seems to have been comfortable and relatively sheltered.[55]

If she could have become a harpist in a symphony orchestra, a career to which she aspired in college, people would have understood her, appreciated her through her art; she would have sensed accomplishment. Unfortunately, the opportunities to earn a living as a musician were limited, particularly for women, and it is unclear whether Dilling had the talent necessary to succeed in music. Her inability to become a professional harpist, leaving a void in her life, probably was profoundly disappointing. Hers was the case of the frustrated artist.[56]

Dilling mechanically accepted the idea that she was to be a housewife, and she found some satisfaction in church service and her family.[57] Her marriage to Albert appears to have been satisfactory from a monetary standpoint, and she and her husband largely agreed on political, moral, and religious issues. (If Albert did not feel called to crusade for his ideals, at least he financed and assisted her crusades.)[58] Still, Albert was weak and superficial, unable to provide the emotional support she needed; he betrayed her trust by commiting adultery. The marriage might have been one in which the partners wanted to love each other but could not connect emotionally, given their different temperaments.[59]

Dilling tried to be a dutiful wife and a good mother, even if her commitment to motherhood was stronger in the abstract than in reality. She provided her children with an environment that was far from harmonious, far from nurturing. Her time-consuming crusades, undertaken as therapy for her frayed nerves, were no remedy, as they provoked conflict and kept her on edge. Although she insisted on being an independent thinker and resented those who limited her options, she did not allow her children to make their own decisions or to express their individuality. She disciplined them not only in a physical sense but in an emotional and intellectual sense, drilling into them her beliefs with no questions asked. She decided where they should attend church and school and tried to influence their choice of friends.[60]

Kirkpatrick embraced Dilling's cause, attacked Jews and communists, and devoted his law career to defending ultraconservative movements. (Whether he shared his mother's religious zealotry is uncertain.) In conflicts between his parents, he usually sided with his mother, particularly when he learned of Albert's infidelity. Growing up amid a mixture of chaos and enforced conformity probably took a toll on Kirkpatrick's peace of mind, however. Twice divorced, he seemed to have been a difficult person. Elizabeth Jane seemed neither to have rejected her mother's causes nor campaigned for them. Shier than her mother or brother, she appeared to have disliked attention and wanted to protect her privacy.[61]

Despite dictating the tone of the child-rearing and the household, Dilling never challenged Albert's position as head of the family, even though she probably resented his status because she knew she was stronger. Too, she believed she was abler than the men who were running the country. She appears to have realized she was at least as capable as were men of making decisions that affected her life. Dilling sensed that women in general, who had little say in matters that affected them, felt this way. But she never rebelled against patriarchy because her conservative values would not permit it.[62]

Dilling's dissent was aimed at a status quo that was relatively liberal in political ideology, a status quo of changing values that imperiled the order that sustained her identity. Her desire was change that would reverse the direction of the country and return it to a simpler, more stable state of fixed values. Thus although Dilling had much in common with Eleanor Roosevelt— especially intellectual independence and activism—she detested Eleanor for transcending the traditional limitations of first ladies, which implicitly challenged Dilling's anchors of religion, family, and stability.[63]

Almost all of the mothers' leaders, even those with more modern views, shared Dilling's commitment to a family and a society that emphasized order. Ironically, their lives, like Dilling's life, were anything but orderly in the public sphere as well as in the private sphere; the friction of political dissent perhaps reinforced their craving for social order. The strain of work and the inability to relax from it must have exacerbated Dilling's internal turmoil. Her private life, further, was less stable than the lives of other movement leaders, not only because of her turbulent marriage to Albert but because of the way it ended.[64]

It is reasonable to assume the divorce aggravated Dilling's anxiety. The breakup of a marriage, inherently stressful in its own right, was particularly stressful to her because it represented an ideological betrayal. In her writing and speaking, she had emphasized the importance of motherhood and family, and of the distinctive realms of men and women, even if she had not observed these distinctions in practice. Now she faced the future alone, with uncertainty over her finances, the education of her children, and her movement, which Albert had subsidized. Worse, the divorce proceedings occasioned immense press coverage that her enemies exploited. For someone as sensitive as Dilling, it must have taken remarkable discipline to persevere with work in the face of this adversity. Her commitment to her cause enabled her to continue leading a meaningful life, albeit an intolerant one.[65]

Dilling did not perceive herself as narrow-minded, of course: she considered herself principled and her opponents stubborn. Like male leaders of the far right, including Smith and Coughlin, she was threatened by people who were more flexible in religious outlook, personality, and political philosophy. Such people were traitors, beholden to undisciplined morality that set bad examples for society.[66] Even the Episcopal Church, containing liberal elements that did not share her antipathy toward communism, came under her fire, however painful it might have been for her to oppose her church.[67] In her mind, no one who opposed her did so in good faith.[68] Although Dilling was correct in believing that most people, particularly men in power, opposed her and dismissed her, she was unduly concerned about her adversaries. Evincing the desire for martyrdom that characterized several of the mothers' leaders, Dilling relished the persecution she perceived, taking it as a sign that she was accomplishing something.[69]

Dilling viewed the world simplistically, but she was not ill-informed. Indeed, she was probably the best-read of the mothers' leaders on religious and political questions, patient enough to spend long hours reading and researching over decades. Still, she lacked intellectual sophistication. She tended to read from unreliable sources in addition to reliable ones, to accept only evidence that reinforced her prejudices, and to react angrily to contrary evidence. Unable to deal with complexity or synthesize her research into logical exposition, Dilling was led to false conclusions. Her hatred of Jews seems to have arisen from a misunderstanding of Judaism and an intolerance of faiths that differed from conventional Christianity, not to mention the convenience of Jews as a scapegoat for changing values that threatened her.[70]

Partly because she simplified issues and furnished her audiences with easy (if incorrect) targets for their hostility, Dilling was an effective writer and speaker for her movement. But her writings and speeches were almost entirely attacks, based upon negative reactions to people and events, rather than attempts to offer constructive alternatives. In all of her condemnations of communism, the only thing she achieved was to evoke moral outrage. She never made clear what she expected Americans to do about communism besides hate it.

Unfulfilled in marriage or in motherhood, Dilling came to a turning point in her life in 1931, when she first traveled to the Soviet Union.[71] There, her inclinations toward prejudice intersected with her need of an outlet for her restless intellect and energy. Shocked by the physical and moral squalor in the USSR, outraged by communist dogma, she decided to devote her life to fighting communism.[72] Communists wished to rule the world, emphasized atheism, and portended class and gender changes that endangered Dilling's cherished beliefs. Jews, Blacks, and other anti-American elements had to be fought as well, for they were part of the conspiracy.

Years before she embraced the anticommunist crusade, Dilling had resolved to help keep the United States out of foreign wars. She had acquired her distaste for intervention during her trips abroad in the 1920s, when she saw that allies showed little gratitude for the American role in bringing World War I to a victorious conclusion. With the coming of World War II and the communist forces that, she believed, sought to lure her country into the conflagration, her mission became more urgent.[73]

Some of Dilling's arguments against American involvement were framed by maternal concerns, including the ideas that war would take young lives, disrupt families, and strain the social fabric. (The belief that mothers had special insights derived from raising children was less prevalent for her than for other mothers' leaders, however.)[74] Yet her enshrinement of motherhood was mostly superficial. When she warned of threats to the family, she always spoke of imagined menaces, such as Jews and communists, instead of genuine perils, such as the changing social environment. She saw less threat to families in divorce, child or spousal abuse, and poverty than in alleged plots to destroy Christianity and enslave Gentiles. Dilling's isolationism likewise was not a major motivation for her antiwar arguments, although she was racist, xenophobic, and particularly angry about British meddling in the United States. Nor was her campaign rooted primarily in a desire to save lives.[75]

Dilling's main anchor was an implicit ideological affinity with Hitler and an antipathy to his foes. Indifferent to Hitler's tyranny, she denied that he persecuted Jews or was guilty of military aggression. She perceived that his Germany was a significant barrier to the spread of communism, a doctrine that was a greater menace than was fascism. Atheism, after all, was integral to communism, whereas Christianity could exist, even flourish, under fascism. (Dilling was especially enamored of Franco's fascism, believing it was sympathetic to Catholicism.) Her fear that war with Germany would cost American lives was secondary to her worry that the United States—perhaps allied with the communist Soviet Union—would make war on a country she supported.

Avoiding war with Germany was the focus of the mothers' movement in general.[76]

Dilling was no pacifist. She would gladly have fought the USSR without complaining that such a war would kill Americans, disrupt families, or make mothers suffer. If saving American lives had been Dilling's chief objective, she should have openly opposed war with Japan as well as war with Germany. Instead, she rarely mentioned the Japanese threat to United States troops and never claimed that the Jews, the British, or international bankers were conspiring to involve her country in a war with Japan.

These omissions were somewhat understandable because everyone from Roosevelt to the internationalists believed war was more likely to come in the Atlantic than in the Pacific. With Dilling, however, the omissions were more significant because of her admiration for Germany. It made sense for her to build up the German armed forces, to portray them as so powerful that her fellow Americans should be unwilling to fight Hitler. Given her fascist sympathies, Dilling also should have approved of Japan and tried to persuade Americans that Japan was too powerful to fight. But her leanings toward Germany were stronger than any she might have felt for Japan; she had visited Germany several times and her racism tied her to White Germans, not to Orientals.

These were not the ideals of a patriot. These were the ideals of one who did her best to undermine her nation's war effort and divide its people. Yet Dilling's excesses, doubtless motivated by her troubled, restless spirit, would have undermined even a worthy cause. "I have rarely seen hatred take complete possession of a woman's face as when Elizabeth Dilling stormed around the corridor shouting," Max Lerner wrote of a 1941 encounter at the Capitol. "She seemed like a woman pursued by the furies. What she did not know was that the furies were not outside her, but in her own mind."[77]

═══ SEVEN ═══
Lyrl Clark Van Hyning and We the Mothers
Mobilize for America

Opposition to intervention reached its apogee in Chicago, where nationalist leaders turned the Midwest's largest city into a place seething with reactionary groups. The catalyst was McCormick's *Chicago Tribune,* which had the largest circulation in the region and styled itself the "World's Greatest Newspaper." Anti-Russian and anti-British, the *Tribune* publicized the nationalists and offered a standard around which everyone from mild isolationists to rabid hatemongers could rally. It consistently maligned Roosevelt and quoted Dilling as an authority on communism. The blessing of the *Tribune* was not the only thing the nationalists had in common, however. Many fed off the America First Committee, and most of the leaders cooperated with businessman William J. Grace's Citizens Keep America Out of War Committee. The women took their lead from Dilling and attended the meetings of various groups.[1]

In this ferment, the largest and most active mothers' organization was We the Mothers Mobilize for America, led primarily by Lyrl Clark Van Hyning. This group did not enter the fray until the debate over Lend-Lease, when it sent women to Washington with Dilling's crusade, but it stepped up activity after Pearl Harbor. In February 1941, We the Mothers was incorporated as an educational, tax-exempt organization by Van Hyning, Lucy Palermo, and Grace Keefe. Dilling was involved in the organizing, as was Barbara Winthrop, a writer who became the group's first president. Due to factional dissension, Dilling and Winthrop resigned in September 1941, although Dilling occasionally spoke to the membership afterward. Within months of its founding, We the Mothers claimed 1,000 members in Chicago and 150,000 nationwide. In addition, it created a male auxiliary called We the Fathers.[2]

We the Mothers organized by congressional district to influence political campaigns although the leaders were less eager to attract masses than they were to plant women in key organizations. Members were encouraged to join five or six isolationist groups and take them over from within. The organization professed to be nonpartisan, yet its leaders included Republicans and opponents of the New Deal. Dues were twenty-five cents per year and subscriptions to the organization's monthly eight-page newsletter, *Women's Voice,*

Barbara Winthrop, president of We the Mothers Mobilize for America, gives her members last-minute instructions before they depart for Washington to protest Lend-Lease in February 1941. Chicago Tribune photo.

were two dollars per year. Other sources of income were contributions from the leaders, sales of printed works by right-wing activists, single copies of *Women's Voice,* and Christmas cards with religious and patriotic themes.[3]

Intelligent, versatile, and forceful, Van Hyning was an effective writer and organizer. One journalist called her "the biggest figure in the war and postwar mothers' movement."[4] Of Scotch-English ancestry, Van Hyning was raised on a farm in Ohio. Her father, William Clark, a descendant of the Revolutionary War General George Rogers Clark, died when she was five years old. (Proud of her heritage, Van Hyning was an officer in the DAR.) She was a schoolteacher before marrying businessman George H. Van Hyning, and they lived in South America for more than a decade before settling in Chicago in 1933. They had three children: a son, Tom, who served in the Army Air Corps during World War II; a daughter, Parrie Ann, who ran unsuccessfully for the Illinois Senate; and a younger daughter, Georgina, who was active in her mother's antiwar work.[5]

Vain about her appearance, the bespectacled Van Hyning dressed fashionably. A chain-smoker, she was energetic, charismatic, and a forceful speaker. Assuming a dominant role, she looked upon her followers as pawns to augment her power. "My women are not intelligent," she said. "In fact, they are rather stupid. But they are a group of women who will work hard for

me and that's what is important. Later, perhaps, we will be able to attract a
higher type of woman to the cause."[6] Van Hyning demanded loyalty from her
mothers: "You have no moral right to refuse to take up this burden. It is your
duty—more binding than feeding your children or being true to your husbands."[7]

Raised a Methodist, Van Hyning professed to be religious, although she
attended no church. She compared herself to Jesus, a Christian martyr ("He
was accused, even as I am accused, of holding the Jewish race, creed, or religion up to ridicule") and even expressed a death wish ("All my life I wished
that I could have gone with him to Calvary").[8] She denied Jesus was a Jew and
said none of the apostles, except for Judas, were Jews. In her view, Christians
were in a fight against Jews, who had caused the Civil War and both world
wars. Moreover, Jews repeatedly tried to destroy the United States. They plotted John Wilkes Booth's assassination of President Abraham Lincoln;
planned to introduce free love so Christian families would be weakened and
communists could take over; and undermined the government. Fifty-two of
FDR's advisers and eighty-six percent of all Washington officials were Jews.
Woodrow Wilson was a Sephardic Jew named "Wohlson." Dwight D.
Eisenhower was a Swedish Jew. Harry S. Truman, whose middle initial stood
for "Solomon," also was a Jew.[9] The New Deal and the "Rosenvelt" administration, however, were the vehicles through which Jews and communists
planned to take over. "The whole gang are the offspring of the old gang that
threw stones at Jesus Christ, wrapped thorns around his head, that flogged
him and finally nailed him to the Cross because he spoke the truth, which
upset their plans for world domination."[10]

Nor was the government the only tool of the Jews, whose conspiracies
were complex, Van Hyning argued. Sometimes they worked through the Masons. Van Hyning used to consider Freemasonry innocent because her husband, father, and grandfather were Masons. Then she learned that "[e]very
password, every explanation, every symbol, every figure in Masonry is Jewish." It had been painful to admit that her family had been involved in a Jewish plot, but she observed, "Truth is a relentless master—once one's hand is
put to that plough, no one can quit, though it takes every earthly possession
and connection."[11]

Nevertheless, Van Hyning insisted she did not despise Jews, she only
loved Christians. "Is the scientist who seeks to find and isolate a disease germ
a hater?" she asked. "Does he hate the germ, or does he love humanity?" It
was unfair to call her anti-Semitic merely because she was exposing Jews as
the germ that caused communism. Indeed, "Communism is Judaism." Marx
had derived his ideas for communism from the Jewish religion; his father had

only pretended to convert to Christianity to mislead Gentiles.[12] Communism was a greater threat than fascism, which was at least pro-Christian and eliminated class warfare. Fascism arose as a defense against Jewish-led communism, "the only successful means for the protection of the Gentiles from Jewish dictatorship."[13] Apparently, it was not an impregnable defense, for Van Hyning thought Hitler became a tool of the Jews, who financed his ascension to power and thus held a whip over him.[14]

Still, Hitler was not a bad man; the führer "probably did the best he could for the German people," Van Hyning believed. That the United States fought him, she wrote after the war, was regrettable. "By choosing to assist Russia to victory rather than Germany, we chose the sinister powers of communism and atheism and fought to ruin the bulwark of Christianity and Germany's great white race."[15] Hitler was not guilty of genocide. The Holocaust was a fabrication that Jews foisted on a gullible American public (there were more Jews after the war than before).[16] Anyway, the fate of European Jews or the effect of Hitler's policies was not so worrisome as Jewish immigration to the United States. Van Hyning called for the deportation of all refugees so their homes could be given to returning soldiers, and she denounced the Community Chest and United Fund because they aided Jewish refugees.[17]

Blacks, too, were enemies of Van Hyning. During the war *Women's Voice* reported that African troops were raping "German Christian women" and published a letter from Knowles, expressing opposition to plans for postwar resettlement of Blacks and other minority groups in Northern cities. Van Hyning was not above recruiting Blacks for her cause, though. She helped create a youth organization and veterans' organization for Blacks, and she peddled *Women's Voice* in Black neighborhoods, hoping the publication would inspire Black anti-Semitism. There is no evidence that she altered the content of her propaganda specifically to appeal to Blacks. Her efforts seem to have made little impact on Blacks, just as the mothers' movement in general made almost no inroads among Blacks. A movement that relied heavily on racist arguments was unlikely to have much appeal to Blacks.[18]

Van Hyning never called for the end of patriarchy, yet it is clear she detested the male-dominated political order. Van Hyning and We the Mothers denounced male politicians and bureaucrats for incompetence ("infant minded males" who were "bungling their affairs"),[19] callousness (men did not join women in mourning the loss of soldiers sent abroad, the American boys "thrown into the breach made of men's stupidity"),[20] and shortsightedness ("old tired men have no imagination and no vision.")[21]

Van Hyning wanted women to think for themselves instead of thinking like men, particularly in politics. Women possessed talents, including experience as mothers, that could enable them to govern better than men. Writing about the mismanagement of veterans' benefits, for instance, Van Hyning concluded, "Only after a mother stepped in was the situation adjusted."[22] Women were obligated to cleanse politics, to abandon the two major parties, in which men held control, and to organize as a pressure group to end war. "The men of the nation cannot be trusted," she wrote in her call for a 1944 women's peace conference. "They have not the moral courage to make a peace settlement with the warring nations and the women must furnish the courage to save their sons from this murderous slaughter."[23]

Although Van Hyning's goal was rule by women on the national level, she did not ignore local politics. Her organization sponsored forums to instruct women on evaluating all political candidates who opposed internationalism, and she discussed foreign policy with Chicago politicians and office-seekers. Moreover, she demanded that women be given representation equal to men's on area draft boards and school boards, and she promised the support of We the Mothers to any qualified woman who sought office in Chicago. Van Hyning was the only major mothers' leader who recruited women to run for office.[24]

Before leading We the Mothers, Van Hyning belonged to the America First Committee and the German American Bund. Evidently she quit the committee and the Bund because she could not become a leader in either group. Then she devoted her activities to women's groups, collaborated with Coughlin, Winrod, and Smith, and became well known among leaders of the ultraright and the mothers' movement (although she lacked Dilling's congressional contacts). Van Hyning knew more women in the movement than did any other leader. She enjoyed a long career, publishing Women's Voice for almost two decades after World War II.[25]

Van Hyning's organization developed an elaborate structure, with members attending annual meetings to elect a president, vice president, secretary, treasurer, and a twenty-nine member board of directors. But the board exercised little control over daily operations, for Van Hyning was firmly in charge. Besides serving as president, she was editor of Women's Voice. Circulation of the newspaper, launched early in 1942 with a list of 1,000 subscribers, grew to 20,000 by 1945, reaching every state and forty-seven foreign countries. Readership went well beyond subscribers, as Van Hyning mailed complimentary copies to each member of Congress. None of the contributors or editors were paid, and volunteers were used for packaging, mailing, sorting, and bookkeeping.[26]

Van Hyning wrote two or three long articles in each issue of Women's Voice, which reprinted articles from the Bulletin, The Cross and the Flag, Conde

McGinley's *Common Sense,* Leon de Aryan's *The Broom,* and other ultraright, anti-Semitic publications. In addition, the tabloid carried antiwar advertisements purchased by Viereck with money from the German government, and ads for bigoted literature. Even more blatantly anti-Semitic than the *Bulletin, Women's Voice* gave less information about its editor than Dilling's publications gave about Dilling. Unlike the *Bulletin,* it was printed professionally, but it had numerous errors in spelling, punctuation, and typography. Investigators considered *Women's Voice* one of the more damaging ultraright publications because it was directed to the wives and mothers of servicemen. (The FBI interviewed more than one hundred members of We the Mothers, including Van Hyning, in its investigation of far-right groups for sedition, yet no indictments were issued.)[27]

Although Van Hyning dominated We the Mothers, she had the assistance of other women and some men. One of her more active associates was Keefe, the organization's secretary. An anti-Semite who was a friend of Dilling and a participant in the National Legion of Mothers of America, Keefe attended meetings of most of the anti-Semitic groups in Chicago; wrote for their publications; campaigned for isolationist political candidates, opposed conscription, the British and the New Deal; and advocated the recall of American armed forces stationed abroad. In 1942 she founded the Women's League for Political Education, which attempted to stop the invasion of Europe by exerting pressure on Congress and inspired Sumner to introduce a resolution prohibiting the invasion. And in 1945 Keefe testified before the Senate Foreign Relations Committee against ratification of the UN Charter. She urged an immediate, negotiated peace with Japan. "When the truth about the merchants of death, the international financers, the diplomatic schemers, and the war-gouging profiteers stands revealed, wars will end," she said.[28]

Adelle Cox of Los Angeles led the California chapter of We the Mothers and wrote a column for *Women's Voice.* She blamed the United States, rather than the Japanese, for the attack at Pearl Harbor and denounced as "Jew inspired" the Federal Council of Churches in America for urging the mobilization of all resources for the war. A friend of Waters, she mailed copies of *The Modern Canaanites,* an anti-Semitic diatribe, to Reverend Jonathan Ellsworth Perkins, who attributed communism and fascism to "the Jewish brain of Karl Marx."[29]

Palermo, the vice president of We the Mothers, was active in Chicago politics, spoke at Townsend's meetings, and attended meetings of the Constitutional Americans. She was chair of the Illinois Bataan Relief organization, an anti-Roosevelt organization created on the pretext of aiding Americans held as prisoners of war by the Japanese.[30]

Mary Catherine Parker took part in We the Mothers as well as in the

Constitutional Americans. A backer of Coughlin, she sold *America Speaks, Women's Voice, The Cross and the Flag,* Court Asher's bigoted *X-Ray,* and numerous anti-Semitic pamphlets at meetings. Parker, who served as the Chicago representative of Asher and Smith, tried to convince mothers to subscribe to their magazines. A Catholic, she was critical of the church hierarchy for supporting the war. Parker was fired from her job with a Chicago print shop because of her nationalist agitation among employees.[31]

Pearl Bussey Phinney, a contributor to *Women's Voice,* was a friend of anti-Semites such as Homer Maertz (who proposed that Jews be sterilized), Sanctuary, and Catherine Baldwin of the Defenders of the Constitution of the U.S.A. A prominent figure in New York City nationalist circles, Phinney termed Arthur V. Terminiello, an Alabama priest who billed himself "the Father Coughlin of the South," as "one of the great patriots in American history." In one of her articles for *Women's Voice,* she wrote, "The State Department is nothing but Jews, as are the post offices and all other government positions. Let's clean them out one way or another, and out of the country for good."[32]

We the Mothers engaged in a variety of antiwar activities, among them lobbying, sending representatives to testify before House and Senate committees, and writing letters. (In its 1943 membership report, the organization claimed to have sent more than six hundred letters per month to local, state, and federal officials.) Like less intense women's groups, We the Mothers conducted political activities through neighborhood networks and social gatherings. Weekly meetings held in members' homes, called "Get Together Parties," offered the opportunity to raise money for the organization.[33]

Van Hyning also organized luncheons at local hotels to draw members. Speakers, often local politicians or visiting women lecturers, discussed topics of national interest. Some luncheons were elaborate social events. One featured a "My Country 'Tis of Thee" pageant that dramatized the first arrival of mothers on American shores. Songs and readings helped the women to celebrate American motherhood.[34]

We the Mothers recruited women who were comfortable working in a religious environment. Besides prayer, meetings featured spiritual talks, worship, and religious songs. Weekly open houses at the group's headquarters included Bible instruction. *Women's Voice* printed religious poetry and biblical stories and employed religious metaphors and imagery.[35]

The weekly meetings, whose attendance varied from a high of 100 to a low of thirty and occasionally included a few men, were concerned chiefly with Jewish conspiracies, communist plots, and British perfidy. At one meeting, Van Hyning charged that the British, not the Spanish, blew up the battleship *Maine* in 1898, precipitating the Spanish-American War. She said American boys were being slaughtered because of the British, who exploited India and would not permit Spain to support the Allies. Guest speakers, including Ingalls, Waters, and Joe McWilliams, were inflammatory. One speaker, who thought the only men fit to be president were Ford, Lindbergh, and Mac-Arthur, advocated that all Blacks be sent to Africa. A candidate for delegate to the 1944 Republican National Convention said her slogan was "bring the boys back" and proclaimed that a bloody revolution might be necessary to remove the Roosevelt administration, although she hoped to accomplish it by ballots. When a reporter and two photographers from the Luce Publications Company covered a 1944 meeting, males who sympathized with the mothers tried to expel them and a scuffle broke out.[36]

The rhetoric and writing of We the Mothers heated up during the war, when the organization campaigned for a negotiated peace. Van Hyning blamed international bankers for starting the war and circulated recall petitions against members of Congress whom she blamed for involving the United States. Calling for women to vote against politicians who led the nation into war, she praised Rankin for voting against the declaration of war on Japan and condemned women who served in the military. Van Hyning said she had been idealistic during World War I, working in a factory, donating her wages to the Red Cross, and buying war bonds. Now she knew better, recognizing that the United States incited the Japanese to attack Pearl Harbor, and that FDR was a war criminal.[37] Van Hyning charged that Pearl Harbor Day had been the happiest day in Roosevelt's life and accused the administration of selling war bonds to make a profit. "Wars are for profits—the profit is in the bonds. No bonds—no profit."[38]

In 1944 Van Hyning opposed the Allied invasion of France and, a few weeks before the Normandy landing, wrote that the war was the antithesis of every mother's hopes: "Those boys who will be forced to throw their young flesh against that impregnable wall of steel, are the same babies mothers cherished and comforted and brought to manhood. Mother's kiss healed all hurts of childhood. But on invasion day no kiss can heal the terrible hurts and 'mother' won't be there. Mothers have betrayed their sons to the butchers. . . . We can turn back to God and stop the invasion or continue with the swine and go down to perdition."[39]

After losing the battle against Lend-Lease, We the Mothers worked to enact a Constitutional amendment to require a public referendum to declare war and circulated petitions for the impeachment of Roosevelt. In July 1941 the group distributed 30,000 cards entitled "A Redeclaration of American Independence" in Chicago. The cards, which the public was asked to sign and mail to the president, stated that although the United States had declared its

Lyrl Clark Van Hyning appears before a federal grand jury in Chicago in April 1942, in connection with a sedition investigation. Acme Newspictures photo.

independence from Britain in 1776, the administration was subordinating American interests to those of the British.[40]

While the organization was roiling the waters, Russell, who had donned a death mask in the Senate during the Lend-Lease debate, turned up in Chicago to promote her antiwar campaign. She paraded in her mask through the streets and staged a mock wedding of the goddess of liberty to Stalin on an altar emblazoned with dollar signs. Russell, who said she wanted to create a "White Army" of young women opposed to American involvement, wore an officer's cap and a white naval uniform with gold braids on the shoulder.[41]

In October We the Mothers launched a letter-writing campaign directed at the parents of sons who had died on American destroyers sunk by German submarines. The group tried to exploit grief, told parents their sadness was part of a "needless slaughter," and concluded, "We the mothers of war age boys, beg you to place the blame for the death of your sons where it belongs, and not to be deceived by propaganda into blaming a foreign power. In the name of justice, we ask you to call to account the real murderers of your loved one, the men who violated the Constitution of the United States by sending him into the war zone. Ask our boys—ask all of us—to call to account the actual murderers and we will bless you and the country will call you blessed."[42] The letter, signed by Van Hyning and Keefe, urged relatives of slain sailors to sue the president and the secretary of war for damages.[43]

Many families resented the attempt to capitalize on personal tragedies. One mother, Mrs. Norbert Larriere of Lafayette, Louisiana, wrote to Van Hyning, "I further wish to say that it is impossible for me to understand how you, who call yourselves 'We the Mothers Mobilize for America, Inc.' and express such un-American thoughts, can ask that I, or any American mother, become a party to such plots against our government and our President. I thank God that you are not representative of the mothers of America."[44] Larriere sent copies of the letter to her congressman, who inserted it in the *Congressional Record*. Secretary of the Navy Frank Knox, outraged by the mothers' tactics, charged that We the Mothers was "part of an organized campaign to undermine civilian morale and the morale of the armed forces." Remorseless, Van Hyning vowed to continue the campaign.[45]

At about the same time, We the Mothers engaged in a debate with newspaper columnist Dorothy Thompson, one of the more vocal advocates of American intervention.[46] In November, Thompson spoke to three thousand persons at a Chicago rally, sponsored by the Fight for Freedom Committee, and read a telegram from We the Mothers, which questioned her patriotism and said its members did not want their sons to fight abroad. The organization accused Thompson of being in the pay of the Communist Party and said FDR was a greater threat to the United States than was Hitler. Thompson responded by accusing the mothers of being paid to spread dissension in the United States. "I know some of these black cockroaches who call themselves American mothers and picket the White House," she said.[47] Keefe wrote to Thompson, challenging her to prove mothers were paid to picket the White

House. Keefe issued a statement to the press: "While Miss Thompson is willing to give a million American boys to defeat Hitler, her own son will not be called upon to make good on her offer, since he is only 11 years old. If Miss Thompson loved America more than she hates Hitler, she wouldn't be so hysterical."[48] A few days later, an organization of women working for the defeat of interventionist congressmen dubbed itself the "Black Cockroach Mothers."[49]

In May 1944 *Women's Voice* issued a call for a national women's peace convention in Chicago to unite the mothers' movement. About 125 women and a few men from sixteen states assembled at the Hotel Hamilton on June 12–14, 1944. Among the leaders present were Katherine Sutter of the Loyal American Mothers (of Flint, Michigan), Waters, Stanley, and Blanche Winters, whose Detroit mansion was a center for women's right-wing antiwar activities.[50]

The conference opened with a silent prayer, a recitation of the Lord's Prayer, a salute to the flag, and the singing of the national anthem. Van Hyning then delivered the keynote address, "Our Duty to Civilization," an indictment of the war that moved her listeners to tears. She said the peace convention was the first ever held in the United States, and warned the world to mind its own business and leave American mothers alone. Reading biblical passages condemning war, she blamed Britain for starting the war and claimed Churchill had devised a plot to destroy Germany back in 1905. The war must be ended by a negotiated peace that would serve the American people rather than the international bankers, she said. Next, Congress should launch an investigation to determine why Roosevelt had led the nation to war, then punish the president.[51]

That evening George Foster, representing the reactionary Constitutional Americans, was the main speaker. He condemned Republicans Dewey and Willkie for collaborating with the New Deal and charged that sinister forces in the United States wanted to follow the doctrines of Marx instead of the Constitution. After Foster spoke, Van Hyning took a collection and closed the session with the reading of a patriotic poem and the Lord's Prayer.[52]

On June 13 delegates at the morning session adopted resolutions urging Congress to petition the president for an immediate armistice and a negotiated peace; condemning the prosecution of "patriots" such as Dilling for sedition; and urging a cessation of immigration for ten years. After an hour of debate, the delegates voted to endorse Ohio Gov. John W. Bricker for the Republican presidential nomination on the condition that he remain a right-wing nationalist. Waters, running for president as an independent, asked the delegates to endorse her but received no support.[53]

Other speakers on the second and third days included Stanley and Brown. Both claimed to have suffered persecution because of their leadership in the mothers' movement. Brown said she had five sons in the armed forces; three of them had participated in the Normandy invasion and one had been wounded. Waters, who also spoke, said she was the only woman whom the New Dealers feared. She claimed to have blocked enaction of a law that would have permitted FDR to deport his enemies, and said there was a communist plot to take over the Republican Party. The mothers agreed to conduct a house-to-house campaign to enlist women to work for a negotiated peace.[54] That was the only peace worth having, Van Hyning said. "Policing the world means that you will never have your boy at home—that is what dictated peace means, what unconditional surrender means." For all the rhetoric, however, the conference accomplished little and Van Hyning did not realize her ambition of forging an organization to unite the mothers' movement.[55]

In 1945 Van Hyning attempted to prevent creation of the UN, which We the Mothers called a creation of Jews, Masons, and communists. She traveled to San Francisco, where she and Cox led a group of women that tried to force their way into the UN organizing conference. Smith was in the city to coordinate the activities of the anti-UN forces, but the groups had little visible effect on the delegates.[56]

Afterward, Van Hyning returned to Chicago to prepare for the second women's peace conference, which met June 14–17 at the LaSalle Hotel. Some two hundred delegates from thirty-six states, including about twenty men, attended. Sanctuary acted as master of ceremonies and sold a suitcase full of anti-Semitic literature. Henry H. Klein, a lawyer who had converted from Judaism to Christianity, spoke twice, one of his speeches lasting two hours. He refused to eat or drink in the hotel for fear that someone would poison him.[57]

Such men, however, were merely sideshows, for Van Hyning dominated the proceedings, delivering several speeches. Waters, who tried to attend without Van Hyning's permission, was thrown out screaming.[58] Van Hyning's messages included the warnings that there was an organized effort to undermine democracy in America, and that it was up to women to save the country. Following her lead, the mothers condemned the international conferences at Dumbarton Oaks, Bretton Woods, and San Francisco. One woman who had accompanied Van Hyning to the UN conference said the gathering was really held to plan wars and most of the delegates were drunk; Anthony Eden attended merely to get whiskey and cigarettes he could not obtain in his England. The mothers adopted resolutions demanding immediate conversion of industry to civilian production, an end to rationing, abolition of the Federal Reserve System, a Constitutional amendment to limit private fortunes, and a pledge to investigate un-American textbooks in public schools. Nevertheless, the convention was no more successful than was the first in creating a united mothers' movement.[59]

Because of scant information, the place Van Hyning occupied in the mothers' movement is easier to determine than her motives for reactionary crusading. Her activism might have owed something to her father's death, which occurred while she was young. Perhaps growing up in a family headed by her mother animated some of Van Hyning's gender consciousness and her desire to compete against men. We know nothing of her mother's political beliefs, however, so it is impossible to determine whether the mother's ideology shaped the daughter's. Nor do we know whether Van Hyning was subjected to harsh discipline as a child, discipline that sometimes contributes to the development of a dogmatic personality.[60]

The Revolutionary War apparently was a strong influence with Van Hyning, a key part of her usable past. An officer in the DAR, she was proud to have an ancestor, a general,[61] who fought for independence from Britain. She was a general in the women's movement, fighting for American independence from Britain, from Jews, from communism. Before a meeting of We the Mothers, she gave a talk entitled "No Place for Tories," in which she condemned British sympathizers and likened them to colonists who supported the British.[62] And it was her organization that asked people to sign "A Redeclaration of American Independence."[63]

Also, it is certain that Van Hyning, like other mothers' leaders, was comfortable only with people she could control, although she had a keen mind and charisma. Despite her determination, though, she was less single-minded than Dilling, her Chicago-area colleague.[64]

There were other differences between Van Hyning and Dilling. First, the former led a more varied life. Whereas Dilling had never worked at a paid job outside her home, Van Hyning had been a schoolteacher; whereas Dilling had only traveled abroad, Van Hyning had lived abroad, in South America. (Their experiences with foreign cultures did not make them tolerant individuals.)[65] Second, Van Hyning's forte was organizing; Dilling, a loner, was strongest as a researcher.[66] Third, Van Hyning did not attend church or read extensively about religious topics, unlike Dilling (but religion was critical to We the Mothers, and Van Hyning, like other mothers' leaders, believed she was a messianic figure who was willing to die for her cause).[67]

Most important, Van Hyning was more interested than was Dilling in issues relating specifically to gender. Van Hyning wanted women to seize the instruments of power, to run for office not merely because they were extreme rightists but because they were women, uniquely qualified to rule. Hence she identified with the interests of women, not just with the interests of the far right. With such women as Curtis, Van Hyning shared ambitions for women's political power that went beyond the mothers' movement. Dilling, by comparison, did not stress the need for women to hold office. To her, the gender of officeholders made little difference so long as they were ultraconservative Christians. She emphasized that women must lead by setting a moral example and by raising children to observe Christian and patriotic values. The writings of the women reflected this split: Dilling's *Bulletin* was limited largely to anticommunist and anti-Jewish invective, yet Van Hyning's *Women's Voice* examined a variety of issues affecting women.

Much like Curtis, Van Hyning was one of the more modern mothers' leaders, pragmatic enough to attempt to succeed in conventional politics. For this reason, she was one of the graver threats to Roosevelt's foreign policies.

═══ EIGHT ═══

The Mothers' Movement in the Midwest: Cincinnati, Cleveland, and Detroit

Outside Chicago, the principal redoubts of the mothers' movement in the Midwest were Cincinnati, Cleveland, and Detroit. Cincinnati was the home of the Mothers of Sons Forum, founded by Josephine Mahler in January 1940 and composed primarily of women who had husbands or sons eligible for conscription. Limited to the city, the group drew from fifty to one hundred women at its weekly meetings, charged no dues, relied on contributions, and operated on a modest budget. Yet the forum, which had a membership of 1,800 and a mailing list of 50,000, could command significant support; in June 1940 it was able to collect 65,000 signatures on a petition against the draft, for instance. Mahler served as vice president, with Ethel Groen president. Among the more active members were Lucinda Benge, Bruneta Gausepohl, and Mary L. Arbogast, a wealthy benefactor.[1]

Groen, the wife of a delicatessen owner and mother of two sons, was of British descent but spent most of her time in the company of Germans. She defined the aim of the forum as "the downfall of the British and the elimination of the Jews."[2] Using material furnished by the German Library of Information, she whipped her women into enthusiasm resembling Nazi rallies. Nothing would stop her, it seemed. Groen claimed to have traveled to Washington to protest extension of the draft despite a skull fracture and concussion suffered in a train accident en route.[3]

Groen fell from favor with the forum after Pearl Harbor, when she changed her mind about the war because of the Japanese attack and signed a waiver to allow her seventeen-year-old son to join the Army. Some mothers argued with her decision, leading to her resignation as president in March 1942. (She remained a member, however.)[4] Groen's successor, Benge, was middle-aged, with a son in the Marines. Anti-Semitic and a member of the America First Committee, Benge detected communism in the YWCA and warned of a government plot to use women to reproduce.[5]

The forum's chief means of expression were the *Bulletin*, a weekly published from 1942 to 1946, and *PS*, a bimonthly published from 1940 to 1942. Costing five cents per month, the *Bulletin* had 1,000 subscribers and reached

Members of the Mothers of the U.S.A. protest a Detroit visit by Lord Halifax, the British ambassador to the United States, in November 1941. The gutter is littered with eggs and tomatoes that the mothers threw at the envoy. Acme Newspictures photo.

readers as far away as Seattle. Free copies were mailed to public officials and to people mentioned in the articles. The mimeographed sheet, which ran from three to five pages, was written chiefly by Groen and Benge and edited by Benge. It used items from the *Congressional Record* and the daily press, given a nationalistic slant, took reactionary stands, and promoted religious fundamentalism.[6]

The Cincinnati mothers amplified their voice through other groups, particularly the America First Committee and the U. S. Selectee Parents Legion, and other leaders, notably Smith, Coughlin, and Dilling. (There was no cooperation with the American Charter, a short-lived group that had splintered from the forum and welcomed men.)[7] Smith spoke several times to the forum and won its support for his America First Party; Benge sat on the platform at the party's first convention. Coughlin never spoke to the organization, but he advised its leaders privately and many of them subscribed to *Social Justice*. As for Dilling, she spoke to the forum, in June 1943, and her books were sold at the meetings.[8]

On March 8, 1941, the forum sponsored its first mass rally, with ex-Sen. Rush Holt as the major speaker. Billed as a rally to defeat Lend-Lease, the gathering was robbed of its purpose when the measure passed the Senate a few hours before Holt spoke. Several thousand women nevertheless showed up to boo Roosevelt and Churchill, cheer Lindbergh and Coughlin, and applaud Holt. The audience was composed mostly of middle-class, middle-aged White women, with a few younger women, and about a dozen priests. Holt attacked Lend-Lease, the Committee to Defend America By Aiding the Allies, Winchell, and Thompson. He vowed not to sacrifice a single American life to save the British Empire. "The president says you cannot believe Hitler's promises; the president has not kept his promises either." Turning to another subject, he said, "I am sick and tired of the refugees enjoying prosperity and life in this country and then trying to involve us and take us over to wars they tried to escape. Let's charter a boat for the refugees and let them fight!"[9]

On May 11 the forum joined with the America First Committee and the Selectee Parents Association, a Cincinnati reactionary group, to sponsor a talk by Curtis at a mass rally. In her introductory remarks, Groen said the 1940 election had been rigged to reelect Roosevelt, who would break his promise not to send Americans to fight a foreign war. Curtis apologized for showing up late because she could not get an earlier plane from Washington. "However, there are hundreds upon hundreds of planes sitting idle in British warehouses, planes that we have sent to them," Curtis said.[10] The mothers cheered when Curtis absolved Hitler of blame for the war, and they encouraged her attacks on Willkie and Glass.[11]

That summer, Benge, Groen, Arbogast, and Mahler went to Washington to testify before the House Military Affairs Committee, in opposition to a bill to extend the term of enlistment of draftees for one year or indefinitely if a national emergency were declared. A delegation of 17 mothers accompanied the leaders and spent time lodging protests with congressmen. Benge testified that if American boys were sent abroad under the terms of the bill, they would spend the rest of their lives in foreign countries. She said soldiers were treated brutally in training camps; 18 were killed in a night convoy on maneuvers in California, and 200 died from bites by poisonous spiders. Groen said she had yet to meet a draftee who wanted to remain in the Army for more than a year. Arbogast said she did not want her four draft-age sons to die in a foreign war. She claimed morale would be poor if draftees were compelled to serve longer than a year. One soldier, she reported, told his mother he would commit suicide rather than remain in the service.[12]

The mothers, having worked feverishly that summer to prevent American involvement in the war, were roused to bitterness by Groen at their November 10 meeting. She read clippings about the first American boy killed in Iceland, and about Pepper's request that Britain give Palestine to the Jews after the war. The mothers booed Pepper and a man arose to say, "Pepper and Wendell Willkie are hired by the Jews. Roosevelt was committed to war by the Jews. The Jews are the ones who cause all our wars. The Christians were taken advantage of by the Jews in Germany. The German Jews exploited German women." Groen responded, "Since Lindbergh's speech, there has never been a denial by a single Jew of the fact that they are interventionists."[13]

Another woman described a trip to New York. She went to see a movie and it was filled with Jewish propaganda. In the lobby after the show she said, "We are getting tired of Jewish propaganda." A patron called her a Nazi and another woman said, "I'm not a Jew, but I am speaking for the Jews. You can't talk that way." The mother replied, "You don't have to tell me what you are. Your physiognomy tells me that." Then the woman told the meeting of a law in New York prohibiting derogatory remarks about Jews. People could say anything about Christians, "but the minute we mention the word 'Jew' we are crucified. We should stand up for Christian rights."[14]

By late 1941 anti-Semitism dominated the forum. "Churchill is a Jew; Roosevelt is a Jew; this is a war of Jewish capitalists!" one member shouted at the November 26 meeting. Benge complained, "Our boys will die on the golden cross of international Jewry!"[15] Roosevelt was especially hated because the mothers believed he was a dictator who wanted to communize the nation. While American soldiers were at war, Roosevelt would undercut democracy at home and plan to restore Prohibition. His administration, which copied its wartime rationing plan from the Soviets, wasted money and soaked people with taxes in an effort to reduce the standard of living to that of India, where workers received seventy-eight cents per month. And while ordinary Americans scrounged for necessities, Bernard Baruch, a Jew who advised Roosevelt, gave a sumptuous feast for the bride of New Dealer Harry Hopkins, including thirty-five items of imported and domestic delicacies such as caviar, coconut pie, four kinds of beef, French wine, and champagne.[16]

To free mothers from Roosevelt's dictatorship, Benge and Groen wrote a new Declaration of Independence. At a meeting on July 2, 1942, they unrolled a six-foot scroll, a document that, among other things, called for the independence of the United States from all other nations, including the Allies. But the members seemed surprised and did not agree totally with its contents. Groen said she wanted to deliver the declaration, with signatures, to Washington and demanded that each mother sign the scroll as a phonograph played the national anthem; then the women would be photographed with the document. Some did not want to be photographed, fearing the government might persecute them and their families. Benge denounced them as cowards and the meeting adjourned with substantial dissent.[17] Still, the members worked to weaken the war effort, complaining about rationing, discouraging the purchase of war bonds, and encouraging men to resist the draft.[18]

Much time at meetings was spent discussing rumors. Benge claimed American boys were freezing in the Aleutians and committing suicide in Panama, and that paratroopers, fed a diet of soda crackers, were dropping dead from hunger. She said she obtained the information from United States senators, but they denied they had told her anything of the kind. In addition, Benge charged that British soldiers sat idle while American troops unloaded ships; that nylon stockings intended for American women were sent to German-occupied countries; and that war bond revenue was used to finance frivolous airplane trips by Eleanor Roosevelt. Groen said wounded White sailors were given blood transfusions from Blacks and Orientals, making them ill and likely to father Black or yellow babies.[19]

In January 1944 the forum sent letters to members of Congress, urging them to block the invasion of France by impeaching Roosevelt and withholding funds. Complaining about the unequal division of invasion forces, which were to be three-quarters American and one-quarter British and Canadian, the mothers urged Congress to rise and "forbid the slaughter of innocent men for a worse than futile cause." Congress was unobliging.[20]

Benge also was unsuccessful in August, when she appeared before the American Legion convention in an effort to prevent the Ohio delegation from condemning the forum as a subversive group and deploring the forum's advocacy of a negotiated peace. Undeterred, the forum sent a letter to Congress, charging Congress with favoring foreign nations and complaining that the patience of American mothers was wearing thin. In July 1945 there were two defeats: Benge failed to persuade the Senate Foreign Relations Committee to reject the UN charter, and the forum then concluded its wartime history by vainly advocating a negotiated peace with Japan.[21]

Cleveland was home to an active mothers group, the United Mothers of America. Patterned after the National Legion of Mothers of America and closely tied to Smith and Coughlin, the organization was founded in 1940 by Frieda Stanley to oppose conscription. United Mothers met twice monthly, notifying its 1,000 members of meetings through the mail. Funding came from donations, some from husbands, brothers, and fathers of members. Stanley was president, with Ella Monreal vice president and Sue Brown secretary. Mike Kelley was "secret correspondent," an honorary office (only women could hold formal office). Stanley, Monreal, and Brown constituted the board of directors, met privately, and made the key decisions. The constitution and bylaws, adopted in July 1941, specified that the group's objective was to preserve the Constitution and government.[22]

Stanley, forty years old in 1940, was married to David Stanley, forty-one, a laborer at the Aluminum Company of America. Born to a German father on a farm in upstate New York, she claimed her father lost his property in Germany "when the communists were in control." She went to Cleveland as a young woman and met David, whom she wed in 1917. They had a son who was drafted and given two honorable discharges. Naive politically and credulous of rumors, Frieda Stanley made up in drive what she lacked in knowledge. She seemed to have a dual personality: harsh when she talked about Jews, Blacks, and FDR; mellow when she praised Coughlin, Smith, Lindbergh, and Hoffman.[23] A devout Catholic, Stanley told of visiting a woman in Canton who was marked with the stigmata and of seeking spiritual guidance from her. Stanley said God was her life and she would give her last drop of blood for God and country.[24]

David Stanley, one of the few men active in the United Mothers, was commander of the Cleveland Post of the Catholic War Veterans. Like his wife, he was devout and he opposed the labor union where he worked; he claimed communists controlled the union and sabotaged defense work. Stanley feared he might lose his job because of his antiwar activities.[25]

Participation in the group's activities cost Kelley his job as a clerk with the Weidman wholesale grocery company. Kelley, thirty-five in 1940, was a member of the America First Committee, the Committee of One Million, and the National Union for Social Justice. Drafted in 1942, he successfully claimed exemption as a conscientious objector. Kelley hoped to follow in Coughlin's footsteps, but he did not want to become a priest because he did not want the Vatican to control him. His religiousness also showed in Kelley's warning that Stalin was the anti-Christ because he encouraged divorce, loose morals, illegitimate children, and the forced labor of women, ideas the Soviet leader wanted to export to the United States.[26]

Other members of the United Mothers were similarly devout. One woman claimed she averted an earthquake in Cleveland by praying and holding her crucifix outside her window. Another said she thought the world would have three days of total darkness, in which the only light would come from blessed candles, to turn the people back to God.[27] The religious fervor gave a revivalistic flavor to the meetings, as when Frieda Stanley denounced criticism of the organization as "lies, lies, and more lies" and told the women, "Be of good faith; the Master was crucified by the same element that now tries to question our loyalty to America first."[28]

Boring meetings could be revived with Stanley's delivery of an anti-Semitic denunciation of Winchell, whom she called "Lipschitz," as an agent of Moscow.[29] A vicious Jew-hater, Stanley used "Christ killer," "kike" or "Judeo-Communism" because "Jew" was too mild, and she encouraged physical attacks on Jews. She saw Jews everywhere in Cleveland: in city hall, the post office, and the Food Boards. Jews were behind evil plots such as Dilling's divorce, a plan to sterilize every Gentile male born in a Massachusetts hospital, and the establishment of blood banks that would weaken Gentiles by draining their blood. In fact, Jews had brought about the war, "controlled on both sides by the Jews so that whichever side wins, the Jews will be the winners." And when the mothers were evicted from the building where they met, due to their notoriety, Stanley attributed the eviction to "the Jews, who are also to blame for getting us into this war."[30]

The British joined the Jews in the ranks of villains. The Rhodes Scholars and the Carnegie Foundation, Monreal said, were responsible for rewriting American history to favor England and their next project would be to discredit George Washington.[31] Further, the mothers claimed British soldiers had come to the United States "to get control of the American Army."[32] One of the women's circular letters declared, "For a number of decades treacherous foreign and pro-foreign elements have conspired against our government, but none so much as the British, who ever since the establishment of our Republic have connived and plotted for what they hoped would be the eventual takeover of our nation as a recovered colony."[33]

Neither the British nor the Jews were as hated as Roosevelt in the mothers' minds, though. Stanley drew wild applause from her audience by suggesting that "the hunk of cheese in the White House be impeached because he is a Jew and is receiving orders from Moscow."[34] When a woman asked why the people trying to destroy the Constitution and American sovereignty could not be prosecuted, Kelley said they were immune because Roosevelt supported them.[35] Race prejudice was combined with anti-Roosevelt venom when Frieda Stanley called Latin Americans "those greasy people for whom Roosevelt likes to play Santa Claus with American money."[36]

Silver Shirts, Coughlinites, and Bundist sympathizers were drawn to the Cleveland mothers, who sold literature written by Kamp, McWilliams, Coughlin, and Dilling.[37] But the far-right figure whom the mothers most admired was Smith. "In our estimation Gerald L. K. Smith is doing more today from the lecture platform to help preserve our form of government than any other person we know," Frieda Stanley said. "We regard Gerald Smith not only as a 100% American but a true Christian gentleman. For the work he is doing in behalf of our country we are deeply grateful."[38]

In the fall of 1941 Smith spoke at a public hall in Cleveland, with Frieda Stanley sitting on the platform. His speech included the assertion that the New Dealers had murdered Senators Lundeen and Huey Long because they opposed FDR. On April 14, 1942, Smith spoke in Cleveland again, with Monreal and Brown on the platform. He warned the United States could lose the war, said a cabinet shakeup was necessary, and asked the women to contribute to his Committee of One Million, noting that Eleanor Roosevelt received $2,000 per speech.[39]

In May 1942 the United Mothers planned another rally for Smith in Cleveland's public auditorium and made a rental deposit, but Mayor Frank J. Lausche refused to permit Smith to speak. The mothers picketed the city council for several days, and about one hundred members of the American Nazi Party demonstrated in support of Smith. On June 24, when the council debated the mayor's decision, about sixty members of the United Mothers packed the chambers to hear Smith defend himself. After the council voted to uphold the decision, women tossed wadded-up newspapers and swatted the council member who led the fight against Smith. A woman ripped a flower off the councilman's coat, tore it up, and threw the petals in his face. He lunged at her and had to be restrained. The council summoned the police to eject the mothers, but they returned and police were called to evict them again. Smith subsequently spoke in a private auditorium.[40]

Smith's colleague in rabble-rousing, Coughlin, was "the greatest religious leader in the country today," according to Stanley. In 1943 she sent him seventy dollars from the treasury of the United Mothers as a birthday gift, saying she hoped he would use the money "to rise above those who persecute him and once again become our national leader."[41] Stanley had personally experienced Coughlin's grace: she took secret trips to Royal Oak to see him, and she said her husband had received a miraculous cure from the priest.[42]

Frieda Stanley also supported Dilling and cooperated in her campaign to defeat Lend-Lease by going to Washington to demonstrate. "God bless your colleagues in your 100 percent patriotic work for us Americans," she wrote Dilling.[43] Waters enjoyed Stanley's support as well. Armed with a one-foot-thick stack of papers that included notes and copies of the *Congressional Record* from which she quoted, Waters spoke to the United Mothers in February 1942—a talk that might have continued indefinitely if people had not begun to leave. Four months later, the mothers applauded when Frieda Stanley said Waters would return to Cleveland to parade in the streets, in a horse-drawn buggy covered with posters announcing her presidential bid. Kelley suggested the United Mothers follow her in the parade, but the mothers declined to participate.[44]

Officeholders had the mothers' backing, among them Hoffman, Rankin, Reynolds, Nye, Dies, and isolationist Congressman Martin L. Sweeney of Ohio. Hoffman agreed to help the organization after conferring with Frieda Stanley in Washington, and the mothers mailed 15,000 copies of one of his isolationist speeches.[45] Rankin, on the other hand, was unaccommodating. The United Mothers praised her for opposing the declaration of war against Japan and, learning that she might not seek reelection, took up a collection to encourage her to run in 1942. Rankin decided not to run.[46]

Once the United States entered the war, the mothers devoted their efforts to fighting international cooperation, such as the UN and proposals for an American union with Britain. They conducted a letter-writing campaign against such a union and world government, called for a federal investigation of groups promoting world government, and collaborated with Smith to oppose internationalism. Some of the mothers and their male allies disrupted a meeting of Union Now, which advocated an Anglo-American union. Fistfights broke out. Monreal charged that New Dealers who professed loyalty to the American flag were hypocritical because they really favored world government. She asked God to strike dead those enemies of the United States before she finished speaking, a request God did not grant.[47]

Religion likewise inspired the mothers' crusade against S. R. 666, a bill authorizing the president to draft laborers for defense work. Claiming that God had labeled the bill "666," the number identified as the "mark of the beast" in Revelation, the group aimed a barrage of letters at Congress. Monreal said she had written more than a hundred letters because the bill would enslave workers and the country would not be worth fighting for if the bill passed. This campaign, too, was unsuccessful.[48]

In 1943 the mothers began seeking a candidate to challenge Roosevelt in 1944. Some of the suggestions were Lindbergh, MacArthur, Taft, and Nye. The organization supported Smith, however, and Frieda Stanley and Monreal sat on the speaker's platform at Smith's America First Party convention in Detroit. Kelley campaigned for Smith.[49] But the United Mothers organization, unable to affect the course of legislation in Congress, was unable to elect a president. Compounding the mothers' ineffectiveness was a serious flaw in their organization: Stanley, an autocrat, disdained delegating authority or grooming a successor. Consequently, when her health failed after the war, the group withered.[50]

A city that possessed great potential for the women's isolationist movement was Detroit, a tinderbox of dissension that rhetoric could set ablaze. Coughlin and Smith made their headquarters there, and in 1943 the city experienced the worst race riot of the war era. The dominant mothers' group in

Detroit was the Mothers of the U.S.A., organized in 1939. Mary A. Decker founded the organization after women wrote in response to her letter to the *Detroit Free Press,* in which she advocated that mothers join to avoid American involvement in a foreign war.[51]

Membership was open to any woman who was a United States citizen, although those who joined were mainly mothers, wives, and sisters of men who fought in World War I. Many of the members had sons of draft age; some had belonged to another right-wing women's group in the city, the Legion of the Blue Cross. Calls and volunteers rushed in as the nation slid toward war, making any membership drive unnecessary. Operating on contributions and charging no membership fee, Decker's group would claim several thousand members in Detroit and attract an average of three hundred women to its weekly meetings.[52]

Decker was the first president, but Rosa Farber, the vice president, was the strongest personality. A tall, attractive, blue-eyed blond of German descent, Farber, thirty-eight in 1940, had two sons, one near draft age, and a daughter. She believed women had stayed home and left politics and diplomacy to men for too long. "We feel that we're just as important to this country as any group alive," Farber said. "It's time we mothers did something."[53] She told her followers that violent revolution might be necessary to purge the government of treacherous New Dealers.[54] Polish Jews, she maintained, had encouraged Hitler to attack their country, and the Sanhedrin—a world Jewish council that existed only in her mind—had elevated the führer to devastate Europe so Jews could offer communism as an alternative to his Nazism.[55]

The first campaign of the Mothers of the U.S.A. was a fruitless effort to retain the embargo on weapons sales to belligerents, provided for in the Neutrality Act of 1939. In October 1939 two busloads of Detroit mothers went to Washington, where they approached congressmen in their offices and urged them to preserve the embargo. "It is not necessary to have a war to obtain prosperity," Decker told them.[56]

In the same month the mothers sent a telegram to Michigan officials, objecting to a change in the date when Thanksgiving was observed. They declared that "the changing of the date to the twenty-third is a subtle attack on religion, a move shot through with atheistic communism and backed by the president." The women intended to celebrate Thanksgiving on the traditional day and keep their children home from school. If the children were recorded absent, the mothers would take the issue up with the Detroit Board of Education.[57]

In May 1940 the mothers sent a delegation to Washington to protest FDR's handling of international affairs. Bringing their case to Republican senators and representatives, the women urged the party to nominate Vandenberg for president and Lindbergh for vice president. In June the mothers intensified their campaign against Roosevelt by adopting a resolution to impeach him, claiming that FDR had delivered a radio address attacking nations at peace with the United States. "We mothers . . . refuse to be stampeded into a war which will slaughter our sons, turn our daughters over to the Department of Labor under Sidney Hillman . . . and thus accomplish the Satanic plot to put the entire nation under the yoke of tyranny," the resolution stated.[58] On June 13 the women began soliciting signatures on an impeachment petition and sent it to all members of the Michigan congressional delegation.[59]

In August hundreds of Detroit mothers went to Washington at their own expense, some hitchhiking, to join demonstrations against a conscription bill. The women demonstrated in shifts around the clock and nine of them, dressed in black crepe, staged a sit-in at the Senate lobby. In testimony before the Senate Military Affairs Committee, Farber complained the bill gave dictatorial power to the president, that the soldiers would not be paid adequately, and that youths would be corrupted by older soldiers. She wanted to add an amendment stating that no one drafted could be sent outside the United States without a referendum of the people. Also, Farber wanted the Army Chief of Staff rather than the president to formulate regulations for conscription.[60]

Farber's testimony did not prevent enactment of conscription, but in March 1941 she returned to Washington to testify against Lend-Lease before the Senate Foreign Relations Committee. Farber said she was not a pacifist, yet she rejected the premise that the government could defend the country by fighting on foreign soil. She demanded that defense be strengthened by keeping American weapons in the United States and termed Lend-Lease part of "a premeditated drive toward ultimate dictatorship"—Roosevelt's goal.[61]

In July Farber testified again, this time before the House Military Affairs Committee, against extending the period of selective service. High morale was essential to the Army, and no one understood the morale of the soldiers like their mothers, she said. Most of the boys had plans that would be interrupted by extending service. Keeping them in the service would surely undermine morale. Furthermore, mothers knew that a national defense must be built to resist invasion; Americans should think carefully before committing their boys and dispersing their forces throughout the world.[62] Once more, Farber was fighting a losing cause.

In November 1941 Farber's mothers made one more public impact, expressing their hostility to Britain by throwing rotten eggs and vegetables at

Lord Halifax, the British ambassador, when he came to Detroit seeking economic aid for his country. They picketed his hotel, carrying signs reading "Halifax is a War Monger" and "Remember the Burning of the Capitol in the War of 1812."[63] Early in 1942 the Mothers of the U.S.A. dissolved because of factional infighting and reorganized as the American Mothers under Beatrice Knowles, who obtained Farber's membership practically intact and added members. To house her organization, which was funded solely by donations, she opened an office in a suite adjoining her husband's headquarters at the Blue Ridge Coal Company.[64]

Knowles, about forty-two in 1945, had been active in nationalist circles locally and nationally. A vibrant woman with charisma, she had been a model, posing in kitchens as the attractive housewife who used the articles that her sponsors produced. During World War I she worked as a purchasing agent for one of the larger coal companies operating in Ohio, Pennsylvania, and West Virginia. Later she and her husband became the chief owners of Blue Ridge. They weathered the depression and built an expensive home in a Detroit suburb. Knowles was the strongest-willed person in her family; her husband was reticent. They had two sons, aged twenty-three and twenty-one in 1945. The oldest son received an honorable discharge from the Army due to a nervous condition, which developed while he was attached to an engineers' unit. The younger son was drafted and served in the Medical Corps, although he opposed the war.[65]

Knowles was not so compulsive as some of the other leaders. Still, she was busy, constantly talking on the telephone, addressing letters, and conferring with business and political allies.[66] Knowles continued Farber's policy of testifying before congressional committees. Well known on Capitol Hill as the inspiration for a bill to give all servicemen and servicewomen free transportation home on furloughs, Knowles was close to Hoffman, who called her when he was in Detroit, visited her at home, and asked for her assistance when he was ill. (In 1945 Knowles told an FBI agent she had been offered a job working for a congressman, apparently Hoffman.)[67]

Knowles was a fervent opponent of the New Deal, particularly of Jewish New Dealers; she once said the New Deal, Nazism, fascism and communism were "one and the same thing."[68] She hated Jews and the British, the latter being a caste-ridden people, as she had discovered when she lived in England before the war.[69] During the war, she fought proposals to draft men and women for war labor—drafting women would destroy homes, she told the House Military Affairs Committee—and opposed the use of textbooks with internationalist viewpoints.[70] The war should be stopped without a military victory, Knowles argued, because a victory with the Soviet Union as an ally would leave the United States worse than if Hitler remained in power. To influence terms of the peace settlement, she continued to hold meetings even after it became obvious the war was coming to an end. "We don't want any internationalists at the peace table," she said.[71]

Because of her temperament, Knowles sometimes clashed with other mothers' leaders, and she was wary of being associated with some. She refused to participate in Van Hyning's peace conventions as a delegate, although she attended as an observer.[72] But Knowles had few misgivings about cooperating with Dilling, Coughlin, and Curtis, to name a few leaders, or about distributing anti-Semitic, isolationist literature, including *The Cross and the Flag,* to the 50,000 people on her mailing list.[73] Smith wrote of Knowles as "a student of the world government conspiracy. . . . perhaps no one is better informed on world-government propaganda than Mrs. Knowles."[74] Smith wanted her support for his 1944 presidential bid, yet Knowles believed that Smith, by opposing Dewey, would only ensure the reelection of Roosevelt. She said Smith's candidacy was hurting the nationalist cause, refused to attend the America First Party Convention, and warned her followers to stay away from Smith.[75]

Knowles became an enemy of Blanche Winters, another leader of the women's ultraright movement in Detroit. Knowles contacted members of Congress whom she thought Winters might approach and confided to them that Winters was a "screwball." Screwball or not, Winters cut a dashing figure in Motor City isolationist circles. A short, gray-haired woman who wore gold-rimmed spectacles, Winters was fifty-five in 1944, when her influence peaked.[76] She lived in a thirty-nine-room, three-story Georgian mansion that reminded visitors of the White House; she called it the "women's White House" and it was the scene of numerous nationalist gatherings. There were several suites, with private kitchens, for women guests. Young girls, whom Winters referred to as "my little friends," flitted in and out of the house. Rooms were furnished elaborately and each was decorated to fit a specific color scheme.[77]

Winters had been born into affluence. She had little patience with less fortunate people, saying that an American-born man who was healthy and had no disastrous luck had only himself to blame if he were without money. Her largesse, however, was not self-made: her family subsidized her activities, she conceded. Winters's crusade also had financial assistance from wealthy men and women. Moreover, she served as a conduit for money from rich individuals to other nationalist leaders, and she gave to those leaders.[78]

Narrow-minded, egotistical, Winters would allow no one else to talk until she finished speaking. Angry at men generally, she said every time she talked to a man, she would bawl him out. During meetings at her mansion, she focused her eyes on men as she denounced males. Some men considered her eccentric. One nationalist even told an American Jewish Committee informant that Winters, once married but childless, was "unnatural" and a lesbian.[79]

To expose men for what they really were, Winters wrote a book, *X-Ray of a Male,* whose thesis was that from early childhood, men permit one or two aggressive individuals to bully them. This submission leads men to fight as children, grow up to become gangsters, and pick fights with other countries, such as World War I. The solutions were to render men harmless by sterilizing them at birth and to put only women in government positions all over the world. If women had been in power in Europe in 1914, Winters argued, there would have been no war because women were not interested in the savage part of life. Indeed, if women governed, war would be banished from the Earth forever. Women, especially mothers, would protect their rights and prevent war because they loved children and would not want them killed later in life.[80]

One male-led government, nevertheless, was praiseworthy. Hitler's, which had put "Jews in their places," appealed to Winters's anti-Semitism. Her enmity toward Jews was also expressed in her belief in *The Protocols,* in the use of the Women's White House as a forum for anti-Semitic speakers, and in her plan to place the Lord's Prayer and Ten Commandments in the Detroit public school curriculum. (Jews, in opposing her plan, would expose their evil nature.) In addition, she believed the Bible commanded that Jews, like Blacks, should not mix with White Gentiles. She confined her racist talk to private moments to protect her public credibility.[81] (One of her allies, Waters, did not share this view. Winters thought she could restrain Waters. But to her chagrin, Waters tiraded against Jews during a rambling speech on June 1, 1945 at the Women's White House, prompting Winters to call off plans to finance a national speaking tour by Waters.)[82]

Befitting a nationalist of her stripe, Winters crusaded against communists. She studied the enemy and attended every communist meeting she could; she said detectives, provided by a Detroit police commissioner who was a close friend of hers, protected her at such gatherings. She had tried to defeat communism as early as 1935, drafting a bill to outlaw communism that was defeated in the Michigan legislature. Ten years later Winters tried again, having her attorney draft several bills for Congress that would treat communism as treason. Once more, her proposals were rejected.[83]

Winters claimed she had a mailing list of hundreds of thousands of names, and that seven nationalist organizations, including the Legion of the

Blue Cross, had been created at her home. Some of those groups had minis-cule memberships and little impact, and the legion disbanded soon after the United States entered World War II. But Winters persisted. Hoping to lay the foundation for a nationwide nationalist movement, she contacted leaders of women's organizations throughout the country and, paying their expenses, brought them to her home in groups of forty to sixty so she could present her ideas to them.[84]

The Women's White House was a meeting place for nationalist leaders when they traveled to Detroit, a center for right-wing literature, and the Mid-western center of the Nationalist Party, led by ex-Senator Reynolds.[85] In 1945 Winters opened her mansion for Friday tea parties, each attended by as many as seven hundred people. The guest lists included anti-Semites and Roosevelt-haters, some of them doctors, lawyers, and other professionals. Among those invited were leaders of the Grand Army of the Republic and the DAR, as well as ethnic Poles, Estonians, Lithuanians, and Latvians from De-troit, whom Winters wanted to shape into an anti-communist coalition. The meetings featured speakers such as Waters, who warned against interna-tional cooperation, and the group would discuss what to do about treach-erous Jews, Blacks, and the labor unions.[86]

Winters was not bothered by the reputation of some of the women she recruited for her causes.

> I have been warned by one of my friends that some of my women are not women of good character. I'll take the huzzies. The com-munists will take in stinking sewer diggers, Negroes, foreigners and the rest. If they are good enough for the communists, they are good enough for my mass movement. And I'll not be too particu-lar about their little private lives either. Let them smear me for this. I can take their smears in my stride, for I have fought com-munism for 25 years and have grown fat in so doing. I love a good fight and will be in one until I die.[87]

More important than the character of Winter's women, she said, was their willingness to crusade.

> We have our beautiful women who'll flirt with the Congressmen and cajole them into supporting our movement. We have our groups who'll even go as far as mass picketing. We have other groups who'll get what they want. And by God, they [members of Congress] are going to listen to us and are going to know what the hell is popping if they don't come across.[88]

In June and July of 1945 Winters and her followers began to plan a monetary congress to meet at the Women's White House in August, a gathering meant to be a rally for fascist sympathizers. The architect of the congress was Leo Charles Donnelly, who had worked for Coughlin and had run for president in 1944 as the Greenback Party candidate. A thin, middle-aged man, with a dreamy disposition, he was a physician and pastor of Westminster Community Church in the Detroit suburb of Highland Park. He frequently quarreled with a committee that Winters had appointed to help plan the congress.[89]

The planners were further plagued by fear. During one discussion, committee member Charles Dexter thought he saw a mysterious car outside and went to check; when he returned, Winters rebuked him for being paranoid. Not immune from paranoia herself, Winters worried that spies might infiltrate the proceedings and tape-record conversations. In addition, she asked her colleagues if they had heard the rumor that a new currency would be printed and all money held in safe-deposit boxes would become worthless. They had not heard of that rumor, but one of them declared Federal Reserve notes were counterfeit.[90]

On August 17 the congress assembled with 136 delegates, a mixture of semiliterates, cranks, and bigots. (Among the group was ninety-one-year-old Jacob Coxey, who had led an army of unemployed in a march on Washington in 1894. Coxey gave an interview to the Detroit newspapers in which he attributed his long life to a laxative he was selling.) Quickly, it became clear that the money-reformers were overwhelmed by anti-Semites, and the meeting degenerated into Jew-hating. Catherine Brown of the Blue Star Mothers of Pennsylvania said she was not interested in monetary issues and had come to condemn Jews; when she criticized Jews, she was applauded. Another delegate, Sanctuary, divided his time between attacking the Talmud and playing his compositions on the piano. Anti-Semitic literature was on sale. One of Smith's assistants was on hand to sell *The Cross and the Flag,* although his boss, jealous because Winters's meeting competed for attention with an America First Party meeting, refused to attend.[91]

Some discussions were incoherent. Donnelly, whom Winters tried to keep away from the press, delivered bigoted, incomprehensible monologues. And despite all the inflated oratory, the congress failed to agree on a program and people could not make sense of the various proposals,[92] a cacophony that fittingly signaled the decline of Winters and the nationalist brigades in her city.

As the activity in Detroit, Cleveland, Cincinnati, and Chicago demonstrated, the mothers' movement found fertile ground in the Midwest. Without extensive publicity, whether favorable or unfavorable, from the *Chicago*

Tribune and other newspapers in the region, the movement would not have reached a mass audience. Ethnic composition, too, was critical. Several states, including Wisconsin, Minnesota, and Illinois, had substantial German populations that opposed war against their native land, opposition reflected in groups such as the German American Bund as well as the mothers' movement. The economy also contributed to isolationism because the largely agricultural region depended less on foreign commerce than did the East and West coasts.

Most important, the Midwest was more rigidly conservative, a hospitable climate for isolationism, nationalism, and xenophobia. Anti-Semitism had deep roots in Midwestern culture.[93] Drawing on such a history, the mothers' groups, largely Protestant with some fundamentalists, fought intervention because they feared the Jewish menace behind the war. There is little statistical evidence that the area was more anti-Semitic than the East or West, though, and quite possibly many Midwestern women who joined the movement were not motivated primarily by anti-Semitic conspiracy theories. There was no question about their leaders' anti-Semitism, however.

Nor was there any question that Midwesterners had long viewed the East Coast with resentment. FDR and fellow eastern elitists had seemingly dominated American life with little or no regard for the rest of the nation. They could not be allowed to drag the United States into another world war that was not vital to the interests of the entire country, a war that would require the Midwest to make the greatest sacrifices—all to serve the East's financial and political imperatives and succor the despised British and other foreigners.

The final element in the strength of the Midwest nationalist crusade was leadership from figures such as Dilling, Van Hyning, Smith, and Coughlin. Smith, in particular, provided a nucleus for the movement. He spoke in all areas of the nation, but his most receptive audiences were in the heartland, and he settled in Detroit in the 1930s partly because of his ideological affinity with Ford. Coughlin, popular nationally, commanded support from his Detroit-area base. The male and female leaders sometimes competed for attention, yet they complemented each other's efforts, making nationalism a formidable presence in Midwestern life.[94]

The growth of the membership in the region created momentum that encouraged women to join and fed optimism about the movement's ability to affect policy. It was in the Midwest that the movement forged its most effective alliances with isolationist organizations, the America First Committee among them, and sympathetic politicians; Dilling, Van Hyning and their female and male supporters enjoyed easy access to their representatives in

Congress. There was conflict among Midwestern isolationists, yet their combined numbers gave them political clout and the potential to affect elections. In no other area did isolationists have a similar degree of influence. Without mass support in the Midwest, the mothers' movement would have been less menacing.

The soil having been cultivated by political access, the presence of crusading leaders, geographic isolation, and ethnic interests, the Midwest yielded a bumper crop of antipathy toward New Deal economic policy, against humanitarianism, and against a foreign policy based on multinational cooperation. But the Midwestern mothers could not make the Roosevelt administration veer from its course, keep the country from a foreign bloodbath, or avert changes that threatened their identity. Failure merely encouraged their belief that the forces behind their defeat—Rooseveltian liberalism, communism, internationalism, and the Jews—would persist. Their anxieties would never wane. Theirs was a bitter harvest.

NINE

The Mothers' Movement in the East:
Philadelphia and New York

Philadelphia and New York were the homes of the more active mothers' organizations in the East. In the former city, the Mothers of Pennsylvania organized to oppose repeal of the arms embargo in 1939. The group originated as a branch of the National Legion of Mothers of America, but with members such as the vicious anti-Semite Bessie R. Burchett, it soon became too extreme for the moderates of the NLMA.[1] Its partisans were "violently anti-British, anti-Semitic, pro-Coughlin, and in some instances outspokenly pro-Nazi," said a member of the Committee to Defend America by Aiding the Allies, who infiltrated the Mothers of Pennsylvania. The mothers, the infiltrator added, "indulge in racial and religious diatribes and [distribute] propaganda tending to excite hatred and create division."[2]

The organization, which had about two thousand members in Philadelphia, attracted seventy-five to one hundred women to its meetings every Wednesday night at the Bellvue-Stratford Hotel. Headquartered in a one-room office, the group communicated through a newsletter edited by Irene Thorne Murphy, a Coughlinite and former secretary to the local America First Committee. The production work was done by volunteers who addressed newsletters to people on a carefully selected list. The volunteers included America First Committee members.[3]

After failing to preserve the embargo, the mothers worked to defeat the Burke-Wadsworth Selective Service bill, urging women to vote against members of Congress who supported it. The bill would enslave the nation "with a slavery worse than that which Hitler has imposed on Germany."[4] Catherine Good warned, "We know if we send our boys we will not be a free country but a colony under Britain." Catherine Brown added that if the bill were enacted, "Our boys will be sent with the regular soldiers to Honolulu to be slaughtered like little pigs that are off to market."[5] Brown asked why the United States sent boys to help England when Germany had not done the United States any harm. She said her group had "proof that all the advisers to the King [of England] are Jews. We don't blame Germany for chasing them out."[6]

The women worked with other antiwar organizations and heard speakers

Bessie Burchett, nicknamed "Two Gun" because she had permits to carry two guns—one in a holster under her skirt—is escorted into a House Un-American Activities Committee hearing in January 1942 in Washington. Acme Newspictures photo.

such as Farber and Catherine Baldwin. They sold the literature of Coughlin, Dilling, Winrod, and Holt, and after the NLMA lapsed, they enjoyed a symbiotic relationship with the mothers' groups that were equally zealous. For instance, they voted to go to Washington to participate in Dilling's campaign against Lend-Lease.[7]

A few months after the group was created, it reorganized as the Mothers and Daughters of Pennsylvania because a Philadelphia newspaper revealed most of the members were not mothers. Change did not end there, for members quarreled among themselves and competed to lead the organization. In May 1941 Brown and the more militant members broke from the parent organization to form the Crusading Mothers of Philadelphia. In March 1943 this group began to call itself the National Blue Star Mothers and, with the end of the war in sight, reorganized in 1945 as the Current Events Club.[8] (This narrative will refer to the group by the name by which it became best known, the National Blue Star Mothers.)

Brown's splinter group, which came to overshadow the Mothers and Daughters of Pennsylvania, held small meetings restricted to members and published a newsletter, *The Cradle of Liberty*, sent to public officials, labor leaders, and other mothers' groups. The organization seemed adequately supplied with funds for circulars, hall rentals, and travel expenses, although she claimed the largest contribution she ever received from a member was five dollars; more funding probably came from wealthy businessmen.[9] The officers of the National Blue Star Mothers included Brown, president; Lillian Parks, executive secretary; Agnes Lewis, corresponding secretary; Marie Goshow, public relations; and Margaret Coyle, membership chair. Like organizations elsewhere, the group was dominated by a single strong personality. Brown made the important decisions, with the other officers serving as a sounding board for her ideas.[10]

Brown was short, chunky, dynamic, feisty—she once told the major of Philadelphia to "kiss my ass"—and anti-Semitic. A Catholic and follower of Coughlin, she was a member of the Social Justice Advocates, a group that supported the priest, sent money to him, and urged Congress to return him to the radio. Brown also joined the Anti-Communist Society of Philadelphia and was one of the more active members of the Christian Front and of the America First Party. She urged her followers to join nationalist organizations and take them over. Opportunistic in her organizing techniques, she would attack the British to appeal to the Irish and, at the next meeting, attack the Irish to appeal to the British. A militant opponent of the war, she charged the America First Committee with being unpatriotic because it disbanded after Pearl Harbor.[11]

Brown went to Washington more than ten times to oppose legislation. While there in October 1941 to protest Roosevelt's foreign policies, Brown joined Waters and Lulu Avery of the Mothers of Minneapolis in a visit to the German and Japanese embassies, at Waters's suggestion, to ask the ambassadors to be patient with the United States and not to declare war. The ambassadors listened politely without replying.[12]

Brown was among Smith's inner circle, and Smith considered her an intelligent woman who had the courage to picket internationalist meetings alone. Brown was deferential to Smith, asked his advice "if I have messed up on anything,"[13] and described him as a fearless man willing to endure the hardships of crusading to save his country. The two shared platforms and addressed each other's groups; in addition, many of Brown's mothers subscribed to *The Cross and the Flag*. Grateful for the support, Smith helped Brown's organization build a mailing list. Mothers who mailed donations to him were asked to write their address and the word "mother" on the envelope, which was then sent to the National Blue Star Mothers.[14] Brown also was close to Dilling, who spoke on the same platform with Brown and Smith at a Christian Front meeting in New York on October 6, 1944. Brown invited Dilling to address the National Blue Star Mothers and sold Dilling's literature at meetings. In fact, almost every major nationalist spoke to the group.[15]

Only one man was very active in the National Blue Star Mothers, the organization's attorney, Charles Edwin Wallington. His chief incentive for aiding the mothers was hatred of Roosevelt; Wallington vowed that if he met the president, he would seize FDR by the throat and shake him. Wallington believed Jews dominated the Roosevelt administration and controlled the media, but anti-Semitism was not his main concern. Nor did he favor a negotiated peace, unlike Brown and Parks. His relationship with them cooled after 1943 and he turned to other issues, including opposition to world government.[16]

Although anti-Semitism was not prominent in Wallington's agenda, it was the prevailing mood of every meeting, in which members decried the Jewish conspiracies that directed communism, the British, international finance, the press, Roosevelt and his advisers, and the war. To warn people about the Jewish threat, the organization distributed thousands of speeches, articles, and pamphlets, and delivered hundreds of talks. Moreover, the mothers picketed Jewish and British meetings; discouraged women from enlisting in the armed forces; called for the impeachment of Roosevelt, Morgenthau, and pro-FDR congressmen; urged boycotts of Jewish businesses; tried to organize veterans; and opposed the UN.[17]

The National Blue Star Mothers outraged loyal members who belonged to similarly named organizations. Sometimes people confused the groups, and women who thought they had signed up for membership in a loyal organization inadvertently joined Brown's group. The Blue Star Mothers of America, a group that worked to uphold morale on the home front and investigated disloyal mothers' organizations, claimed the National Blue Star Mothers had mimicked its name to take advantage of its good reputation.[18]

Perhaps the biggest irritant in Philadelphia was Burchett. No member of the Mothers and Daughters of Pennsylvania was so virulently anti-Semitic, or so divisive, as the pro-Nazi Burchett, whose extremism was largely responsible for the break between the NLMA and its Philadelphia chapter. A gray-haired, elderly woman who carried guns and vowed that communists would not take her alive, she was so fanatical that she appeared comical. Yet there was nothing comical about the views of someone who said Hitler should target New York Jews by dropping a bomb in "the right place" and implied there were seven million lampposts in the country—enough hanging posts for every Jew.[19]

Holder of a doctorate in education from the University of Pennsylvania, Burchett had embarked on a teaching career in 1903 and worked at Temple University, a private high school, and public high schools in Philadelphia. Most of her career was spent in public schools, but Burchett was no friend of democratic mass education, believing that education "should be limited to a select few white Protestant Americans of high IQ." (After she became a Coughlinite, though, she decided it was permissible to teach Catholics.)[20] Furthermore, she was angry because communism and internationalism were being taught in the schools. Burchett thought she had a duty to teach Christian values in the classroom and recruit students for reactionary groups.[21]

At South Philadelphia High School, 105 of the 120 teachers were incensed at Burchett's activities and asked for her dismissal. Seventeen "patriotic" societies came to her defense and the school board compromised, removing her as head of the social sciences department and transferring her to West Philadelphia High School.[22] Burchett blamed Jews for the move and refused to go quietly; a few days after arriving at the school, she addressed a Nazi rally and invited teachers to join the Silver Shirts. More than two hundred students went on strike and signed a petition to get her fired. Some of her colleagues suggested she see a psychiatrist. The board nonetheless permitted Burchett to teach until her retirement, six months before the Pearl Harbor attack. Dilling called her "a real 100% sound American Christian who has suffered martyrdom in Philadelphia and had been retired from her important teaching position because of her patriotic opposition to Red influences in the schools."[23]

In retirement, Burchett wrote a book, *Education for Destruction,* about her experiences fighting communism in the schools. Her friend Joseph Gallagher raised money to print the work and Dilling advertised it. An assault on her enemies in the school system and a diatribe against Jews, real and imagined, the book seemed unworthy of someone who had a doctorate. Not surprisingly, it sold well among nationalists.[24]

Burchett also inspired the Anti-Communism Society, led by Gallagher, and created the Committee for the Preservation of Constitutional Rights, led by Thomas A. Blissard, an intimate of Gallagher. Burchett served as vice president of the Anti-Communism Society and financed the organization, saying she was interested in preventing a communist takeover of the United States.[25] But a detective who investigated the group said, "This anti-Communist title is just a blind for anti-Semitic propaganda."[26] Burchett saw nothing wrong with spreading anti-Semitic propaganda, of course. She told HUAC she was proud to have distributed a statement attributed to Benjamin Franklin, opposing Jewish immigration. The immigrants took jobs and charity that should have gone to Americans, she said.[27]

Burchett despised Jews and communists because their beliefs conflicted with Christianity, which she thought should be the national religion. She urged women to join her in picketing radio stations that would not carry Coughlin's broadcasts.[28] And she said Aryan Christians had to learn to defend themselves against Jews, communists and blacks. Toward that end, Burchett built a rifle range on her farm outside Philadelphia and taught Aryan children to handle firearms. Like other far-right figures, however, she loathed Roosevelt the most, labeling him a traitor, a stooge for the Jews, for the British, and for the communists. Burchett agitated during the war, although she grew less vigorous with age.[29]

In New York City, the largest nationalist women's organization was Women United, started in 1939 by Beatrice Brown, who selected Mrs. Hall Herrick as president. Norris became honorary vice president of the group, which had close ties to the NLMA. Headquartered on Fifth Avenue in Manhattan, Women United said it had members in every state and branches in Long Island, New Jersey and throughout New England. About seventy-six women attended weekly meetings in the Bronx and ninety-six in Scarsdale. Members were expected to contribute a minimum of fifty cents per month, but most financing came from business interests.[30]

Herrick, a divorced portrait painter with two children, was a figurehead for Brown, the real leader. Brown, forty-five in 1940, ran a mimeograph business on Lexington Avenue and poured most of her wealth into women's isolationist groups. She talked compulsively and dressed unfashionably. Brown did not marry and had contempt for men, wanting to prove she could be as efficient as any of them. A Republican reactionary, she considered Herbert Hoover too liberal, yet her real anger was reserved for the New Deal, Roosevelt, and his allies, the Jews and the internationalists.[31]

A Catholic and a Coughlinite, Brown claimed influence in the church, particularly with Bishop Francis Spellman, who she said was an isolationist.[32] She worked to save Christian America from the Jewish threat. Brown said she once had a Jewish secretary and worked with Jews, but privately she hated Jews because they tried to cheat her, argued with her, and did not obey orders. Half of all draft evaders were Jews. Jewish refugees who fled Germany for the United States turned traitor by giving American military secrets to the Germans.[33]

Brown also boasted of political connections, such as her friendship with James Farley, a former Roosevelt adviser. Farley broke with FDR over the president's decision to run for a third term—as far as the public knew. The real reasons for the split, Farley supposedly told Brown, were the Jewish influence in the administration and Eleanor Roosevelt's use of dirty tricks to get votes. Like Farley, Thomas Dewey, another friend of Brown, was wise to the Jews. Dewey, she knew, would not appoint Jews to government positions.[34]

Elizabeth Nixdorff, the treasurer of Women United, and Charles Nixdorff, the organization's attorney, had long been nationalists. The couple had a Manhattan apartment filled with antiwar literature and a circle of friends including Lindbergh and Sanctuary. Elizabeth Nixdorff believed the Japanese, threatened by FDR, were right to have attacked Pearl Harbor. Charles Nixdorff hoped the United States would be defeated quickly. They raised money for Women United to send propaganda letters, to visit congressmen, and to collect and disseminate literature.[35]

One of the more active nonofficers in Women United, Cooper likewise had a long involvement in the nationalist movement and an apartment well stocked with extreme rightist literature. Active in the Bund, Cooper received information from Germany, was connected with Zoll's American Patriots, and defended Burchett. She did research for Smith in New York, sold *The Cross and the Flag* on commission, and distributed 2,000 copies of one of Smith's pamphlets at a communist meeting before the communists realized what was happening. Her closest friend, however, was Dilling. Cooper served as Dilling's East Coast representative, joined the New York branch of Dilling's Paul Revere Sentinels, and raised money for Dilling.[36]

Women United began modestly, headquartered in an eight-by-twelve-foot room with a table, a desk, and three chairs. In February 1942 the group moved into more commodious offices on Fifth Avenue: a two-room suite with desks, filing cabinets, card indexes, and a mailing list. The organization collected books on communism, held mass meetings, kept members informed of bills before Congress, and campaigned to defeat internationalists and New Dealers. Members organized study groups in their neighborhoods, with the national office providing speakers. Brown believed that organizing the grass roots would pressure Congress. She employed volunteers but appealed for money for rent, telephones, printing, paper, stamps, books, marches, and speakers such as Ingalls.[37]

In March 1941 Women United distributed 138,000 copies of a *Congressional Record* edition that contained isolationist testimony against Lend-Lease. One month later, the organization staged a mass meeting at Carnegie Hall, attended by twenty-three hundred women. The speakers included Senators Reynolds and Clark and Mrs. Taft. "Must the sons of our American mothers give their lives again on alien shores for a war that I swear is not ours?" Reynolds asked. Clark commended Women United for its opposition to a foreign war and Taft urged the members to write the president and demand that he honor his pledge to keep the peace. The speeches were punctuated by pro-German and anti-Semitic remarks from the audience that included Bundists, Christian Mobilizers, and Coughlinites, who hissed at the mention of Roosevelt and Churchill. One audience member shouted, "What's wrong with this country is all the Jews in it!"[38]

In May Women United announced a plan to send 1,000 women to Washington to demonstrate against convoys. Ann Schumacher, in charge of reservations, said delegations from New Jersey, Pennsylvania, Connecticut, and Maryland would join New York mothers at the Dodge Hotel, then break into small groups to lobby senators and congressmen. Mothers who could not go could give money. A full-page advertisement was placed in the *New York Times,* yet only 400 New York women joined 500 from other cities in traveling to Washington. Trailed by FBI agents, they posed for photographs on the Capitol steps and heard speeches from Fish, Rankin, Curtis, and Mrs. Wheeler. A group that walked to the White House and demanded to see the president was permitted to present a petition to a secretary. The women then returned to the Capitol to seek the New York congressional delegation, but the representatives and senators evaded them. The pilgrimage a failure, Cooper blamed Herrick, charging that she was more interested in publicity than in the organization's objectives.[39]

Also in May 500 women participated in a second journey to Washington to demand passage of the Ludlow Amendment (which would require a national referendum to declare war) and an end to Soviet propaganda in the United States. Exasperated because they received no results, Brown threatened to quit, complaining she was smeared in the press and lost money because Women United failed to pay for printing.[40] A protest in November was feebler; only seven women, drawn from Women United and We the Mothers, showed up to picket at the White House, calling FDR a traitor and urging his impeachment. A group of British sailors watched them wave a sign that read "Drive the British From Washington Again."[41]

On December 19, 1941 Brown announced that Women United would not disband in the wake of Pearl Harbor. The war made fund-raising difficult, though, and Women United had difficulty paying debts.[42] In 1943 the organization finally dissolved because Charles Nixdorff, alarmed over public hostility to the group, forbade his wife to work at the Women United office, which she ran. Her subsequent resignation made it impossible for Brown to continue, so she decided to work quietly, trying to keep members together by meeting in homes. Brown remained in contact with her followers throughout the war.[43]

Another New York nationalist group that peaked during the war was the American Women Against Communism, led by Marguerite Snow Morrison, a tall, gaunt, aristocratic woman. A member of the Mayflower Descendants Society and the DAR, she was the second wife of A. Cressy Morrison, a retired executive of the Union Carbide Company. The Morrisons lived in a luxurious Park Avenue apartment and gave money to nationalists. Their support kept the American Women Against Communism solvent, although their contributions to that organization and similar groups drained them of funds.[44]

In 1934 Marguerite Morrison founded American Women Against Communism with several aims: to stir women to greater interest in politics; to ban radicals from public office; to oppose subversion in colleges, churches, and the YMCA; to prohibit immigration; and to prosecute leftist agitators. She believed communists were the primary danger to American freedom because they were against private property, inheritance, free speech, and the family. Communists also had seized farmland in the Midwest, infiltrated the Federal Council of Churches, and planned a Black republic in the South, she thought.[45]

Morrison and her husband were close to Dilling, and Marguerite Morrison read and quoted from Dilling's books. Dilling urged her readers to send for Morrison's pamphlets. Too, Morrison collaborated with Smith, Pelley, Sanctuary, and Smythe, among others. Her closest allies were Beatrice Brown, Cooper, and Van Hyning. She enjoyed cordial relations with Hoffman, Reynolds, and FBI Director J. Edgar Hoover, and mailed all of her anticommunist literature to the FBI.[46]

Morrison's lieutenants in American Women Against Communism included fellow aristocrats Charlotte Aycrigg and Mrs. Charles A. Ransom. Aycrigg, a past president of the DAR and a friend of Curtis, joined the nationalist movement out of naïveté. She financed luncheons for the American

Patriots, but when their leader, Zoll, was indicted for extortion in 1939, she quit supporting him, declaring that he was ruining her reputation. Aycrigg cut off her generous support of American Women Against Communism under similar circumstances, resigning in July 1941 after the *New York Post* published an exposé of the group.[47] Ransom, secretary-treasurer of the American Women Against Communism, had no reason to fear for her image, since she was a fanatic who said Roosevelt received orders from Moscow—she had seen them. Viewing communism as a greater evil than fascism, she wanted FDR to stop criticizing Hitler and to expose communists.[48]

Morrison's organization trafficked in the standard charges of anti-Semitism: motivated mainly by money, Jews controlled a disproportionate share of national wealth; Jews dominated the Roosevelt administration and manipulated the New Deal; Jews were behind communism. Morrison cited *The Red Network* as evidence that 600 Jewish communist groups were active in the United States. Anyone who required further proof need only look in *The Protocols,* available from American Women Against Communism for fifty cents. In 1943 Morrison campaigned against the "world conspiracy" involving B'nai B'rith.[49] Still, this fulmination belied Morrison's concern that criticizing Jews would damage her reputation and prompt them to take revenge.[50] Morrison herself was not disloyal. She did not favor a negotiated peace and supported American aid to help the Soviet Union defeat Hitler. Perhaps reflecting these anomalies, in 1945, the year before her death, she changed the name of her organization to the American League for Good Government. The league disbanded after Morrison's death due to lack of leadership and insufficient funding.[51]

New York made an additional contribution to the isolationist network with the Peace Now movement, which promoted a negotiated peace with Germany and Japan. Open to any American, Peace Now differed from its far-right allies by including socialists and pacifists as well as Bundists, Nazi agents, Christian Fronters, Christian Mobilizers, and America Firsters. The group was not officially anti-Semitic, but many members were anti-Semites.[52]

A speech by Dorothy H. Hutchinson to a Quaker meeting in Philadelphia on July 11, 1943 launched Peace Now. The address was published as a pamphlet entitled *A Call to Peace Now.* The pamphlet, and a booklet that Hutchinson later published, *Must the Killing Go On?,* became the essential literature of the movement.[53] New York was the national headquarters, with branches in Philadelphia, Los Angeles, and St. Louis, and a few members in Massachusetts, Maryland, New Jersey, Illinois, Ohio, Indiana, and Michigan. By March 1, 1944 Peace Now claimed 6,000 members.[54]

Most of the members and officers were women, although the president was George W. Hartman, a professor of psychology who had worked at Columbia University, Harvard University, Pennsylvania State University and Dartmouth College. He ran unsuccessfully as a socialist for lieutenant governor of New York in 1938 and for mayor of New York City in 1941. Hartman opposed communism and resigned from the New York College Teachers Union in 1939, claiming it was a front for the Communist Party.[55] His work for Peace Now was important, he believed, because there was no social order in the world worth the five million to ten million lives that would be lost in an effort to defeat the Axis; furthermore, a peace with military victory would not last so long as peace by mutual consent. As for the criticism that Americans could not do business with Hitler, Hartman replied they did business with Stalin, Franco, and other dictators whom they did not completely trust. "If we continue fighting, we'll get one dictator instead of another, Stalin instead of Hitler," Hartman wrote.[56]

Bessie Simon, the executive secretary, ran routine activities for Peace Now. She had Washington experience from her work as a staffer for government agencies, as a congressional secretary, and as office manager for the America First Committee. Simon tried to revive the committee by recruiting its former members for Peace Now; among those she attracted were Mrs. Wheeler and Alice Roosevelt Longworth.[57] Hutchinson, the treasurer, had an academic background—her father was professor of classics at Wesleyan University, and she was a scientist who held a Ph.D. in zoology from Yale University. She believed that just as social problems could be solved by scientific means, world peace could be preserved by the application of scientific research.[58] The field secretary who traveled to sign up members was John Collette, a Norwegian who fled his home when the Nazis invaded. His reputation was less than stellar. On an organizing tour in September 1943 Collette was arrested for peeping into the shower room of a Cincinnati sorority house and fined $100 for disorderly conduct.[59]

Peace Now operated on a meager budget. Between August and December of 1943, the organization had just eleven contributions of as much as $50 and raised only $2,565.70, of which a little more than $100 was left at the end of the year. Nor was funding the only problem. Many crackpots tried to sign up for membership and Simon usually avoided them by referring them to her assistant, Elizabeth Nixdorff, the former treasurer for Women United. Simon said she was not worried about the quality of her members, but she was concerned with secrecy; letters to Senator Wheeler, Lindbergh, and Wood had been stolen from her files. In June 1944 Peace Now became less secure, evicted from its New York headquarters after fellow tenants complained about sharing a building with a group that HUAC had labeled disloyal. The organization, which by this time was dominated by extreme bigots, moved its headquarters to Hartman's home in Cambridge, Massachusetts.[60]

Peace Now argued the United States was fighting an unjust war for power and profits. Leaders misled the public about the war, according to Hutchinson: it was the Americans, not the Germans, who believed they were a master race; it was the Americans, the British, and their allies who had taken more territory by conquest than had the Germans or the Japanese. If the Allies had treated Germany generously after World War I, they would have prevented grievances that led to the rise of Hitler. Japan also had received unfair treatment from the Allies. Japan was overcrowded and dependent on imports, yet the United States closed its markets to Japan and prevented Tokyo from gaining needed capital. Goaded by Roosevelt into attacking Pearl Harbor, Japan had to fight or submit to economic slavery. Japan and Germany did not pose threats to the United States; the only threat was to British-American economic domination of the world.[61]

The Allies might be winning the war, Hutchinson wrote, but the bloodiest days were ahead. Bloodshed only guaranteed more fighting, and the possibility of a durable peace grew dimmer each week the war continued. Even the most generous terms, if dictated by the victors, would not enlist the support of the vanquished. A disarmed Germany would leave Europe vulnerable to the Soviets, and execution of Nazi leaders would make them martyrs to their own people. If United States bombers would drop leaflets calling for peace, Hutchinson said, Germans and Japanese would take the appeal to heart and force their governments to consider it.[62]

Through Simon, Peace Now leaders maintained close contact with former America First Committee officials, including Wood and Lindbergh. Simon also traveled to Washington to confer with Nye, Rankin, and Senator Wheeler. The group distributed Rankin's antiwar speeches, and Hoffman and Rankin inserted Peace Now's propaganda in the *Congressional Record*.[63] In addition, Peace Now held numerous small meetings and two mass rallies, one at Carnegie Hall on December 30, 1943 and one at the Old South Meeting House in Boston on September 27, 1944. A half million peace flyers were mailed out after the rallies.[64]

Ironically, the organization advocated peace when the defeat of Hitler appeared certain. In late 1943 a Peace Now letter to congressmen opposed the Allied invasion of France. "Like a mouse transfixed by the paralyzing gaze of a snake, the American Christian watches the relentless approach of D-Day," wrote Hutchinson, who urged Congress to stop "this meaningless slaughter."[65] Other letters went to prominent clergymen, asking them to request that all Christians lay down their arms. "We would so much rather Christians would be guilty of treason to this administration than guilty of treason to the Christ," Hartman wrote.[66]

One more irony: Peace Now, HUAC concluded, encouraged the Germans and Japanese to continue the war because its propaganda was seen as a sign that American morale was disintegrating. After an investigation of Peace Now files under subpoena, HUAC found the group's activities did indeed undermine morale at home, and that the Nazis used Peace Now propaganda to agitate against the United States in neutral countries.[67] Hartman's group was exactly what the Axis wanted, the St. Louis *Globe-Democrat* charged. A negotiated peace would not eliminate fascism; it would merely give Germany and Japan time to consolidate their gains and prepare for the next war, the newspaper argued.[68]

In 1944 Simon went to Washington to speak with isolationist politicians. Rankin, now retired, told Simon Peace Now should be converted from a propaganda organization into a political party, but Simon feared the war would be over before members would have time to form a party. She favored throwing the group's support behind the Republican presidential nominee unless the GOP chose an internationalist.[69] Her movement, though, was not around for the election. In October the difficulty of raising money during the final phase of the European war, coupled with Hartman's poor health, made it necessary to suspend activities. Hartman and Simon asked members to support organizations such as the National Council for the Prevention of War and the Women's International League for Peace and Freedom.[70]

Appealing to the left as well as to the right, Peace Now had a greater potential for undermining home front morale than did the pro-fascist mothers' groups. Fortunately, it did not begin large-scale operations until after the war had turned in favor of the Allies. Had it started during the series of American defeats in the Pacific in 1942, it might have become a major headache for the administration.

Catherine Baldwin was a headache all by herself. The most virulent nationalist woman in New York, she lad the Defenders of the Constitution of the U.S.A. Raised in the shadow of Bunker Hill, Baldwin was a superpatriot whose father's family had been in the country for thirteen generations. Baldwin's five children were nationalists; one of her three sons was employed in Albany, where he kept tabs on the legislature. But her energies turned in a nationalist direction only after the death of her husband, Thomas. Thomas's business was hurt by regulations during World War I, his health declined, and he died in 1926. Catherine Baldwin still was wealthy, although she came to resent government interference in business and joined the nationalist movement.[71]

In the 1930s Baldwin attended meetings of the American Patriots, the American Nationalist Party, the Christian Front, the Paul Reveres, and mothers' organizations. In 1934 she created an organization, the Defenders of the Constitution, to fight world government. The group, which had branches in Philadelphia, Pittsburgh, and Boston, had no officers and never held large meetings; members met in their homes. Baldwin preferred it that way, believing the only productive nationalist work was done by small, secretive organizations that investigated potential members. "The big public outfits are all run by Jewish stooges who themselves are immune from federal prosecution but operate their outfits as traps to get good people in, who will all be prosecuted at a later date," she said. "They suck in a lot of innocent people." Baldwin attracted some of the more militant members of other nationalist organizations. There were no dues, yet Baldwin had money to finance the group. It was rumored that she received funds from Germany.[72]

Hating Britain was another cause that engaged Baldwin. She investigated British propaganda in the United States, supported the Sinn Fein movement for liberation of Ireland from British control,[73] and opposed the British Israel World Federation of London. The federation, a religious cult, claimed the British were the people of Israel, descendants of the Ten Lost Tribes and ordained by God to rule the world. Little was heard about the movement in the United States until after World War I, although it had been founded in Britain in the eighteenth century. In the United States, the movement was known as the Anglo-Saxon Federation of America, headed by Howard Rand in Haverhill, Massachusetts.[74]

Baldwin charged the British sought to rule the United States through the British Israel World Federation, a plot that involved the Boy Scouts, the Jehovah's Witnesses, the World Court, the League of Nations, the UN, Churchill, Roosevelt, and American aid to Britain during World War II.[75] To expose the scheme, Baldwin published ten charts and wrote a seven-page pamphlet comprised of excerpts from *Destiny,* the magazine of Rand's group. The pamphlet made the familiar right-wing arguments about London's desire to control world finance and its potential to threaten the United States, but Baldwin added a twist: Pelley, Smith, and other nationalists collaborated in the British Israel movement! Proud of her writing yet gullible in accepting notorious forgeries as sources, Baldwin was unoriginal in her conclusions, mimicking the books and magazines she read. Her style would have embarrassed a young child.[76]

In related allegations, Baldwin labeled Roosevelt a British dupe who had given away everything of value in the United States. His treason was due to his position as exalted ruler of the Masons or to his syphilis. Baldwin could find no word "violent enough to describe the viciousness and imbecility of FDR."[77] She spoke of possessing transcripts of telephone conversations between Roosevelt and William Bullitt, the American ambassador to Germany, proving the president had plotted war on the Germans before Hitler invaded Poland. The Nazi government had turned these "Polish documents" over to Baldwin, knowing she would make good use of them.[78]

Baldwin's lack of discernment also showed when she said she had discovered a plan to replace the American flag with the British Israel flag. The new flag had a yellow Star of David in place of the American stars, stripes like those on the American flag, and a Union Jack. Baldwin, whose younger daughter sewed one British Israel flag to show at meetings, complained that Smith was exposing the plot, showing the banner at his meetings without giving her, Catherine Baldwin, any credit for discovering it. (Strangely, she never explained why Smith, whom she identified as a British Israel supporter, would want to betray the group.)[79]

With her hostile temperament, Baldwin made more enemies in the nationalist movement and was so difficult that nationalists accused her of being an operative for internationalists. She considered other nationalists her competitors and said they stole her followers. Some of her shriller comments were reserved for these adversaries. Ford was a patriot, but his wife was an internationalist and he was wrong to support the "skunk" Smith. Kamp was a "dirty little rat," a double-crosser in the pay of the Carnegie Foundation. Jung was a Smith disciple, reason enough to hate him. Hoffman, once her friend, reneged on a promise to publicize her material. Fish was a coward. Curtis refused to expose British Israel because her Woman Investors had British members. Baldwin even turned against her onetime ally Dilling, falsely claiming Dilling had a grandmother in England and "has spies checking on me all the time."[80]

Despite the discord she provoked among nationalists, Baldwin did have her favorites. A Coughlinite, she worked with Hart on a committee to support Franco and was a friend of True. She liked Marshall and said he was "put away in an insane asylum by the Jews"; Marshall tried to expose British Israel at an antiwar meeting but the presiding officer impeded him. Baldwin considered anti-Semitic Congressman Lewis McFadden a martyr, a victim of the Jewish plan to kill patriots. She wanted Lindbergh to rule the United States because Jews could not dictate to him.[81] Baldwin continued to work in New York nationalist circles after the Pearl Harbor attack, even though she had suspended operation of the Defenders of the Constitution.[82]

One of Baldwin's colleagues in the New York nationalist community, Maude DeLand, was "the most vicious woman alive who actually shows her teeth and snarls defiance at the United States," in the words of an opponent.[83] About seventy-three in 1940, DeLand was a graduate of the Women's Medical College of Philadelphia. While she lived in Kansas, she met Winrod and became a Germanophile. Then DeLand learned to read German and lived in Germany, which she preferred to any other country, from 1933 to 1935. She said she saw no anti-Semitism there and felt that too much was written about persecution of Jews, too little about how Hitler saved his nation from Bolshevism.[84]

In New York DeLand made the nationalist movement her life.[85] She lived in a hotel room surrounded by newspapers and books, including a large Nazi collection; her favorites included *Mein Kampf,* picture books of Hitler, a biography of Hermann Göring, and books by General Erich von Ludendorff. She had a trunk full of anti-Semitic papers, a letter from Göring, and an autographed photo of Hitler.[86] When she was not reading, DeLand recruited followers, joined the Bund and attended meetings of the American Patriots, the American Nationalist Party, the Christian Crusaders for Americanism, and the American Immigration Conference Board. She also was active in the Steuben Society and in Kurt Mertig's Citizens Protective League, an organization of Nazi sympathizers who raised money for Bruno Richard Hauptmann, a German American convicted of kidnapping and murdering the Lindbergh baby. Mertig blamed Jews for the crime and said he must clear Hauptmann to vindicate Germany.[87]

DeLand consorted with some of the more notorious fascist sympathizers in the United States. She worked on Winrod's campaign for the United States Senate, distributed the antiwar speeches of her friend Rankin, and knew Congressman Stephen Day and Sen. Rufus Holman. From DeLand, Holman received a book, *Money, Politics, and the Future,* a defense of the German financial system, and he inserted it into the *Congressional Record.* Other friends of DeLand were Kuhn, Sanctuary, True, Dilling, Fry, Morrison, Curtis, Knowles, and Mrs. Adam Kunze, a hostess of Bund meetings. DeLand met De Aryan and sent propaganda to Coughlin from the German Library of Information, the Fascist League of London, and British Fascists Limited.[88]

When the war started, DeLand despaired, hating to see German soldiers killed because she thought they could spread German civilization around the world. Hitler wanted peace but international bankers forced him to fight; he had done nothing wrong. She rationalized the führer's racism: "They condemn Hitler because of his racist ideas. But the Jews also think themselves a superior people so they must be worse than Hitler. It was Jehovah who made the Jews a 'chosen race,' so God must be even worse than Hitler. Now what's wrong with that logic?" After the United States entered the war, a federal grand jury investigating sedition interviewed DeLand but did not indict her. In the postwar era, age and ill health forced her to curtail her activities.[89]

Like DeLand, Mrs. Rudyard Uzzell recruited followers for the pro-Nazi movement. About fifty in 1940, she lived the comfortable life of an artistocrat in Jamaica, Long Island, where her husband sold equipment to amusement parks. Her appearance suggested mystery. She dressed entirely in black and had heavy black eyebrows, black hair beginning to turn gray, a dark olive complexion, and a prominent nose.[90]

Uzzell joined the pro-Nazi movement in the 1930s and emerged as a leader around 1937. Her chief activity was to enlist followers from the upper-middle and wealthy classes, women who hated the New Deal, at meetings of the Allied Patriotic Societies and the American Federation Against Communism. Recruits confirmed their loyalty at private sessions of an organization called the Study Group Conference, which gathered at a different place each week, sometimes at Uzzell's house. Meeting notices announced gatherings to discuss "the secret forces behind world revolution," *The Protocols,* and "pending legislation designed to Sovietize America."[91]

Uzzell's closest collaborator was her son Bud, who was twenty-eight in 1940. A graduate of the University of Pennsylvania, Bud had his mother's dark hair and piercing eyes. He considered himself an expert on Jews and Masons who wanted to control the world. Secretary to an Army officer, Bud gave secret military information to his mother, who turned it over to Kuhn. The Uzzells used a shortwave broadcasting set in their home to communicate with German officials.[92]

Journalist Alice May Kimball saw the Uzzells' fanaticism when she interviewed the mother and son in their house, which was surrounded by guards. Books and pamphlets issued by the German Library of Information filled bookcases and were piled on a table. The Uzzells praised conditions in Germany since Hitler had come to power, saying life there was better than in the United States. Bud said he hoped Germany would crush Britain. His mother said her meetings were designed to combat Jewish communists who threatened America, constituted thirty percent of the Navy, ran the Boy Scouts, dominated the Roosevelt administration, and controlled the Republican Party.[93]

Mrs. Uzzell also made her mark as a leader in the movement to make George Van Horn Moseley an American dictator. For the cause, she obtained contributions from industrialists, among them Howard Pew of Sun Oil and E. T. Weir of Weirton Steel. In May 1939 Uzzell arranged for Moseley to meet secretly with nationalists in an effort to create a confederation of nationalist organizations headed by the general. About fifty persons attended, including

Fritz Kuhn, Gerhard Kunze, Cooper, and Aycrigg. Moseley made an anti-Semitic speech; when he recommended that Jews be sterilized, Uzzell suggested killing them. Unfortunately for Uzzell, who disliked attention, news of the meeting leaked out, prompting her to withdraw from public activities.[94]

Women such as Uzzell, DeLand, Baldwin, and their colleagues in New York and Philadelphia gave considerable fervor to the nationalist crusade in the East. Their views found adherents because their region, thickly populated with Coughlinites and followers of Smith, abounded with discontent and ethnic strife. Appeals to prejudice in the name of keeping the country independent of foreign influence had potential; divisiveness was an effective recruiting tactic. Without converting significant numbers of women in the East, the mothers' movement, despite its large following in the Midwest, could not hope to succeed as a national crusade.

Nonetheless, the movement in the East suffered by comparison with the movement in the Midwest. The former region was generally more sympathetic to Britain and had a smaller percentage of German immigrants who would favor their native land. Many Eastern women seemed more tolerant of ethnic and ideological diversity. Some Catholics, citing the example of the 1920s KKK, identified right-wing extremism with anti-Catholicism and rejected such activity. Anti-Semitism was of limited resonance. The major newspapers were far more hostile toward this bigotry, as well as toward isolationism, and the concentration of Jews in some cities gave them political might that made officeholders reluctant to alienate them. Politicians on the whole were more liberal, more internationalist, and more loyal to the Roosevelt administration, hence beyond nationalist appeals.

The Eastern mothers' movement was also weakened from within. There was no women's isolationist paper with the readership of *Women's Voice* and no woman writer with the following of Dilling. Especially significant, the guidance was ineffective. The leaders dissipated much of their energy in internal power struggles and the movement had fewer potential male allies, such as those who spearheaded the America First Committee.

That the isolationists in the East and Midwest were annoyances rather than revolutionaries was due not only to their deficiencies but to Roosevelt's popularity, strong leadership, and relatively successful foreign policy, particularly after the United States entered the war. Success, like failure, feeds on itself, and the more optimistic Americans became about winning, the less chance the mothers had of changing the course of history. The balloon of discontent about involvement in a foreign war was punctured at Pearl Harbor, and as Americans grew confident about suppressing tyranny, much of the hot air went out of the movement. Additionally, as Hitler's atrocities drew increasing publicity, few reasonable people could remain neutral in their attitudes toward the war or remain unsympathetic to the führer's victims.

These developments were not inevitable. If Hitler's villainy had not been so obvious, or if he had been more generous toward conquered peoples, those Americans who considered him less of a threat than Soviet communism might have reached a larger audience. And had the war dragged on indecisively or stalemated, the nationalist movement could have become a force on the scale of the antiwar movement of the Vietnam era. The mothers and their allies encouraged the enemy and mobilized dissidents to an extent that could have hamstrung Roosevelt as protesters in the 1960s distracted President Lyndon Johnson.

═══ TEN ═══

Agnes Waters: The Lone Wolf of Dissent

Like Dilling, Agnes Waters had a flaming temper and an antipathy to Jews, blacks, communists, liberals, internationalists, and the Roosevelts. She was even more volatile than Dilling or Curtis. A highly nervous woman, Waters pulled constantly at her hair and clothes and, while delivering talks, removed her glasses every other minute. She spoke intemperately, swore compulsively—and was the most inflammatory lecturer on the mothers' circuit in the 1930s and 1940s. Working alone, sometimes ostracized because she was so intense, Waters appointed herself the Washington representative of the National Blue Star Mothers, the Mothers of the U.S.A., and We the Mothers Mobilize for America. She maintained a high profile in the capital, where she appeared before congressional committees and heckled representatives and senators. Her testimony, which included her vow to "arrest, try, and hang for treason any bureaucrat or other communist guilty of the crime of conspiracy to get us into this war," shocked the legislators.[1]

Waters was born Agnes Murphy Mulligan in New York City on July 1, 1893. Tracing her lineage to the patriots who fought in the American Revolution, she said her ancestors had fought in every American war, and that one had written the Bill of Rights. She also claimed descendancy from British royalty, saying she was a direct descendant of King James II and was a relative of the first Duke of Marlborough, yet she hated the British and blamed them for dragging the United States into war. Waters received her early education from private tutors and read law in her father's office, although she never earned a college degree. During World War I she moved to Washington, where she worked in the War Department and the Justice Department, campaigned for women's suffrage, and served as secretary to Alice Paul of the National Woman's Party. After the war she married a veteran, John E. Waters, and was widowed within a decade. Waters then sold real estate and was fabulously successful, earning $40,000 her first year and $130,000 her second. In the 1920s she closed millions of dollars in land deals in Chevy Chase, Maryland.[2]

Waters might have gotten her flair for real estate and her feistiness from her parents. Waters's mother, Agnes Murphy, took over her father's tiny real estate agency in New York City, oversaw some of the larger sales in the Bronx, and built one of the more successful firms in the city. Believing she could earn

Testifying before the House Military Affairs Committee in October 1942 in Washington, Agnes Waters vehemently objects to a measure to lower the draft age from twenty to eighteen. Associated Press photo.

more if she knew the law, Murphy entered New York University Law School and earned the first law degree ever awarded to a woman in the state. She met W. G. Mulligan, the class valedictorian, and they married in 1892, the year they graduated. Mulligan compiled a brilliant academic record. A prodigy who entered high school at age eleven, he had attended Hamilton College, graduated as valedictorian in 1886 and received a master's degree in 1888. After he married Agnes Murphy she converted to his faith, Catholicism, and he became a partner in her real estate firm.[3]

The Mulligans were successful, albeit shady and erratic. On December 16, 1915 they were arrested and accused of defrauding an elderly couple of $12,000; they allegedly took money to invest, then kept it. They did not serve prison time, but in 1917 W. G. Mulligan was disbarred in New York State for unethical conduct. After he died in 1930, Agnes Mulligan continued in real estate, only to go bankrupt in 1932. She gained a victory before the United States Supreme Court, however. Challenging a property tax assessment, she argued the case herself and won because, she explained, she could not live without a fight. Prepared to defend herself outside a courtroom as well, Mulligan received a license to carry a gun and demonstrated expert marksmanship. She lived to see most of her seven children succeed in business; three of them, including two of her daughters, became attorneys.[4]

Mulligan's daughter Agnes could not settle for a quiet life. In the 1920s she was a socialite in Winchester, Virginia, buying fancy clothes and driving big cars. In 1928 she organized women against Democratic presidential candidate Al Smith because Smith opposed Prohibition. In 1930 she asked the city council to withhold appropriations for the Red Cross, charging the organization was subversive. On October 30, 1930 Waters was arrested in Winchester for an armed robbery in New York City in 1926. Instead of accompanying the police to the courthouse calmly, she fled in her car and was apprehended after a long chase. She accused her mother of having instigated her arrest, but her mother denied it. There is no record that Waters was convicted and no further mention of the incident in newspapers or court proceedings.[5]

In the late 1930s Waters moved to a small apartment in Washington, where she lived with her two daughters, who worked for the government and took no part in her crusades. A devout Catholic who viewed herself as "God's instrument," Waters filled the apartment with paintings and statues of Jesus and the saints. For her, though, cleanliness was not next to godliness. A reporter who interviewed her in 1943 found the apartment littered with papers, the tables greasy, and the floor filthy.[6]

In the mid-1930s Waters became involved in the nationalist movement, retired as a real estate agent, and devoted herself to politics. She began to read about communism, to testify before congressional committees against bills she considered communistic, and to attract women supporters for her campaigns. After World War II began she attended a rally for the British and claimed to find Jews and communists in control. Also, Waters tirelessly circulated antiwar pamphlets; aided Hitler's cause by creating dissension and duping women into supporting the führer; and published *The White Papers* (1940), a collection of antiwar congressional speeches, newspaper articles, letters she had written to public figures and newspapers, and her testimony before congressional committees. Her thesis was that it would be folly to go to war with Germany, for the country had nothing at stake and could not defeat the Nazis. Moreover, the Japanese were too far away to threaten the United States, whose Navy was too weak to fight Japan. Waters was no pacifist, but she did not want to fight a war the United States could not win.[7]

To avoid being pulled into a fruitless war, Waters argued, the nation should refuse to come to Britain's or France's aid. She called for Washington to take British islands in the Caribbean and the Atlantic in payment for World War I debts, and to seize British and French ships entering American waters. Nor should the United States defend Latin America. Her nation should clean house of all communists and subversives and follow an isolationist course even if attacked. The United States could obtain all the defense it needed by permitting Ford, who should replace Roosevelt as commander in chief, to mechanize the American Legion. "Let the American Legion drill our children, if need be—not communists," she said. Waters knew she was advocating unpopular policies, although she was not afraid. "My life is worth very little," she said. "It has been threatened many times, but if I die, it will be for liberty."[8]

Waters uncovered numerous plots to undermine American liberty and put undesirable elements in control of the globe. She claimed the drive to stop Hitler was led by the Federal Council of Churches, which was a communist front backed by the British and composed of Blacks and Jews. London planned to embroil the United States in war with Germany, make a separate peace with the Nazis, and dominate world trade while Americans fought the führer. The British made a deal with Hitler at Dunkirk, so he let them evacuate their troops, Waters explained. But there would be no deals to save American boys, sent abroad to die for Jewish bankers and Washington bureaucrats. "As long as I have breath in my body I will continue to cry out against the injustices of this horrible plot!"[9]

Hitler was also involved with Neville Chamberlain in a scheme to create an emergency so the British prime minister could raise taxes, Waters believed. London paid Hitler to pose as a danger so it could bleed Britons.[10] The plan grew intricate as Waters retold it: "In April 1939, I discovered this world plot being blueprinted by a group of world anarchists, communists, alien enemies of ours, parlor pinks, and New Deal brain trusters in the Shoreham Hotel."[11] Roosevelt, Churchill, and Stalin, needing an outside threat, had invited Hitler to invade the USSR. At the war's end, Hitler would reveal himself a Bolshevik.[12]

Jews had been involved in such plans for a long time, according to Waters. It was to fulfill a master plan outlined in *The Protocols* that Benjamin Disraeli, a British Jew, had introduced the concept of world government. Now England plotted with the Jews to regain its colonies in the United States. Jews would bring the United States into the British Empire, unite the empire with Russia, then get the world under their control. The USSR would mop up after Hitler, a tool of the Jews, then become part of the world Jewish empire planned by Roosevelt and Churchill, disciples of Lenin.[13] Waters claimed to be one of hundreds of witnesses to another plot to take control of United States; she had seen a map on which the country was carved up, with Germany control-ling the Atlantic coast and Japan controlling the Pacific coast. She vainly begged the Justice Department to investigate.[14]

Further, Waters believed the British Israel movement, a movement that controlled gold, narcotics traffic and international white slavery, was schem-ing to build a world government led by the Duke of Windsor. In her country, the movement was spearheaded by the Carnegie and Rockefeller foundations and Columbia University President Nicholas Murray Butler, and symbolized by the eye atop the unfinished pyramid, placed on the back of the dollar bill in 1935.[15]

Inspired by the devil, communist Jews had persecuted patriots such as Coughlin, Waters said. Coughlin told the truth about Jews and exposed their plans for world domination, so they retaliated by suspending his mailing privileges. In the office of the Solicitor of the Post Office, Waters found a ring of Jews sitting around the assistant postmaster general, giving him instruc-tions. The discovery proved there was an alliance of Jews and New Dealers who would destroy the Bill of Rights and abolish the government.[16]

Roosevelt was another puppet of Jews, possibly a Jew himself. Waters had voted for FDR in 1932 and attended the 1936 Democratic National Conven-tion as a Roosevelt supporter. She saw the party, and Roosevelt, in a different light after Democratic leaders refused her request to adopt a platform plank condemning communism. The rejection showed her how much influence communists had in the party, but she did not abandon the Democrats.[17]

FDR wanted to wreck the United States and engineer a global government dominated by Jews and Britons, Waters alleged. He had plotted with the king and queen of Britain to start World War II, a pretext to forge the world gov-ernment outlined in *The Protocols*. Waters knew of the unholy alliance be-cause the monarchs had come to the United States just before hostilities erupted. Also, she knew the 1938 Munich conference was part of a scheme under Hitler—who, coincidentally, became führer shortly after FDR became president—to bring to power disciples of Lenin. The United States could not win a world war instigated by these forces. Even if the nation achieved a military victory, it would lose because it would be ruled by homegrown communists.[18]

Roosevelt had betrayed his country, Waters complained, just as a fifth col-umn had betrayed France. He was an honorary member of the Third Interna-tional, and when Americans elected him to their highest office, the Soviets hailed him "as the first Communist President of the United States." Surely the Soviets' faith in him was justified; he implemented a New Deal written in Moscow and appointed thousands of communists to government positions.

With World War II looming, he compromised the military by plunging the United States into debt to feed and arm aliens, and by handing over American defenses to communists Leon Henderson and Sidney Hillman.[19] Roosevelt and the secretaries of state, Army and the Navy had prior knowledge of the Pearl Harbor attack, which was an inside job. Jews were directly involved; they had piloted the planes that did the bombing.[20]

Roosevelt was insane to run for a third term. Thinking he owned the nation and could continue to grab power, he followed the path of Mussolini and Stalin: win election, then abuse the power of his office.[21] FDR sought to silence all of his critics, especially Waters ("They tell me I won't even have a trial, that I'll be put into an insane asylum").[22] Still, she swore to keep fighting "even if I have to rot in jail to clean this government of the Jews who are running this country." She wanted to impeach Roosevelt, remove everyone he had appointed to office, and turn the government over to peoples' committees named by Congress.[23] But more violent means were permissible against Roosevelt and his cohorts, she believed. In fact, they should be shot to death. "This would be easier than to fool with the elections and a lot more certain of getting all traitors out of office because we are constantly betrayed by having stooges in both parties for candidates."[24] Waters's firing squad would take aim at not only Roosevelt but his internationalist allies, including Clare Boothe Luce and Pepper. "That Senator Pepper hangs around with Moscow Jews and Negroes. Also, he is part Indian, I hear. We want real Americans."[25]

Waters was ejected from the offices of congressmen and senators who considered her a nuisance. She was persistent, nevertheless. Between 1939 and 1946 she testified against repeal of the arms embargo, against Selective Service, against Lend-Lease, against the mobilization of labor, against extension of enlistments, and against the UN charter. The congressmen who were subjected to her tirades were too dense to heed her warnings of elaborate plots against the United States. "Most of you are a bunch of jackasses anyhow," Waters said.[26] Another time, she asked, "Are you all asleep at your posts? Why are you all so dumb and blind? Doomed! Just because you were so dumb or so stubborn you would not listen to me!" Only the likes of Wheeler, Nye, Hoffman, and Rankin took her seriously. But in the summer of 1939 Waters and other far-right leaders worked to defeat a bill to provide a haven for twenty thousand German Jewish children. On January 9 a delegation of clergymen presented a petition to Roosevelt, asking him to open the doors of the United States to the children. Sen. Robert F. Wagner of New York and Congressman Edith Nourse Rogers of Massachusetts introduced the Wagner-Rogers Bill, or Child Refugee Bill, providing that a maximum of ten thousand children under the age of fourteen be admitted in 1939, and an ad-

ditional ten thousand be admitted in 1940, apart from the German quota for
those years. They would be adopted temporarily by American families, with
costs assumed by individuals and private organizations. The children would
not be permitted to work—a provision designed to mollify labor unions—
and would return to their parents when conditions in Europe were safe. The
American Friends Service Committee would supervise the operation.[27]

A committee of distinguished Americans, including former President
Hoover, Landon, and publisher William Allen White, lobbied for the bill; Eleanor Roosevelt, too, supported it (although her husband, who feared antago-
nizing Congress, remained silent). The day after the plan was announced,
four thousand families offered to adopt children. After advocates of the bill
had testified, however, opponents had their turn.[28]

The most hostile witness was Waters, who testified on April 22, claiming
to represent the widows of World War I veterans. "The refugees have a heritage of hate," she said. "They could never become loyal Americans." She
characterized the youths as "thousands of motherless, embittered, persecuted children of undesirable foreigners" and called them "potential
leaders of a revolt against our American form of government. . . . Why
should we give preference to these potential communists? Already we have
too many of their kind in our country now trying to overthrow our government."[29] Those who welcomed the children, she said, were communists and
would raise the children as communists. "Of course the communist house
would welcome a child."[30]

On July 1 the bill was reported out of the House Committee on Immigration, but it had been amended to count the twenty thousand children against
the quota. Wagner opposed the amendment, believing the twenty thousand
children would deprive twenty thousand adults of places, so he withdrew the
bill. Waters, the mothers, and their anti-Semitic allies had won. As a result,
some twenty thousand children were left to their fates in Nazi-occupied
countries.[31]

Waters joined the fray again, when FDR called a special session of Congress in September 1939 to repeal the arms embargo. Repeal, she wrote, was
part of an international conspiracy that involved Jews, communists, New
Dealers, Blacks, anarchists, radicals, and Roosevelt, guided by the "hidden
hand" of Baruch. Loyal to the Soviet Union, FDR wanted to sell arms so the
United States would be drawn into war with Germany and softened up for a
communist revolution. Waters maintained that it was ridiculous to consider
Britain the first line of American defense, as proponents of repeal argued, because the Nazis were no threat to the United States. If Germany tried to invade, women could repel the Nazis without help from men.[32]

Waters declared that communists were getting ministers and college professors to testify in favor of repeal, and she sent Congressman Martin Dies a list of subversives who had appeared before Congress on behalf of repeal. She warned that Sen. Theodore Bilbo, who supported the president, had threatened to confine her to an asylum if she proved repeal was communist-inspired. Waters felt like David fighting against Goliath, but she knew she would win because God was on her side. She knew this was so because she had seen God.[33]

Goliath and his forces somehow won the battle, yet the setback did not discourage Waters. Comparing herself to Joan of Arc, a heroic woman fighting to save her country, she opposed the conscription bill in 1940, arguing there was no reason for a draft because no one would attack the country. The only explanation for conscription was that Roosevelt wanted to send troops abroad. Amounting to slavery, conscription would drain Americans of their will to resist subversion and raise an Army that FDR would use to perpetuate his dictatorship. "The proposed so-called Selective Training and Service Bill would put our American manhood in a strait-jacket, if not in a shroud," Waters charged. "For thousands it will mean suffering, disease, insanity, and death."[34] After conscription was approved, she suggested to Gen. Louis Hersey, who directed the draft, that communists and Jews be selected instead of Gentiles. Hersey supposedly said they would only run under fire. Waters replied that if they did, he should shoot them.[35]

Waters also testified against Roosevelt's plan to extend military enlistments. She complained that the bill was part of a Jewish plot mentioned in *The Protocols,* which she had shown to Congress many times, only to be ignored. She lost this round, too, although she continued to oppose conscription even after Pearl Harbor. On December 15, 1941, she wrote to her friends, urging an end to the draft and an investigation of a conspiracy to drag the nation into war. Smith praised Waters's letter, saying it took courage to publish such a letter after war had been declared. He gave a copy of Waters's letter to the FBI and urged his followers to copy and distribute the letter because it belonged in every home.[36]

In April 1943 Waters's rhetoric reached a crescendo. Opposing the bill to conscript civilians for war labor, she told a Senate committee that the government should abolish conscription altogether and draft convicts to do the fighting. The Army should use Mexicans, "greasers," to fight and seize Mexican and Latin resources such as quinine, rubber, and tin. "Why, my ancestors were kings on this earth for a thousand years and when they wanted slaves, if they ever had them," Waters explained, "the ancient kings went out and took somebody else's people, they did not take their own, and that is what I propose we should do—take Mexico, Central, and all of South America." It would be simple. "I propose to take an army of millions of men that are ready to fight and take them there and take every country from the North to the South Pole and make them do the fighting." The time had come to fly the Stars and Stripes over the entire Western Hemisphere.[37]

Waters opposed Lend-Lease and tried to testify when it came up for renewal. In February 1943, while the House Foreign Affairs Committee was holding hearings on a bill to extend Lend-Lease, Waters went to the hearing room every day, but chairman Sol Bloom, who considered her a crackpot, refused to permit her to testify. Shocked to find that Clare Boothe Luce was preparing to testify, Waters ran to the witness table and shouted: "I demand this bill be killed! I demand to be heard against it! I also object to the presence of this bloody vampire of a Luce woman whose husband hides in her skirts!" Bloom cut off Waters and had a policeman eject her from the Capitol. "This stopped my circulation and almost made me faint," she said. "I had heart attacks after. I feel sure this was a deliberately planned attempt to murder me."[38]

Waters was not cowed when the bill passed the House. She moved her opposition to the Senate Foreign Relations Committee and fired a salvo.

> Take a look around this soft-carpeted room and see for yourself the superficial, sophisticated foreign looking radicals and Rhodes scholars from the State Department, the cocktail joints and the drawing-rooms of the world, who look down their Roman noses at the American people and parade around in the uniform of the American Army and Navy although they have never seen and never will see a battle! . . . Can you see Christ in any of them? . . . With their slick, well-groomed, whiskey-infested bodies and their manicured hands holding fancy cigarettes, while in some heads there are little bows, and on others there are no hairs, much less no brains.[39]

In May 1943 Waters created another furor, when she went before the House Immigration Committee to testify against allowing Chinese refugees to enter the United States. (Waters said she represented the National Blue Star Mothers, which provoked a congressman to say he knew many mothers who disagreed with Waters. "They might be called black star mothers if they are Negroes and Jews," she responded.) Waters claimed there was room for the Chinese in China, where they were needed to fight the Japanese and, after the war, the Jews. "Why flood this country with yellow races? Why, Chinese can never become Americans." Waters charged that "practically all of the Chinese are communists and when they come in here, they come to ruin this country."

She refused to leave the witness stand when her time expired, and the chair implored, "Now, lady, will you please leave the witness stand? You have finished your testimony. Why can't you act like a lady and stop screaming?" Eventually she departed voluntarily.[40]

In 1944 Waters testified that a bill to reorganize the District of Columbia and permit its residents to vote was communistic, backed by Moscow money. "You see nothing but Jews before every committee meeting in the last ten years," said Waters, who added, "The first thing I knew I saw the District Committee, in committee packed with Jews, Moscow Jews, just as black as these two sitting here." Waters said Jews had better not come to Capitol Hill again because she had ropes with which to hang them. "Just let the Jews come in and the pistol-packing mamas will take care of them. There will be nothing left of them."[41]

As for Blacks, Waters promised that if she were elected president, she would shoot every Black person in the country. Most Blacks were traitors and communists, with ties to Moscow; the NAACP was a front for Moscow-directed communism, and the University of Moscow had a branch in North Carolina, where Blacks were indoctrinated into communism.[42] Nor were the "niggers" of Africa worthy of her sympathy. "Why should we save the niggers?" she asked. "We have enough here now."[43]

Also like Jews, Blacks were given the jobs of White Gentile American men who went off to fight the war. Still, malevolent Jews were more dangerous than Blacks in the United States. "The Jews control everything in America," she said. After coming to the United States as poor peddlers, they rose to ownership of stores, theaters, and movies. "If we wanted to really deal with them . . . we would quit buying at their stores . . . or buying their newspapers— and we will if they get obnoxious."[44] A Chicago group heard Waters warn of "200,000 Communist Jews at the Mexican border" waiting to get into the United States and rape every unprotected woman and child in the country. Waters was so excited she sputtered and forgot the words to patriotic songs and the Pledge of Allegiance. The moderator had to calm her before she could continue.[45]

Audiences sometimes walked out after hours of Waters's diatribes. More often, though, mothers' groups received her enthusiastically when she condemned Jews. A woman who heard her speak to the National Blue Star Mothers told her she agreed with everything Waters said. The admirer said that when she visited the mothers or wives of men killed or wounded in action, she would tell them that while their sons and husbands were fighting, Jewish men stayed home. Another woman in the audience told Waters she had sent three dollars to Smith and received no acknowledgment; she suspected Jews in the post office took the money. Others agreed who had sent money to Smith and received no acknowledgment.[46]

There was just one way to rescue the United States from all the dangers it confronted. "What this country needs is an American revolution. A good, old-fashioned American revolution of mothers," Waters argued.[47] She proposed to lead one. Pledging to "drive out all corruption and graft," she announced on May 19, 1942 that she was running for the Democratic and Republican presidential nominations in 1944. "It is high time the women of America took over the driver's seat since the men have made a hell of a mess of things everywhere," she said during the campaign.[48]

A woman could be president in wartime because the female of the species was more deadly than the male, Waters believed. "Maybe that's why these enemies of our form of government do not want a woman in the White House, especially a pistol-packin' mama like me." A woman had a divine right to rule "and, like Joan of Arc, to lead our armies to victory. I am going to be that woman, and the gates of hell shall not prevail against us." Women must take their place as leaders, as God intended. "America was placed under the guidance and protection of a woman since her discovery by St. Christopher Columbus," Waters said. "The figure of a woman stands at all our mastheads above the Stars and Stripes. She is 'Columbia, the gem of the ocean.'"[49]

Waters was "a died-in-the-wool born Jeffersonian Democrat, but I am also a strong supporter of that brave little band of isolationists in Congress who are Republicans." Therefore, she sought the nominations of both major parties.[50] Considering that she saw no other candidate who was not "an old hack-horse of a politician,"[51] she expected to win them, which would be tantamount to election. Next, she would select a cabinet of experienced, patriotic men, "not old 'red' doodle-wits, doddering old fools, aliens, communists, nazis, fascists, 'brain-trusters,' parlor pinks, radicals, liberals and civilians outstanding for their mistakes." In short, "I want only Americans that are real men and women, not idiots and incompetents and dirty Jews!"[52]

Waters proposed to negotiate peace for her country and let the rest of the world fight. She would repeal Lend-Lease, demand return of Lend-Lease materials from England, keep servicemen and weapons at home, withdraw the Pacific Fleet to San Francisco, and end diplomatic relations with the USSR. She vowed to expel all Englishmen and Russians from the United States, arrest communists, Nazis, and Jews so they could not obstruct national defense, and prohibit all immigration. Finally, she would provide a gas mask to every Christian because she feared Jewish plots to gas Gentiles.[53]

To Waters's surprise, neither major party nominated her, so she ran a write-in campaign. Most of her campaigning was done before mothers'

groups. She addressed meetings in Cleveland, Chicago, Baltimore, and Philadelphia, staged forums in Washington, spoke at Winters's mansion, and hired
a publicity agent. If she did not win, at least she could use the campaign to
deliver antiwar, anti-Roosevelt speeches with a candidate's immunity from
prosecution, she said, adding that her notoriety would encourage people to
attend rallies. Her effort accomplished little else.[54]

In the waning months of the war, Waters devoted her efforts to thwarting
plans for the UN. She warned the Senate Foreign Relations Committee that
the UN charter would create a superstate, that the organization would enable
the Soviets to emerge supreme, and that it would pave the way for World War
III. She termed the charter a "fraudulent, deceitful, collusive contract that has
been signed by 50 nations under force of duress, under propaganda to overthrow this republic and every nation upon the face of the earth." The communist blueprint had been established by novelist and historian H. G. Wells, "a
'Red' Englishman who visited Lenin in Moscow just before Lenin died." A
vote for the charter was treason.[55] When Waters continued shouting after her
time had expired, the chair, Tom Connally, banged his gavel and said he could
make as much noise as she could. Waters was escorted to a seat in the spectators' section.[56]

Waters was the loudest mothers' leader. All of the leaders were highly motivated, even compulsive, in their crusades, but Waters, thriving on conflict
and unable to find another outlet for her tremendous energy, was the most
defiant, the most determined. She lacked Dilling's patience to plow through
long, complicated books or spend hours at her desk doing research. Her
drive, combined with her sense of showmanship and thirst for attention (bor-
dering on exhibitionism), led her to oratory that was more bombastic than
any other mother's.

Nonetheless, Waters never led an organization of her creation. She could
not cooperate with partisans in planning and implementing activity; many
women distanced themselves from Waters, unable to tolerate her intense personality. She thus had to free-lance as a leader and concentrate on lobbying
Congress. Away from the lecture circuit and Capitol Hill, Waters seemed
rather lonely, having few personal friends and little warmth, compassion,
humor, or hobbies. She was indifferent about her appearance and about keeping an orderly house.[57] She had no time for relaxation or idle conversation.
Her agitation might have been intended partly to compensate for what she
missed in close friendships.

But Waters was unlikely to have listened to anyone who would tell her she
needed interests outside the mothers' movement. She would not fit into anyone's paradigm; she insisted the world fit into hers. Contrary evidence and

arguments could not make her yield. Out of the chaos in the world, Waters detected patterns of conspiracies that made events seem comprehensible. Her ability to find sinister meaning behind the words and deeds of Jews and communists, however, exceeded her ability to rally people against the threats. Those who disagreed with her were treated as scapegoats or confederates of the anti-Christ. She never let her foes rest in peace.

From the little information available on Waters, it appears she was proud of her family, particularly of her purported royal ancestry,[58] yet she apparently lacked love in her childhood home. Perhaps she engaged in a contest with her mother. Agnes Murphy seemed to be an ambitious woman whose accomplishments were substantial.[59] Perhaps Waters wanted to escape her mother's shadow and exceed her mother's achievements. Waters's resentment of those in authority, as well as her refusal to accept advice or admit mistakes, might have started with resentment of her mother.

Religion, too, was essential to Waters. Her convictions were more emotional than learned and do not seem to have resulted from serious study. But religion was one of the few things that provided her with comfort; more than anything else, it helped temporarily to alleviate her anxiety. The dark side of that faith was militant animosity toward non-Christians—especially Jews— and Christians who did not share her views. If Waters could not convert the apostates, she would destroy them.

Religion and crusading gave Waters direction and satisfaction, which were lacking even in her successful career in real estate. Christianity and patriotism, she believed, were inseparable; it was God's will that the United States be saved from the intrigues of Jews and communists. In this crusade she saw herself as God's instrument.[60] Her temper was most aroused by those who appeared to endanger orthodox Christianity—and, of course, the United States. To this messianic complex Waters added a desire for martyrdom, her rhetoric sprinkled with references to herself as Joan of Arc.[61] Frustrated when men in power treated her with condescension, or when her views were dismissed or ignored, she could nonetheless withstand a succession of defeats because of her confidence that she was doing God's work and that with divine help, she would be triumphant, rewarded in the end.[62]

Waters's gender consciousness, in turn, complemented this faith. Part of the reason God selected her to help rescue humanity, she thought, was her sex. A consistent theme of her oratory was that God wanted women to be the moral leaders of the nation. Unlike some of the mothers' chief figures, she rarely emphasized the moral superiority of mothers, yet she stressed the moral superiority of all women.[63] Considering that she almost never mentioned her family in her speeches, and that her daughters were not active in her crusades,[64] Waters probably believed women received their special gifts directly from God rather than from the experience of raising families. She denounced not only men such as FDR for failing to be moral exemplars but women such as Eleanor Roosevelt, who had betrayed womanhood by failing to conform to the proper Christian female role. Ironically, Waters's career and lifestyle were hardly those of a conventional Christian mother. With some of the other mothers' leaders, she shared a commitment to motherhood that was more evident in her rhetoric than in her life.[65]

A major part of her identity, gender consciousness ran like a thread throughout her career. Again, Waters might have felt challenged to emulate her mother, who was a pioneer among women attorneys and real estate agents. Her work in the National Woman's Party[66] also suggests her gender consciousness antedated her public battles against Jews and communism. Once she decided to fight those battles, she worked mainly through women. Her politics changed, with her transformation from a liberal (at least in her mind) active in the Democratic Party into an agitator on the far right.[67] Waters seems to have been one of the few mothers' leaders who was a Democrat. Probably World War II crystallized her opinions, causing her to focus on ideas that had been only subthemes in her ideology earlier.

One might be tempted to dismiss Waters as a lot of noise. For all of her bigotry and crackpot ideas, however, she helped kill the child refugee measure and convinced some women that she was an asset to their causes. To Waters, it was the world, not she, that was idiosyncratic and menacing.

═══ ELEVEN ═══
The Mass Sedition Trial

The far-right attacks on Roosevelt and his defense program infuriated the president, who had mobilized the FBI as early as 1935 to investigate pro-Nazi organizations. FBI Director J. Edgar Hoover kept the White House well informed about suspicious individuals and groups, yet Roosevelt sometimes was dissatisfied with the FBI, thinking it was too lenient on subversion, and asked Attorney General Francis Biddle to look into far-right agitators. Biddle demurred out of concern for civil liberties and a belief that convictions would be difficult to obtain. Roosevelt "was not much interested . . . in the constitutional right to criticize the government in wartime," Biddle commented. FDR prodded him to prosecute, showering him with memos and asking him brusquely, "When are you going to indict the seditionists?"[1]

In early 1941 Biddle selected William Power Maloney as his special assistant to investigate fascist propaganda. Maloney, who detested the far right, investigated for three months, decided there was enough evidence to convene a grand jury, and kept the panel in session into 1942. Some of the more prominent mothers' leaders were called to testify before the grand jury, including Dilling, Curtis, Stanley, Van Hyning, and Cooper.[2]

Maloney's plan was to prosecute under the Sedition Act of 1917, which outlawed attempts to undermine the morale of the armed services in wartime, and under the Smith Act of 1940, which prohibited activities to undermine the morale of fighting men in peacetime. This prosecution would be the first under the latter law. The Justice Department decided to start with small fry as a prelude to prosecuting more important fascist sympathizers, among them Coughlin and Smith. Senators such as Wheeler, Nye, and William L. Langer of North Dakota, and congressmen such as Fish and Hoffman disliked the strategy, believing attempts to prosecute minor figures were intended to intimidate the administration's congressional opponents. But on July 21, 1942 the grand jury indicted twenty-eight German agents, Bundists, and far rightists, including Dilling, Pelley and Winrod, on two counts of conspiracy to cause insubordination of the military in peacetime and wartime. Conviction on each count would bring a maximum penalty of thirty years in prison and a fine of $20,000. To establish venue in the District of Columbia, Dillard Stokes, a journalist who worked with the Justice Department, used aliases to

Lois de Lafayette Washburn gives a Nazi salute as she leaves a Washington courtroom on the first day of the mass sedition trial in April 1944. Associated Press photo.

solicit propaganda that the defendants mailed to him in the district. The case, known as *U.S. vs. Winrod*, would be tried in Washington.[3]

In 1943, six months after the first indictment, the government produced a second indictment with broader charges. It named the twenty-eight individuals in the first indictment and five others. The new indictees included two women, Lois de Lafayette Washburn, who operated anti-Semitic, pro-Nazi organizations in Chicago and Tacoma, Washington, and West Coast nationalist Paquita Louise de Shismareff, who preferred to be known as Leslie Fry.[4]

The second indictment, like the first, had two counts but moved the date of the conspiracy from June 28, 1940, when the Smith Act became law, to

January 1, 1933, the date Hitler came to power. Also, the second indictment alleged there was a continuing conspiracy after December 7, 1941, when the United States was at war. Again, many congressmen were angered. Nye insisted the defendants, although crackpots, were no more guilty than he of conspiracy. Wheeler and Senator Taft demanded the removal of Maloney, whom they accused of bias. After Wheeler threatened a congressional investigation of the Justice Department, Biddle agreed to remove Maloney. His successor, O. John Rogge, was a famous trial lawyer who had won convictions against Long's corrupt successors in Louisiana in 1939.[5]

After hearing preliminary defense motions seeking dismissal of the charges, District Judge Jesse C. Adkins emasculated the second indictment by eliminating all acts that occurred before approval of the Smith Act. On March 5, 1943 he ruled that by dating the conspiracy to 1933, the government was attempting to prosecute on the grounds of an ex post facto law— prosecution for acts that were not crimes when they were committed. Later Adkins ruled that no actions taken before the United States went to war could be included.[6]

Rather than going to trial on reduced charges, Rogge decided to seek a third indictment. Returned on January 3, 1944, this bill reindicted twenty-two defendants, dropped eleven, and included eight new ones; Dilling and Washburn were reindicted but Fry was not. The new indictment, known as *U.S. vs. McWilliams,* differed from the first two by attempting to link the defendants with Hitler's agents in a plot to overthrow the government and establish a Nazi dictatorship. Hitler and his lieutenants were named as coconspirators. The government claimed it could prove the defendants had received instructions and funds from Germany.[7]

Washburn, a widow of fifty in 1944, said she was descended from the Marquis de Lafayette, the French general who fought for the colonists in the American Revolution. She had a history of involvement in nationalist politics. In 1936 and 1937 she joined with George W. Christian in organizing the Crusaders for Economic Liberty in Chicago. After Christian was sentenced to prison for inciting insubordination in the armed forces, she became executive secretary of the National Gentile League. In October 1937 Washburn set up her own organization in Chicago, the American Gentile Protective Association, and hired Frank W. Clark as her assistant. Clark had been secretary of Pelley's Christian Party, a member of the Silver Shirts, and an assistant to Deatherage in the American Nationalist Confederation. After working for Washburn, he moved to Tacoma, where he founded the Young Buffaloes and led the western division of the National Gentile League.[8]

In 1943 Washburn moved to Tacoma and helped Clark organize the National Liberty Party, later renamed the Yankee Freeman. She and Clark claimed the Axis cause was just and supported a negotiated peace and pogroms against Jews. Washburn vowed the National Liberty Party would remain active "as long as a single Jew remains alive on the North American continent." She said her program was an "all-American Aryan movement to defend Christians against Lucifer" in "this Jewunited States of America," and concluded that "we are going to have to resort to Civil War" to overthrow the Jew-dominated government.[9]

Washburn, who believed every president since Lincoln had been corrupt, thought Jews were trying to sell her into "white slavery," claimed Boy Scouts were training young people to serve Jews, and denounced the anti-Semite de Aryan for carrying advertisements of Yellow Cabs in his publications because everyone knew the taxicabs were "Jew-controlled."[10] She was so notorious that Homer Maertz, a Bund leader who saw nothing wrong with anti-Semitism, considered her a crackpot. Asked how his position on Jews differed from Washburn's, he said, "I try to go about it in a sensible way, and she goes about it in more or less a hysterical way."[11] Even Dilling would have nothing to do with her.[12]

Like Washburn, though, Dilling thought she had done nothing unpatriotic. In July 1942 Dilling heard of her indictment on the car radio while she and her daughter were returning home from a visit to Kirkpatrick. She telephoned lawyers to arrange for the $5,000 bail but several bondsmen, fearing adverse publicity, refused to serve her, and Dilling had difficulty raising $500 as a bond fee. She arrived at the Federal District Court in Chicago, where about 150 supporters packed the courtroom, and she was photographed, fingerprinted, and questioned. Dilling said she was a loyal American whose only crime was fighting communism. She compared her arrest to the persecution of Jesus and her fight against the government to the battle between David and Goliath.[13]

Dilling was charged with mailing seditious material to the District of Columbia: a copy of The Octopus and a reprint of a cartoon ridiculing Lend-Lease. The indictment also charged her with making seditious statements. First, she had reprinted in her Bulletin part of a speech by Hoffman, in which he quoted an American soldier in the Philippines who complained his outfit lacked bombers because the planes had been given to Britain. Dilling protested she could not be prosecuted for reprinting a speech delivered in Congress. Second, Dilling was charged with writing that "Any professed servant of Christ who could aid the church-burning, clergy-murdering, God-hating Soviet regime belongs either in the ranks of the blind leaders of the blind or in the ancient and dishonorable order of Judas."[14] She admitted to writing the

Elizabeth Dilling, her daughter, Elizabeth Jane, and her attorney and former husband, Albert Dilling, arrive at court for the opening of the sedition trial. Associated Press photo.

statement but said it was not intended to undermine military morale. If there was a morale problem, she said, it was due to New Deal bungling of the war effort, not to her writing. The *Chicago Tribune* defended Dilling and portrayed her struggle sympathetically. Also in support of Dilling, the American Women Against Communism published a flyer charging Roosevelt with destroying free speech.[15]

Dilling denied she was party to a conspiracy; she said she did not even know most of the defendants. If she were to be tried, she argued, the trial should be in Chicago because a Washington jury would be packed with New Deal sympathizers. In addition, she complained it would be expensive to travel to Washington, that she would not be able to keep house or write her *Bulletins,* and that she would not have access to documents necessary for her defense. She hired attorneys Floyd Lanham of Chicago and Dellmore Lessard of Portland, Oregon, yet they soon quit and her ex-husband Albert took over as her chief attorney.[16]

On July 29, 1942 Dilling appeared in Chicago before United States Commissioner Edwin K. Walker, who ruled she must stand trial in Washington but permitted her to appeal to the District Court in Chicago. District Judge William H. Holly was sympathetic to Dilling's case, doubted her guilt, and reduced her bail to $200. He said his authority would not permit him to block a Washington trial, however. At the end of the hearing, fifty of Dilling's women followers rushed forward to congratulate her on a moral victory. The Circuit Court of Appeals upheld Holly's order and Dilling dropped plans to appeal to the Supreme Court. On October 26 about seventy-five women and Albert accompanied Dilling to the train station as she left for arraignment in Washington.[17]

Dilling expressed confidence she would be acquitted, although she worried about money for her defense. During the early days of the trial (which would not begin until 1944, after the third indictment), she delivered talks and continued to publish tracts and her *Bulletin,* appealing for contributions. Her friends on the far right published advertisements urging people to contribute to a defense fund. Mothers' groups held dances, dinners, and bake sales to raise funds. Dilling received $10,500 from Alice T. Whitney of Massachusetts, a wealthy sympathizer who gave money to other defendants. Without furnishing proof, Rogge claimed Dilling got money for her defense from Germany.[18]

At her arraignment in October 1942, Dilling pleaded "absolutely not guilty" and bail was raised to $5,000; she posted it and was told to remain in the city. The hearing featured sharp exchanges. Maloney termed Dilling an "ink spot on the apron of American womanhood" and said the government had "ink remover amply to remove the spot." When he accused Dilling of being a tool for the German Propaganda Ministry, she started to rise from her chair but Albert restrained her. In Congress, Dilling's supporters, including Wheeler and Taft, accused the Justice Department of trying to entrap the defendants. If the defendants had violated the law, Wheeler argued, they should be tried individually in their own localities, not in Washington on nebulous conspiracy charges.[19]

On March 1, 1943, preliminary motions in the case were argued before Adkins, who quashed all moves for dismissal and denied the defendants the right to examine the ten thousand pages of grand jury documents. Washburn appeared for arraignment without counsel and said she would not hire an attorney "until the revolution." When Adkins offered to appoint one, she complained she could not get a fair trial before a prejudiced court. (Ultimately, though, two-thirds of the defendants, including Washburn, were represented by court-appointed attorneys.) Refusing to pay bail because she considered all bonding companies Jewish, Washburn remained for a few days in the District of Columbia jail. She complained about conditions and appeared in court wearing a blue nightgown under her dress, explaining that jailers had confiscated her clothes. (Adkins promised to investigate.) Seven other defendants were in jail on previous convictions and three others could not raise bail; the ten were incarcerated throughout the trial.[20]

After Adkins weakened the second indictment, the defendants who were free dispersed until the third indictment was returned. When the government went to trial on the indictment, the case was assigned to District Judge Edward C. Eicher, a former New Deal congressman from Iowa. Eicher had given up his seat in the House to challenge Guy Gillette in 1938, when FDR attempted to purge conservatives from the Senate. After Eicher lost, Roosevelt appointed him to the Securities and Exchange Commission and, later, to the Eighth Circuit Court of Appeals. But Gillette blocked the appointment to the appellate court, so FDR named Eicher to the District of Columbia seat. Eicher, sixty-five, lacked the stamina and temperament to preside over the rowdy *McWilliams* case, his first major criminal trial. He tried to be fair to the defendants, who disrupted the proceedings and attempted to make a farce of the trial. Yet most of his rulings favored the government, and by trial's end, Eicher had fined four attorneys and three defendants more than twelve hundred dollars for contempt.[21]

When Eicher took over, Albert Dilling filed demurrers to the indictment. Nine members of the grand jury, he said, were federal employees biased in favor of the government. He also said the indictment was so vague it was impossible to prepare a defense. The government demonstrated only that his ex-wife had said and written certain things; it failed to connect her to any act of conspiracy or to an attempt to undermine military morale.[22]

Moreover, Albert Dilling argued, the government gave two dates for the beginning of the alleged conspiracy: 1933, when Hitler came to power, and June 28, 1940, when the Smith Act became law. But any actions taken before the law went into effect could not be included in the indictment, he said. And if the conspiracy had originated on June 28, 1940, the three-year statute of limitations had expired before the trial. Nor could the government prosecute for a continuing conspiracy, for any actions after June 28, 1940 were merely means of implementing the conspiracy, not the conspiracy itself.[23]

Eicher quashed Dilling's demurrers but asked for a bill of particulars from the government. The subsequent bill was vague and had little direct relevance to the charges in the indictment; there was nothing to indicate the defendants had conspired with Nazis to weaken the military. Some twenty-five of the bill's thirty-two pages were devoted to a history of the Nazi Party in Germany, consisting of excerpts from scholarly books about the country and quotations from Nazi letters. The bill listed publications in which purport-edly seditious statements appeared but did not specify the writers. "By attack-ing the Jews the Nazi conspirators hoped to destroy the feeling for law and order in the whole world," the government argued.[24]

The defense denounced the bill and sought to strike it from the record. Also, Dilling's counsel asked that the trial be postponed until after the war because the case might require officials to testify about classified documents. On March 27 Eicher rebuffed those bids, clearing the way for the trial to start on April 17.[25] As the defendants entered the courtroom for jury selection that day, Washburn gave a Nazi salute. The woman who billed herself as "90 pounds of TNT," said, "Lafayette, we are here to defend what you gave us: our freedom from tyranny." She tried to continue but her attorney tugged at her and she stopped. When court recessed, Washburn walked into a cluster of photographers. They started taking pictures and Washburn became angry, put her handbag in front of her face, and lunged at a reporter. Reaching the sidewalk, she gave the fascist salute and shouted, "I am a fascist!" Her oppo-nents were "a bunch of communists!" Then she thumbed her nose at the courthouse.[26]

At noon proceedings were halted because one defendant, Edward James Smythe, had not appeared. The next day Smythe was apprehended in a small New York town near the Canadian border. He said he had gone there to fish and was unaware the trial had started because the FBI had stolen his mail. Smythe gave Eicher cause to regret dragging him into court. A constant irri-tant, he shouted objections, refused to cooperate with his attorneys, and showed up drunk. He was no worse than codefendant Sanctuary, who some-times slept through sessions.[27]

Washburn's outbursts continued. Waving her hand like a student to gain recognition, she said she wanted to explain her Nazi salute. "That was given for the scandal scavengers, Judge," she said, "for the smear sheets, *PM* and all the others, the smear artists. They have hounded me from coast to coast."[28] Later, Washburn leaped up, pointed to a spectator, and shouted, "There's an-other government stooge! Throw him out!"[29] Washburn's disruptions of-fended some defendants who thought their identification with her might prejudice their cases. Dennis requested that Washburn be required to submit to a lunacy test and asked that her case be severed from his. Eicher refused.[30]

When she was not shouting, Washburn sat sewing ornamental ribbons, which she sold to defray expenses. After posting bond and leaving jail, she taught stenography at a secretarial school and skipped some sessions with court permission. She complained it was difficult to earn a living because when an employer learned she was a defendant, she would be fired.[31]

Washburn made up a set of questions she wanted Eicher to ask potential jurors. She wanted to know whether they were Christian, what they knew about the Jewish religion, including the Talmud, and whether they considered Jesus a Jew. Defense attorneys accommodated Washburn's concerns, using their preemptory challenges to exclude Jews and Blacks from the jury. Selection of the jury took a month and exhausted three pools of potential jurors. Eicher dismissed the first pool because Rogge prejudiced it by mentioning the first and second indictments. The second pool was dismissed because its call expired before a jury was chosen. Finally, ten men and two women were impaneled. Most of them read only newspapers and magazines; only one was a college graduate. None of the jurors was a New Dealer and only one worked for the government.[32]

The day after jury selection was completed, the prosecution made its opening statement. Rogge wanted to prove there was a web of conspiracy whose center was in Berlin and whose strands reached Washington. He described a scheme featuring George Van Horn Moseley as führer, Pelley, McWilliams, Baxter, and Kunze as subführers, and Dennis as the intellectual inspiration. The German-American Bund leaders took orders from Berlin and passed them on to the defendants. Moreover, some defendants had been to Germany for indoctrination and received mail from Germany.[33]

Rogge said the defendants wanted to foment a revolution that would culminate in the physical seizure of power, using storm troopers, Silver Shirts, paramilitary groups, and treasonous members of the armed forces. As a prelude, the social structure would be undermined. Hitler instructed the conspirators to make fascist foes appear to be Jews allied with communists who conspired together to take over the United States. The Nazi sympathizers would then insist that support for Nazism was the only way to save the nation; they would call their revolution a counterrevolution to forestall communism.[34]

To block measures to prepare American defenses, Rogge argued, the conspirators would try to convince the public the Axis cause was just and the Allied cause was unjust. The defendants preached to soldiers that they were being trained not because the country needed defenders but because Roosevelt and Congress were betraying the United States. This attempt peaked during congressional consideration of Lend-Lease, when the conspirators published cartoons showing Uncle Sam crucified on a cross, implying that the government was crucifying its people. The cartoons originated in Chicago, where Dilling and the Bund distributed them.[35]

Attorney Henry Klein, representing Sanctuary, summarized the defense position. The defendants had not tried to destroy democracy, he said; they had merely opposed the government. Rogge had demonstrated Hitler was anti-Semitic in Europe and the defendants were anti-Semitic in the United States, yet he had not proved there were links, and he had not proved they conspired to subvert the armed services. There was no law in the United States against anti-Semitism, which had existed throughout the Christian world for two thousand years. Echoing Albert Dilling, Klein said the indictment specified no crime and did not identify which defendants had written which statements, preventing preparation of a defense. In fact, there was more propaganda in the indictment than in the defendants' publications.[36]

To that point, Klein's argument was sensible. The government's charges were vague and lacked evidence of a conspiracy with Hitler. Further, much of the subsequent presentation, consisting of the history of Hitler and Nazi Germany or condemnations of the führer, was irrelevant. The prosecution's case was a syllogism: the Nazis wanted to keep the United States out of the war; the defendants wanted to keep the United States out of the war; therefore, the defendants were members of a worldwide Nazi conspiracy. Had he stopped after outlining the prosecution's flaws, Klein might have won sympathy for the defendants. Instead, he proceeded to outline another conspiracy, asserting the defendants' persecution had been masterminded by "so-called professional Jews." As a Jew, Klein said, he knew Jews who made a practice of raising money from fellow believers by frightening them with false charges of anti-Semitism. The real danger was from communism, and the defendants opposed FDR because Stalin controlled him.[37]

Perhaps trying to compensate in volume for what it lacked in clarity, the prosecution introduced thousands of unlabeled exhibits; the government could not print enough copies for the defense attorneys.[38] Nor could the government's witnesses bolster a vague, rambling case. Peter Gissibl, one of the founders of the Bund and its predecessors, testified on cross-examination that none of the defendants had plotted with the Bund to overthrow the government. Henry J. Nord, deputy customs collector from Los Angeles, identified subversive documents mailed from Germany to the defendants but had no knowledge of whether the defendants requested the papers, read them, or used them in their writing. William Luedtke, national secretary of the Bund, testified that a few of the defendants were Bund members and others attended Bund meetings, yet he knew nothing of a conspiracy involving Hitler. Other witnesses testified some defendants had written anti-Semitic articles, yet they could not show the articles were aimed at weakening the morale of the armed forces.[39]

Like the prosecution, the defense presented a disorganized case and raised irrelevancies: repeated requests that Eicher disqualify himself, claims that

Roosevelt was a Jew, attempts to introduce *The Protocols* as evidence, and demands to subpoena New Dealers and generals.[40] Mixed with the propaganda were some valid points, however. Albert Dilling falsely said he would show the prosecution was the work of the Anti-Defamation League of B'nai B'rith, and that his former wife, a lone crusader unconnected with other opponents of communism, had criticized Jews only because they interfered with Christians' rights. More germanely, Dennis pointed out his beliefs could hardly have differed more from Pelley's—Dennis did not share his belief in the supernatural—weakening the argument that the two were part of the same conspiracy. Similarly, Winrod's attorney pointed out his client and Pelley were not on speaking terms.[41]

Soon the trial degenerated into vaudeville, even if some of the original characters were no longer on stage. On the second day of the trial, one defendant, Elmer J. Garner, eighty, died of a heart attack. Later the cases of three defendants were severed: Robert Noble's because he was disruptive; David Baxter's because his partial deafness prevented him from following the proceedings; and True's because of illness. Also, Eicher dismissed attorney James J. Laughlin for filing a petition to impeach the judge, and Klein resigned, frustrated and exhausted by the trial.[42]

Many of the defense attorneys were liberals unsympathetic with their clients' beliefs. But they came to see the defendants' side on a human basis, and instead of conducting a perfunctory defense, as many observers had expected, they put up a vigorous defense. When Dennis, acting as his own counsel, would raise an objection, several of the court-appointed attorneys would join him. With a few exceptions, morale among the defense attorneys was higher than morale among the prosecutors.[43]

By mid-June Eicher had fined several attorneys and defendants, including Albert Dilling, for contempt. In response, Albert formed an "Eicher Contempt Club," whose members wore badges of white ribbon, reading "E.C.C.," under their lapels. One star was added to the badges each time an attorney was fined. Eicher had a one-hour discussion of the badges in open court after the *New York Times* reported on the club. After Albert Dilling explained he had formed the club to maintain the morale of the defense, Eicher decided to ignore the badges.[44]

Albert's client was feisty, too. During one session, Elizabeth Dilling spotted Theodore Pope in the spectators' section. Pope, minister of a Universalist church in Wisconsin, was an active member of the Communist Party. Elizabeth looked at Pope and remarked to Albert, "All those kikes have big ears, don't they?" Pope replied angrily, "I'm not a Jew; I'm a communist!" Elizabeth responded, "You're both a kike and a communist!"[45]

On June 13 the prosecution received what could have been a fatal blow: the Supreme Court overturned the sedition conviction of Elmer Hartzel, who had insulted Roosevelt, Britain, and the Jews in spurious pamphlets similar to the defendants'. Nothing in Hartzel's pamphlets was directed at the armed forces and he never mentioned military insubordination. The pamphlets were malicious, but they fell into the category of hyperbolic propaganda, not sedition, and were protected by the Constitutional guarantee of free speech. Mere intent to influence public opinion was not equivalent to sedition, the Court declared. On June 21 Eicher ruled that *Hartzel* did not require a directed verdict of acquittal because Hartzel had acted alone, whereas the defendants were accused of participating in a conspiracy. *Hartzel* gave the defendants hope that the Court might overturn any convictions in their case, though.[46]

In October the defense asked for a mistrial after Roosevelt discussed the Silver Shirts in a radio speech. He compared them to Mussolini's Black Shirts and Hitler's Brown Shirts and said groups such as the defendants' were a part of the "lunatic fringe." Pelley's attorney complained the president had prejudiced the case against his client. Eicher denied the motion for a mistrial.[47]

Continuing into the fall, the trial became a routine of legalistic fencing and public interest waned. Jurors had been confused and bored since the early days of the case. On August 2 the *Washington Post,* which condemned the trial as "a sorry spectacle" and "a courtroom farce," announced the trial had lost news value and deserved only intermittent coverage. Under the circumstances, the *Post* declared, justice could not be obtained and the proceedings should be terminated.[48]

The trial ended in unexpected fashion. On November 29 Eicher died of a heart attack. The trial was recessed until early December, while District Judge James M. Proctor considered whether to declare a mistrial. The odds against continuing were high: a new judge would have to read nearly eighteen thousand pages of testimony and examine more than eleven hundred exhibits. Furthermore, the case could not continue unless all the defendants agreed, and only one, Prescott Dennett, was willing to proceed under a new judge. Proctor therefore declared a mistrial. By that time, the stenographic record of more than seven months of proceedings, including five hundred motions for mistrials, weighed some 150 pounds. The government was not yet halfway through its case, having put thirty-nine witnesses on the stand and expecting to present sixty-seven more. The defense had not begun.[49]

The case lingered into the Truman administration, which was hesitant to retry it, but the end of the war raised hopes in the Justice Department that evidence of a conspiracy could be found in Germany. In 1946 Rogge requested delays in setting a trial date so he could collect evidence in Germany. When he returned, he leaked some of his findings to the press and was fired for the indiscretion. Yet nothing Rogge found proved the existence of a conspiracy among Germans and Nazi sympathizers in the United States. Finally, on November 22, 1946 District Judge Bolitha Laws dismissed the charges because the defendants had not received a speedy trial. Because of the length of the delay, Laws said, witnesses were scattered and the defendants did not have the financial resources for a second trial. On June 30, 1947, the Circuit Court of Appeals upheld Laws's dismissal.[50]

The intriguing question is whether convictions could have been obtained had the case gone to the jury. There was little question that the prosecution had shown the defendants to be despicable characters, some of whom had committed the acts of which they were accused. The defendants nevertheless did not conspire as a group or with Hitler. They were mainly minor bigots who would not have known what to do if a revolution had occurred. As they wrote for an audience that agreed with them, it would have been difficult to prove they made many converts, particularly in the armed forces, even if their message reached soldiers and sailors. The jury was split and might have compromised by convicting the more notorious defendants (such as Dilling) and acquitting others. But no conviction, Rogge believed, could have withstood an appeal.[51]

Biddle claimed that although the trial ended without convictions, it served Roosevelt's purpose by tying up the defendants and making it difficult for them to produce propaganda.[52] It could also be said the government punished them by subjecting them to a long, expensive trial far from their homes. Still, the trial enabled the defendants to obtain more publicity than they could have attracted on their own—publicity that might have encouraged the curious to read their propaganda. And the unfairness of prosecuting lesser figures, while individuals such as Smith and Coughlin were not prosecuted, might have evoked more sympathy for the defendants. Most of the accused were not serious dangers to the nation and many of their pronouncements, however bigoted, were protected by Constitutional free-speech guarantees. Generally they were annoyances, not miniature Hitlers, and in his frustration, Roosevelt overreacted by insisting on their prosecution. The resulting trial emulated the title of Shakespeare's farce "Much Ado About Nothing."

═══ TWELVE ═══
The Postwar Mothers' Movement

The mothers' movement waned after World War II, for the Holocaust had exposed the darkest side of anti-Semitism, Roosevelt's death had deprived the mothers of their archenemy, and the mothers had failed to avert the social change they feared, a failure that led to declining enthusiasm for the cause. Even without these developments, the movement might have become obsolete because the mothers' extreme rhetoric and lack of funds would have prevented them from getting their message on the key medium of television. Most of the mothers' followers returned to the mainstream in the 1950s, remaining right of center. Some of the leaders and organizations lasted into the 1960s, finding new foes, yet the leaders lost the prominence they had in the 1930s and 1940s. Some faded into the obscurity they richly deserved, leaving no obituaries in major newspapers.

Dilling had the most active postwar career. She remained bitter because of her personal setbacks, including her divorce and the sedition prosecutions. Her alienation grew and her sense of humor was less evident in her writing, which became pedantic, obscure, and repetitious. Dilling's beliefs did not change—if anything, she was more anti-Semitic in the 1950s and 1960s—and she continued to research with great industry. Buried in her work, she seldom left her home and office to speak, preferring to reach the public by writing. Her only friends were other bigots, and some of the people whom she considered close friends were people with whom she only corresponded.

Dilling's personal life remained turbulent. After the divorce, Albert lived with her briefly before moving out for good. (He continued to serve as her attorney, however.) Following his departure, Ellis O. Jones, a codefendant in the sedition trial, moved in with her. She said their relationship was platonic and he was only her editorial assistant, despite rumors that they were lovers.[1] Then in January 1948, Dilling, fifty-three, married Jeremiah Stokes, seventy, a lawyer from Salt Lake City who had succeeded Jones as her live-in companion. Stokes came highly recommended by other nationalists, and she feared she could not live up to the expectations of such a good man. A close friend of Smith, Stokes won a libel suit against John Roy Carlson, author of *Under Cover,* although the decision was overturned. He helped Dilling revise her books and write the *Bulletin,* and joined Albert's and Kirk's law firm.[2]

The sedition trial left loose ends that took Dilling years to settle. She sued the Chicago *Herald-American* for publishing an article implying that she was guilty of sedition. An Illinois court dismissed the suit on the grounds that she was a public figure subject to reasonable criticism. Dilling sued the Chicago *Star* and the Billboard Publishing Company for libel, but both suits were settled out of court for undisclosed terms. Her most publicized lawsuit was brought against the Jewish *Sentinel,* a small Chicago weekly. Joined by several sedition trial defendants, she claimed the *Sentinel* presumed their guilt. On the witness stand she made numerous anti-Semitic statements and her attorney, Kirk, tried to turn the trial into a confrontation between Christians and Jews, arguing "a verdict for my mother, Mrs. Dilling, and the rest of these people is a verdict against Communism and for Christianity and Americanism." Some of the plaintiffs were awarded small damages. Dilling settled out of court after her suit resulted in a hung jury.[3]

For more than two decades, Dilling wrote about issues arising from World War II and crusaded against the elements of the communist conspiracy: the North Atlantic Treaty Organization (NATO), foreign aid, the income tax, racial mixing, flouridation of drinking water, and federal power. And she detected a conspiracy between German Nazis, including her hero, Hitler, and Jews (a conspiracy of which others on the far right had warned.) "Evidence piles up and up that Hitler himself was not only of Jewish ancestry, but had Jewish financing from the very beginning," Dilling wrote. The führer could have conquered the Soviet Union but did not, and "[a]t no time did Hitler disturb the great Jewish bankers who own and run German industry."[4] Claims that six million Jews had perished in the Holocaust were false, part of a plot to admit thousands of Jews to the United States, where they would undermine the government. Germans had tried to expose the Jewish scheming, only to be punished in the Nuremberg war crimes trials.[5]

The Japanese, too, had received unduly harsh treatment, at the hands of the Americans. Dilling had traveled to Japan in the 1930s and thought it was the only Christian nation in Asia. Unfortunately, General MacArthur and President Truman had introduced communism to Japan after the war. They plotted to arrange for Jewish domination of the Japanese; the two had merely pretended to break over Korean War strategy.[6]

Also in the 1950s, Dilling backed Sen. Joseph McCarthy's crusade against communism and attacked President Eisenhower. Disappointed over Eisenhower's election, she said "Ike the kike" was the candidate of the Jews.[7] In 1960 Eisenhower was not on the presidential ballot, although Dilling found several reasons to complain about the major candidates, Democrat

John F. Kennedy and Republican Richard M. Nixon, Eisenhower's vice president. Kennedy was denounced for reviewing favorably a book that condemned McCarthy, for addressing the National Conference of Christians and Jews, for accepting an honorary degree from Brandeis University, and for advocating the sale of Israel bonds. Furthermore, Dilling believed Kennedy wanted to admit more refugees to get more Jews into the country. Dilling nonetheless concluded that "The only candidate who can excel Kennedy in service to the synagogue is perhaps Nixon."[8]

After Kennedy was elected, Dilling became one of his more vicious critics. She claimed that Jews, blacks, and communists had provided JFK's margin of victory; condemned the Peace Corps; labelled Kennedy's New Frontier program the "Jew frontier"; and criticized the appointment of Arthur M. Schlesinger Jr. to the White House staff because the historian had written books praising FDR. Dilling demanded to know what Kennedy and Soviet President Nikita Khrushchev, a Jewish puppet, said over the "hot line" set up between Washington and Moscow.[9]

More than she hated liberals such as JFK, Dilling hated politicians whom she considered false conservatives, and during the 1960s she directed diatribes at one of them, Arizona Senator Barry Goldwater. In 1960 Dilling feared Goldwater might win the Republican presidential nomination and led a campaign to defeat him. She disliked Goldwater because he had a Jewish grandfather and had belonged to the NAACP, yet her chief complaint concerned his membership in the National Municipal League. The league supported a council-manager form of city government, which she equated with communism. That type of government, she said, permitted more than one thousand six hundred communists to become local officials. The league's use of the term "standard metropolitan statistical areas," moreover, signalled a plot to obliterate state and national boundaries and place communities under the rule of "commissars." In the 1964 presidential election, Dilling was relieved when Democrat Lyndon Johnson defeated Goldwater because the Republican had been backed by Jews, had communist advisers, had supported NATO, and had a running mate, Congressman William E. Miller, who was a prosecutor at Nuremberg.[10]

Dilling wrote less about the Johnson administration than she wrote about Goldwater, but she was in declining health during Johnson's presidency. She was appalled to hear that LBJ swam nude in the White House pool, condemned the War on Poverty as a waste of money, denounced Vice President Hubert Humphrey for accepting an honorary degree at a Jewish university, and considered the Vietnam War a plot to divert American resources abroad and facilitate a communist takeover in the United States. When LBJ committed troops to fight in Vietnam without a declaration of war, she argued, he was fulfilling Protocol X of *The Protocols*.[11]

Castigating politicians, however, was not Dilling's chief activity in the postwar period. Her obsessions were anti-Semitism and the Talmud. She claimed to have read all volumes in English translation and began to sign her name "Elizabeth Dilling, D.D.T.," meaning "Doctor of Damned Talmud."[12] The strain of hours reading material she detested made her nervous and bitter—she scribbled "lies!" and "anti-Christian!" in the margins—but she could not stop searching for anti-Gentile references. It took an eye such as hers to detect the duplicity of the authors who made the Talmud obscure to befuddle Gentiles.[13]

Dilling believed the purpose of Judaism was to exterminate or enslave Christians, and that Jews studied the Talmud to learn how to undermine Christianity. She was drawn to discussions of sex, which she misinterpreted, and of Jesus, who is not mentioned by name. Dilling complained of the "Talmudic teaching that Christ's mother was a hairdresser named Miriam who was a whore and adultress; that all Christians are consigned to eternal hell under 'boiling semen.'" The Talmud permitted adultery, sodomy, sex with children, corpses, and dogs; cheating and murdering non-Jews; and burning of babies as human sacrifices. Incest was the least serious sin a Jew could commit. The most serious was to become a Christian. In short, "Talmudism is a conglomeration of all the demonology of ancient time."[14]

Dilling said Jews practiced voodoo, used black magic against her family, and communicated with the devil.[15] Their tactics for world domination included not only communism but the civil rights movement that stirred in the 1950s (thanks in part to the UN-mandated *Brown* decision). Blacks would not have come to America in the first place, except for Jewish slave traders. It followed that desegregation was a Jewish plot. "Any habitual reader of the American Jewish press knows that forced integration is strictly a Talmudic plot, the design and program to create a bowl of stew out of racial opposites which the Talmudist may stir at will, as his own," she wrote.[16]

Dilling commented on the Talmud in the *Bulletin* and in her last book, *The Plot Against Christianity*, privately published in 1954. (After her death, the title was changed to the less inflammatory *The Jewish Religion: Its Influence Today*.) The work "reveals the satanic hatred of Christ and Christians responsible for their mass murder, torture and slave labor in all Iron Curtain countries—all of which are ruled by Talmudists—believe it or not!" proclaimed an advertisement in *Women's Voice*, which offered the book for one dollar.[17] Like Dilling's other books, this work was more of a compilation than a narrative. The book consisted largely of 299 photostats of Judaica and included alleged State Department documents "proving" that Jews financed the Bolshevik Revolution. These documents, Dilling wrote, constituted the raw material she intended to use in writing an irrefutable exposé, but she never got around to writing it.[18]

As for the *Bulletin* it was more disjointed than Dilling's earlier writing, skipping from one subject to another. Everything she turned out was an unrevised first draft written in stream-of-consciousness fury. Her series of articles on Jews for *Women's Voice* was so long it had to be spread over several issues. The articles sometimes stopped in the middle of a sentence, requiring the reader to wait for the next issue to read the rest.[19] It is difficult to conceive of anyone deriving enjoyment from Dilling's writing, although she had readers and influenced their lives. One Catholic wrote to her, thanking her for changing his point of view. He had always been taught to love his enemies, but after reading Dilling, he realized it was all right to hate Jews.[20]

If her fanaticism found favor with readers, it alienated Dilling from some anticommunists on the right. She criticized William F. Buckley Jr. as a "kosher conservative" who let Jews on the staff of his *National Review;* denounced Robert Welch's John Birch Society for being insufficiently militant and for failing to deal with the "Jewish Question"; and chastised Fred Schwartz, leader of the Christian Anti-Communist Crusade, for not teaching that communism was Jewish. Dilling even broke with two longtime allies, the *Chicago Tribune* and Smith. She faulted the newspaper because "Talmudists" had infiltrated it, but her split with Smith was prompted by money rather than ideology.[21]

Albert Dilling represented Smith in a number of trials arising over the arrest of Smith and Arthur Terminiello during a riot at a Terminiello speech in Chicago in 1946. After devoting months to the cases, Albert won, yet Smith refused to pay him. Albert successfully sued for fees of $18,000 and settled out of court for $7,500. The dispute brought recriminations because Dilling sided with Albert. Smith's supporter Wesley Swift aggravated things, Dilling claimed, by spreading rumors that she was living in a basement under the influence of dope, with a Negro lover.[22]

In 1954 Stokes died. Dilling then sold her home and moved in with Kirk. Her son aided her work, but Dilling was troubled by poor health, exacerbated by her compulsive work habits, and in the 1960s, the *Bulletin* appeared sporadically. Still, she kept researching and writing until her death at seventy-two on April 29, 1966. Her books are still in print.[23]

Van Hyning likewise remained active until the 1960s. By 1952 circulation of *Women's Voice* had shrunk from twenty thousand to about ten thousand.

But the paper remained an outlet for anti-Semitic, anticommunist writers such as Dilling, Waters, and Washburn, and as late as 1956, We the Mothers had chapters in thirty-nine states. Van Hyning's core beliefs about World War II also persisted: Hitler was a slandered man who had never murdered Jews, and Germans and Japanese were unfairly punished for a conflict that was the United States's fault. She also crusaded against the UN, NATO, the income tax, the Federal Reserve System, politicians, coexistence with the Soviet Union, arms limitation treaties, racial mixing, water flouridation, and all amendments to the Constitution except the first ten.[24]

Additionally, Van Hyning found herself opposing another war that was a communist plot to weaken the United States and make it ripe for a takeover. American soldiers in Korea were traitors for fighting for the money changers under the UN flag, she said, and Americans should do nothing to help them, a proscription that covered such gestures as rolling bandages or contributing to the Red Cross. The true enemies of the United States were not overseas in Korea but at home, in New York and Washington.[25]

In 1950 Van Hyning and her mothers scored a political victory: they were volunteers in the campaign of Everett M. Dirksen, the Illinois Republican who defeated Lucas, leader of the Democratic majority in the United States Senate.[26] Generally, however, Van Hyning thought the GOP was as pernicious as the Democratic Party because both were controlled by Jews; Eisenhower and Nixon, as well as Woodrow Wilson, FDR, and Harry "Solomon" Truman were Jews.[27] Compounding the Republicans' problems, in 1952 the New Dealer Eisenhower ran on a platform written by the New Dealer John Foster Dulles.[28]

On July 4–6, 1952, We the Mothers and the Constitutional Americans, led by George T. Foster, held a nationalist convention in Chicago to prevent the election of Eisenhower—who had not a single qualification for the White House, Van Hyning said—or of Democrat Adlai Stevenson. Extremists came from around the country to read the Declaration of Independence, sing patriotic songs, and hear speeches against politicians who had sold out to Wall Street, international bankers, England, aliens, and, of course, Jews. Delegates adopted resolutions calling for an investigation of the Anti-Defamation League of B'nai B'rith and for American withdrawal from the UN. Van Hyning urged her supporters to cast write-in votes for MacArthur, the only man who was strong enough "physically, mentally and spiritually" for the presidency, and for McCarthy as vice president.[29]

Women's Voice was a strong supporter of McCarthy and his anti-communist forays. "McCarthyism is now definitely Americanism," Van Hyning wrote. "I can well believe the lady who wrote that she saw Jesus standing above Senator McCarthy." The Wisconsin Republican had tried to prevent Eisenhower from leading the nation into World War III, and for his efforts, Eisenhower wanted to destroy him.[30] That the Senate would censure such a patriot was regrettable. McCarthy had fought "the entrenched wealth of the world Rothschild-Warburg-Kubh-Loeb-Rockefeller-Lehman-Baruch-et al.—for that is all Communism is," and exposing communists was his only "crime."[31]

The heart attack Eisenhower had suffered in 1955 was fatal, yet only Van Hyning, Dilling, and Waters noticed he had died and a double had replaced him. *Women's Voice* printed photographs that "proved" the switch had been made so the substitute would run for president in 1956. To prevent others from discovering the truth, Van Hyning explained, the Secret Service would not let anyone near Eisenhower's hospital or his farm in Gettysburg, Pennsylvania; his body had been smuggled out of the hospital and buried at Gettysburg. (Eisenhower's widow, Mamie, was powerless to prevent the plot.)[32] Mystery also clouded McCarthy's death in 1957. It was the result of foul play, no doubt the work of communists, Van Hyning suggested. When she heard of his demise, she immediately suspected Baruch. She consoled herself that McCarthy was in heaven and urged Wisconsinites to elect McCarthy's widow to succeed him.[33]

The only death that seemed to sadden Van Hyning more was that of her son Tom, killed in a plane crash at age thirty-five in 1955. Tom, whom Van Hyning claimed had an IQ of 165, reluctantly served in the military in World War II, then worked for the Goodyear Rubber Company in Venezuela. He aided his mother's crusades by protesting the income tax. Tom filed blank tax returns, and when the Internal Revenue Service questioned him, he refused to answer, pleading the Fifth Amendment. He was not prosecuted. "Adoption of the Marxian-Lenin income tax, in open defiance of the Constitution, makes people pay for their own destruction," said his mother, who warned that "you are not a loyal American when you pay your hard-earned money so that the despoilers of your country will have more money to waste and meddle in the affairs of others and bring on wars."[34]

Van Hyning said Jews also meddled in American affairs by instigating the civil rights movement and encouraging mongrelization to weaken the country's ruling race.[35] She believed, as did Dilling, that the Supreme Court issued the *Brown* decision because the UN called for racial equality. Roosevelt had committed the United States to the UN and many southerners had foolishly supported him. "The South can well weep, but they brought it on themselves in their support of the Jew-Communist F. D. Roosevelt."[36] Nor was Eisenhower immune from the spell of the civil rights proposal that would create a police state; already, the government had begun to build concentration camps. There was a race problem, Van Hyning believed, although the solution was to deport blacks to Africa.[37]

That course, obviously, would not be followed by a sick country under the influence of Jews and Masons. "[T]oday the U.S.A. is no longer a republic, but a Freemasonic State ruled by the statute of King Solomon," claimed a pamphlet published by We the Mothers. Van Hyning knew the Masons ran the Anti-Defamation League for the Jews. The Great Seal of the United States was based on the seal of freemasonry, which Morgenthau had put on currency. A photograph of Truman shaking hands with a Soviet diplomat showed them using the secret Masonic grip.[38]

Jews sought to increase their numbers in the United States, via immigration, so they could enslave Gentiles and abolish Christianity—the goal of the Jewish-controlled Soviet government. "This growth of Jewish immigration constitutes a swarm of human locusts just as foretold in the second chapter of the Book of Joel," Van Hyning believed. "They destroy as they come and that is the purpose of having them come here."[39]

If she had even a shred of credibility—and that is a very generous estimate —left after years of invective, Van Hyning destroyed it by writing of a government plot to prevent Americans from learning that flying saucers from Venus had visited Earth as many as seven hundred times per week. The visitors, whose civilization was five hundred years ahead of Earthlings', had come to help people, but the government concealed the visits because they would prove the existence of God. "Our guests from Venus reveal more of God and the more he is revealed, the more Almighty he becomes. The faceless little men in Washington are cut down to their size—nothing."[40] In the early 1960s, though, it was Van Hyning who was cut down to nothing. She faded from the political scene and, in 1962, ceased publishing *Women's Voice,* whose main office had moved to Albuquerque, New Mexico.[41]

Waters also carried the mothers' fight into the 1960s. After the war, she remained a popular speaker before nationalist groups and testified before Congress against every major foreign policy initiative that had White House backing. In 1947, for instance, she opposed Truman's appointment of the "arch-fiends and anarchists and Jews" David E. Lilienthal and Lewis L. Strauss to the Atomic Energy Commission. Her alarms were ignored, the Senate confirmed the two, and atomic bombs were subsequently dropped on Texas City, Texas, and other American cities. This was part of Lilienthal's slaughter of Gentiles, as forecast in *The Protocols.*[42]

It was no accident that all the so-called natural disasters since the Jews were appointed had been explosions, Waters said; that, too, was part of the grand Jewish scheme. In addition, Jews were planning to use germ warfare against cities on the East Coast. For appointing Jewish killers to high office, Truman should be tried for treason, espionage, and mass murder. Waters did her part to stop the carnage by appealing for money, warning "You may be next." She promised the money would be well invested as national insurance against a Jewish revolution. The appeal letter was signed "Love, Agnes Waters."[43]

On another occasion in 1947, Waters testified against military aid to any nation. Truman had proposed such aid to Greece, Turkey, and other nations threatened by communism. His policy, which came to be known as the Truman Doctrine, was designed by Jews to give away money that would fall into communist hands and therefore weaken the United States, Waters said. Trying to exploit American hatred of communism, Jews hoped to involve White Gentile nations in a third world war that would destroy these countries and pave the way for a global government. If Greece and Turkey really needed money, the government should take it from Jews, a tactic that also would yield enough funds to alleviate all poverty in the United States. Waters vowed to save her country from this Jewish threat, as Joan of Arc had saved France, if people would send her enough money to pay the postage for mailing millions of copies of her testimony. "The war lords and the 'hidden hand' government of the Jews are in a mortal terror of this awakening and its subsequent avenging wrath."[44]

Waters opposed the other facet of Truman's anticommunist program, the Marshall Plan for economic aid to rebuild war-torn Europe. She saw Truman's real intention: the United States would send supplies that communists would seize, and then the president would send troops to save the goods, embroiling the country in another European war. Before attacking communism abroad, however, Americans had to clean out communism at home. Anyone who testified for the Marshall Plan, therefore, should be arrested for treason and tried as a war criminal, she said. Waters offered an alternate plan whereby the government would promote immigration of non-Jewish Germans and use Marshall Plan money to build cities for them in Alaska. These Germans would be hard-working citizens who would erase the national debt and make the United States invulnerable to invasion, deterring war.[45]

In 1948 Waters made a second race for president. Attempting to distribute anti-Semitic pamphlets at the Republican and Democratic conventions, she found few takers. At the Democratic conclave in Philadelphia, she forced her way into the hall and charged the rostrum, shouting "Get rid of the Jews and the New Deal!" but the sergeant at arms ejected her and forbade her to reenter the building. Having failed to secure the nomination of either party, Waters campaigned for write-in votes. She received no contributions, spent $100 of her own money and traveled twenty-five hundred miles by bus from Washington as far west as St. Louis. On the day before the election, Waters campaigned on the streets of Philadelphia, marching and carrying signs that read "The pistol-packin' Mama—Agnes Waters, only Woman Candidate for President of the United States."[46]

The next year Waters testified before the Senate Foreign Relations Committee against approval of NATO. Ostensibly an alliance against the Soviet Union, NATO actually was a Soviet plot. While the United States was protecting Norway and Europe, the USSR would invade through Alaska and Canada. "Why, if this pact is ratified, it becomes the greatest military triumph as well as a diplomatic and bureaucratic coup for Russia," Waters said. The Bible admonished against the treaty. "Nineteen centuries ago, our Lord Jesus Christ anticipated the North Atlantic Pact and similar treaties of internationalists and He said: 'When they shall say peace and security, the sudden destruction cometh upon them.'" Waters refused to stop talking after her allotted five minutes and police had to drag her from the hearing room. Traitors, she complained, had been given entire days to testify in favor of the treaty.[47]

In 1950 Waters opposed the Korean War, argued that it caused the mass murder of Americans, and asked, "How do you think we can win the war with these 'Red Jews' in power?" Harry "Solomon" Truman initiated the war. The Army quartermaster was a Jew, which explained why the guns were bad. The Strategic Air Command failed under its Jewish commander, Gen. Curtis LeMay. The secretary of state was "the Jew stooge and British Jew Dean Acheson." The UN Security Council that brought the United States into the war was dominated by Jews. To no avail, Waters submitted a petition to impeach the president and all cabinet members, to try them as war criminals, to bring home American troops, to end the war, and to repeal the UN charter.[48]

The UN was the epitome of Jewish communism, charged Waters, who fought every activity of the organization. In 1950 she appeared before the Senate Foreign Relations Committee to testify against a UN treaty that would make genocide a violation of international law. Under the "vile treaty" drafted "by the enemies of the Christian peoples of the United States," Americans could be deported, tried in a foreign court, and executed; federal, state, and local authorities would be prevented from suppressing strikes and riots. The treaty, in short, would guarantee a Russian victory in World War III.[49]

In 1951 Waters took pride in causing another disruption before the Senate Foreign Relations Committee, which led to her expulsion from the hearing room. "And while I was waiting for the police to take me to jail, I made an awful commotion in public," said Waters, who wanted to testify against a foreign aid bill. "I stopped everybody! I raised all the hell I could in the corridors of the Capitol, and I used every breath against! I caught several of the Kikes as they were flying by, and I yelled at them that if any more materials of war or other supplies went to the enemy, there would be some hangings in Washington, D.C.!" She wrote down the names of Jews who had attended the hearing and blocked the path of the Israeli ambassador, whom she accused of representing the USSR.[50]

In 1954 Waters struck a major blow against the nefarious Jews. God, she said, arranged for her to meet Churchill, Eden, and Baruch as they were leaving the Statler Hotel in New York. She shouted "No war! No war!" at Churchill and Eden, and when she saw Baruch, "I almost grabbed that big horsey-looking Jew by the throat." Furious at seeing her archenemies, she sobbed uncontrollably and left the stunned Baruch "as white as a sheet!" That God enabled Waters to confront them convinced her that God still ruled the universe.[51]

In 1955 Waters appeared before the Senate Foreign Relations Committee again, to testify in vain against approval of the Southeast Asia Treaty Organization. This agreement was part of a communist plot to weaken the United States by promoting revolutions in Asia at the instigation of the State Department. The pact committed Americans to the defense of six hundred million Asians who would not defend themselves and were not worth the life of a single American.[52]

Nor were Blacks worthy of defending, Waters declared in 1955, when she testified before the Senate Armed Services Committee against a bill authorizing the president to call Army reservists into active duty. If the reservists were sent abroad, the Soviets would take over; besides, there was no danger that required calling up reserves. "What if the enemy did bomb our cities? What would they destroy? Only our internationalists, our Jews and our niggers who are heavy concentrations in every city. These people are mostly on welfare, and it would be no loss to us to lose them." In the event of danger, farmers could defend the country because there was a machine gun on every farm. And if the Reds tried anything, Waters would retaliate by instigating "open hunting" on Blacks and Jews.[53]

Furthermore, Waters said New Dealers had arranged the immigration of hundreds of thousands of Black Africans and built airfields in the heart of Africa to facilitate it.[54] The immigration continued under Truman and Eisenhower. "These are not American niggers. And they should be made to swim back to Africa. Yet President Eisenhower has filled our government departments with these niggers until the United States government is now black." Coming from Eisenhower, this was not surprising because he had turned "niggers loose on the defeated and helpless women of Berlin. Which to a white woman is worse than death." Eisenhower and his opponent in the 1952 and 1956 presidential elections, Adlai "Sweet Adeline" Stevenson— who was "in Africa secretly conferring for some other mischief he is cooking up against the white race"—wanted to carry out the world government plan to mongrelize Whites through intermarriage with Blacks.⁵⁵

In 1954 Waters used a long article in *Women's Voice* to announce she would be a write-in candidate for president again in 1956. Among other things, she claimed the United States had turned its armed forces over to the Soviet-controlled NATO. She urged women to run for every office from Congress to dogcatcher because men had ruined things. Eisenhower's reelection meant he could continue to ruin foreign policy, and Waters continued to criticize his diplomacy. In 1957, invoking the objections she had raised against the Truman Doctrine, she condemned the Eisenhower Doctrine. Giving military and economic aid to the Middle East, the doctrine was part of a conspiracy to establish a communist world government "with our money and our blood." With Eisenhower as commander in chief, the United States would get into a war to "save the 'persecuted' belly-aching treasonous Jews." Waters also denounced his "Open Skies" proposal to permit mutual surveillance of the United States and the Soviet Union. The plan would lead to the takeover of the United States by the Russian Air Force. Americans would be strafed from the air with machine guns and survivors would be driven into cattle cars for transportation to Siberia.⁵⁶

Waters said she was assured of the 1960 Democratic presidential nomination; West Virginia Sen. Harry F. Byrd had told her so. And she told a reporter, "Carmine De Sapio, the leader of Tammany Hall, had me nominated at the Democratic convention in Chicago in 1956, but they gave it to that silly Adlai. De Sapio said, 'Come back in 1960 and we'll put you over.'" Declaring she could easily defeat JFK, who was only a boy, Waters invited the reporter to visit her in the White House in 1961. But in 1961, her address was still her three-story row house in Washington, where she quietly lived the rest of her life.⁵⁷

In the postwar era, Curtis remained outspoken for a time on public affairs. She opposed the UN, the Truman Doctrine, the Marshall Plan, Truman's economic policies, and the *Brown* decision. She favored McCarthy's anticommunist crusades and, when the Senate threatened to censure McCarthy, came to his defense with a pamphlet entitled "Is McCarthy Censure Case Another Nuremburg Trial?" Curtis's influence among women declined rapidly after the war, however, and in the 1950s and 1960s she lost much of her credibility as an expert on finances and foreign policy. Her papers contain no correspondence with members of Congress after the 1940s. She withdrew from public life and returned to the world of business and club women.[58]

Washburn continued her activities in the early 1940s and 1950s, although her organizing efforts ceased after the sedition trial, her health failed, and her influence was limited to occasional articles in *Women's Voice*. In a long article published in 1946 and reprinted in 1955, Washburn denounced the Red Cross as communistic. The American Red Cross was controlled by the International Red Cross headquartered in Geneva, Switzerland, "the hot-bed of internationalism that gave birth to that infamous League of Nations." For years after the American Red Cross was founded in the 1860s, internationalists had tried to absorb it into their group. When American presidents refused to hand it over, they grew desperate. "Finally they became vicious enough to do a dirty job of murder in cold blood to remove President James A. Garfield, because he refused to amalgamate. . . . while he lay a corpse, over his dead body in the 1882, these Geneva gangsters moved in and took over the American Red Cross—lock, stock and barrel."[59]

Winters's career also went into eclipse after the war. In the winter of 1946, she suffered leg injuries in an auto accident and suspended meetings at the Women's White House for several months. Once the meetings resumed, they no longer attracted big crowds. Winters concentrated on local activities and remained prominent in Detroit, but her national stature declined. On March 8, 1957, she died of a stroke at seventy-seven.[60]

Knowles kept the American Mothers of Detroit active into the late 1940s. Her group campaigned against economic and military aid to Europe and demanded that Truman create a cabinet position: secretary of peace. Knowles stayed in contact with the leaders of the American Mothers and corresponded extensively with them, but after 1946 her group held no mass meetings and attracted negligible publicity.[61]

In Philadelphia, the National Blue Star Mothers reorganized as the Current Events Club and stayed active through the 1950s. Catherine Brown and Parks continued to lead the group, with Wallington as the chief male stalwart. The club had a weekly newspaper with several thousand subscribers, and weekly meetings featuring speakers such as Smith, Terminiello, and Waters.[62] As usual, the meetings were a forum for rumormongers. In March 1947, for example, a Mr. Rowland said all information going to FBI Director Hoover went through his secretary, a Jew, who passed it on to the Anti-Defamation League of B'nai B'rith. Jews also knew when Christians whispered conversations in tall buildings; they could hear everything via dictaphones. Jews had even replaced light bulbs in motel rooms with midget cameras so they could photograph everyone present at ostensibly secret meetings.[63] These warnings did not make an impression on Attorney General Tom Clark. In 1949 he classified the club as a subversive, profascist group and the organization withered away afterward.[64]

In New York, the mothers' movement was reduced to a skeletal remnant of its prewar influence, as only Catherine Baldwin was active. Baldwin opposed the UN and foreign aid, sponsored speakers such as Fish and Holt, and maintained contact with Cox and Monreal, among other allies. Her efforts, though, could not revive the movement.[65]

In the postwar period women still were attracted to the right, but the moderate right was more successful in gaining women than was the bigoted right represented by the likes of Dilling. The best-known leader of the women's postwar right, Phyllis Schlafly, resembles Dilling in being a staunch anticommunist who publishes prolifically and leads an upper-middle-class lifestyle. Because of these similarities, she has been compared to Dilling, a comparison that is unfair to Schlafly. A child of working-class parents, Schlafly is a lawyer who wrote a best-selling defense of Goldwater's 1964 campaign and ran two unsuccessful races for Congress, activities that distinguish her from Dilling. Although her views are inflexibly conservative—she stresses family values, opposes feminism, and was instrumental in the defeat of the proposed Equal Rights Amendment to the Constitution—she has none of the anti-Semitic or subversive tendencies of the mothers' movement, and her views reflect those of many women.[66] Moreover, none of the major leaders of the postwar women's right wing base their ideology on anti-Semitism.

The mass movement of profascist women who opposed World War II has no major counterpart in postwar politics. The mothers' movement was confined to the past, based on issues that most women now consider obsolete.

THIRTEEN

The Significance of the Mothers' Movement

Although the mothers forged a mass movement and energized the crusade against intervention—despite opposition from much of the press and the two major parties, and despite a lack of abundant funding—they did not disable the body politic. Weakened by fanaticism, factionalism, and inept leadership, they never blocked a troop train, obstructed the draft, or seriously jeopardized the war effort. They had political connections but were no match for their experienced and resourceful foes in government; they swayed few votes in Congress, they could not defeat FDR in 1940 or 1944, and they rarely changed administration policy. They influenced the pace of policy, reinforcing White House caution against getting ahead of public opinion, but they did not have the impact their adversaries feared.[1]

Still, the mothers' movement had significance beyond its failure. For one thing, it alters the historical conception of isolationism. Most isolationists were not hatemongers, yet their ranks included a sizable number of far-right women and people who sympathized with the mothers' ideology. The substantial presence of anti-Semites and bigots, a presence that is not usually recognized, robbed isolationism of its moral credibility in the short run and should discredit isolationism in the view of history.[2]

The mothers similarly had a harmful effect upon the political culture. With their infusion of strength, the far right became more dynamic and seemingly more formidable. Foes overestimated the right's potential and launched the Brown Scare campaign against domestic subversion. The effort, which included the sedition trial, trampled civil liberties and carved paths for Cold War measures. By augmenting the right, the mothers helped create the conditions that led to McCarthyism and government suppression of suspected internal enemies.[3]

Additionally, the mothers' story compels us to reconsider twentieth-century women's history, in particular the overestimated belief that women are peace oriented and view all wars as inimical to their interests. This idea had currency early in the century, among women who spearheaded social reform groups. Catherine Marshall, a leader in the British peace movement of the World War I era, held that "militarism by its nature implied the subservience of women."[4] In the United States, prominent activists such as Addams and Catt made world peace and demilitarization a feminist priority, underscoring the notion that women, especially mothers, had a special role to play as peacemakers. The Women's International League for Peace and Freedom (WILPF), the Women's Peace Society, the Women's Peace Union, and the National Committee on the Cause and Cure of War worked successfully for treaties that limited naval armaments, provided for arbitration of disputes, and outlawed aggression. Women also were instrumental in the creation of the Nye Committee, formed in 1934 to investigate the attempts of munitions manufacturers to involve the United States in World War I.[5]

With the ascendance of Hitler, Mussolini, and the Japanese militarists, faith in world peace began to wane. Membership in peace groups dwindled and only the WILPF survived.[6] The idea that women had a unique competence and responsibility for peacemaking, D'Ann Campbell asserts, had lost its force. "By 1940 (and probably earlier)," Campbell writes in an original and informative study of women's roles in World War II, "the special link between morality and gender roles had dissolved. . . . No women peace leaders of the stature of Jane Addams or Emily Balch emerged, nor did anything resembling the large peace movement of the 1920s. . . . The central moral issues of the war were not specifically linked to gender."[7]

Dilling was hardly a Jane Addams, to be sure, but her movement dwarfed the elitist feminine peace movement of the 1920s. Moreover, the perception of a relationship between morality and gender roles had not faded with the passing of Addams and her allies. Again, to the millions of far-right women who agitated against World War II, gender issues, especially maternalism, were essential to their case. Neither men nor women, they believed, could question the mothers' gender-influenced morality.[8]

During the early years of the Cold War, women resumed their involvement in leftist antiwar campaigns. The WILPF continued its work, even though it was unpopular in the age of McCarthyism. In the 1960s, the Vietnam conflict became the chief focus of the women's peace movement, which welcomed the Voice of Women, Women Strike for Peace, and Another Mother for Peace, the last an organization that emphasized maternalism as an argument against war. Rankin lent her name to the Jeannette Rankin Brigade, a coalition of women who marched on Washington in 1968, calling for an end to the Vietnam War.[9]

In the next two decades, feminists kept conflating war and sexism. Women's antiwar organizations, like the feminist movement, remained largely White and middle-class. Among groups that formed in the 1980s were Women Against Military Madness and the peace encampment movement, which had a base at Seneca Falls, New York, birthplace of the women's rights movement. WILPF celebrated its seventy-fifth anniversary in 1990, yet in 1991, Women Strike for Peace dissolved, having lost much of its impetus with the American withdrawal from Vietnam and the end of the Cold War. Women turned their attention from the peace movement and toward other issues.[10]

The question of women and war nevertheless persisted. Some feminists continued to argue that only the demise of patriarchy would bring the dawn of lasting peace, and war still was equated with male violence against women. The power to make war was considered the ultimate male power and therefore the most potent weapon in the arsenal of men who oppressed women.[11] "Imperialist actions do seem to me, more and more clearly, to be patriarchical acts, acts of rape," feminist peace activist Barbara Demming writes.[12] Another argument was that women suffer more than did men from war. Josephine Donovan, for example, writes that "future studies on 'wartime women' may well find that women's fortunes rise and fall in inverse proportion to the degree of militarism in society, and that there is a correlation between denigration of women and glorification of war."[13]

Other feminists brand such analysis as obsolete. Jean Bethke Elshtain notes the ironies of growing up in a family in which a little girl wanted a gun and a brother did not; in which another brother liked to hunt but detested war; in which the father would never kill a deer.[14] Author of the thorough and penetrating study *Women and War*, she argues that "the old myths [of men as warriors and women as peacemakers]—flattering to both men and women—will not do. They are defied by the reality of female bellicosity and sacrificial male love, and undermined by ambiguous issues—from the role of women in combat, to the moral imperatives of just wars."[15] Elshtain implies that blaming war on men is a form of scapegoating, and that there is no factual basis for believing that individual acts of violence (usually committed by men) and war have common origins. Countries have geopolitical reasons for going to war, whose stakes are not simply the deaths of individuals but national survival. No nation, not even a morally depraved nation such as Nazi Germany, wages war merely to wreak gratuitous violence.[16]

The proposition that women's wartime misery exceeds men's is debatable as well. At a scholarly conference several years ago, after delivering a paper on women who opposed war, I was moved by a conversation with a woman who told me her fiancé had been killed in World War II. I brooded about our conversation for some time because her pain was genuine and enduring. After his death, however, she resumed her life, married, had children, earned a Ph.D., and became a professor of history. Her fiancé's pain ended once he died and entered heaven (if one believes in a glorious afterlife), although he was denied the opportunity to spend life with his beloved. Is it fair to say her suffering was greater than his?[17]

Equally questionable is the idea that men wage war because it feeds their egos or proves their manhood. The aim of the good soldier is to preserve his nation, much as the good mother seeks to preserve her offspring. When men go to war, they do so reluctantly and few enjoy killing, especially when it accompanies the risk of being killed. Elshtain points out that fear of killing, rather than fear of being killed, was the most common cause of battle failure among American troops in World War II. [18] "Indeed, history suggests that men have an even more ambivalent reaction to the fighting expected of them than women do to the mothering for which they are said to be 'naturally suited,'" Sara Ruddick writes.[19]

As for the generalization that females are inherently pacifist, it, too, is dubious. Women realize some wars are just, offering the only alternatives to tyranny, and must be waged. World War II, fought to save the planet from a totalitarian menace, was a just war, won with the help of American women. "Most women, like most men, believe that violence must be met by violence and that the virtues of a cause justify the horror done in its name," Ruddick states.[20] Some feminists insist women have the right to serve as combat soldiers. The National Organization for Women supported a legal challenge to all-male draft registration in 1981, on the grounds that if women are first-class citizens, they must be conscripted. The challenge failed, but women did not abandon the armed forces. Today the United States has the largest percentage of women in the military (ten percent) of any major industrialized nation, raising the possibility that they will change the military more from within than from outside.[21]

The use of maternal arguments to justify opposition to war further divides contemporary feminists. Elshtain, who says there is a feminist animus against maternal voices, believes it is sentimental even to pose the question of whether women can prevent wars by refusing to offer their sons as cannon fodder.[22] Gerda Lerner and Andrea Dworkin reject the concept of maternal thinking. Lerner writes, "Maternalist theory is built upon the acceptance of biological sex differences as a given." Dworkin thinks praise of motherhood is an insult to women, a tool men use to keep women in line: "Precisely because she is good, she is unfit to do the same things [as men]."[23] Shulamith Firestone argues that biological motherhood lay at the heart of women's oppression and rejects the claim that motherhood endows women with special wisdom. Nancy Chodorow strongly contests the idea that mothering is instinctive. "Politically, then, the right not to become a mother was central to feminist analysis," Eisenstein summarizes.[24]

But some modern feminists share the belief that motherhood has a bearing on peacemaking. Carol Gilligan says thinking comes from experience, and the experience of raising children provides lessons in conflict resolution. Describing her talks and interviews with mothers in the course of her research, Gilligan is struck by their "wish not to hurt others and the hope that in morality lies a way of solving conflicts so that no one will be hurt."[25] Harriet Hyman Alonso, in a 1993 work, traces the history of female pacifism from the 1910s to the 1990s and concludes, "Certainly the emphasis on the role of women as peacemakers plays an important role in the [women's peace] movement: motherhood is the one continuous theme running through every organization represented in this book and through every historical work covered."[26]

The peace-oriented perspective of mothers is no panacea for a violent world, Gilligan counsels, although it could help by producing innovative diplomacy that forestalls war. "Some maternal characteristics are especially appropriate to peacemaking: resiliency, caring, tolerance of ambiguity and ambivalence, preservative love, the knowledge of the value and the vulnerability of human life."[27] Dramatizing the depth of a mother's love, Gilligan quotes a Victorian poem:

> There was a young man loved a maid
> who taunted him. "Are you afraid,"
> She asked, "to bring me today
> Your mother's head upon a tray?"
> He went and slew his mother dead,
> Tore from her breast her heart so red,
> Then toward his lady love fell in all his haste.
> As the heart rolled on the ground
> It gave forth a plaintive sound.
> And it spoke in accents mild:
> "Did you hurt yourself, my child?"[28]

The far-right women of the 1930s would have understood the poet completely, even though their personal lives marked them as questionable nurturers and their bigotry tainted their maternal antiwar position. Their capacity for hate did not mean they were incapable of love, or that their arguments were hypocritical or irrelevant. People of their intensity might well feel different emotions with comparable fervor; hatemongers often are superpatriots. The greater the attachment to one's group, be it family or nation, the more hostile one is likely to be toward anything that imperils it, Gordon Allport shows. "One must first overestimate the things one loves before one can underestimate their contraries," he writes. "Fences are built primarily for the protection of what we cherish."[29]

Historians have built fences that keep us from comprehending the far right, and the mothers' story reminds them to pay closer attention to right-wing women. Generally, the right baffles left-learning scholars, who dislike it and cannot understand its attraction to reasonable persons. Those who are drawn to the right are marginalized and works on them are relegated to an intellectual ghetto, writes Ribuffo (who stands out among liberal historians for his fair and honest treatment of the right).[30]

Women of the right seem especially vexing. Some writers find it inconceivable that women could willingly embrace Schlafly's New Christian Right, let alone Dilling's extremist movement. Women who support bastions of patriarchy, including conservatism, Christianity, the nuclear family, and conventional morality, are portrayed as dupes of males, ignoramuses, charlatans, or betrayers of the true interests of women. Lerner states, "Women have for millennia participated in the process of their own subordination because they have been psychologically shaped so as to internalize the idea of their own inferiority." Eisenstein argues that since women have been brainwashed to believe they need men to protect them, they exchange their freedom for the security of a police state. And Dworkin maintains that "Moralism is the moral sphere designated to women, who are supposed to learn the rules of their own, proper, circumscribed behavior by rote." Women who oppose feminism are particularly reprehensible, in Dworkin's eyes. "Antifeminism is a direct expression of misogyny; it is the political defense of woman hating."[31]

But the premise that women cannot willingly join the right is mistaken, as wrong as the idea that because the right is monolithic, without variations, the reactionary mothers can be likened to conservatives. To believe that rightist women lack free will is to imply that women cannot have priorities that differ from those of liberalism; cannot think for themselves, a notion that demeans all women; and cannot harbor prejudices or a desire for power, as can men. These suppositions have no basis in reality. The experience of decades confounds expectations that women will vote consistently as a bloc for liberal measures. If men did not vote as a bloc, it was unrealistic to expect women to do so. It was unrealistic to expect women to unite in a single movement—even to expect feminists to agree on goals and strategies when they are divided by class, race, religion, occupation, age, and culture. (Consider, for instance, that many poor women and minority women do not mesh with feminism, considering it unresponsive to their needs.)

As we have seen, women have gravitated to nonfeminist groups such as the DAR and the Ku Klux Klan, besides the mothers' movement. "The success of these organizations, however fleeting, demands that historians re-examine women's attraction to conservative and right-wing causes," Kari Frederickson observes.[32] This attraction remained strong for women of the 1960s and 1970s who rejected feminism. Chafe explains, "To women who had spent a lifetime devoting themselves to the culturally sanctioned roles of homemaker and helpmate, the feminist charge that women had been en-slaved frequently appeared as a direct attack on their own personal experi-ence. Such women did not believe that they had wasted their lives or had been duped by malevolent husbands. Many enjoyed the nurturant and sup-portive roles of wife and mother."[33]

Nor were the mothers dupes of men. They sincerely adhered to the anti-Semitism, racism, Nazism, and conspiracy theories they repeated incessantly. They were as secure in these beliefs as their enemies, Jews, were secure in knowing Jesus was not the messiah.[34] Laura McEnaney, one of the few femi-nist historians who has studied the far right women of the 1930s, loathes the mothers for their views yet finds no evidence they were insincere or male puppets. Stasia Von Zwisler, another feminist and author of the only study of Dilling, discovers nothing that indicates Dilling was insincere. Zwisler came to a grudging admiration of Dilling's tenacity, even though she deplores Dill-ing's opinions.[35] Perhaps the mothers' venomous prejudice, which distin-guishes them from most of the figures who preceded and followed them on the right, defies understanding because it is so disturbing. We should remem-ber, however, that human behavior runs the gamut from the bizarre to the rational.

Dworkin believes men of the New Christian Right use religion to keep women subservient, to keep them faithful to Jesus, "the one male to whom one can submit absolutely,"[36] so she might answer that the mothers' piety was a product of scheming men. True believers ready to die for God and Jesus, the mothers would have found this suggestion insulting. Willingly they em-braced Christianity, a source of comfort and purpose. Male bigots, also believ-ing in "the one male to whom one can submit absolutely," likewise found sustenance in Christianity. Religion is not an exclusively negative force, con-trary to Dworkin's assertion. It can be used for worthy ends, including spiri-tual nourishment, or wickedness, including persecution of nonbelievers.[37]

About anti-Semitic women, Dworkin might say they hate men instead of Jews but are manipulated by men to displace their enmity onto Jews. "Women cling to irrational hatreds, focused primarily on the unfamiliar, so that they will not murder their fathers, husbands, sons, brothers, lovers, the men with whom they are intimate, those who hurt them and cause them grief," she writes.[38] Dworkin presents no evidence for her theory, whose logical conclusions lead to blind alleys. There is nothing in her analysis to account for left-wing anti-Semitism. More seriously, how can she explain male anti-Semites? Her logic would imply that male anti-Semites hate women but are manipulated by women to project their hatred onto Jews. As for homosexual anti-Semites, Dworkin's thought points in two directions. Perhaps it is impossible in her mind for homosexuals to be anti-Semites if they hate neither men nor women. On the other hand, her reasoning might lead us to declare that homosexual anti-Semites hate men and women yet direct that hatred against Jews. That still leaves the question of who manipulates them.[39]

Finally, Dworkin and others who attribute bad faith to ideological opposites distort reality, as did the far-right women who considered history an endless series of conspiracies. If Dworkin thinks conservatism is a male conspiracy to enslave women, presumably it would be in the interest of all men to be conservatives. How, then, can she account for moderate or liberal males?

Historians' analysis of the right should be more sophisticated. As a Jew, a supporter of the New Deal and Democratic presidential candidates, the husband of a feminist theologian, and the father of two daughters, I have far more sympathy for feminists than opponents of feminism, and no sympathy at all for the far right. I have devoted much of my academic career to exposing bigots and anti-Semites. Still, the simplistic writing about the right troubles me. We are rapidly approaching the point at which scholarship becomes propaganda, ceases to liberate the spirit of human individuality, and simply replaces old dogmas with new ones.[40]

As history deserves better from those who write it, womanhood and maternalism deserve better than the mothers' movement. Understandably frustrated with a political system that ignored their voices, the mothers pursued objectives and tactics that contradicted their maternal values and reinforced the stereotype that women were hysterical. Their contention that they had to be strident to overcome intransigent rulers was but a variation on the theme that "the devil made me do it."

Those who believe additional knowledge inevitably results in superior wisdom, however, are likely to be humbled by the tides of history. If history teaches anything, it teaches humility. It teaches that victory and defeat can be ephemeral and that every day we must fight the furies within ourselves—furies that overcame the mothers.

═══ EPILOGUE ═══

"Can We All Get Along?"

Pleading for an end to riots that broke out around the nation in 1992, riots triggered by the acquittal of four White Los Angeles policemen tried for beating him, Rodney King, a Black man, asked a question with a simple answer but complex ramifications. "People, I just want to say . . . can we all get along?" King said, choking back tears. "Can we get along? . . . We've just got to, just got to. We're all stuck here for a while. Let's try to work it out. Let's try to work it out."[1] The answer to King's question is that we often have trouble getting along because we want some of the same things, for which we must compete, as well as different things. We are divided by conflict, prejudices, and suspicions. Maybe bigotry is as inevitable as death and taxes.

If there were an ideal way to eliminate hate, it would be to ensure no one would lack love or experience anxiety and frustration, to guarantee respect, opportunity, and security for all. In the real world, these promises cannot be kept, and attempts to create this utopia might well result in an Orwellian nightmare in which Big Brother rules over us to maintain a veneer of happiness. Believing that we can better get along if we understand the sources of bigotry, however, I would like to offer some observations from my research and writing about racist, anti-Semitic leaders of the far right.[2]

Extreme bigots are not simply victims of ignorance, as the examples of Dilling and Smith show. Dilling studied the Jewish religion obsessively, reading an entire set of the Talmud in English; Smith read the works of his enemies, including Jews.[3] But nothing they learned about Judaism dispelled their anti-Semitism. Viewing the world through a glass darkly, bigots are not open to enlightenment from education about adversaries. New information only strengthens their prejudices.

Nor is extreme bigotry a result of economic deprivation, for social forces tend to accentuate bigotry instead of producing it. Prejudice waxes during times of hardship and wanes during times of prosperity.[4] Hard-core bigots endure because the more extreme the prejudice, the less important are external factors. (This applies to individuals as opposed to movements, which are partly shaped by social forces.) Thus the mothers' followers abandoned their movement after the war, whereas the leaders continued to crusade.[5]

To fathom fervent racists and anti-Semites, we must comprehend the role of anxiety. Everyone has anxieties, although stable, happy, fulfilled people can deal with their fears constructively and are unlikely to become bigots. Among bigots, anxiety is obsessive and unrealistic, giving rise to a need for scapegoating and temperament that compels them to act upon their prejudice. Bigots cling to their biases tenaciously, regardless of the opposition, because dogmas provide security.[6] The mothers' leaders, riven by insecurities, were not comforted or satisfied by conventional politics, economic independence, or raising a family. In their minds, their differences with their adversaries, whether economic, political, or theological, threatened their serenity, their security, their identities.

The idea that prejudice is due to anxiety instead of ignorance was borne out in the Germany of the 1930s, the most sophisticated nation in Europe, a land rich in learning, art, culture, philosophy, and technology. Germans suffered from hyperinflation, economic decline, unstable governments, the psychological wounds left by defeat in World War I, and the subsequent hard peace. Hitler's career coincided with the growth of these tensions. He offered scapegoats, revenge, nationalism, racial superiority, and prowess at arms— pablums for a nervous people.[7]

The United States, too, was troubled by economic dislocation and attendant self-doubt, and like Germany the nation rallied under a charismatic leader whose most effective weapon against the emergencies was psychology. Nevertheless, the United States did not resort to radical doctrines such as Hitler's. The spiritual crisis in Germany was far more dangerous, far more conducive to a dictator, than the depression that Americans faced. FDR was often devious and overbearing, but he was no dictator, his critics notwithstanding, and he forestalled radicalism by championing liberal democracy.

Not long after the challenges of the Great Depression and World War II, the United States experienced anxieties that fed prejudices. First came the Cold War. Like individuals, nations define themselves in relation to their enemies: the creators of the mothers' movement sensed they were at risk because of Jews and communists; the United States believed it was jeopardized by the Soviet Union. One superpower could not feel secure while the other existed, even if the opposition did not resort to arms. What began with genuine disagreements, economic and moral, grew into obsessions. Ideological differences, threatening the core values of people and countries, can be subdued but not eliminated by diplomacy, hence they are more difficult to reconcile than economic or political divisions.[8]

Then there was the civil rights movement that attacked southern segregation in the 1950s and 1960s. Growing into adulthood as a White in Louisiana during those decades, I was aware of Whites' fears about this movement. To many of the people I knew, integration would lead to promiscuous mis-cegenation and destroy civilization, a foreboding that was eased long before Cold War worries were soothed. Once we realized, however slowly, that civil rights laws would not bring cultural destruction, desegregation was accepted as a fact of life and prejudice against Blacks declined. Among later genera-tions of Whites, apprehension over interracial sex never disappeared, but it was less stressful.[9] Herein lay the key to eradicating prejudice: dissipating people's anxieties about those who happen to be different. Alas, there is no quick, simple way to this goal.

Exhortations in favor of tolerance, for instance, are not irrelevant to cam-paigns for social justice, such as the civil rights movement, yet among ex-treme bigots these efforts will probably harden hatreds, just as learning about Jews merely exacerbated Dilling's and Smith's anti-Semitism. It follows that courses on cultural diversity, a remedy that became popular in the 1980s and 1990s, will raise unrealistic expectations that might lead to disappointment and backlash. We cannot teach tolerance in schools as we teach driver educa-tion because prejudice is based on complex attitudes and indoctrination. Only the mildly prejudiced are likely to be influenced by these courses, and if the classes could shape attitudes easily, students would be sufficiently gull-ible to change their minds again when confronted by contrary propaganda. Moreover, if classes on diversity are poorly taught or used to assert cultural chauvinism, students will resent them. It is simpler to win a revolution by arms than by intellectual or ethical conversion, to my mind.

Protest demonstrations also will be ineffective in converting bigots to the cause of tolerance. Showing the community stands against the haters, the demonstrations can be useful in unifying advocates of tolerance and in deter-ring acts of hatred. We do not have to reform bigots to minimize the damage from their deeds. But we should recognize the limits and possible liabilities of militant defiance of bigots. This strategy, which might be effective against less determined bigots, could encourage the fanatical by throwing a gauntlet at them.[10]

Tolerance is an attitude that evolves over a lifetime, an evolution that de-pends greatly on one's sense of security and on reinforcement from families, friends, peers and religious institutions (schools, government, and the media have a limited impact). Time, patience, and persistence are required in this cultivation. We must start anew with each birth. A few years of neglect and the weeds will take over the garden.

Whatever our shortcomings, we should acknowledge that we have made considerable progress in fighting prejudice and discrimination, and that weeds have not overrun the American garden. Generalizations such as "The

United States is a racist nation" are meaningless without context. Is there a major nation with comparable diversity that is or has been less prejudiced? With regard to anti-Semitism, to take but one case, I believe that although it will not disappear, it must be seen in a comparative perspective. Leonard Dinnerstein, author of a comprehensive study of anti-Semitism in this nation, remarks that "in no Christian country has anti-Semitism been weaker than it has been in the United States. . . . There never have been pogroms in America; there never have been any federal laws curtailing Jewish opportunities in America."[11] This balanced outlook reminds us that groups of the mothers' stripe are fortunately atypical. The peace-loving and the tolerant seem to outnumber the warmongers and bigots, even in the twentieth-century United States, where the problem of prejudice has no definitive solutions.

It is difficult to realize the magnificent ideal of tolerance. Perhaps the things that are difficult are the things that we should strive hardest to accomplish.

≡ NOTES ≡

Chapter One

1. Among the accounts describing the contributions and problems of women in wartime are Karen Anderson, *Wartime Women: Sex Roles, Family Relations, and the Status of Women During World War II* (Westport, Conn.: Greenwood Press, 1981); Susan Hartmann, *The Home Front and Beyond: American Women in the 1940s* (Boston: Twayne Publishers, 1982); Alice Kessler-Harris, *Out to Work: A History of Wage-Earning Women in the United States* (New York: Oxford University Press, 1982), 273–99; Ruth Milkman, *Gender at Work: The Dynamics of Job Segregation by Sex During World War II* (Urbana: University of Illinois Press, 1987); and Doris Weatherford, *American Women and World War II* (New York: Facts on File, 1990). Personal perspectives are provided by Judy Barrett Litoff and David C. Smith, *Since You Went Away: World War II Letters From American Women on the Home Front* (New York: Oxford University Press, 1991).

2. Harriet Hyman Alonso, *Peace as a Women's Issue: A History of the U.S. Movement for World Peace and Women's Rights* (Syracuse, N.Y.: Syracuse University Press, 1993) traces the involvement of women in peace activities since the nineteenth century, emphasizing the use of maternal arguments. She does not include any women's peace movements of the right and admires her subjects, who were quite unlike the mothers I describe. Little of the literature on women's peace activists is critical of its subjects. For another example, see Temma Kaplan, "Female Consciousness and Collective Action: The Case of Barcelona, 1910–1918," *Signs* 7 (spring 1982), 54–66.

3. My estimate is a composite from articles in the *Chicago Tribune,* the Hearst papers, the *New York Times,* and Midwestern papers that did not sympathize with the movement yet covered it in detail, such as the *Detroit Free Press* and the *St. Louis Post-Dispatch.* Additional information was gleaned from reports of meetings compiled by investigators from the American Jewish Committee, the Anti-Defamation League of B'nai B'rith, and investigative reporters. I do not accept the membership figures of the leaders of the movement at face value. I know of no surviving membership lists. Some NLMA chapters did not keep detailed records.

Unfortunately, a number of patriotic groups had names similar to ultraright groups and some women joined subversive organizations by mistake. The National Blue Star Mothers, for example, were confused with the patriotic Blue Star Mothers. See Patricia Lochridge, "The Mother Racket," *Woman's Home Companion* 71 (July 1944), 20–1, 71–4; E. A. Piller, *Time Bomb* (New York: Arco Publishing Company, 1945), 114; and Memorandum on Mothers' Groups, File: (hereafter F) Mothers' Groups, American Jewish Committee (hereafter AJC), New York City.

4. For profiles of three leaders, see Glen Jeansonne, "Furies: Women Isolationists in the Era of FDR," *Journal of History and Politics* 8 (1990), 67–96. The movement is

described in John Roy Carlson (pseudonym for Avedis Derounian) *Under Cover* (New York: E. P. Dutton and Company, 1943), and *The Plotters* (New York: E. P. Dutton and Company, 1946); Nathaniel Weyl, *Treason: The Story of Disloyalty and Betrayal in American History* (Washington, D.C.: Public Affairs Press, 1950); Lochridge; and Russell Whelan and Thomas M. Johnson, "The Menace of the 'Mothers'," *Liberty* (July 26, 1944), 18–9, 72–3. Also see Janet Saltzman Chafetz and Anthony Dworkin, *Female Revolt: Women's Movements in Worldwide and Historical Perspective* (Totowa, N.J.: Littlefield, Adams, and Company, 1986), 73–7; McEnaney, "Defending the Family Altar," 49; Jeansonne, *Gerald L. K. Smith*, 12; McEnaney, "He-Men and Christian Mothers," 49; Wayne S. Cole, *America First: The Battle Against Intervention, 1940–1941* (Madison: University of Wisconsin Press, 1953), 6–8; Lillian Greenwald, "Fascism in America: The Distaff Side," *Contemporary Jewish Record* (1941), 616–24; and Ribuffo, *The Old Christian Right*, 178–215.

5. Cole, *Roosevelt and the Isolationists, 1932–1945* (Lincoln: University of Nebraska Press, 1983); Cole, *America First*; Henry Hoke, *It's a Secret* (New York: Reynal and Hitchcock, 1946), 181. Cole's works, a major contribution, are the most detailed treatments of the whole isolationist movement.

6. Roosevelt's frustration and caution in the face of opposition to his foreign policies are described in James MacGregor Burns, *Roosevelt: The Soldier of Freedom, 1940–1945* (New York: Harcourt Brace Jovanovich, Inc., 1970); Robert Dallek, *Franklin Roosevelt and American Foreign Policy, 1931–1945* (New York: Oxford University Press, 1979); Kenneth S. Davis, *FDR: Into the Storm, 1937–1940* (New York: Random House, 1993); and Cole, *Roosevelt and the Isolationists*. Jeansonne, *Gerald L. K. Smith*; and Alan Brinkley, *Voices of Protest: Huey Long, Father Coughlin and the Great Depression* (New York: Vintage Books, 1983), conclude that such ultraright critics as Smith and Coughlin were annoyances rather than major barriers to Roosevelt's foreign policies. Ribuffo, *The Old Christian Right*, argues that FDR's fears of his critics on the far right were excessive. Charles Dexter, "Wreckers of American Morale," *Magazine Digest* 24:6 (June 1942), 37–44, is an excellent summary of the anti-Roosevelt, antiwar groups. The above interpretations stress that although the extreme isolationists' power lay more in the perceptions of their opponents than in tangible threats, these perceptions, as well as the isolationists' potential to inflame the masses, were by no means inconsequential. No realistic formulation of foreign policy could have excluded consideration of their potential as a mass movement.

7. Hoke, *It's a Secret*, 181.

8. William Chafe, *Women and Equality: Changing Patterns in American Culture* (New York: Oxford University Press, 1977), 8, 115–43; Robyn Muncy, *Creating a Female Dominion in American Reform, 1890–1935* (New York: Oxford University Press, 1991); and Robert L. Daniel, *American Women in the Twentieth Century: The Festival of Life* (New York: Harcourt Brace Jovanovich Publishers, 1987), 4–35. Chafetz and Dworkin, *Female Revolt*, is especially useful in placing the work of women reformers, and the role of women in broad reform movements, in a context that is limited neither to the United States nor to the twentieth century. See especially 3–4 for an analysis of the role of religion as a vehicle for women reformers.

9. Nancy F. Cott, *The Grounding of Modern Feminism* (New Haven: Yale University Press, 1987), 3, 6–7, 16–8.

10. Chafetz and Dworkin, *Female Revolt*, 21–7; Chafe, *Women and Equality*, 24–9.

11. Chafe discusses the American antipathy to group identity in *The Paradox of Change: American Women in the 20th Century* (New York: Oxford University Press, 1991), xi, 203. Chafetz and Dworkin discuss the frustration of women who have been expected to suppress their gender identity and interests in service to reform movements. See Chafetz and Dworkin, *Female Revolt*, 39–45.

12. Patriarchy is discussed in Gerda Lerner, *The Creation of Patriarchy* (New York: Oxford University Press, 1986); Simone de Beauvoir, *The Second Sex* (New York: Random House, 1974); Kate Millet, *Sexual Politics* (Garden City, N.Y.: Doubleday, 1970); and Hester Eisenstein, *Contemporary Feminist Thought* (Boston: G. K. Hall and Co., 1983). I use the work "patriarchy" to denote a society based on male-dominated families and organized around male leadership. For a discussion of uses of the term, see Linda Gordon and Allen Hunter, "Sex, Family and the New Right: Anti-Feminism as a Political Force," *Radical America* 11–2 (November 1977–February 1978), 9, 25; and Rosalind Pollack Petchesky, "AntiAbortion, AntiFeminism, and the Rise of the New Right," *Feminist Studies* 7 (summer 1981), 210. Also see Cott, *The Grounding of Modern Feminism*, 276.

13. Chafe, *Women and Equality*, 171.

14. For the contrasts between the woman movement and feminism, see Cott, *The Grounding of Modern Feminism*, 3, 5, 15, 36, 37, 42, 96–7, 151, 277.

15. Ibid., 4–6.

16. Gordon is quoted in Cott, "What's in a Name? The Limits of 'Social Feminism': or, Expanding the Vocabulary of Women's History," *Journal of American History* 76 (December 1989), 76. See also Claire Goldberg Moses, "Debating the Present, Writing the Past: 'Feminism' in French History and Historiography," *Radical History Review* 52 (winter 1992), 79–94.

17. Sara Ruddick, *Maternal Thinking: Toward a Politics of Peace* (Boston: Beacon Press, 1989), 234–5.

18. Cott, *The Grounding of Modern Feminism*, 36, 46.

19. Chafe, *The Paradox of Change*, viii–ix; Cott, *The Grounding of Modern Feminism*, 278–82.

20. Eisenstein, *Contemporary Feminist Thought*, xvi.

Perhaps Kari Frederickson is correct in arguing that accepted definitions of feminism are too narrow, and that with more scholarship on right-wing women, a more flexible and inclusive definition will emerge, one the mothers would fit. To define the mothers as feminists, however, would require a permutation of the historic identity of feminism with the left. Defined so broadly, feminism would lose its focus and usefulness as an analytical tool. See Frederickson, "Voices on the Right: Cathrine Curtis and the Women Against World War II," unpublished paper, December 1991, 26. In "Furies: Women Isolationists in the Era of FDR," *Journal of History and Politics*, 8 (1990), 67–96, I discuss three of the more prominent leaders, Dilling, Van Hyning, and Waters. Contemporary feminists such as Andrea Dworkin and Rebecca Klatch, who have studied conservative women in the period since the 1970s, find the beliefs of such women incompatible with feminism. See Dworkin, *Right-Wing Women* (New York: G. P. Putnam's Sons, 1983); and Klatch, *Women of the New Right* (Philadelphia: Temple University Press, 1987).

Jean Bethke Elshtain observes that "Feminism is destined to remain what it has always been; an essentially contested concept, whose meaning admits of no final and definitive resolution." Elshtain makes this point in a joint review of a book by Gloria Steinem, who celebrates the success of feminism, and a book by Christina Hoff Sommers, who charges that feminism has betrayed women. Sommers, Steinem, and Elshtain, all longtime feminists, differ drastically. See Elshtain, "Sic Transit Gloria," *The New Republic* (July 11, 1994), 36.

21. Cott, *The Grounding of Modern Feminism,* 35.

22. Susan Ware, *American Women in the 1930s: Holding Their Own* (Boston: Twayne Publishers, 1982), 87.

23. Chafe, *The Paradox of Change,* 20–5.

24. Ware, *American Women in the 1930s,* 88.

25. Cott, *The Grounding of Modern Feminism,* 264. Also see Hester Eisenstein, xi–xiii; and Chafe, *The Paradox of Change,* vii–x. For an example of the degree to which the issue of gender differences continues to divide feminists, see Alan Wolfe, "The Gender Question," *The New Republic* (June 6, 1994), 27–34. Wolfe's essay examines three books that view the question of gender differences from distinct perspectives: Sandra Lipsitz–Ben, *The Lenses of Gender: Debate on Sexual Inequality* (New Haven: Yale University Press, 1994); Helen Haste, *The Sexual Metaphor* (Cambridge, Mass.: Harvard University Press, 1994); and Judith Lorber, *Paradoxes of Gender* (New Haven: Yale University Press, 1994).

26. Ibid., 255–57; Alonso, *Peace as a Women's Issue;* Kathleen M. Blee, *Women of the Klan: Racism and Gender in the 1920s* (Berkeley: University of California Press, 1991); Nancy MacLean, *Behind the Mask of Chivalry: The Making of the Second Ku Klux Klan* (New York: Oxford University Press, 1994); Frederickson, 25.

27. Cott, *The Grounding of Modern Feminism,* 260.

28. Ibid., 255–7; Jeansonne, *Gerald L. K. Smith,* chapters 4 and 5; McEnaney, "He-Men and Christian Mothers," 47–57.

29. Chafe, *The Paradox of Change,* viii–xi, 24–5, 39–44, 53–5; McEnaney, "Defending the Family Altar," 63, 76, 81–92; Cott, *The Grounding of Modern Feminism,* 17–30; McEnaney, "He-Men and Christian Women," 50; Alonso; Ruddick, 115; Stasia Von Zwisler, "Elizabeth Dilling and the Rose-Colored Spy Glass," M.A. thesis, University of Wisconsin—Milwaukee, 1986.

30. Chafetz and Dworkin, *Female Revolt,* 193.

31. Jeansonne, "Furies," 67–96; Dworkin, *Right-Wing Women;* Klatch, *Women of the New Right;* Chafetz and Dworkin, *Female Revolt,* 49; Myra Marx Ferree and Beth B. Hess, *Controversy and Coalition: The New Feminist Movement* (Boston: Twayne Publishers, 1985), 27–8.

32. Chafetz and Dworkin, *Female Revolt,* 65–6; Ferree and Hess, 27–8; McEnaney, "Defending the Family Altar," 76; Alonso, 11. Lyrl Clark Van Hyning was the only major leader of the mothers' movement to recruit women to run for office. But when Agnes Waters sought to become the first woman president in 1944 and requested Van Hyning's endorsement, Van Hyning rejected Waters and supported Republican nominee Thomas E. Dewey. See chapter 7 for a discussion of Van Hyning and her relationship with Waters.

33. Chafetz and Dworkin, 65–6; Eisentstein, 48; Betty A. Reardon, *Sexism and the War System* (New York: Teachers College, Columbia University, 1985), 21.

34. Ware, *American Women in the 1930s,* 171–2. On Eleanor Roosevelt's encouragement to women to enter politics, see Roosevelt, "Women in Politics," *Good House-*

keeping 110 (March 1940), 45. For an excellent account of the formative years of Eleanor Roosevelt, see Blanche Wiesen Cook, *Eleanor Roosevelt,* Vol. I, *1884–1933* (New York: Viking, 1992).

Of all the ultraright women leaders, Dilling was the most critical of Eleanor Roosevelt. In *The Roosevelt Red Record and Its Background* (Chicago: self-published, 1936), Dilling devoted more space to criticizing Eleanor Roosevelt than she devoted to denouncing Franklin Roosevelt. Among her charges were that Eleanor entertained prostitutes, fraternized with Blacks, joined communist organizations, neglected her children, dominated her weak husband, and associated with Jews. Perhaps there was no better litmus test of a woman's political ideology than a woman's opinion of Eleanor Roosevelt.

35. See, for example, Daniel Bell, ed. *The Radical Right: The New American Right Expanded and Updated* (Garden City, N.Y.: Doubleday and Company, 1963); David H. Bennett, *The Party of Fear: From Nativist Movements to the New Right in American History* (Chapel Hill: The University of North Carolina Press, 1988); Richard Hofstatder, *The Paranoid Style in American Politics and Other Essays* (New York: Vintage Books, 1967); Jeansonne, *Gerald L. K. Smith;* Seymour Martin Lipset and Earl Raab, *The Politics of Unreason: Right-Wing Extremism in America, 1790–1977,* 2nd ed. (Chicago: University of Chicago Press, 1978); and Ribuffo, *the Old Christian Right.*

There has been little work on the relationship of women and the right, particularly the far right. The studies by Blee and MacLean are useful, yet women were chiefly followers rather than leaders in the gender-integrated movements these scholars describe. There is more on the connection of women to the New Right of the 1970s and 1980s than to the Old Right of the 1930s and 1940s. Studies that link the questions of gender and the right include Pamela Johnson Conover and Virginia Gray, *Feminism and the New Right: Conflict Over the American Family* (New York: Praeger, 1983); Gordon and Hunter, "Sex, Family and the New Right"; and Petchesky, "Anti-Abortion, AntiFeminism, and the Rise of the New Right." On Phyllis Schlafly, see Carol Felsenthal, *The Sweetheart of the Silent Majority: The Biography of Phyllis Schlafly* (Garden City, N.Y.: Doubleday, 1981). I discuss Schlafly briefly in chapter 12 on the postwar mothers' movement. In the chapter, I also discuss Dilling's bitter opposition to Barry Goldwater, whom Schlafly supported.

36. Chafetz and Dworkin believe urbanization and dislocation concentrate people with similar life experiences and expectations, enabling a social movement to emerge. See Chafetz and Dworkin, *Female Revolt,* 69. It is significant, then, that the mothers' movement was largely urban. Rural women might have been even more threatened by change but lacked the infrastructure and numbers to organize. The urban media, particularly the Hearst press and the *Chicago Tribune,* played a crucial role in incubating the movement with favorable publicity.

Jill Conway emphasizes that some women who participate in social movements are motivated by their own needs as much as by the needs of those they intend to help. Her argument appears applicable to many of the mothers' leaders. See Conway, "Women Reformers and the American Culture, 1870–1930," *Journal of Social History* 5 (Winter 1973), 171.

37. McEnaney emphasizes the mothers' fears of changes to gender and family relations, and she stresses that right-wing women wanted to return to simpler, stabler times. See McEnaney, "Defending the Family Altar," 121–2, 136. McEnaney also be-

lieves the ultraright women were threatened by changes in relations between Blacks and Whites, induced by the relocation of war industry workers. See ibid., 117–21.

In *Transformation and Reaction: America, 1921–1945* (New York: HarperCollins, 1994), I argue that the period from the end of World War I to the end of World War II was characterized by rapid change and by resistance to change, and that women were among those most affected by the dynamic tension between transformation and reaction. The greatest traumas were produced by the war itself. See 3–14, 197–232.

Useful accounts of changes in the lives of women during the interwar era include Dorothy M. Brown, *American Women in the 1920s: Setting a Course* (Boston: Twayne, 1987); J. Stanley Lemons, *The Woman Citizen: Social Feminism in the 1920s* (Charlottesville: University of Virginia Press, 1973); Ware, *American Women in the 1930s;* and Ware, *Beyond Suffrage: Women in the New Deal* (Cambridge: Harvard University Press, 1981).

A number of excellent works focus on the social and cultural rebellions particularly as they affected young people. Among these are Paula S. Fass, *The Damned and the Beautiful: American Youth in the 1920s* (New York: Oxford University Press, 1991); Beth L. Bailey, *From Front Porch to Back Seat: Courtship in Twentieth Century America* (Baltimore: The Johns Hopkins University Press, 1988); and Virginia Scharf, *Taking the Wheel: Women and the Coming of the Motor Age* (New York: Free Press, 1991).

D'Ann Campbell, *Women at War with America: Private Lives in a Patriotic Era* (Cambridge: Harvard University Press, 1984), emphasizes the stress placed upon women by the war. See especially 8–15, 170–9, and 190–208.

Chafe describes how the women's liberation movement of the 1960s aroused the anxieties of traditionalists. "Perhaps the most profound obstacle was the extent to which the movement threatened the sense of identity millions of people had derived from the culture and from the primary transmitter of social values, the family." His analysis helps explain the emotional intensity with which ultraright women responded to changes that threatened their values, beliefs, and psychological security. "It seems logical to assume that the more central a social pattern is to the perpetuation of a way of life, the more difficult will be the process of altering that pattern." See Chafe, *Women and Equality,* 132, 171. In *The Paradox of Change,* Chafe argues that changes in American society and politics are more likely to receive social approval when the gains and the losses appear marginal rather than fundamental.

38. The role of Christianity in providing focus for the movement of ultraright, isolationist women is the theme of McEnaney's article and thesis. McEnaney notes that Christian motherhood was central to the identity of far-right women isolationists and that their rhetoric and writing were replete with religious metaphors. She argues that the mothers' desire to maintain a White, Christian, patriarchal society based upon the nuclear family led them to demand the infusion of Christian values into government policy. See McEnaney, "Defending the Family Altar," 78.

Women's Voice, Dilling's *Bulletin,* and Smith's *The Cross and the Flag* were sprinkled with references linking Christian faith to patriotism and motherhood. The belief that national strength was dependent upon Christian principles, especially family values, was integral to the ideology of ultraright males such as Smith, as well as to that of ultraright women. Like some of the mothers' leaders, Smith came to politics through religion, incorporating his training as a minister in his patriotic crusades. His propaganda merged Christianity and supernationalistic patriotism. In his declining years

Smith collected bibles, built a seven-story statue of Jesus, the "Christ of the Ozarks," and staged an outdoor Passion Play catering to religiously inspired tourists at Eureka Springs, Arkansas. See Jeansonne, *Gerald L. K. Smith,* particularly chapters 1 and 11.

In *The Old Christian Right,* Ribuffo describes the role of intense religious convictions in shaping the careers of Smith and ultraright contemporaries Gerald B. Winrod and William Dudley Pelley. In his epilogue, "From the 'Radical Right' to the 'New Christian Right,'" Ribuffo discusses the role of religion in the ideologies of various elements of the right.

Erling Jorstad, *The Politics of Doomsday: Fundamentalists of the Far Right* (Nashville, Tenn., and New York: Abingdon Press, 1970), discusses the connection between Christian fundamentalists and right-wing politics. For an analysis of the interaction between religion and politics in the New Christian Right, see Richard John Neuhaus and Michael Cromartie, eds., *Piety and Politics: Evangelicals and Fundamentalists Confront the World* (Washington, D.C.: Ethics and Public Policy Center, 1987).

Not all of the mothers' leaders were equally devout, and their motives varied, at least in degree. Dilling, for example, was motivated by religion to a greater degree than was Cathrine Curtis or Kathleen Norris. Waters peppered her speeches with profanity as well as with biblical quotations.

From the ultraright of the 1930s to the present, religious differences have played a major role in divisions between women of the right and women of the left. Also, such differences have helped shape the identities of women's movements, establish their priorities, and motivate women to become activists.

39. Christians have condemned Jews as Christ-killers; as aliens whose principal loyalty is to Judaism rather than to the United States; as the inventors of communism and the exploitative international bankers; and as cheaters of Gentiles. Jews are also seen as tainted by their identification with urban values, machine politics, and Hollywood. Alas, anti-Semitism has a momentum of its own.

The mothers' books, magazines, and pamphlets focus on specific scapegoats for social changes. Dilling's books, her *Bulletin,* and *Women's Voice* direct their venom at human targets rather than at abstract forces. The mothers concentrated on the evil and malign nature of their enemies to a greater degree than on the virtues of Christianity or the lifestyle of the patriarchal family. They appeared more concerned with discrediting their foes than in defending the virtues of tradition and the status quo.

Dilling frequently argued that Hitler protected Christianity against atheistic communism. Francisco Franco likewise was a Christian enemy of atheism. I discuss Dilling's use of conspiracy theories to justify her beliefs and her work in chapter 2 and in chapter 6. In chapter 12, I emphasize that her obsessions with Judaism and communism were lifelong and that she refused to believe Hitler had perpetrated the Holocaust.

The body of work on prejudice and anti-Semitism, some of it focusing on the role of Christianity, is extensive and much is of high quality. Still the best general work on prejudice is Gordon Allport, *The Nature of Prejudice,* 25th anniversary edition (Reading, Mass.: Addison-Wesley Publishing Company, Inc., 1987). See also Allport, *The Person in Psychology: Selected Essays* (Boston: Beacon Press, 1968). Other valuable studies include Howard J. Ehrlich, *The Social Psychology of Prejudice* (New York: John Wiley and Sons, 1973); Malcolm Hay, *The Roots of Christian Anti-Semitism* (New York: Philosophical Library, 1978); and Hannah Arendt, *Antisemitism,* part I of *The Origins of Totalitarianism* (New York: Harcourt, Brace, & World, 1968). An older work by an observer who was not an academic expert is useful in understanding fanaticism: Eric Hoffer, *The True Believer* (New York: Harper and Row, 1966).

The most recent and comprehensive study of American anti-Semitism is Leonard Dinnerstein, *Anti-Semitism in America* (New York: Oxford University Press, 1994). Other important works include Harold E. Quinley and Charles Y. Glock, *Anti-Semitism in America* (New York: Free Press, 1979); Nathan Perlmutter and Ruth Ann Perlmutter, *The Real Anti-Semitism in America* (New York: Arbor House, 1982); Ernest Volkman, *A Legacy of Hate: Anti-Semitism in America* (New York: Franklin Watts, 1982); Stephen D. Isaacs, *Jews and American Politics* (Garden City, N.Y.: Doubleday, 1974); and David A. Gerber, ed., *Anti-Semitism in American History* (Urbana and Chicago: University of Illinois Press, 1986).

40. The mothers added the perspective of White, middle-class, chiefly middle-aged women to the classic conspiracy theories of the far right that linked Jews, communists, liberals, international bankers, Masons, Blacks, and others. The mothers' views resembled those of such male ultraright leaders as Smith, Coughlin, Winrod, and Pelley. The tradition of far-right conspiracy theories has continued with more recent hatemongers such as George Lincoln Rockwell and David Duke.

Indeed, the works of Dilling and Smith, as well as *The Protocols of the Learned Elders of Zion,* are still sold by ultraright groups. They are available at some far-right bookstores and through mail orders.

For the conspiratorial outlook that has permeated the propaganda of the far right, see Jeansonne, *Gerald L. K. Smith;* Ribuffo, *The Old Christian Right;* Dinnerstein; Morris Kominsky, *The Hoaxers: Plain Liars, Fancy Liars, and Damned Liars* (Boston: Branden Press, 1970); David Brion Davis, ed., *The Fear of Conspiracy* (Ithaca, N.Y.: Cornell University Press, 1971); Solomon Andhil Fineberg, *Overcoming Anti-Semitism* (New York: Harper and Brothers, 1943); Herman Berstein, *The Truth About "The Protocols of Zion": A Complete Exposure* (New York: Covici, Friede, 1935); Arnold Forster and Benjamin R. Epstein, *The Trouble-Makers* (Garden City, N.Y.: Doubleday & Company, 1952); Forster and Epstein, *Cross-Currents* (Westport: Greenwood Press, 1956); Gertrude J. Selznick and Stephen Steinberg, *The Tenacity of Prejudice: Anti-Semitism in Contemporary America* (New York: Harper & Row, 1969); and Erich Fromm, *Escape From Freedom* (New York: Avon Books, 1941). Fromm discusses the appeal of totalitarian and absolutist ideologies to those who crave security.

Chapter Two

1. Arthur M. Schlesinger Jr., *The Age of Roosevelt,* Vol. 3: *The Politics of Upheaval* (Boston: Houghton Mifflin Company, 1960), 39; McEnaney, "Defending the Family Altar," 59.

2. Elizabeth Dilling to Henry B. Joy, October 5, 1936, Box (hereafter B) 7, F: October 1–11, 1936, Joy papers, Bentley Historical Library, University of Michigan, Ann Arbor; "Mrs. Elizabeth Dilling and the Mothers of America," AJC F: Dilling, n.d., New York City.

3. Federal Bureau of Investigation file on Dilling, part 16, 70.

4. Dilling, *The Roosevelt Red Record,* 145.

5. *Cleveland Press,* October 30, 1934.

6. Cleveland *Plain Dealer,* June 8, 1936.

7. Zwisler, 36–7, 40.

8. Dilling to the Rev. George Craig Stewart, November 26, 1932, Dilling papers, School of Christian Liberty, Arlington Heights, Illinois.

9. Zwisler, 36–7, 40.

10. Zwisler, 1–2; Albert Dilling, opening statement in *U.S. vs. McWilliams,* FBI file, pt. 9, 95. Also see *Elizabeth Dilling vs. the Billboard Publishing Company et al.,* transcript in AJC F: Dilling.

11. Zwisler, 12.

12. Ibid.; Harry Thornton Moore, "A Study in Dillingsgate," New York *PM,* March 30, 1941; unmarked clipping by Moore from *The New Republic* in FBI file, pt. 15, 12–3; "About Elizabeth Dilling," press release, n.d., Dilling papers; Durwood Howes, ed., *American Women: The Official Who's Who Among the Women of the Nation,* Vol. 2 (Los Angeles: American Publications, Inc., 1937–1938), 176.

13. Ware writes, "While women could study and train on their chosen instruments, they were barred from almost all major orchestras. The first (and only) women hired for an orchestra was usually a harpist, a position considered suitable for women's sensitivity and talents." See Ware, *American Women in the 1930s,* 164.

14. FBI file, pt. 9, 96; New York *PM,* March 30, 1941.

15. Zwisler, 2; "About Elizabeth Dilling"; Patriotic Research Bureau *Bulletin,* 1.

16. Zwisler, 3–4; FBI file, pt. 9, 97; Dilling to Mrs. Henry B. Joy, November 16, 1936, B 8, F: November 3–17, 1936, Joy papers.

17. Zwisler, 4; Dilling to Joy, November 2, 1936, B 8 F: October 26–November 2, 1936, Joy papers; *Bulletin,* July 8, 1940, 4; *Chicago Daily News,* October 21, 1939.

18. *Chicago Herald and Examiner,* December 28, 1937; *Chicago American,* December 28, 1937; Ithaca, New York *Cornell Daily Sun,* May 6, 1940; *Chicago Tribune,* May 7, 1940; *Dilling vs. Billboard,* 1–2.

19. Dilling to Joy, November 1, 1936, B 8 F: October 26–November 2, 1936, Joy papers; Zwisler, 4.

20. "About Elizabeth Dilling"; FBI file, pt. 9, 96.

21. Dilling to unknown addressee, November 11, 1937, FBI file, pt. 1, 39.

22. YIVO Trends Analysis Files (hereafter TAF) 1938, 361, YIVO Institute for Jewish Research, New York City.

23. *Bulletin,* summer 1939, 1–2; Dilling biographical statement, 3, Dilling papers; Dilling to "Dear Friends," July 11, 1939, Dilling papers; Albert Dilling, opening statement in *U.S. vs. McWilliams,* 2160–1.

24. Dilling, *Red Network,* 9–13; Cleveland *Plain Dealer,* June 8, 1936; Albert Dilling, opening statement in *U.S. vs. McWilliams,* 2161–2; Milton S. Mayer, "Mrs. Dilling: Lady of the Red Network," *American Mercury* (July 1939), 296.

25. Dilling, *Red Network,* 9–13.

26. McEnaney, "Defending the Family Altar," 113.

27. Mayer, 296.

28. Ibid.

29. Boston *Evening Transcript,* June 8, 1938.

30. *Bulletin,* August 1941, 2.

31. "About Elizabeth Dilling," 2.

32. *Dilling vs. Billboard,* 61; Dilling to Joy, September 23, 1936, B 7 F: September 16–30, 1936, Joy papers.

33. Dilling, *Red Network*, 64.

34. *Bulletin*, May 4, 1940, 10.

35. Ibid., March 1946, 8. Dilling was hostile to religions other than Christianity. She complained that among subversive groups "speakers for the debasing and degrading Hindu, Mohammedan, pagan, and agnostic cults are placed in fellowship and on an equal footing with speakers for Jesus Christ. The audiences chant a mixture of prayers and ritual from all these. The savage Mohammedan call of the Mezzin as heard in darkest Asia is mingled with the propaganda of the Hindu, Jew, and agnostic." See Committee on Un-American Activities, House of Representatives, 75th Cong., Third Sess.; 76th Cong., 1st Sess., *Investigation of Un-American Activities in the United States*, Vol. I (Washington, D.C.: Government Printing Office, 1938–9), 698.

36. Dilling, "Should Christians Support the Communistic Propaganda of the Y's?", 1–4, Dilling papers; FBI file, pt. 20, 107.

37. *St. Louis Star-Times*, July 28, 1943.

38. *Bulletin*, August 1941, 2; Flyer, "Elizabeth Dilling, Author of *The Red Network*," B 9, F: Misc. Pub., Dilling and Extremists, Joy papers.

39. Flyer, "Elizabeth Dilling, Author of *The Red Network*."

40. Zwisler, 6; Moore, "The Lady Patriot's Book," *The New Republic* (January 8, 1936), 243.

41. Moore, "Lady Patriot's Book," 243; *Bulletin*, February 21, 1939, 21, and April 4, 1939, 1; Dilling to "Dear Friends," December 8, 1938, FBI file, pt. 10, 64; Los Angeles *Evening Express*, November 11, 1934.

42. Zwisler, 9–10; "Report on Elizabeth Dilling," Mothers of Minnesota Collection, Jewish Community Council of Minnesota papers, B 16, Minnesota Historical Society, St. Paul; Dilling, *Red Revolution: Do We Want It Here?* (Kenilworth, Illinois: self-published, 1932), 5, in Dilling papers.

43. "About Elizabeth Dilling."

44. "Elizabeth Dilling, Author of the Red Network," B 9, F: Misc. Pub., E. Dilling and Extremists, Joy papers.

45. Dilling to Joy, September 21 and 22 and October 7 and 12, 1936, B 8, F: September 16–October 13, 1936, Joy papers.

46. *Bulletin*, July 4, 1941, 21; Dilling to Joy, October 15, 1936, B 8, F: October 14–30, 1936, Joy papers. My observations about Dilling's tastes in reading are based partly on an examination of her library at the School of Christian Liberty.

47. *Bulletin*, July 4, 1941, 21; Dilling to Joy, October 15, 1936; quote from Upton Sinclair, "Mrs. Dilling Entertains," *Common Sense* (November 1936), 13.

48. *Bulletin*, February 21, 1939, 1.

49. Dilling to Joy, October 19 and November 2, 1936, B 8, F: October 14–November 4, 1936, Joy papers.

50. Dilling to William M. Smith, January 7, 1940, Dilling papers.

51. *Bulletin*, November 1946, in FBI file, pt. 10, 84; *Bulletin*, Christmas 1940, 16.

52. Dilling to Joy, August 25, 1936, B 8 F: July 20–August 26, 1936, Joy papers; FBI file, pt. 4, 7, pt. 15, 28–9, and pt. 16, 82; *Bulletin*, December 1939, 5; Dilling to "Dear Friend," January 23, 1939, Dilling papers; Dilling biographical statement, 2; Dilling to E. F. Webber, December 7, 1940, Dilling papers.

53. *New York Times*, May 1, 1966.

54. George Seldes, *Witch Hunt: The Technique and Profits of Redbaiting* (New York: Modern Age Books, 1940), 158–60.

55. Ibid.

56. *Chicago Tribune,* June 8, 1935.

57. Ibid.; Cleveland *Plain Dealer,* June 8, 1935.

58. Harry S. Ashmore, *Unreasonable Truths: The Life of Robert Maynard Hutchins* (Boston: Little, Brown and Company, 1989), 129–32.

59. *Chicago Herald and Examiner,* December 28, 1937; Chicago *American,* December 28, 1937; *Cornell Daily Sun,* May 6, 1940; *Chicago Tribune,* May 7, 1940.

60. *Chicago Tribune,* May 7, 1940.

61. Dilling, *Reds at Cornell University,* n.p., n.d., 1–11, Dilling papers.

62. Dilling to Mrs. James Cunningham Gray, November 27, 1940, Dilling papers.

63. *Nashville Banner,* October 10, 1941; *Bulletin,* March 1947, 5–11.

64. Zwisler, 22–23; Dilling, *The Red Network* (Chicago: self-published, 1934).

65. Ware, *American Women in the 1930s,* 103–4.

66. Dilling, *Red Network,* 48–50, 259–81, 306–15; Mayer, "Mrs. Dilling," 297; *Dayton Daily News,* February 20, 1941.

67. Quotes from Dilling, *The Red Network,* 74, 79–80. See also *The Red Network,* 111, 116, 139, 149, 189, 193.

68. Review of *Red Network* in *Chicago Press,* undated clipping, Dilling papers; Independence, Kansas *Daily Reporter,* October 3, 1936.

69. *Dilling vs. Billboard,* 45–7; *In Fact,* 21:4 (April 24, 1950), 1–4; Mayer, "Mrs. Dilling," 298; Leland V. Bell, *In Hitler's Shadow: The Anatomy of American Nazism* (Port Washington, N.Y.: Kennikat Press, 1973), 50, 101; "Some of Hundreds of Favorable Comments on *The Red Network,*" B 8 F: 1943, Dilling, Gerald L. K. Smith papers, Bentley Historical Library.

70. Seldes, 65–8; Greenwald, "Fascism in America," 620.

71. Dilling, "Answer of Elizabeth Dilling, Author of *The Red Network,* to radio attack by Bishop G. Bromley Oxnam," 1938, AJC F: Dilling.

72. Miles M. Goldberg to Samuel L. Scheiner, June 13, 1940, B 16, Jewish Community Relations Council of Minnesota papers.

73. Allport, *The Nature of Prejudice,* 186.

74. Heywood Broun, "Redder Than the Roosevelts," *The Nation* (July 17, 1935), 78.

75. Dilling, *Red Network,* 33.

76. Dilling, "The Lady Patriot Replies," 1936, B 9 F: Misc. Pub., Dilling and Extremists, Joy papers.

77. Wilmette, Illinois *Life,* October 1, 1936.

78. Dilling to Joy, August 1936, n.d., B 7 F: August 4–13, 1936, Joy papers; Dilling advertisement for *Roosevelt Red Record,* Jewish Community Relations Council of Minnesota Papers.

79. Dilling to Joy, July 2, 1936, B 7 F: July 1–11, 1936, Joy papers.

80. Dilling to Joy, October 1, 1936, B 7, F: October 1–11, 1936, Joy papers.

81. *Dilling vs. Billboard,* 44–45.

82. Sinclair, "Mrs. Dilling Entertains," 15.

83. New York *Journal,* January 11, 1939.

84. Dilling, *Roosevelt Red Record,* 217.

85. Ibid., 350.

86. Dilling to Joy, July 20, 1936, B 7 F: July 12–22, 1936, Joy papers.

87. Zwisler, 27–8; Wilmette *Life,* October 1, 1936, B 9 F: Misc. Pub., E. Dilling and Extremists, Joy papers; Dilling, *Roosevelt Red Record,* 13, 28, 32.

88. Dilling, *Roosevelt Red Record,* 13.

89. Ibid., 394–426; *Nashville Tennessean,* October 10, 1941.

90. Dilling, *Roosevelt,* 3, 26–7, 350; Mayer, "Mrs. Dilling," 297; Richard M. Ketchum, *The Borrowed Years: 1938–1941: America on the Way to War* (New York: Random House, 1989), 379; McEnaney, "Defending the Family Altar," 87–8.

91. Dilling, *Borah: "Borer from Within" the G.O.P.,* B 11 F: Papers and Pamphlets; Dilling to Joy, June 17, 1936, B 7, F: June 13–30, 1936, Joy papers; *Bulletin,* November 23, 1935; Cleveland *Plain Dealer,* June 8, 1936.

92. Dilling to Joy, June 17 and June 19, 1936, B 7 F: June 13–30, 1936, Joy papers; Dilling to Mrs. Joy, September 21, 1936, B 7, F: September 16–30, 1936, Joy papers.

93. Dilling to Joy, October 5, 1936, B 7, F: October 1–11, 1936; Dilling to Joy, October 15, 1936, B 7, F: October 12–16, 1936; Dilling to Joy, November 1, 1936, B 8, F: October 26–November 2, 1936; and Dilling to Joy, November 4, 1936, B 8, F: November 3–17, 1936, Joy papers.

94. *Bulletin,* June 1940, 13, and July 1940, 1–2; "Elizabeth Dilling," report by AJC, F: Dilling; Dilling, *Wanted—A Presidential 'Man on a White Horse,'* 1–8, Dilling papers.

95. FBI file, pt. 22, 89–98; Dilling biographical statement, Dilling papers; Herbert S. Parmet and Marie B. Hecht, *Never Again: A President Runs for a Third Term* (New York: The Macmillan Company, 1968), 218.

96. John Roy Carlson (pseudonym for Avedis Derounian), *Under Cover: My Four Years in the Nazi Underworld of America* (New York: E. P. Dutton, 1943), 216; Rev. Frank Woodruff Johnson (pseudonym for Dilling) *The Octopus* (Omaha, Nebraska: self-published, 1940), 67.

97. Johnson, 67.

98. Ibid., 79.

99. *Bulletin,* August 1947, 6.

100. Johnson, *Is God Anti-Semitic or Just?* (Chicago: self-published, 1940), 7–8.

101. Dilling, open letter to Congress, 1949, Jewish Community Relations Council of Minnesota papers.

102. *Dilling vs. Billboard,* 52.

103. Ibid., 53–5.

104. Davis, *The Fear of Conspiracy,* 275.

105. Dilling, *Roosevelt Red Record,* 229.

106. Davis, *Fear of Conspiracy,* 276.

107. Dilling, *Roosevelt Red Record,* 234.

108. *Bulletin,* May 1940, 1.

109. Zwisler, "Elizabeth Dilling," 7–11.

Chapter Three

1. Susan Canedy, *America's Nazis: A Democratic Dilemma* (Menlo Park, Calif.: Markgraf Publications Group, 1990), 38–9.

2. Ibid., 139–43.

3. Ibid., 50–65.

4. Ibid., 73.

5. Ibid., 73–97.

6. Ibid., 120–4; TAF 1939, 535.

7. Canedy, 194–6.

8. Ibid.

9. Undated memo on G. Wilhelm Kunze, AJC F: Kunze, 6. Also see Canedy, 159–61, 175, 194, 204.

10. Niel M. Johnson, *George Sylvester Viereck: German-American Propagandist* (Urbana: University of Illinois Press, 1972): Charles Higham, *American Swastika* (Garden City, N.Y.: Doubleday, 1985), 40–3.

11. Ibid., 197–9; Cole, *Roosevelt and the Isolationists,* 472, 533; Michael Sayers and Albert E. Kahn, *Sabotage! The Secret War Against America* (New York: Harper & Brothers, 1942), 186–187; *Washington Post,* July 17, 1943.

12. *Propaganda Analysis,* 2:4 (January 1, 1939), 8; "Anti-Semitic Propaganda," AJC, 1939, 3–16.

13. "Anti-Semitic Propaganda," 3–16.

14. George Wolfskill and John A. Hudson, *All But the People: Franklin D. Roosevelt and His Critics, 1933–39* (London: The Macmillan Company, 1969), 64; Walter Winchell, "Americans We Can Do Without," *Liberty,* August 1, 1942, 10; Friends of Democracy, "Pattern for Revolution," 8 (obtained from American Jewish Historical Society, Waltham, Mass.); Nathaniel Weyl, *Treason: The Story of Disloyalty and Betrayal in American History* (Washington, D.C.: Public Affairs Press, 1950), 321; *McWilliams et al. vs. Sentinel Publishing Co. et al.,* N. 4450, Appellate Court of Illinois, First District, Second Division, November 18, 1949, 276.

15. Raymond W. Stebbins, Memo on Henry Ford and Edwin Pipp, 1–7, AJC F: Ford; Henry Simonoff, *The First Henry Ford and His Dearborn Independent* (New York: Bloch Publishing Co., n.d.), 3–4.

16. Dilling, *Bulletin,* July 8, 1940, 3. See also Report on Henry Ford (1940), AJC F: Ford.

17. Sheldon Marcus, *Father Coughlin: The Tumultuous Life of the Priest of the Little Flower* (Boston: Little, Brown and Company, 1973), 1–40.

18. Higham, *American Swastika,* 2; AJC F: Fundamentalism, 1939, 2.

19. Marcus, 169, 186–96, 202.

20. "Summary of Coughlin influence in mothers movement by the League for Human Rights," Cleveland, Ohio (September 1940), 1–5, World War II Collection, Mothers of America file, Pennsylvania Historical Society, Philadelphia.

21. See Jeansonne, *Gerald L. K. Smith,* chapters 2–5.

22. Ribuffo, *The Old Christian Right,* 158–9.

23. Jeansonne, *Gerald L. K. Smith,* 89.

24. Ibid., 88.

25. Ibid.

26. Ibid.

27. Ibid., 87.

28. Ibid., 88.

29. Ibid., 87.

30. Ibid.

31. *The Cross and the Flag,* 2 (March 1944), 363 and 3 (August 1944), 426.

32. McEnaney, "Defending the Family Altar," 56–7, 72.

33. Ibid.

34. Ibid., 54.

35. Jeansonne, *Gerald L. K. Smith,* 149, 250–1; McEnaney, "Defending the Family Altar," 50–2; *The Cross and the Flag,* 2 (March 1944), 363.

36. Jeansonne, *Gerald L. K. Smith,* 47, 50–64, 82–90.

37. Ribuffo, *The Old Christian Right,* 1–49, 81.

38. Sayers and Kahn, *Sabotage!,* 136. Also see Ribuffo, *The Old Christian Right,* 57.

39. Sayers and Kahn, *Sabotage!,* 136; Ribuffo, *The Old Christian Right,* 57.

40. Ribuffo, "Protestants on the Right," Ph.D. dissertation, Yale University, 1976, 298.

41. Ribuffo, *The Old Christian Right,* 63–70; *Minneapolis Journal,* September 12, 1936.

42. Ibid.

43. *Minneapolis Journal,* September 11, 12, 15, 1936.

44. Ibid., September 13 and 16, 1936; Ribuffo, *The Old Christian Right,* 72–3.

45. Ribuffo, *The Old Christian Right,* 76–8.

46. AJC *News Letter* (Los Angeles), 5:135 (March 19, 1941), 1–3.

47. Ribuffo, *The Old Christian Right,* 80–7.

48. Ibid., 102–5, 107–18.

49. Ibid., 120–5.

50. Ibid., 125–7.

51. Report on Elizabeth Dilling, n.d., 3, Jewish Community Relations Council of Minnesota papers.

52. Dilling, *Bulletin,* March 1942, 10.

53. Akron *Beacon Journal,* August 8, 1943.

54. Winchell, 45–6; George Deatherage to Dilling, December 11, 1939 and Dilling to Deatherage, December 28, 1939, both in Dilling papers; Hoke, *It's a Secret,* 200.

55. Carlson, *The Plotters* (New York: E. P. Dutton & Company, Inc., 1946), 20.

56. Ralph Lord Roy, *Apostles of Discord* (Boston: Beacon Press, 1953), 82.

57. Paul E. Grosser and Edwin G. Halperin, *The Causes and Effects of Anti-Semitism* (New York: Philosophical Library, 1978), 261; Sayers and Kahn, *Sabotage!,* 149.

58. Rogers, "Isolationalist Propaganda," 107–15; Cole, *Roosevelt and the Isolationists,* 379–481. The most comprehensive study of the movement is Cole, *America First,* but it deals only tangentially with the subjects of this book.

59. Rogers, "Isolationist Propaganda," 107–15.

60. Ribuffo, *The Old Christian Right,* 185; *New York Daily News,* January 6, 1941.

61. Minutes of America First Committee meeting, Philadelphia, August 20, 1941, AJC F: National Legion of Mothers.

62. Rogers, "Isolationist Propaganda," 133–5; Walter S. Roos, *The Last Hero: Charles A. Lindbergh* (New York: Harper & Row, 1976), 304.

63. Roos, 295–8; Rogers, "Isolationist Propaganda," 136.

64. Roos, 295–8, 304; Rogers, "Isolationist Propaganda," 136; Dorothy Thompson, "An Open Letter to Anne Lindbergh," *Look,* March 25, 1941, 10–11.

65. Cole, *Roosevelt and the Isolationists,* 460.

66. Roos, 299–300.

67. Gerald L. K. Smith to Charles A. Lindbergh, October 9, 1941, B 3, F: 1939–1942, Lindbergh, Charles, Smith papers.

68. Smith to Barbara Herman and Mary Jane Heals, December 9, 1942, B 6, F: 1939–1942, Smith family, Smith papers.

69. Ketchum, 620.

70. Memo on Verne Marshall, undated, AJC F: No Foreign War Committee, 1–15; Hoke, *It's a Secret,* 208–10; Sayers and Kahn, *Sabotage!,* 165.

71. Memo on Verne Marshall, 18.

72. Ibid., 16–7.

73. Hoke, *It's a Secret,* 210–2.

Chapter Four

1. Los Angeles *Herald-Express,* October 10 and November 10, 1939.

2. Gordon W. Allport and Janet M. Faden, "The Psychology of Newspapers," *Public Opinion Quarterly* 4 (1940), 695.

3. Los Angeles *Herald-Express,* October 12, 1939.

4. Ibid., October 13, 1939.

5. Ibid., October 11, 1939, October 19, 1939.

6. Ibid., October 11, 12, 18, 1939.

7. Ibid., November 23, 1939.

8. Chicago *Herald-American,* November 12, 1939.

9. Los Angeles *Herald-Express,* November 23, 1939.

10. *American Mothers National Weekly,* September 7, 1940, Pennsylvania Historical Society; Allport and Faden, 695; Los Angeles *Herald-Express,* June 15, 1940.

11. *American Mothers National Weekly,* September 7, 1940.

12. *New York Times,* January 19, 1966; *Washington Evening Star,* (obituary), undated clipping; "Norris, Kathleen Thomason," *Notable American Women, The Modern Period: A Biographical Dictionary* (Cambridge: Belknap Press, 1980), 509–11.

13. Rogers, "Isolationist Propaganda," 145.

14. *San Francisco Examiner,* January 25, 1940.

15. Los Angeles *Herald-Express,* April 23, 1940.

16. Ibid., February 1, 1940.

17. Ibid., April 23, 1940.

18. Ibid., April 12, 1940.

19. Chicago *Herald-American,* August 4, 5, 1940.

20. Ibid., August 16, 21, 1940.

21. Testimony of Hannah M. Connors on Conscription, House Military Affairs Committee, 76th. Cong., 3rd Sess., *Hearings* (Washington, D.C.: Government Printing Office, 1940), 371–5.

22. Memo, League for Human Rights, AJC F: Women Fascists.

23. *San Francisco Examiner,* June 5, 1940.

24. Chicago *Herald-American,* October 22, 1939.

25. Ibid., October 15, 22, 23, 27, and November 4, 5, and 15, 1940.

26. Ibid.; quote from ibid., November 20, 1939.

27. Ibid., November 25 and December 14 and 15, 1939, and January 9, 1941; *San*

Francisco Examiner, February 2, 1940; Los Angeles *Herald-Express,* December 26, 1939; *Chicago Herald-Tribune,* June 1, 1940.

28. Dilling to Lillian E. Fiss, December 30, 1940, Dilling papers.

29. "Daughters of Dissension and Defeat," unmarked clipping, YIVO, F: 1944, 10–11.

30. Whelan and Johnson, "The Menace of the 'Mothers,'" 19; Carlson, *The Plotters,* 168.

31. Memorandum on Philadelphia NLMA meeting, May 26, 1941, 1, Pennsylvania Historical Society.

32. "Memorandum on 'Mothers' Groups," 1944, AJC Vertical Files, F: Fascism—U.S., Mothers' Groups; Meeting Report, National Legion of Mothers of America, August 26, 1940, AJC F: National Legion of Mothers of America (hereafter NLMA).

33. Greenwald, 616–24. I was unable to determine from the available sources which of the founders was Catholic and which was Jewish.

34. *San Francisco Chronicle,* June 9, 1940.

35. *New York Times,* May 23, 1940; New York *Herald-Tribune,* May 25, 1940; *New York Post,* May 28, 1940.

36. Undated flyer by Molly Pitcher Christian Women's Brigade, AJC F: Molly Pitcher Christian Women's Brigade.

37. Flyer by Molly Pitcher Christian Women's Brigade, June 2, 1941, AJC F: Molly Pitcher Christian Women's Brigade.

38. Washington *Evening Star,* April 26, 1941; New York *Herald Tribune,* May 10, 1941; Anne Morrow Lindbergh, *War Within and Without: Diaries and Letters of Anne Morrow Lindbergh, 1939–1944* (New York: Harcourt Brace Jovanovich, 1980), 199; *New York Times,* January 19, 1966.

39. Greenwald, 616–24.

40. Meeting Report, Philadelphia NLMA, June 30, 1941, 1–2, AJC F: NLMA; Meeting Report, Philadelphia NLMA, December 5, 1941, 881, YIVO F: Misc., 1941.

41. Meeting Report, Philadelphia NLMA, July 14, 1941, p. 3, AJC F: NLMA.

42. Ibid., October 27, 1941, 3.

43. Ibid., September 15, 1941, 3.

44. Ibid., August 18, 1941, 4; October 6, 1941, 1–4. There are no surviving membership lists, much less a breakdown of membership by race and ethnicity, and no newspaper account made an estimate of the number of Blacks and other minorities who joined the NLMA. The number was probably very small because the organization's atmosphere was elitist and at least implicitly racist. Even so, the NLMA probably had more minority members than had any of its smaller, more extremist successors.

45. Ibid., October 13, 1941, 1–4.

46. Ibid., September 8, 1941, 1–3.

47. Meeting report, Philadelphia NLMA, December 1, 1941, 807–11, YIVO F: Misc., 1941.

48. Meeting report, September 17, 1942, 5, AJC F: NLMA.

49. Ibid.

50. Meeting report, December 8, 1941, 812–5, YIVO F: Misc., 1941.

51. *New York Times,* January 19, 1966; *Washington Evening Star* (obit.), undated clipping; "Norris," *Notable American Women,* 509–11.

52. *San Francisco Examiner,* January 25, 1940; Los Angeles *Herald-Express,* April 23, 1940.

53. *New York Times,* January 19, 1966; Rogers, "Isolationist Propaganda," 145; Memorandum on Philadelphia NLMA meeting, May 26, 1941, 1.

54. Memorandum on Philadelphia NLMA meeting, May 26, 1941, 1; Los Angeles *Herald-Express,* April 12, 1940.

55. Rogers, "Isolationist Propaganda," 145; Chicago *Herald-American,* August 4, 5, 1940.

56. Los Angeles *Herald-Express,* October 10, November 10, 1939; June 15, 1940; Allport and Faden, 695.

57. Los Angeles *Herald-Express,* October 12, 1939; Chicago *Herald-American,* August 4, 5, 1940.

Chapter Five

1. Frederickson, 1–4.

2. Ibid., 4–6; *American Women,* vol. 3 (1939–40) (Los Angeles: America Publishers, 1939), 207; *New York Times,* June 6 and 7, 1922; May 26, 1924; June 6 and 7, 1927; TAF 1939, F: Misc., 365; "They Stand Out from the Crowd," *Literary Digest* 118: 10 (November 10, 1934), 12.

3. Frederickson, 4–6.

4. Ibid., 6. For an excellent account of the role of women in the American economy from colonial times to 1929, see W. Elliot Brownlee and Mary M. Brownlee, *Women in the American Economy: A Documentary History, 1675 to 1929* (New Haven: Yale University Press, 1976).

5. Frederickson, 7; *What Is Women Investors in America?* n.p., n.d., Reel (hereafter R) 2, 1–3, Cathrine Curtis microfilm, New York Public Library.

6. Frederickson, 8; Curtis, *Women Investors,* 1–6, R 2; Women Investors Statement of Purpose, undated, 1–6, R 2; Membership form, R 2; "Women," *Time,* May 27, 1935, 64–8; Michael Ahearn to S. Clay Williams, November 15, 1936, R 3.

7. Frederickson, 8; *Women Investors,* 1–6; Ahearn to Williams, November 15, 1936.

8. "Women," *Time,* 64.

9. Frederickson, 9; Testimony of Curtis, "Revenue Act of 1935," U.S. 74th Congress, 1st Sess., Senate Finance Committee, *Hearings,* August 2, 1934 (Washington D.C.: Government Printing Office, 1934), 151–154; Curtis, *What Is Women Investors?* 3–4; "Women's Declaration of Independence," undated, 1–2 R 2; Women Investor's Press Release, January 6, 1937, R 2. Despite Curtis's efforts, the Wealth Tax bill was enacted. Curtis was militantly opposed to organized labor, which she equated with the far left. For example, in 1940, the Women Investors investigated Brookwood Labor College in Katonah, New York and concluded it was a communist front financed by Jewish bankers from New York. See Women Investors Research Institute, "Memorandum in Re: Brookwood Labor College, Katonah, New York," January 15, 1939, B 1, Curtis papers.

10. "Congress," *Time,* June 15, 1936, 63–4.

11. Frederickson, 12; *New York Times,* October 23, 1937.

12. Wolfskill and Hudson, 69.

13. Based on a survey of the Jewry file on R 2.

14. Curtis to Helen Forest, May 13, 1939, Curtis papers, cited in Frederickson, 13; Statement of Cathrine Curtis before Senate Foreign Relations Committee, May 6, 1939, R 2; Curtis to Herbert Darlington, September 23, 1939, R 2.

15. Curtis press release, September 20, 1939, R 2; Frederickson, 16. Curtis's belief that women had to provide the moral leadership to keep the United States out of war did not extend to women who were her ideological opponents. She severely criticized the testimony of members of the liberal Women's International League for Peace and Freedom, who "recommended unlimited powers for the President [and] encouraged international alliances." See Curtis to John J. Watson, May 9, 1939, B 3, Curtis papers.

16. Frederickson, 16; Curtis press release, September 20, 1939; Curtis to Mrs. Marty Z. Bentley, October 15, 1939, R 2; Curtis to Robert E. Edmondson, April 17, 1939, R 1; Frederickson, 16–17; Curtis to Darlington, September 23, 1939, R 2.

17. *New York Times,* September 27 and 29, 1939, April 26, 1934, March 23, 1935, and December 19, 1941; Mildred Adams, "Woman Makes Good Her Claim for a Place in the Skies," *New York Times Magazine,* June 7, 1931, 6, 20.

18. *Cleveland Press,* October 7 and 9, 1939.

19. Unmarked clipping, *Cleveland Press; Cleveland Press,* April 16, 1935; Cleveland *Plain Dealer,* April 5, May 26, and July 12, 1935; biography prepared by United Press, undated.

20. Cleveland *Plain Dealer,* September 27 and 29, 1939; *Cleveland Press,* October 7 and 9, and December 23, 1939; *New York Times,* September 27 and 29, 1939; Memorandum on Behalf of Laura Ingalls, Holder of Solo Pilot Certificate No. 9330, Docket No. SR-30, R 2.

21. *New York Times,* September 29, 1939.

22. *Chicago Tribune,* September 29, 1939.

23. Curtis to Sumner, May 21, 1941, R 3; Curtis to Farber, December 12, 1940, R 1; Curtis to Reynolds, July 16, 1941; Curtis to Johnson, July 14, 1939, R 1; Marie R. Smith to Curtis, February 6, 1941, R 1.

24. Curtis to Farber, December 12, 1940; Dilling *Bulletin,* May 4, 1940, 8; Curtis to Dilling, January 10, 1941, R 1.

25. Mrs. William A. Wendelburg, "Mothers Fight War Plans," American Mothers' *National Weekly,* September 7, 1940, 4–5, World War II collection, B 11, F: Mothers of Pennsylvania, cited in Frederickson, 19.

26. "A Mother," to Mrs. George S. Patterson, May 5, 1941, B 11, F: Mothers of Pennsylvania, cited in Frederickson, 20.

27. Wendelburg, "Mothers Fight War Plans," 4–5, cited in Frederickson, 18.

28. Mrs. H. Ernestine Bulger Ripley to Gerald P. Nye, August 19, 1941, 1, Curtis papers, cited in Frederickson, 21; Curtis, *Your Answers to the War Dancers* (Washington, D.C.: Women's National Committee to Keep the U.S. Out of War, 1941), 3–4.

29. Curtis, *Undermining America* (Washington, D.C.: Women's National Committee to Keep the U.S. Out of War, 1940), 1.

30. Curtis, *Britain's War Aims* (Washington, D.C.: Women's National Committee to Keep the U.S. Out of War, 1940), 3, 13, 25.

31. Curtis, *The March of Democracy* (Washington, D.C.: Women's National Committee to Keep the U.S. Out of War, 1940), 1–2.

32. *American Jewish Committee News Letter* (Los Angeles), 5:139 (April 9, 1941), AJC F: Newsletter.

33. Curtis, *Military Capitalism vs. Industrial Capitalism* (Washington, D.C.: Women's National Committee to Keep the U.S. Out of War, 1941), 5, in AJC F: Newsletter.

34. Curtis, *Your Answers to the War Dancers!,* 1–8, 25–9.

35. Curtis to Davis H. Crowley, October 11, 1940, R 1; Suggested Program for the Minority Party in the Seventy-Seventh Congress, prepared by Women Investors Research Institute, Inc., January 8, 1941, R 3.

36. Curtis, *A. D. 1776 for Liberty: H. R. 1776 for Dictatorship* (Washington, D.C.: Women's National Committee to Keep the U.S. Out of War, 1941), 1–15, R 3. This is a reprint of testimony given by Curtis to the Senate Foreign Relations Committee on H. R. 1776 on February 10, 1941.

37. Special Washington Letter from Curtis to members of the Women's National Committee to Keep the U.S. Out of War, February 18, 1941, R 3.

38. Carlson, *Under Cover,* 225, 309; Mary Hallock Wellmang to Curtis, February 11, 1940, B 1, F: 25, Curtis papers.

39. Carlson, *Under Cover,* 225.

40. Curtis to Mrs. Jeremiah Millbank, March 2, 1941, R 1.

41. *New York Post,* July 9, 1941.

42. Quoted from Curtis to Sen. Rufus Holman, March 18, 1941, B 6, F 10, Curtis papers; Curtis to Mrs. H. R. Parkinson, March 18, 1941, R 1.

43. *American Jewish Committee News Letter* (Los Angeles), 5:139 (April 9, 1941), 8, F: AJC *News Letter;* TAF 1941, 129.

44. Mother's Day Petition, May 1941, B 1, Curtis papers, cited in Frederickson, 32.

45. *Congressional Digest,* 20: 6–7 (June–July 1941), 186; Campbell, 6–7.

46. Irene Pennington to Curtis, June 10, 1941, R 1.

47. *Los Angeles Examiner,* May 26, 1941.

48. Sayers and Kahn, *Sabotage!,* 219; Curtis to Mrs. John F. Hooker, May 21, 1941, R 3.

49. *Cincinnati Post,* May 10, 1941.

50. Report on Mothers of Sons Meeting, May 11, 1941, B 37, F: Mothers of America, Jewish Community Relations Council of Minnesota papers.

51. Curtis, *Goodbye America,* (pamphlet opposing property seizure bill), undated, R 2; Frederickson, 33; Testimony of Curtis, House Committee on Military Affairs, 77th Congress, 1st Sess., *Hearings,* July 21, 1941 (Washington, D.C.: Government Printing Office, 1941), 214–35.

52. See, for example, Curtis to Members and Friends of Women Investors, November 24, 1941, and other letters in B 4 of the Curtis papers condemning price controls. Neither the major accounts focusing on women during the war, nor the more general accounts of women on the home front, discuss the activities of women such as Curtis. The best account of women on the home front (as well as those who went to war) is Campbell. General accounts emphasizing the home front include John Morton Blum, *V Was for Victory: Politics and American Culture During World War II* (New York: Harcourt Brace Jovanovich, 1976); Geoffrey Perrett, *Days of Sadness, Years of Triumph: The American People 1939–1945* (Baltimore: Penguin Books, Inc., 1973); and Richard

Polenberg, *War and Society: The United States, 1941–1945* (Philadelphia: J. B. Lippincott Company, 1972). Michael C. C. Adams, *The Best War Ever* (Baltimore: The Johns Hopkins University Press, 1994) asserts there was more home front suffering and dissension in wartime America than we like to believe. For other interpretations, see Chafe, *The Paradox of Change;* Jeansonne, *Transformation and Reaction;* Hartmann, "Women's Organizations During World War II: The Interaction of Class, Race, and Feminism," in *Women's Being, Woman's Place,* ed. by Mary Kelly (Boston: G. K. Hall and Co., 1979), 313–28. Chafe and Jeansonne emphasize the positive aspects of changes on the home front for women and others. Hartmann notes that the experience of women varied widely, in part due to factors such as their class and race.

53. Ingalls to Curtis, June 7, 1941, R 3; Sayers and Kahn, *Sabotage!,* 211, 214.

54. *Cleveland Press,* February 10, 1942; Sayers and Kahn, *Sabotage!,* 214; *Cleveland Plain Dealer,* February 12, 1942.

55. *Cleveland Plain Dealer,* February 12, 1942; Sayers and Kahn, *Sabotage!,* 214.

56. Sayers and Kahn, *Sabotage!,* 214. There is no record that von Gienanth actually gave Ingalls the names of German agents.

57. *Cleveland Plain Dealer,* February 10, 1942; *New York Times,* February 10, 1942.

58. O. John Rogge, *The Official German Report: Nazi Penetration 1924–1942; Pan-Arabism 1930–Today* (New York: Thomas Yoseloff, 1961), 308.

59. Frederickson, 1–6; *American Women,* 207; TAF 1939, 207.

60. Frederickson, 4–6; "They Stand Out From the Crowd," 12.

61. Frederickson, 4–6; "They Stand Out From the Crowd," 12; TAF 1939, F: Misc., 365.

62. Statement of Cathrine Curtis before Senate Foreign Relations Committee, May 6, 1939; Curtis press release, September 20, 1939, R 2; Curtis, *Undermining America,* 1; Curtis, *Britain's War Aims,* 3, 13, 25; Curtis, *The March of Democracy,* 1–2; Curtis, *Goodbye America,* 2.

63. Frederickson, 9; Testimony of Curtis, "Revenue Act of 1935," 151–4; Women Investors Press Release, January 6, 1937; Wendelburg, "Mothers Fight War Plans," 4–5.

64. Frederickson, 4–6; "They Stand Out From the Crowd," 12.

65. Carlson, *Under Cover,* 225; *New York Post,* July 9, 1941.

66. For a discussion of the theme that the entire interwar period was characterized by convulsive social change, see Jeansonne, *Transformation and Reaction.*

67. Curtis, *Goodbye America;* Testimony of Curtis, House Committee on Military Affairs.

68. Jewry file, R 2; Wendelburg, "Mothers Fight War Plans," 4–5; Curtis, *Undermining America,* 1; Curtis, *Britain's War Aims;* Curtis, *The March of Democracy;* Curtis, *Your Answers to the War Dancers!;* Campbell. Chafe, *The Paradox of Change,* discusses the paradox of women seeking gender solidarity while divided by class, racial, ethnic, and occupational differences. Indeed, Chafe views this paradox as one of the central themes in feminism.

Chapter Six

1. "About Elizabeth Dilling," 3; Dilling to Joy, July 20, 1936, B 7, F: July 12–22, 1936, Joy Papers; Zwisler, 57.

2. *Dilling vs. Billboard,* 22.

3. Johnson, *The Octopus*, 127.

4. *PM*, July 27, 1943; Henry Hoke, *It's a Secret*, 177; E. A. Piller, *Time Bomb* (New York: Arco Publishing Company, 1945), 69.

5. *Bulletin*, March 1946, 14.

6. FBI file on Dilling, pt. 15, 91; Rogge, 216; *German Report*; Carlson, *Under Cover*, 132–3; "Mrs. Elizabeth Dilling and the 'Mothers of America' Demonstrations," 1, Dilling papers; Mayer, "Mrs. Dilling," 294; Johnson, *The Octopus*, 199–200; Dilling to Charlene Barrett, June 26, 1940, Dilling papers.

7. Dilling, *The Roosevelt Red Record*, 161; *Dilling vs. Billboard*, 21; Dilling, *The Red Network*, 99.

8. *Philadelphia Public Ledger*, February 16, 1939.

9. "Elizabeth Dilling," report by American Jewish Committee, n.d., 3, AJC; Dilling, *The Roosevelt Red Record*, 63.

10. *Bulletin*, March 1942, 7.

11. *Dilling vs. Billboard*, 14–5; *Bulletin*, 3–4.

12. *Bulletin*, August 1941, 12–3.

13. *Dilling vs. Billboard*, 16.

14. Dilling, *The Roosevelt Red Record*, 50.

15. *Bulletin*, August 1941, 12–3.

16. Johnson, *The Octopus*, 226.

17. FBI file on Dilling, pt. 15, 91; Rogge, 216; Carlson, *Under Cover*, 132–3.

18. Rogge, 170, 187–91.

19. FBI file on Dilling, pt. 21, 279–88; *Dilling vs. Billboard*, 117–8; *New York Times*, October 31, 1938.

20. FBI file on Dilling, pt. 105, 9,621, pt. 16, 117, pt. 18, 141–2; Dilling biographical statement, Dilling papers; *Bulletin*, March 1942, 14; TAF 1941, 150.

21. *Bulletin*, Christmas 1940, 10–11; May 1941, 2; October 1942, 3, 13; FBI file on Dilling, pt. 15, 232–3; Carlson, *Under Cover*, 245.

22. *Dilling vs. Billboard*, 67.

23. "The March on Washington," September 15, 1941, AJC F: Women Fascists, 1; "Mrs. Elizabeth Dilling and the 'Mothers of America' Demonstrations," 1–2, Dilling papers; Zwisler, 66.

24. Zwisler, 66.

25. *Chicago Tribune*, February 5, 1941.

26. Ibid., February 1, 1941; Rogers, 24.

27. *PM*, February 16, 1941; *Chicago Tribune*, February 6, 1941; TAF 1941, 182–4.

28. *Dilling vs. Billboard*, 68; Carlson, *Under Cover*, 213; *Chicago Tribune*, February 9, 1941; *New York Post*, February 27, 1941.

29. *Bulletin*, March 1941, 5.

30. *Chicago Herald-American*, February 12, 1941.

31. *New York Daily Mirror*, February 25, 1941; Dilling *Bulletin*, March 1941, 8.

32. *Bulletin*, March 1941, 9.

33. *PM*, March 30, 1941.

34. *Bulletin*, March 1941, 5–7; TAF 1941, 184–5; FBI file on Dilling, pt. 21, 179; Carlson, *Under Cover*, 211–3.

35. *Bulletin*, March 1941, 11–2; Chicago *Herald-American*, February 28, 1941; *Chicago Tribune*, February 28, 1941.

36. *New York Times*, March 2, 1941.

37. *New York Times*, March 2, 7, 1941; *Washington Sunday Star*, March 1, 1941; Zwisler, 67.

38. *New York Times*, March 2, 1941.

39. *Cleveland Press*, March 1, 1941.

40. *New York Times*, March 2, 7, 1941; *Washington Sunday Star*, March 1, 1941; Zwisler, 67.

41. *New York Times*, March 9, 1941.

42. Warren F. Kimball, *The Most Unsordid Act: Lend-Lease, 1939-1941* (Baltimore: The Johns Hopkins Press, 1969), 216-20.

43. *PM*, March 30, 1941; *New York Daily Mirror*, March 30, 1941; Zwisler, 67.

44. *Chicago Tribune*, March 13, 1941.

45. *Dilling vs. Billboard*, 80; *Chicago Tribune*, March 17, 19, and 20, 1942; Dilling, "They Have Struck," (1942), 1-4, AJC F: Dilling.

46. *Albert Dilling vs. Elizabeth Dilling*, Complaint for Divorce, State of Illinois, Superior Court of Cook County, No. 42 S 2876, February 27, 1942, 1-5.

47. *Dilling vs. Billboard*, 80-1; *Chicago Tribune*, March 17 and 19, 1941; Dilling to "Dear Friends," February 28, 1942, Dilling papers.

48. *Dilling vs. Billboard*, 81-2; New York *PM*, March 31, 1942; *Chicago Tribune*, March 27, 1941; *New York Times*, March 27, 1942.

49. *Chicago Tribune*, April 10, 1942; *New York World-Telegram*, April 10, 1942; *New York Herald Tribune*, April 10, 1942; *Dilling vs. Billboard*, 82.

50. *Dilling vs. Billboard*, 83-4; *Washington Evening Star*, April 22, 1942; *Washington Times-Herald*, April 24, 1942; New York *PM*, April 25, 1942.

51. *Dilling vs. Billboard*, 83-5; *Washington Times-Herald*, September 18, 1943; Albert Dilling, "To Whomsoever It May Concern," June 19, 1942, in FBI file pt. 4, 11A.

52. *Dilling vs. Billboard*, 86; Dilling *Bulletin*, September 1943, 1; Chicago *Sun*, September 18, October 8, 1943; *New York Times*, October 20, 1943.

53. *Bulletin*, April 1944, 3-6, and December 1944, 2.

54. "From Dewey's college days when he was a cantor in a synagogue he has been fawning at the feet of international Jewry," Dilling wrote in the April 1944 *Bulletin*, 6. For Dilling's comment on FDR leading the United States to hell, see *Bulletin*, December 1944, 2. Upon learning of FDR's death, Dilling said, "You are well aware, I know, that Jewry's most perfect responsive instrument left us. He is continuing his 'fireside chats,' it is reported, with Old Nick in a new location. The chief mourners' long faces have matched their noses." See *PM*, May 27, 1945. Dilling wrote of the United Nations, "The UN Charter and treaties are constructed to make way for the 'man of sin,' the Anti-Christ who will hold supreme power over life or death as he briefly heads this last Red satanic world empire." See *Bulletin*, September-October 1954, 6.

55. Zwisler, 1-12; Moore, "A Study in Dillingsgate"; FBI file on Dilling, pt. 9, 96; "About Elizabeth Dilling," 1-2.

56. *PM*, March 30, 1941; Ware, *American Women in the 1930s*, 163-6.

57. Zwisler, 3-4.

58. Ibid.; FBI file, pt. 9, 97; Dilling to Mrs. Joy, November 16, 1936, B 8, F: November 3-17, Joy papers.

59. *Chicago Herald and Examiner*, December 28, 1937; *Chicago American*, Decem-

ber 28, 1937; Ithaca, N.Y. *Cornell Daily Sun*, May 6, 1940; *Chicago Tribune*, May 7, 1940.

60. *Chicago Herald and Examiner*, December 28, 1937; *Chicago American*, December 28, 1937; *Cornell Daily Sun*, May 6, 1940; *Chicago Tribune*, May 7, 1940; Elizabeth Dilling, *Reds at Cornell University*, n.p., n.d., 1–11, Dilling papers; Dilling to Mrs. James Cunningham Gray, November 27, 1940, Dilling papers.

61. Zwisler, 1–4; *Dilling vs. Billboard*, 81–2; New York *PM*, March 31, 1942; *Chicago Tribune*, March 27, 1941; and April 10, 1942; *New York Times*, March 27, 1942; *New York Herald-Tribune*, April 10, 1942.

62. Zwisler, 2; "About Elizabeth Dilling"; *Chicago Tribune*, June 8, 1935; *Cleveland Plain Dealer*, June 8, 1935; Dilling, *Wanted—A Presidential "Man on a White Horse,"* 1–8, Dilling papers; *Cleveland Press*, March 1, 1941.

63. Zwisler, "Dilling," 6; Moore, "The Lady Patriot's Book," 243; Dilling to "Dear Friend," January 23, 1939, Dilling papers; Dilling biographical statement, 2; Dilling, *Roosevelt*, 3, 26–7, 350.

64. FBI file on Dilling, pt. 16, 70; Zwisler, 1–12; Moore, "A Study in Dillingsgate"; "About Elizabeth Dilling," 1–4; Dilling *Bulletin*, May 4, 1940, 10; Christmas 1940, 16; December 1939, 5.

65. *Bulletin*, February 21, 1939, 1; Christmas 1940, 16; Dilling to "Dear Friend," January 23, 1939, Dilling papers; *New York Times*, May 1, 1966; Seldes, 158–60.

66. Zwisler, "Dilling," 36–7, 40; Dilling to the Rev. George Craig Stewart, November 26, 1932, Dilling papers; *Dilling vs. Billboard*, 61; Dilling to Joy, September 23, 1936, B 7, F: September 16–30, 1936, Joy papers; Dilling *Bulletin*, March 1946, 8.

67. *Dilling vs. Billboard*, 61; Dilling, *Red Network*, 64; Dilling *Bulletin*, May 1940, 10; March 1946, 8.

68. *Cleveland Plain Dealer*, June 8, 1936; Dilling to Stewart, November 26, 1932, Dilling papers; Zwisler, 36–37, 40.

69. Zwisler, 36–7, 40; *Bulletin*, February 21, 1939, 21; April 4, 1939, 1; Dilling to "Dear Friends," December 8, 1938; Los Angeles *Evening Express*, November 11, 1934.

70. *Bulletin*, July 4, 1941, 21; November 1946, 1; Christmas 1940, 16; Dilling to Joy, October 15, 19, and November 2, 1936, B 8, F: October 14–30, 1936, Joy papers; Sinclair, 13.

71. Dilling, *The Red Network*, 9–13; *Cleveland Plain Dealer*, June 8, 1936; Mayer, "Mrs. Dilling: Lady of *The Red Network*," 296; Dilling *Bulletin*, August 1941, 2; "About Elizabeth Dilling," 2.

72. *St. Louis Star-Times*, July 28, 1943; Dilling *Bulletin*, August 1941, 2; Flyer, "Elizabeth Dilling, Author of *The Red Network*," B 9, F: Misc. Pub., Dilling and Extremists, Joy papers.

73. "About Elizabeth Dilling," 1–4.

74. Zwisler, 66; "The March on Washington," September 15, 1941, AJC F: Women Fascists, 1; *Chicago Tribune*, February 5, 1941; *New York Times*, March 2, 9, 1941; *Cleveland Press*, March 1, 1941.

75. "About Elizabeth Dilling," 1–4; Dilling *Bulletin*, summer 1939, 1–2; Dilling to "Dear Friends," July 11, 1939, Dilling papers; Dilling, *Roosevelt Red Record*, 229–34.

76. TAF 1938, 361; Dilling biographical statement, 3; Dilling to "Dear Friends,"

July 11, 1939, Dilling papers; *Dilling vs. Billboard,* 22; Zwisler, 57; FBI file on Dilling, pt. 15, 91; Carlson, *Under Cover,* 132–3; "Mrs. Elizabeth Dilling and the 'Mothers of America' Demonstrations," 1, Dilling papers; Mayer, "Mrs. Dilling," 294; *Bulletin,* summer 1939, 1–3; August 1941, 12–3, March 1942, 7; Dilling, *The Octopus,* 199–200, 226.

77. Max Lerner, *Public Journal: Marginal Notes on Wartime America* (New York: Viking Press, 1945), 48.

Chapter Seven

1. Piller, *Time Bomb,* 65–72; James C. Schneider, *Should America Go to War? The Debate Over Foreign Policy in Chicago, 1939–1941* (Chapel Hill: University of North Carolina Press, 1989), 2–5.

2. *Chicago Tribune,* February 5, March 5, and March 8, 1941; FBI file on We the Mothers, pt. 21, 70, 247; *Cincinnati Enquirer,* July 29, 1943.

3. *New York Post,* March 20, 1944; Sayers and Kahn, *The Plot Against the Peace: A Warning to the Nation* (New York: Dial Press, 1945), 207–9; McEnaney, "Defending the Family Altar," 46–7; FBI file on We the Mothers, pt. 1, 8. None of the Christmas cards survived, to my knowledge, so I cannot analyze their specific content. The secondary sources did not describe the cards in more than a general way.

4. Hoke, *It's a Secret,* 180.

5. "Lyrl Clark Van Hyning, 1942–1946," AJC F: Van Hyning, 2; John L. Spivak, "Senator Langer's Secret Meeting," *New Masses,* April 3, 1944, 3–8; *Women's Voice,* July 31, 1952, 2–3.

6. Lochridge, 21.

7. "We the Mothers Mobilize for America," AJC F: We the Mothers, 1.

8. *Women's Voice,* July 31, 1952, 3.

9. Ibid., July 31, 1952, 3, October 12, 1954, 5–12, December 25, 1952, 2, May 24, 1945, 2; December 27, 1945, 2; "Lyrl Clark Van Hyning," (April 1946), AJC F: Van Hyning, 5–7; FBI file on We the Mothers, pt. 1, 22.

10. FBI file on We the Mothers, pt. 1, 22.

11. *Women's Voice,* October 12, 1954, 12 and October 29, 1953, 7–9; Van Hyning, "Is Masonry Jewish?", reprint from *Women's Voice,* November 29, 1945, 1–2.

12. *Women's Voice,* March 27, 1952, 2.

13. Ibid., December 30, 1948, 2.

14. FBI file on We the Mothers, pt. 1, 61.

15. Ibid., 72.

16. "Van Hyning," (April 1946), AJC F: Van Hyning, 2.

17. FBI file on We the Mothers, pt. 1, 22, 26; *Women's Voice,* October 12, 1954, 15.

18. *Women's Voice,* August 30, 1945, 9; TAF 1945, 1386–7.

19. *Women's Voice,* December 30, 1943, 2.

20. Ibid., August 26, 1943, 1; December 30, 1943, 2.

21. Ibid., April 26, 1945, 2.

22. Ibid., March 18, 1943, 5.

23. Ibid., April 27, 1944, 1.

24. McEnaney, "Defending the Family Altar," 46–7, 95–7; *Women's Voice,* March 27, 1952, 9; April 27, 1944, 2, 5.

25. "Nationalists," AJC F: Mother's Groups, 1–5; Piller, *Time Bomb,* 69; Carlson, "They Praise the Lord and Pass the Poison Leaflets," *The Woman with Woman's Digest* (October 1944), 10.

26. *Women's Voice,* March–April, 1957, 2, October 29, 1953, 9; McEnaney, "Defending the Family Altar," 46.

27. *Women's Voice,* March–April, 1957, 2; Piller, *Time Bomb,* 143; *U.S. vs. Joseph E. McWilliams,* U.S. District Court, District of Columbia, Criminal No. 73086, Box 1371, p. 17995, McWilliams Case File; Chicago *Sun,* January 13, 1945.

28. Quotations from testimony of Grace Keefe, U.S. Senate Committee on Foreign Relations, *Hearings,* 79th Cong., 1st Sess., July 11, 1945, 390. Also see FBI file on We the Mothers, pt. 21, 63–5 and pt. 14, 99–100; TAF, 1943, 919; Piller, *Time Bomb,* 164; *PM,* June 12, 1944.

29. Carlson, 173–4; TAF 1945, 595, 1343.

30. New York *PM,* September 19, 1943; FBI file on We the Mothers, pt. 19, 301.

31. YIVO TAF, 1944, 562, 722.

32. Carlson, *The Plotters,* 174.

33. McEnaney, "Defending the Family Altar," 44, 50; TAF 1943, 29; TAF 1944, 471; TAF 1945, 533.

34. McEnaney, "Defending the Family Altar," 44. The precise content of the pageant cannot be described because neither a program nor a script is available. The secondary sources do not describe the songs and readings. The songs and readings likely combined a celebration of Christianity with patriotic and maternal praise.

35. McEnaney, "Defending the Family Altar," 45.

36. YIVO TAF 1944, 254, 351, 562, 722; FBI file on We the Mothers, pt. 18, 130; *Chicago Tribune,* April 26 and 27, 1944.

37. FBI file on We the Mothers, pt. 21, 43–4; Van Hyning speech to 1944 Women's National Peace Convention, B 57, Jewish Community Relations Council of Minnesota papers.

38. *Propaganda Battlefront,* March 31, 1945, 1; Sayers and Kahn, *The Plot Against the Peace,* 209.

39. Carlson, "They Praise the Lord and Pass the Poison Leaflets," 9–10.

40. *Chicago Tribune,* March 9, July 3, 1941.

41. Ibid., November 1, 1941.

42. Sayers and Kahn, *The Plot Against the Peace,* 208.

43. Ibid.; *Chicago Tribune,* November 30, 1941.

44. "Daughters of Dissension and Defeat," unmarked clipping, TAF 1944, 11–2.

45. *New York Times,* November 30, 1941, quoted in McEnaney, "Defending the Family Altar," 41–3.

46. Ware writes that "probably the preeminent female foreign correspondent of the 1930s was Dorothy Thompson." Thompson earned a reputation in the 1920s in Europe, reporting on wars and revolutions and interviewing European leaders. In 1928 she married novelist Sinclair Lewis. In 1931 she returned to Europe and interviewed Hitler in Germany. Three years later Hitler expelled her from Germany for writing a series of articles critical of the Nazi regime. After she returned to the United States, Thompson became a successful columnist and radio commentator who condemned fascism and called for American intervention against the European dictators. See Ware, *American Women in the 1930s,* 78.

47. *Chicago Tribune,* November 20, 1942.

48. Ibid., November 21, 1941.

49. Ibid., November 26, 1941.

50. TAF 1944, 644, 732–4.

51. Ibid.

52. Ibid., 736.

53. Ibid., 645–6.

54. Ibid., 648–738.

55. Whelan and Johnson, "The Menace of the 'Mothers'," 73.

56. Hoke, *Black Mail* (New York: Reader's Book Service, Inc., 1944), p. 60; *Women's Voice,* January 31, 1946, 1, and October 26, 1950, 3; TAF 1945, 334, 398, 532–3; "We the Mothers Mobilize for America," (1945), AJC F: We the Mothers, 6.

57. TAF 1945, 689–90, 718.

58. *Milwaukee Journal,* June 17, 1945.

59. "We the Mothers Mobilize for America," AJC F: We the Mothers, 5; TAF 1945, 523–6.

60. For an analysis of the effect authoritarian parents can have on the personality development of children, see Allport, *The Nature of Prejudice,* and Theodor W. Adorno, et al., *The Authoritarian Personality* (New York: Harper, 1950).

61. "Lyrl Clark Van Hyning," AJC F: Van Hyning, 2.

62. FBI file on We the Mothers, pt. 18, 130; TAF 1944, 254, 341.

63. *Chicago Tribune,* March 9 and July 3, 1941.

64. "Lyrl Clark Van Hyning," AJC, 2; Spivak, "Senator Langer's Secret Meeting," 3–8; *Women's Voice,* July 31, 1942, 2–3.

65. "Lyrl Clark Van Hyning," AJC, 2.

66. Carlson, "They Praise the Lord and Pass the Poison Leaflets," 10.

67. *Women's Voice,* July 31, 1952, 3; McEnaney, "Defending the Family Altar," 44, 50.

Chapter Eight

1. "Mothers of Sons Forum," B 56, 6, Jewish Community Relations Council of Minnesota papers; Memo, Mothers of Sons Forum, 1–4, AJC F: Mothers of Sons Forum.

2. Carlson, *Under Cover,* 509.

3. Ibid.; "Hitler's Petticoat Brigade," April 7, 1941, YIVO F: Misc., 169–170; AJC *News Letter* (Los Angeles) 6:158 (August 6, 1941), 1, AJC F: AJC News Letter; TAF 1942, 881; Confidential Report on Mothers of Sons Rally, Taft Auditorium, March 1941, 1, AJC F: Women fascists; Testimony of Mrs. Ethel Groen on Removing Restrictions on Numbers and Length of Service of Draftees, *Hearings,* House Committee on Military Affairs, 76th Cong., 1st Sess. (Washington D.C.: Government Printing Office, 1941), 143–5.

4. TAF 1942, 881; Confidential Report on Mothers of Sons Rally, 1; AJC F: Women fascists; Testimony of Groen, 143–5.

5. Lochridge, 20; Hoke, *Black Mail,* 56; Carlson, *The Plotters,* 177.

6. Topical Study Memorandum, Mothers of Sons Forum, U.S. Naval Intelligence,

Ninth Naval District, June 28, 1943, 6; Report on Mothers of Sons *Bulletin,* May 11, 1943, YIVO F: Misc., 1943, 227.

7. FBI file on Elizabeth Dilling, pt. 23, 140; Topical Study Memorandum, 3.

8. Meeting Report, America First Party, Dayton, Ohio, May 6, 1943, YIVO F: 1943, Misc., 287; "Nationalist Congress Assembles in St. Louis," 1944, B 9, F: Duplicates, Smith papers; Topical Study Memorandum, 3, 9; Dilling *Bulletin,* August 1943, 16–7.

9. Quotes from "Hitler's Petticoat Brigade," 168; Confidential Report on Mothers of Sons Rally, 1, Jewish Community Relations Council of Minnesota papers.

10. Meeting report, May 11, 1941, 1, Jewish Community Relations Council of Minnesota papers.

11. "Hitler's Petticoat Brigade," 169.

12. AJC *News Letter* (Los Angeles) 6:158 (August 6, 1941), 4, AJC F: AJC News Letter; testimony of Groen, 143–5; and testimony of Arbogast, ibid., 150–1; editorial, *Cincinnati Post,* July 29, 1941.

13. Meeting report, November 10, 1941, 3, Jewish Community Relations Council of Minnesota papers. Groen was referring to the speech Lindbergh delivered at Des Moines, Iowa on September 11, 1941, in which he blamed the British, the Jews, and the Roosevelt administration for leading the United States into war. See Roos, 299–300.

14. Meeting report, November 10, 1941; Roos, 299–300.

15. TAF 1941, 881; "Hitler's Petticoat Brigade," 162.

16. TAF 1941, 881; *Cincinnati Times-Star,* September 4, 1943; TAF 1942, 250; Meeting report, Mothers of Sons Forum, July 13, 1943, YIVO F: Misc., 1943, 364; Report of woman investigator, Mothers of Sons Forum, F: Misc., 1942, 497; Mothers of Sons Forum *Bulletin,* January 12, 1943, 2–3, Department of the Army File.

17. Meeting report, Mothers of Sons Forum, July 2, 1942, AJC F: Mothers of American Sons, 1–2.

18. "Hitler's Petticoat Brigade," 170; Topical Study Memorandum, 9; *Cincinnati Post,* March 5, 1943.

19. Carlson, "Daughters of Dissension and Defeat," *The Woman with Woman's Digest* (November 1944), 10, in AJC Vertical File, F: Fascism—U. S., Mothers' Groups; *Cincinnati Post,* April 16 and November 29, 1943; "Hitler's Petticoat Brigade," 165; Meeting report, Mothers of Sons Forum, June 23, 1942, 665, YIVO F: Misc.

20. *Women's Voice,* January 27, 1944, 4.

21. "Gentlemen of Congress, arise and answer the questions of the American Mother," letter to Congress, undated, Department of the Army File; Washington *Times-Herald,* July 13, 1945; *Cincinnati Post,* July 25, 1945.

22. Meeting report, Fall 1941, YIVO, F: Misc., 1941, 1; Meeting report, June 24, 1943, YIVO F: Misc., 1943, 337; FBI file on United Mothers of America, pt. 14, 87.

23. Stanley to Smith, June 3, 1946, Reel 13, Smith microfilm (in author's possession), F: Mrs. David Stanley; Meeting report, United Mothers of Cleveland, May 13, 1942, YIVO F: Misc., 1942, 507–8; Stanley to Smith, September 17, 1942, B 7, F: 1939–42, Stanley, Mrs. David, Smith papers; TAF 1945, 56. The conclusion that Freida Stanley was politically naive and less intelligent than some other mothers' leaders is based on the evaluation of the American Jewish Committee, found in the Trends Analysis Files, which concluded her lack of ability made her less threatening than women such as Van Hyning.

24. Stanley to Smith, June 3, 1946, Smith microfilm (in author's possession), Reel 13, F: Mrs. David Stanley; Meeting report, United Mothers of Cleveland, May 13, 1942, YIVO, F: Misc., 1942, 507–8; Stanley to Smith, September 17, 1942, B 7, F: 1939–42, Stanley, Mrs. David, Smith papers; TAF 1945, 56, Meeting report, May 13, 1942, YIVO F: Misc., 1942, 508–9; Stanley to Smith, August 2, 1941, B 7, F: 1939–42, Stanley, Mrs. David, Smith papers; Meeting report, March 9, 1943, YIVO F: Misc., 1943, 3.

25. Meeting report, May 13, 1942, YIVO F: Misc., 1942, 506.

26. Report on conversation at headquarters of United Mothers, January 21, 1943, YIVO F: Misc., 1943, 1; Topical Study Memorandum, America First Party, U.S. Naval Intelligence, Ninth Naval District, September 6, 1943, 9; TAF 1944, 404, and TAF 1942, 888; Meeting report, April 21, 1942, AJC F: United Mothers, 3; *Cleveland Press,* September 16, 1942.

27. Meeting report, May 13, 1942, YIVO, F: Misc., 1942, 508–9; Stanley to Smith, August 2, 1941, B 7, F: 1939–42, Stanley, Mrs. David, Smith papers; Meeting report, March 9, 1943, YIVO F: Misc., 1943, 3.

28. *Cleveland Press,* March 14 and 15, 1944.

29. TAF 1942, 872, 948, and 1945, 901; Meeting report, June 8, 1943, YIVO F: Misc., 1943, 315; *Cleveland Press,* March 14, 1944; Meeting report, May 13, 1942, YIVO, F: Misc., 1942, 509.

30. Carlson, *The Plotters,* 170; Statement of the League for Human Rights on Un-American Leaflets in Cleveland, August 26, 1942, AJC F: National Legion of Mothers and Women of America, 2; Meeting report, August 26, 1943, YIVO, F: Misc., 1943, 438; Johnson and Whelan, "The Menace of the Mothers," 1.

31. Meeting report, October 26, 1943, YIVO F: Misc., 1943, 635.

32. Carlson, *The Plotters,* 170.

33. *Cleveland Press,* March 14, 1944.

34. Ibid.

35. Meeting report, August (undated) 1944, YIVO F: Misc., 1943, 441.

36. Joanna Steinmetz, "America Firster Gerald L. K. Smith is Hero of United Mothers Group," *Washington Daily News,* March 28, 1944, Smith microfilm, R 8, F: Cleveland Meeting.

37. Anti-Defamation League of B'nai B'rith (hereafter ADL), *Anti-Semitism in the United States in 1947* (New York: ADL, 1948), 180.

38. "A Public Statement by the United Mothers of America," 1944, Smith microfilm, R 9, F: Mrs. David Stanley.

39. Meeting report, fall (undated) 1941, YIVO F: Misc., 1942, 2; Meeting report, April 14, 1942, YIVO F: Misc., 1942, 335.

40. Meeting report, June 24, 1942, YIVO F: Misc., 1942, 656; *Cleveland Plain Dealer,* August 20, 1943; editorial, *Cleveland News,* June 25, 1942; *Detroit News,* June 25, 1942.

41. *Cleveland Press,* March 14, 1944.

42. Meeting report, November 30, 1943, YIVO F: Misc., 1943, 677; Meeting report, May 13, 1942, YIVO F: Misc., 1942, 509; TAF 1942, 872.

43. Hoke, *It's a Secret,* 180.

44. Confidential memo on United Mothers meeting, February 19, 1942, AJC F: United Mothers, 1; TAF 1942, 890.

45. Memo on Clare Hoffman, undated, AJC F: Hoffman, 4; TAF 1942, 877–8;

Cleveland Press, June 4, 1941; *Cleveland Plain Dealer,* September 4, 1941; Report on Beatrice M. Knowles, ADL, July 23, 1943, YIVO F: Misc., 1943, 1; *The Catholic Universe Weekly,* June 6, 1941, B 7, F: 1939–42, Stanley, Mrs. David, Smith papers.

46. Meeting report, March 3, 1942, AJC F: United Mothers, 1.

47. Resolution of United Mothers of America, March 17, 1942, B 7 F: 1939–42, Smith papers; and Stanley to Smith, March 26, 1942, F: 1939–42, Smith papers; *Cleveland News,* May 17, 1941; Ella Monreal, "A Tribute to Old Glory," June 15, 1943, YIVO F: Misc., 1943, 436.

48. Meeting report, United Mothers of America, August 26, 1943, YIVO F: Misc., 1943, 438.

49. Meeting report, July 27, 1943, YIVO F: Misc., 1943, 369; *Cleveland Press,* March 15, 1944.

50. ADL, *Anti-Semitism in the United States in 1947,* 89.

51. Testimony of Mrs. Rosa M. Farber on Removing Restrictions on Numbers and Length of Service of Draftees, *Hearings,* 140; Piller, *Time Bomb,* 119; Memo, National Legion of Mothers of American and Other Mothers' Organizations, AJC F: Mothers, 4; Dilling, *Bulletin,* Christmas 1940, 9; Mothers of the U.S.A. to "Dear Patriot," November 26, 1940, in AJC *News Letter* (Los Angeles) 5:127 (January 29, 1941), 1, AJC F: AJC Newsletter.

52. Testimony of Farber, 140; Memo, National Legion of Mothers of America and Other Mothers' Organizations.

53. Testimony of Farber, 140; Memo, National Legion of Mothers of America and Other Mothers' Organizations.

54. Carlson, *Under Cover,* 310.

55. Ibid.; Memo, National Legion of Mothers of America and Other Mothers' Organizations, 4.

56. *Los Angeles Herald Express,* October 23 and 24, 1939.

57. Ibid., October 24, 1939.

58. Memo, National Legion of Mothers of America and Other Mothers' Organizations, 4.

59. Resolution to Impeach the President, Mothers of the United States of America, 1943, AJC F: Mothers of the United States of America.

60. Ibid.; Testimony of Mrs. Rosa Farber on S. 4164, Compulsory Military Training and Service, *Hearings,* Senate Military Affairs Committee, 76th Cong., 3rd Sess. (Washington, D.C.: Government Printing Office, 1940), pp. 278–84; *New York Times,* August 23, 1940.

61. Statement of Rosa M. Farber, U.S. Senate, 77th Cong., 1st Sess., Committee on Foreign Relations, *Hearings* (Washington: Government Printing Office, 1941), pp. 770–2.

62. Testimony of Farber on Removing Restrictions on Numbers and Length of Service of Draftees, 141–3.

63. Greenwald, 622; *New York Times,* November 4 and 5, 1941.

64. Lochridge, 72; Beatrice Knowles Biography, AJC F: Beatrice Knowles, 1.

65. TAF 1943, 1270–1; Knowles Testimony to Military Affairs Committee, undated and unmarked, AJC F: Beatrice Knowles, 1–2.

66. TAF 1943, 1270–1; Carlson, *Under Cover,* 312.

67. TAF 1945, 179; Mothers of the United States of America, AJC F: Mothers of

the U.S.A., 4; Knowles testimony to Military Affairs Committee in AJC F: Beatrice Knowles, 6–8.

68. Whelan and Johnson, "The Menace of the 'Mothers,'" 72; TAF 1942, 108; Knowles testimony to Military Affairs Committee in AJC F: Beatrice Knowles, 6–8.

69. TAF 1945, 640–1; Lochridge, 72.

70. TAF 1943, 881; TAF 1944, 68–9, 233, 413; and TAF 1945, 641.

71. TAF 1942, 332; TAF 1945, 122; Carlson, "Daughters of Dissension and Defeat," 8.

72. TAF 1944, 556.

73. TAF 1945, 640–1; Lochridge, 72.

74. Curt Riess, *The Nazis Go Underground* (Garden City, N.Y.: Doubleday, 1944), 124.

75. Memo, Mothers of the United States of America, AJC F: Mothers of the U.S.A., 3.

76. Dorothy Roberts, "Old Anti-Semites in New Clothes," *New Masses* 57 (October 23, 1945), 6; Meeting report, July 27, 1945, YIVO F: Misc., 1945, 2; TAF 1944, 655, 917.

77. TAF 1944, 916; TAF 1945, 62, 180; Meeting report, August 31, 1945, YIVO F: Misc., 1945, 1–2.

78. TAF 1944, 920–3; and 1945, 1353.

79. TAF 1945, 180, 62; Meeting report, August 31, 1945, YIVO F: Misc., 1945, 1–2.

80. Memo, Women's White House: Blanche Winters, in AJC F: Blanche Winters, 3; Meeting report, August 3, 1945, 1–3; and September 7, 1945, 4, YIVO F: Misc., 1945.

81. Meeting report, August 31, 1945, YIVO F: Misc., 1945, 2; TAF 1945, 1327, 2242; and 1946, 974.

82. TAF 1945, 576.

83. Meeting report, September 14, 1945, YIVO F: Misc., 1945, 1–3; TAF 1944, 141, 920; TAF 1945, 1068, 1072.

84. Piller, *Time Bomb,* 119; Memo, Women's White House: Blanche Winters, in AJC F: Blanche Winters, 1–2; Meeting report, August 31, 1945, YIVO F: Misc., 1945, 1; TAF 1944, 918; TAF 1945, 1137.

85. TAF 1944, 649, 923–4; TAF 1945, 1011, 1067, 1155–7; 1240, and 1353.

86. Memo, Women's White House: Blanche Winters, 1–3; Johnson and Whelan, "The Menace of the 'Mothers,'" 72; New York *World-Telegram*, July 19, 1945; Report on activities in Detroit, December 24, 1945, AJC F: Misc., 1946, 1; Memo on Blanche Winters in F: Lois Washburn, undated, 1; TAF 1945, 471.

87. TAF 1944, 919.

88. Ibid.

89. Roberts, "Old Anti-Semites in New Clothes," 7–8.

90. TAF 1945, 33, 1049; Meeting report, August 3, 1945, YIVO F: Misc., 1945, 3.

91. TAF 1945, 898–901, 1096–7, 1108–9; Roberts, "Old Anti-Semites in New Clothes," 8–9.

92. TAF 1945, 898–901.

93. Brinkley, 270.

94. My study of Smith suggests the Midwest was receptive to nationalist and isolationist appeals. See Jeansonne, *Gerald L. K. Smith,* 67. Several contemporary press ac-

counts emphasized the potency of isolationism in the Midwest. See, for example, *The Nation*, July 27, 1940, 73–4; March 11, 1944, 298; May 6, 1944, 530–1; March 31, 1945, 347; May 26, 1945, 597–8; *The New Republic*, August 2, 1943, 129–30; and the *St. Louis Post Dispatch*, February 13, 1944. Cole's studies of the America First Committee and of the broader isolationist movement also stress isolationist activities in the Midwest. See Cole, *America First*, and *Roosevelt and the Isolationists*.

Chapter Nine

1. Greenwald, 620; B 11, F: Mothers of Pennsylvania, 1–3, Pennsylvania Historical Society; Memo, National Legion of Mothers of America and Other Mothers' Organizations, 4, AJC F: Women Fascists.

Another mothers' organization was the Pittsburgh-based Defenders of George Washington's Principles. The organization was directed by Marie Lohle, although Charles Madden was the nominal president. Lohle, a militant feminist and the wealthy wife of a salesman, devoted her time and money to holding nationalist meetings at her large suburban estate. She was a confidante of Baldwin and Nye and a collaborator with the American Women Against Communism. Smith was her closest ally in the nationalist movement, however. Lohle sponsored meetings at which Smith spoke and distributed his magazines. Like Madden she was active in Smith's America First Party and National Emergency Committee.

Lohle organized her group in 1939 and soon collected 15,000 signatures on a petition against repeal of the Neutrality Act. The group met twice weekly to alert women about the perils of the New Deal, socialism, and world government. For accounts of the organization, see TAF 1943, 666; Piller, *Time Bomb*, 82; Carlson, *The Plotters*, 176–7; FBI file on Defenders of George Washington's Principles, pt. 20, 109–11.

2. Memo re: Mothers of Pennsylvania (1940), 1, B 11, F: Mothers of Pennsylvania, Pennsylvania Historical Society.

3. Ibid.; TAF 1943, 396.

4. Flyer, October 6, 1940, AJC F: Mothers of Pennsylvania.

5. B 4, 11, F: Mothers of America, Pennsylvania Historical Society.

6. Meeting report, November 20, 1940, AJC F: Mothers of Pennsylvania, 1.

7. Memo, National Legion of Mothers of America and Other Mothers Organizations, 4, AJC F: Women Fascists; Meeting report, October 1, 1941, 2, AJC F: National Legion of Mothers and Women of America; Meeting report, January 22, 1941, 3, AJC F: Mothers of Pennsylvania; Meeting report, March 6, 1941, 3, AJC F: Mothers of Pennsylvania.

8. TAF 1944, 153–164; Aims and Purposes, National Blue Star Mothers, 1, AJC F: National Blue Star Mothers; Memo on Mothers' Groups, 1944, 1, AJC Vertical Files F: Fascism—U.S., Mothers' Groups; Interview with C. E. Wallington, February 4, 1944, 6, AJC F: National Blue Star Mothers; Crusading Mothers of Pennsylvania, B 37, F: Mothers of America, 8, Jewish Community Relations Council of Minnesota papers; TAF 1941, 814; FBI file on National Blue Star Mothers, 9.

9. TAF 1941, 814, FBI file on National Blue Star Mothers, 9.

10. Interview with Wallington, 5; National Blue Star Mothers, 2–5, AJC F: National Blue Star Mothers; TAF 1945, 1097; Meeting report, November 9, 1943, 2, AJC F: National Blue Star Mothers.

11. National Blue Star Mothers, 2–5, AJC F: National Blue Star Mothers; TAF 1945, 1097.

12. Testimony of Catherine Veronica Brown, House Un-American Activities Committee, 78th Cong., 1st Sess., on H. R. 282, *Executive Hearings,* 6, January 15, 1942 (Washington, D.C.: Government Printing Office, 1943, 2648–51.

13. Brown to Smith, October 19, 1943, B 8, F: 1943, Crusading Mothers of Pennsylvania, Smith papers.

14. *Friends of Democracy Congressional Bulletin,* 1:15 (June 26, 1946), 1; TAF 1944, 316; Memo, Mrs. Catherine Veronica Brown, 3, AJC F: National Blue Star Mothers; Johnson and Whelan, "The Menace of the Mothers," 163; FBI file on National Blue Star Mothers, 10; Memo on Mothers' Groups, 3, AJC Vertical Files, F: Fascism—U.S., Mothers' Groups.

15. *American Jewish Year Book,* 46 (1944–5) (Philadelphia: Jewish Publications Society of America, 1945), 139; *Friends of Democracy Congressional Bulletin,* 1:15 (June 26, 1946), 1; TAF 1945, 879 and 1940, 710.

16. TAF 1944, 164; interview with Wallington, 4–5; Wallington to Gov. Edward Martin, November 6, 1943; Meeting report, November 9, 1943, 1, AJC F: National Blue Star Mothers; Wallington to *Chicago Tribune,* October 25, 1944.

17. Memo on Brown, 3, AJC F: National Blue Star Mothers; TAF 1941, 1169 and 1945, 229; Hoke, *Black Mail,* 52; Riess, *The Nazis Go Underground,* 124; New York *Daily News,* March 3, 1944; Meeting report, November, 1941, YIVO F: Misc., 1941, 868.

The Blue Star Mothers also took an interest in the Tyler Kent case, a cause célèbre of the far right. Kent, a code clerk for Joseph P. Kennedy, the American ambassador to Britain, handled Kennedy's and Churchill's confidential telegrams to Roosevelt before the war. Disturbed by warlike statements from American leaders, Kent passed secret documents to Germany, saying he wanted them published to discredit Roosevelt. British intelligence arrested Kent, and after incriminating documents were found in his apartment, he was convicted of espionage and sentenced to seven years in prison. Kent claimed he had taken the documents only to reveal plans to get the United States into the war. His mother, joined by far-right organizations, sought to get him released. Kent was released after the war, but Brown complained his return to the United States, set back on the pretense that no transportation was available, was really engineered by Jews because they knew he would expose their plot to embroil the country in the war before the Pearl Harbor attack. See Higham, *American Swastika,* 32; Meeting report, October 26, 1945, 1, AJC F: Current Events Club.

18. *New York Times,* June 25, 1944; TAF 1943, 590; Flint *News Advertiser,* December 7, 1943 and April 4, 1944; Cleveland *Press,* March 30, 1944; "Blue Star Mother Facts," FBI file: Blue Star Mothers, 1–2.

19. Testimony of Dr. Bessie R. Burchett, Special Committee on Un-American Activities House of Representatives, *Hearings,* 78th Cong., 1st Session, 15 (Washington: Government Printing Office, 1942), 2542–5; Memo on Women Fascists, 3–4, AJC F: Women Fascists; Earl McCoy, "Bessie and the Bund," *New Masses,* June 6, 1939, 15; Gordon Sager, "Swastika Over Philadelphia," *Equality,* n.d., 8; Memo on the National Blue Star Mothers, 7, AJC F: National Blue Star Mothers.

20. Testimony of Burchett, 2542–5.

21. Ibid.

22. Dilling, *Bulletin,* October 1941, 27; McCoy, "Bessie and the Bund," 15.

23. Dilling, *Bulletin,* October 1941, 27; McCoy, "Bessie and the Bund," 15.

24. TAF 1941, 740.

25. Special Committee on Un-American Activities, Testimony of Burchett, 2542–5; "Bessie and the Bund," 15; Sager, "Swastika Over Philadelphia," 7.

26. Sager, "Swastika Over Philadelphia," 7.

27. Testimony of Bessie Burchett, House Un-American Activities Committee, *Executive Hearings* on H. R. 282, 78th Cong., 1st Sess., 6, October 1941–April 1942 (Washington: Government Printing Office, 1943), 2559.

28. TAF 1941, 904; Dilling to "Dear Friends," February 21, 1939, Dilling papers.

29. Memo on Women Fascists, 3–4, Box 11, F: Mothers of America, 1, Pennsylvania Historical Society; Testimony of Burchett before House Un-American Activities Committee, 2548–51; Meeting report, November 20, 1941, 1–2 and January 22, 1941, 1, AJC F: Mothers of Pennsylvania.

30. TAF 1941, 373 and 304, and 1943, 56; Beatrice Brown to members of Women United, February 19, 1942, 1, AJC F: Women United.

31. TAF 1943, 28–31.

32. TAF 1940, 30 and 1943, 640, 918; Hoke, *Black Mail,* 85.

33. TAF 1943, 55, 639.

34. Ibid., 260.

35. TAF 1942, 200–1.

36. TAF 1941, 514 and 878; TAF 1943, 68–9, 97; TAF 1944, 651; FBI file: Cooper, 36–9, 49–51, 59–63.

37. TAF 1941, 490 and TAF 1942, 208; Mrs. Beatrice Brown to members of Women United, February 19, 1942, AJC F: Women United; Memo to members of Women United, June 12, 1941, AJC F: Women United.

38. Memo on Women United, May 2, 1942, 1–3, AJC F: Women United.

39. Memo on Women United, May 10, 1941, 1, AJC F: Women United; TAF 1942, 490–1, 583; Memo 2 on Women United, 3, AJC F: Women United.

40. TAF 1941, 714; "Items on Parade," unmarked clipping in AJC F: Bound Clippings, 1941, 700.

41. *New York Times,* November 6, 1941.

42. AJC *News Letter,* March 23, 1942, AJC Bound Clippings, 1942 (page number illegible).

43. TAF 1941, 632.

44. Carlson, *Under Cover,* 144, 197; TAF 1943, 165; Memo on Mrs. A. Cressy Morrison and American Women Against Communism, October 8, 1940, 1, AJC F: Mrs. A. Cressy Morrison; *New York Post,* July 8, 1941.

45. Carlson, *Under Cover,* 197–8; AJC *News Letter* (Los Angeles) 5:144 (May 7, 1941), 6, AJC F: AJC Newsletter.

46. Dilling *Bulletin,* May 4, 1940, 7; Reiss, *The Nazis Go Underground* (New York, 1944), 124; TAF 1939, 377, and 1943, 117, 165; Memo on Mrs. A. Cressy Morrison, June 22, 1943, 1, U.S. War Department.

47. TAF 1939, 1301, and 1941, 713.

48. *New York Post,* July 8, 1941.

49. *Why Are Jews Persecuted for Their Religion?* (Bremerton, Wash.: American Publishing Society, n.d.), AJC F: American Women Against Communism; FBI file: Ameri-

can Women Against Communism, 111, TAF 1943, 117, 165; Whelan and Johnson, "The Menace of the Mothers," 73; Hoke, *Black Mail,* 50; Piller, 117; FBI file: American Women Against Communism, 111; *New York Times,* May 5, 1946.

50. TAF 1943, 165; Memo on Mrs. A. Cressy Morrison and American Women Against Communism, October 8, 1940, 3, AJC F: Mrs. A. Cressy Morrison.

51. *New York Times,* May 5, 1946; FBI F: American Women Against Communism, 111.

52. Memo on Bessie Simon and Peace Now, Eastern Regional Office, ADL, New York, January 25, 1944, 1; Louis A. Novins to ADL Regional Offices, January 19, 1944, 1; Dorothy H. Hutchinson, *Must the Killing Go On?* (New York: The Peace Now Movement, 1943), 22, AJC F: Peace Now Movement.

53. House Un-American Activities Committee, *The Peace Now Movement,* Report No. 1161, 78th Cong., 2nd sess., February 17, 1944 (Washington, D.C.: Government Printing Office, 1944), 2; St. Louis *Star-Times,* February 10, 1944; "Peace Now Movement," 1944, p. 1, AJC F: Peace Now Movement; Riess, *The Nazis Go Underground,* 132; Carlson, *The Plotters,* 180.

54. House Un-American Activities Committee, *The Peace Now Movement,* Report No. 1161, 78th Cong., 2nd Sess., February 17, 1944 (Washington, D.C.: Government Printing Office, 1944), 2; St. Louis *Star-Times,* February 10, 1944; "Peace Now Movement," 1944, p. 1, AJC F: Peace Now Movement; Riess, *The Nazis Go Underground,* 132; Carlson, *The Plotters,* 180.

55. *New York Times,* December 19, 1943; *New York Post,* January 28, 1944; Peace Now Movement, 1944, 1–2, AJC F: Peace Now Movement.

56. Riess, *The Nazis Go Underground,* 132.

57. *New York Post,* January 27, 1944.

58. Testimony of Mrs. Dorothy Hutchinson, U.S. Senate Committee on Foreign Relations, 86th Cong., 2nd Sess., *Hearings,* Pt. 1, January 28, 1960 (Washington, D.C.: Government Printing Office, 1960), 41–4.

59. Peace Now Movement, 1944, 2, AJC F: Peace Now Movement.

60. Carlson, *Under Cover,* 85; *New York Post,* January 28, 1944; New York *PM,* January 26, February 1, March 16 and June 26, 1944.

61. Hutchinson, *Must the Killing Go On?,* 9–12, AJC F: Peace Now Movement.

62. Ibid., 2, 14–6, 19–21.

63. Sayers and Kahn, *The Plot Against the Peace,* 201–2.

64. Derounian, "Petticoat Peace Plotters," *News Story* (November 1944), 34; *Peace Now* (October 1944), 1, AJC F: Peace Now Movement.

65. Editorial, St. Louis *Globe-Democrat,* February 18, 1944.

66. Dorothy Hutchinson, *Peace Now* (New York: Peace Now Movement, n.d.), 2, AJC F: Peace Now Movement.

67. HUAC Report, 10–2; Washington *Times-Herald,* February 17, 1944.

68. Editorial, St. Louis *Globe-Democrat,* February 18, 1944.

69. *New York Post,* January 28, 1944.

70. Flyer, "Peace Now," October 1944, 1, AJC F: Peace Now Movement.

71. FBI file: Catherine Baldwin, 17–8; Memo on Catherine P. Baldwin (1941), 1–3, AJC F: Catherine Baldwin; TAF 1943, 797, 922; Catherine P. Baldwin, *And Men Wept* (New York: Our Publications, 1954), 1.

72. FBI file: Baldwin, 18–9; TAF 1943, 928–9.

73. Baldwin, *And Men Wept*, 1; TAF 1943, 797, 922.

74. Baldwin, *And Men Wept*.

75. Ibid., 24–35, 77–87, 113, 130–3.

76. M. S. Pratiner to N. Goodrich, memo on *Undermining America*, November 13, 1940, 1–2, AJC F: Catherine Baldwin; FBI file: Baldwin, 18–9; Memo on Catherine P. Baldwin (1941), 3, AJC F: Catherine Baldwin.

77. TAF 1943, 922.

78. Ibid., 923.

79. Ibid., 922.

80. Ibid., 922–3, 928–9.

81. Ibid., 922–3; Memo on Catherine P. Baldwin (1941), 5, AJC F: Catherine Baldwin.

82. FBI F: Baldwin, 19; Statement of Catherine P. Baldwin, U.S. Senate, Committee on Foreign Relations, 79th Cong., 1st Sess., July 11, 1945, *Hearings* (Washington, D.C.: Government Printing Office, 1945), 367–70.

83. TAF 1939, p. 412.

84. "Dr. Maude DeLand," 1–2, AJC F: Maude DeLand; "Communism in Germany," February 24, 1939, clipping in AJC F: Maude DeLand. There is no evidence that DeLand ever practiced medicine.

85. Memo on Women Fascists, 5, AJC F: Women Fascists; "Dr. Maude DeLand," 2, AJC F: American Women Against Communism.

86. Carlson, *Under Cover*, 192–3; TAF 1939, 662; TAF 1940, 569, 745; TAF 1942, 162; TAF 1943, 162.

87. Memo on Women Fascists, 5, AJC F: Women Fascists; "Dr. Maude DeLand," 2, AJC F: American Women Against Communism.

88. "Dr. Maude DeLand," 1–2, AJC F: Maude DeLand; Carlson, *Under Cover*, 87, 193, 488, and 236; TAF 1940, p. 709, 4491; 1943, 162.

89. Carlson, *Under Cover*, 193, 488; Hoke, *It's a Secret*, 28; TAF 1940, 491.

90. Memo, Mrs. Rudyard Uzzell, June 1940, 1–2, AJC F: Mrs. Rudyard Uzzell.

91. Ibid.

92. Memo on Mrs. Uzzell's Son, 1–2, AJC F: Mrs. Rudyard Uzzell; Memo on Uzzell, 3–4, AJC F: Mrs. Rudyard Uzzell.

93. Deposition of Alice May Kimball, April 13, 1943, 1–3, AJC F: Mrs. Uzzell's meeting for General Moseley.

94. Memo, Mrs. Rudyard Uzzell, June 1940, 1–2, AJC F: Mrs. Rudyard Uzzell; Harold Lavine, *Fifth Column in America* (New York: Doubleday, Doran and Company, 1940), 53–4; Memo, Women Fascists, 1–2, AJC F: Women Fascists; Testimony of General George Van Horn Moseley, Special Committee on Un-American Activities, House of Representatives, 76th Cong., 1st Sess., *Hearings*, 3, May 22, 1939 (Washington, D.C.: Government Printing Office, 1939), 3561.

Chapter Ten

1. Carlson, "Daughters of Dissension and Defeat," 8–12.

2. Agnes Waters, *The White Papers* (Washington, D.C., n.p., 1940, 56–7, 70–1, 90; Statement of Agnes Waters at Viereck Trial, March 4, 1942, AJC Vertical File, F: Agnes Waters; Testimony of Agnes Waters on S. 666, Senate Military Affairs Committee,

78th Cong., 1st Sess., April 8, 1943, *Hearings* (Washington D.C.: Government Printing Office, 1943), 871–5. That Waters participated in the activities of the National
Woman's Party indicates gender consciousness was an important facet of her personality. In *The White Papers* she mentions her role in the party yet does not describe
exactly what she did or how long her affiliation lasted. No other primary or secondary
source provides specific information about her involvement in the party.

3. *New York Times,* May 10, 1888, June 4, 1892 and August 30, 1930. There is no
record indicating Agnes Murphy's religious affiliation before she converted to Catholicism.

4. Ibid., November 25, 1935, May 26, 1941.

5. Ibid., October 31, 1930.

6. TAF 1943, 128.

7. TAF 1945, 577; Waters, *The White Papers,* 11–32, 39.

8. Waters, *The White Papers,* 57; Hoke, *It's a Secret,* 172; Piller, 112–3.

9. Waters, *The White Papers,* 55–61.

10. Ibid., 39.

11. Waters to Congress, July 6, 1942, B 59, Jewish Community Relations Council
of Minnesota papers.

12. Waters, *The White Papers,* 803.

13. Waters to Congress, July 6, 1942, B 59, Jewish Community Relations Council
of Minnesota papers.

14. Waters, *The White Papers,* 803.

15. Ibid., 73.

16. Waters to Postmaster General, May 4, 1942, AJC F: Agnes Waters.

17. Testimony of Agnes Waters on S. 666, 874.

18. Waters, *The White Papers,* 55–61.

19. Testimony of Agnes Waters on S. 666, 876, 902–4; Meeting report, April 15,
1942, YIVO F: Misc., 367.

20. YIVO F: Misc., 259.

21. *New York Times,* April 23, 1939.

22. New York *PM,* April 17, 1942.

23. Meeting report, April 15, 1942, YIVO F: Misc., 367; Waters, *The White Papers,*
65.

24. Lochridge, 73.

25. Sayers and Kahn, *Sabotage!,* 243–4; *PM,* June 13, 1943.

26. Waters, *The White Papers,* 57; Hoke, *Its a Secret,* 172; Piller, 112–3.

27. Arthur D. Morse, *While Six Million Died: A Chronicle of American Apathy*
(Woodstock, N.Y.: Overlook Press, 1983), 253.

28. Ibid., 259.

29. Ibid., 260.

30. *New York Times,* April 23, 1939. Also testifying were Winters; Margaret Hopkins Worrell, national legislative chair of the Grand Army of the Republic and a close
friend of Smith; and John B. Trevor, representing the American Coalition of Patriotic
Societies. Winters said, "I say if we are going to keep this country as it is and not lose
our liberty in the future, we have got to keep not only these children out of it, but the
whole damned Europe." Worrell said, "The women of America should arise and defend their own children." Other foes of the bill were Reynolds, the American Legion

national executive committee, Kuhn, and the American Vigilant Intelligence Federation, headed by Jung. See *New York Times,* April 23, 1939 and Morse, 260.

31. Morse, 268.

32. Waters, *The White Papers,* 67, 86–9.

33. Ibid., 93–7.

34. Ibid., 11–32, 79–83.

35. Unmarked clipping, AFC F: Agnes Waters.

36. Testimony of Agnes Waters Before the Committee on Military Affairs, House of Representatives, 77th Cong., 1st Sess., on H. J. Res. 217, 218, 220, and 222, To Declare a National Emergency and Extend Terms of Enlistments, *Hearings* (Washington, D.C.: Government Printing Office, 1941), 156–8; Agnes Waters to friends, December 15, 1941, B 7, F: 1939–42, Sutter, Katherine, Smith Papers.

37. Testimony of Agnes Waters on S. 666, 872, 902–6.

38. Letter to the Congress from Waters, February 19, 1943, B 59, Jewish Community Relations Council of Minnesota papers.

39. Memo on Agnes Waters, AJC F: Agnes Waters.

40. Testimony of Agnes Waters before House Committee on Immigration and Naturalization, 78th Cong., 1st Sess., on H. R. 1882 and H. R. 2308, May 26, 1943, *Hearings* (Washington, D.C.: Government Printing Office, 1943), 185–6.

41. Testimony of Agnes Waters on Reorganization of the Government of the District of Columbia, n.d., 1, B 59, Jewish Community Relations Council of Minnesota papers.

42. Meeting report, n.d., AJC F: United Mothers; Testimony of Agnes Waters before Senate Committee on Military Affairs on S. 666, *Hearings,* 902.

43. New York *PM,* April 17, 1942; Meeting report, n.d., AJC F: United Mothers; Testimony of Agnes Waters before Senate Committee.

44. *PM,* April 17, 1942; ADL Report on Agnes Waters, July 17, 1947, 2.

45. *Philadelphia Record,* April 17, 1942.

46. Report on National Blue Star Mothers, 2–3, AJC F: National Blue Star Mothers.

47. Lochridge, 73.

48. Press release by Agnes Waters, May 19, 1942, AJC Vertical File, F: Agnes Waters; *PM,* February 28, 1944.

49. *PM,* February 28, 1944.

50. Ibid.; press release by Agnes Waters, May 19, 1942, AJC Vertical File, F: Agnes Waters.

51. *PM,* February 28, 1944.

52. Press release by Waters, May 19, 1942.

53. Ibid.; Waters, "An All-American Program for Defense of the United States of America," January 14, 1942, AJC F: Agnes Waters.

54. Carlson, *The Plotters,* 186; TAF 1942, 708.

55. Testimony of Mrs. Agnes Waters, U.S. Senate Committee on Foreign Relations, 79th Cong., 1st Sess., The Charter of the United Nations, July 11, 1945, *Hearings* (Washington: Government Printing Office, 1945), pp. 351–4.

56. New York *Herald Tribune,* July 11, 1945.

57. TAF 1943, 128.

58. Testimony of Waters on S. 666, 871–5.

59. *New York Times,* October 31, 1930, November 25, 1935 and May 26, 1941.

60. Waters, *The White Papers*, 11, 32, 39, 55–61, 65, 93–7; Letter to Congress from Waters, February 19, 1943.

61. Waters, *The White Papers*, 11–32, 79–83; New York *PM*, February 28, 1944.

62. Waters, *The White Papers*, 93–7.

63. Ibid., 67, 86–9; Lochridge, 73; press release by Waters, May 19, 1942; New York *PM*, February 28, 1944.

64. TAF 1943, 128.

65. Lochridge, 73; Waters, *The White Papers*, 57; Hoke, *It's a Secret*, 172; Piller, 112–3; Press release by Waters, May 19, 1942.

66. Waters, *The White Papers*, 56–7, 70–1, 90; Testimony of Waters on S. 666, 871–5.

67. Testimony of Waters on S. 666, 874.

Chapter Eleven

1. Hoke, *It's a Secret*, pp. 12–4, 176–80, 200. Biddle is quoted in Ribuffo, *The Old Christian Right*, 188. Also see Ribuffo, 184–9. Biddle discusses his reluctance to indict such dissenters, and his failure to persuade Roosevelt that convictions would be difficult, in Francis Biddle, *In Brief Authority* (Garden City, N.Y.: Doubleday and Company, 1960), 238–43.

2. Ribuffo, *The Old Christian Right*, 184–9.

3. Ibid.

4. Fry was a shadowy personality, a mystery to most women nationalists. Born in Paris to American parents, she married a Russian prince who was killed in the Bolshevik Revolution. She lived in Britain and Canada, countries where she was well known to fascists, before coming to California with her two sons in 1926. Extremely rich, she lived opulently and bankrolled nationalists despite having no visible means of income. Another Californian, Elizabeth Jewett, helped fund some of Fry's schemes and they were rumored to be lovers.

Fry believed the New Deal represented "the transformation of the Constitutional form of American government into that of the Kahal or Jewish form of government. It has been called the New Deal and the Jew Deal: both are correct and synonymous." She accused Jews of trying to take over the United States as they had enslaved Russia; not only the New Deal but the Supreme Court, the Federal Reserve Bank, and the ACLU were Jew-dominated. Still, she warned that if war broke out between Christians and Jews, American Christians would be ready. In addition, in 1938 Fry wrote to the American Jewish Committee, insisting that Jewish immigration cease.

During the 1930s Fry, a virulent anticommunist, cooperated with the Russian Fascist Union and German Nazis. She received the backing of the German Ministry of Propaganda in trying to prove *The Protocols* valid. Moreover, she founded a monthly newspaper, the isolationist, anti-Semitic *Christian Free Press*, published in Britain and the United States; became a consulting editor of the Bund organ, the *Deutscher Weckruf and Beobachter;* and wrote a book, *Waters Flowing Eastward,* which argued that communism and capitalism were Jewish inventions, and that communists and capitalists were collaborating to create a world Jewish state with a capital in the Middle East.

Fry's most ambitious research effort, however, was the compilation of charts to document the Jewish conspiracy. Rooted in the eighteenth century, the far-ranging conspiracy included Freemasonry, the Illuminati, the Rothschilds, Disraeli, and the League of Nations. Among the results of this conspiracy were several overseas wars, including World War II, labeled the "European War for Jewish control of world's resources, financial, economic, and political, and for the destruction of Christian civilization and Aryan cultural genius."

In 1937 Fry attempted to unite nationalist forces in the United States, sending Henry D. Allen to consult with Deatherage, True, Winrod, Edmondson, and Kuhn. At Fry's instruction, Allen tried to purchase the copyrights and mailing lists of the KKK, part of her plan to rejuvenate the Klan, but Klan leaders rebuffed the overture. Then Allen broke with Fry, charging that she had paid him to attack the Los Angeles home of a prominent anti-Nazi lawyer. She wanted Allen and a dozen men to heave rocks with threatening notes attached to them and buckets of cement through the windows, then escape in a car with a false license plate. When Allen rejected the scheme, Fry dismissed him.

Also in 1937, Fry participated in a convention of the American Nationalist Confederation in Kansas City, Missouri, to unify pro-fascist organizations. Deatherage, who worked for Fry, was the organizer. The objective was to make Moseley a military dictator under the pretense of protecting the United States from communism. And in 1938, Fry collaborated with Herman Schwinn, the West Coast Bund leader, to organize a well-attended, three-day nationalist convention in Los Angeles. One of the sedition trial defendants, Frank W. Clark, wrote a letter to the gathering to advise, "You people in Los Angeles have over 70,000 Jews to deal with and twice as many communists, and the Pacific Ocean is a pretty good place for them to start swimming or go down." The convention apparently did not need to be reminded about violence. Names of prominent citizens who were to be purged were written on a blackboard, and one of Fry's assistants suggested kidnapping the children of a well-known Los Angeles man who condemned Hitler.

In 1940, when the Dies Committee subpoenaed Fry, she fled to Italy. After the Pearl Harbor attack, she returned to the United States and was interned at Ellis Island for the duration of the war as a dangerous alien. While there, she was indicted for sedition, but the Justice Department concluded there was insufficient evidence to try her.

On Fry's background and views, see Lavine, 50–3, 197–9; Confidential memo on Paquita Louise de Shishmareff, November 1947, 1, AJC F: Mrs. Leslie Fry; Testimony of Henry D. Allen, Special Committee on Un-American Activities, House of Representatives, 76th Cong., 1st Sess., August 22, 1939, *Hearings* (Washington D.C.: Government Printing Office, 1939), 4014–33; Leslie Fry, "The New Order: How America Lost Its Power to Jewry," 1–3, ADL F: Leslie Fry; Mrs. Leslie Fry to Dr. Cyrus Adler and Rabbi Stephen S. Wise, March 28, 1938, AJC F: Militant Christian Patriots.

On Fry's publications and research activities, see New York *PM,* June 15, 1943; Testimony of Allen, 3989–4013; AJC *News Letter* (Los Angeles) 5: 135 (March 19, 1941), 3–4, AJC F: AJC Newsletter; *Christian Free Press,* October, November, and December 1937. Photocopies of Fry's charts were obtained from the ADL.

On Fry's attempts to unite nationalists and her legal problems, see press release of November 27, 1944, J. L. Martin News Research Service, Inc., B 56, Jewish Community Relations Council of Minnesota papers; Greenwald, 616–7; Fry, "The New Order," 1–3; Fry to Adler and Wise, March 28, 1938; *Boston Daily Globe,* January 24, 1940; *Democracy's Battle,* February 1, 1940, in YIVO F: 1948, 87; Confidential Memo on Madame Paquita Louise de Sishmareff, 2–3.

5. Chicago *Tribune,* January 5 and 29, 1943 and October 12, 1952; *New York Times,* January 4, 1944; Dilling *Bulletin,* January 1943, 1–8; Richard Polenberg, *War and Society: The United States, 1941–1945* (Philadelphia: J. B. Lippincott Company, 1972), 48. On Rogge's role in prosecuting corruption in Louisiana, see Harnett T. Kane, *Louisiana Hayride: The American Rehearsal for Dictatorship, 1928–1940* (Gretna, La.: Pelican Publishing Company, 1971), chapters 11–17. The Louisiana prosecutions established Rogge as a brilliant attorney. Yet in Louisiana and in the sedition prosecutions, he showed signs of overzealousness driven by ambition and arrogance.

6. Chicago *Tribune,* March 6, 18, 19, 1943 and October 12, 1952.

7. Ibid., January 4, 1944; Ribuffo, *The Old Christian Right,* 196; Hoke, *It's a Secret,* 59; *New York Times,* January 4, 1944. Previously indicated individuals included in the third indictment were David J. Baxter, H. Victor Broenstrupp, Prescott Freese Dennett, Hans Diebel, Dilling, Robert Edward Edmondson, Elmer J. Garner, Charles B. Hudson, Ellis O. Jones, William Robert Lyman Jr., Robert Noble, Pelley, Sanctuary, Herman Max Schwinn, Edward James Smythe, True, George Sylvester Viereck, Winrod, Clark, Deatherage, Frank K. Ferenz, and Lois de Lafayette Washburn. Included in the third indictment and not indicted previously were Garland L. Alderman, Lawrence Dennis, Ernest Frederick Elmhurst, August Klapprott, Gerhard Wilhelm Kunze, Joseph E. McWilliams, E. J. Parker Sage, and Peter Stahrenberg. For a list of those included in each of the three indictments, see Hoke, *It's a Secret,* 48.

8. Hoke, *It's a Secret,* 31, 114–5; New York *PM,* June 17, 1943.

In April 1943, Clark wrote to Washburn in Chicago and asked her to arrange a meeting of ten of her best friends in her home so he could address them. Hitler had always met in private homes when he was building the Nazi Party, Clark said. "I will give them a talk straight from the shoulder—what the nation is up against and what we will have to organize to do, to combat the arising situation. Of course, I shall talk about guns and other things, that ultimately must be our weapons to safely guarantee our security when the communists start their bloody overthrow." Clark also said he had been building a "revolutionary army" in Washington and vowed to expand it nationwide. See press release of October 4, 1944, J. L. Martin News Service, B 56, Jewish Community Relations Council of Minnesota papers.

9. *PM,* June 17, 1943.

10. *Women's Voice,* October 30, 1947, 5; Report on Elizabeth Dilling, 3, B 56, Jewish Community Relations Council of Minnesota papers.

11. Testimony of Homer Maertz, Special Committee on Un-American Activities, House of Representatives, 76th Cong., 3rd Sess., on H. Res. 282, October 2, 1939, *Hearings,* 4 (Washington, D.C.: Government Printing Office, 1939), 1666.

12. Report on Elizabeth Dilling, 3.

13. FBI file on Dilling, pt. 4, 7–11, 25; Dilling appeal letter, July 29, 1942, B 16, Jewish Community Relations Council of Minnesota papers, 1–3; *Chicago Tribune,* July 24, 1942.

14. *Chicago Tribune,* July 24, 1942. The statement was probably published in Dilling's *Bulletin* but neither news accounts nor the trial transcript identifies the source.

15. *The People vs. the Chicago Tribune* (Chicago: Union for Democratic Action, 1942), 36; flyer, "Free Speech," AJC F: American Women Against Communism.

16. *Chicago Tribune,* July 24, 1942.

17. Ibid., July 30, August 21, September 11, 12, 19, 29, and October 6, 1942.

18. *Bulletin,* September 3, 1942, 1–2, and November 25, 1942, 1–3; *Chicago Tribune,* August 5, 1942; Rogge, 314–5.

19. *Chicago Tribune,* October 28, December 9, 18, 1942. The Washington judge who raised Dilling's bail seemed to consider her a more serious threat than did the authorities in Chicago.

20. *Chicago Tribune,* March 2 and 3, 1943; Biddle, 242.

21. "Edward C. Eicher," *Current Biography,* 1941, 256; *Biographical Dictionary of the American Congress, 1774–1971* (Washington, D.C.: Government Printing Office, 1971), 903; *Chicago Tribune,* November 30, December 1, 1944.

22. Additional Memorandum in Support of Demurrer by the Defendant, Elizabeth Dilling, *U.S. vs. Joseph E. McWilliams, et al.,* Criminal No. 73086 in the District Court of the United States for the District of Columbia, February 18, 1944, pp. 3421–5.

23. Ibid.

24. Bill of Particulars, *U.S. vs. McWilliams,* 1–2; *Chicago Tribune,* March 8, 1944.

25. *Chicago Tribune,* March 21 and 28, 1944.

26. New York *PM,* April 18, 1944.

27. Hoke, *It's a Secret,* 186; *Chicago Tribune,* April 19, 1944; New York *PM,* June 4, 1944.

28. *Chicago Tribune,* April 19, 1944.

29. Sayers and Kahn, *The Plot Against the Peace,* 219.

30. *Chicago Tribune,* May 17, 1944.

31. Ibid., August 9, 1944, December 10, 1944.

32. List of Interrogatories submitted by Ira Chase Koehne, attorney for Washburn, 1–3, Box 1371, transcript of *U.S. vs. McWilliams,* Washington National Records Center, Suitland, Maryland; Ribuffo, *The Old Christian Right,* 199–201. I want to thank Ribuffo for making available his notes on the trial transcripts.

33. Opening statement to the jury, Rogge, *U.S. vs. McWilliams,* B 56, Jewish Community Relations Council of Minnesota papers, 1–6.

34. Ibid., 6–40.

35. Ibid.

36. *U.S. vs. McWilliams* transcript, 2232–5.

37. Ibid., 2236–42; Maximilian J. St. George and Lawrence Dennis, *A Trial on Trial: The Great Sedition Trial of 1944* (Chicago: Haddon-Craftsman, 1946), 34.

38. Ribuffo, *The Old Christian Right,* 207; *New York Times,* June 30, July 6, 1944.

39. *Chicago Tribune,* May 24, June 8, 12, and 15, 1944; *New York Times,* May 24, June 3, 9, September 7, 1944.

40. Transcript of *U.S. vs. McWilliams.*

41. Ribuffo, *The Old Christian Right,* 203; *Chicago Tribune,* May 23, 1944.

42. *Chicago Tribune,* May 5, July 6, July 14, August 8, 1944; St. George and Dennis, 348–9.

43. *Chicago Tribune,* May 5, July 6, July 14, August 8, 1944; St. George and Dennis, 348–9.

44. Ribuffo, *The Old Christian Right,* 203; *Chicago Tribune,* May 23, 1944.

45. Ribuffo, *The Old Christian Right,* 203; *Chicago Tribune,* May 23, 1944.

46. *Chicago Tribune,* June 13, 21, 1944; *New York Times,* June 13, 1944; Harold Norris, *Mr. Justice Murphy and the Bill of Rights* (Dobbs Ferry, N.Y.: Oceans Publications, Inc., n.d.), 152–7.

47. *New York Times,* October 7, 1944.

48. *Chicago Tribune,* August 3, 8, 1944.

49. Ibid., November 30, December 5, 1944; *New York Times,* December 1, 8, 1944; Higham, 66; Ribuffo, *The Old Christian Right,* 211.

50. Ribuffo, *The Old Christian Right,* 212–3; Weyl, *The Battle Against Disloyalty* (New York: Thomas Y. Crowell Company, 1951), 163–4.

51. Ribuffo, *The Old Christian Right,* 274.

52. Biddle, 232.

Chapter Twelve

1. TAF 1946, 231–3, 384–7, 993–4; *Chicago Tribune,* January 7, 1946; December 15, 1948.

2. *Chicago Tribune,* January 22, 23, 1948; Washington *Times-Herald,* January 22, 1948; AJC report on meeting of Christian Youth of America, April 14, 1946, AJC F: Christian Youth of America; *New York Times,* November 1, 1954.

3. *Dilling vs. Illinois Publishing and Printing, et al.* No. 44695, Appellate Court of Illinois, First District, Third Division, March 8, 1950, 635–7; *McWilliams et al. vs. Sentinel Publishing Co. et al.,* No. 44500, Appellate Court of Illinois, First District, Second Division, November 18, 1949, 266–76; *Dilling vs. Billboard,* No. 47 S 11210, Superior Court of Cook County, State of Illinois, 1947 (unpaginated); *Bulletin,* January 1948, 2–12; *Common Sense,* May 15, 1966, 1.

4. *Bulletin,* June 1954, 5.

5. Ibid., April 1947, 10; August 1947, 5; January–February 1960, 20, 38, 43; May–June 1963, 6; May–June 1964, 11.

6. Ibid., May–June 1960, 13, 17, 19.

7. Ibid., August 1952, 1.

8. Ibid., May–June 1960, 11–2; September–October 1960, 20.

9. Ibid., May–June 1960, 11–2; September–October 1960, 16, 20; January–February 1961, 11; July–August 1963, 2.

10. Goldwater to Dilling, September 20, 1960 and Goldwater to Harry T. Everingham, October 20, 1960, Dilling papers; *Bulletin,* May–June, 1960, 8–9; July–August, 1960, 2, 9; July–August 1964, 14–9; Dilling, *The Conscience of that "1313" Conservative Goldwater* (Chicago: self-published, 1961), 1.

11. *Bulletin,* March–April 1964, 4; January–February 1965, 13; September–December 1965, 28.

12. Dilling to Arthur E. Summerfield, July 2, 1954, ADL F: Dilling, 1953–1954; *Bulletin,* Christmas 1962, 8.

13. Dilling to Summerfield, July 2, 1954.

14. *Bulletin,* June 1954, 1–2; Christmas 1954, 1; January–February 1964, 3; Dilling, "Brotherhood," (Chicago: self-published, 1954), 4; "An Open Letter from Elizabeth Dilling, n.d. (1953), 24–8, ADL F: Dilling.

15. "An Open Letter from Dilling," n.d. (1953), 24–28.

16. Dilling *Bulletin,* August 1954, 12; November–December 1960, 11; September–December 1965, 19.

17. *Women's Voice,* June–July, 1954, 1.

18. Dilling, *The Plot Against Christianity* (Chicago: self-published, 1954).

19. *Women's Voice,* June–July, 1954, 1.

20. *Bulletin,* March–April, 1963, 7.

21. Ibid., January–February, 1960, 3, 7, 10; November–December 1960, 26.

22. *Bulletin,* September 1955; January–February 1960, 3, 7, 10; November–December, 1960, 26; *Chicago Tribune,* June 4, 1955; Stokes to Smith, May 16, 1947, Dilling papers; Chicago *Sun,* October 25, 1946, August 1, 1948; Dilling, "Open Letter Concerning Gerald L. K. Smith," to Frank L. Britton, April 4, 1954, B 54 F: D (misc.), Smith papers.

23. *New York Times,* May 1, 1966.

24. *Women's Voice,* February 1955, 1; Membership chart of We the Mothers, 1956, B 57, Jewish Community Relations Council of Minnesota papers.

25. Minutes of Van Hyning speech to former Mothers of Minnesota, January 30, 1951, B 57, unpaginated, and Mothers to Humphrey, April 3, 1951, Jewish Community Relations Council of Minnesota papers.

26. Van Hyning to "Dear Fellow American," December 1950, B 57, Jewish Community Relations Council of Minnesota papers.

27. *Women's Voice,* March 1952; July 1952.

28. Ibid., July 1952.

29. Ibid., March 1952, July 1952; Arnold Forster and Benjamin R. Epstein, *Cross-Currents* (Garden City, N.Y.: Doubleday & Company, Inc., 1956), 48; Mark Sherwin, *The Extremists* (New York: St. Martin's Press, 1963), 16–8; Roy, *Apostles of Discord,* 18–23.

30. *Women's Voice,* June 1954.

31. Ibid., May 1957.

32. Ibid., November–December 1955.

33. Ibid., May 1957.

34. Ibid., February 1955; June 1955.

35. Minutes of meeting of Parents' Group, April 24, 1951, Jewish Community Relations Council of Minnesota papers.

36. *Women's Voice,* May 1954.

37. Ibid., July–August, 1957; August–September, 1959.

38. Minutes of Meeting of January 30, 1951, 2 and April 28, 1951, 1, B 57, Jewish Community Relations Council of Minnesota papers; "Anti-Gentilism," n.d., 12, Jewish Community Relations Council of Minnesota papers.

39. "Anti-Gentilism," 7, 15–6.

40. *Women's Voice,* October 1950; November–December 1954; November–December 1955; and January–February 1956.

41. H. K. Thompson Jr., "A Survey of the Right Wing," *The Independent* 124 (August 1962), 7.

42. Letter from Mrs. Agnes Waters to supporters, April 17, 1947, AJC Vertical File, F: Agnes Waters.

43. Ibid.

44. Prepared Statement of Mrs. Agnes Waters, U.S. Senate Committee on Foreign Relations, 80th Cong., 1st Sess., "Assistance to Greece and Turkey," *Hearings,* March 27, 1947 (Washington, D.C.: Government Printing Office, 1947), 164–70.

45. Testimony of Agnes Waters, Senate Foreign Relations Committee, 80th Cong., 2nd Sess., *Hearings,* Pt. 3, February 3, 1948 (Washington D.C.: Government Printing Office, 1948), 1333–40.

46. *New York Times,* November 2, November 3, 1948; *New York Sun,* November 8, 1948; press release, "Anti-Semites Picketing Convention Ignored by Press and Public," June 1948, Jewish Community Relations Council of Philadelphia, YIVO F: 1948.

47. Statement of Mrs. Agnes Waters, Senate Committee on Foreign Relations, 81st Cong., 1st Sess., "North Atlantic Treaty," *Hearings,* Pt. 3, May 18, 1949 (Washington, D.C.: Government Printing Office), pp. 1144–54.

48. Waters, "Petition for Redress of Wrongs," *Women's Voice,* July 1950.

49. Statement of Mrs. Agnes Waters, Senate Committee on Foreign Relations, 81st Cong., 2nd Sess., "The Genocide Convention," *Hearings,* January 25, 1950 (Washington, D.C.: Government Printing Office, 1950), 293–4.

50. Waters to Congress, August 2, 1951, AJC F: Agnes Waters.

51. *Women's Voice,* August 1954.

52. Testimony of Agnes Waters, Senate Committee on Foreign Relations, 84th Cong., 1st Sess., *Hearings,* Pt. 2, January 19, 1955 (Washington, D.C.: Government Printing Office, 1955), 59–61.

53. *Women's Voice,* December 1955.

54. Ibid., April 1954.

55. Ibid., April 1954, January–February 1956.

56. Ibid., March 1954, September 1957; Statement of Mrs. Agnes Waters to the Senate Foreign Relations Committee against "The Eisenhower Doctrine," February 4, 1957, 1–4, Dilling papers.

57. *Washington Evening Star,* March 12, 1959; Thompson, "A Survey of the Right Wing," *The Independent,* 11.

58. Frederickson, 22–38; Curtis to Lewis Haney, October 19, 1950, B 3, Curtis papers; Curtis to Ethel Barber, November 8, 1950, B 2, Curtis papers; Curtis, "Is McCarthy Censure Case Another Nuremburg Trial?" November 18, 1954, Curtis papers.

59. *Women's Voice,* May 1946, April 1955. Fry also contributed articles to *Women's Voice,* which continued to advertise her *Waters Flowing Eastward,* and she continued organizational work on the local level in California until the 1960s. Her articles included "Who Put Hitler in Power?" which argued that the führer had been a puppet of Jewish bankers. In 1962 Fry was running the California League of Christian Parents of San Bernardino. The league produced tracts and pamphlets advocating that Christianity be put back into public schools. See *Women's Voice,* January and February 1956, October 1956, and May 1957; Thompson, "A Survey of the Right Wing," 9.

60. Meeting report, September 1945, YIVO F: Misc., 1945, 1–2; Walter E. Klein to Solomon A. Fineberg, April 21, 1946, AJC F: Misc., 1946, 1–2; Report on Blanche Winters, May 12, 1946, AJC F: Misc., 1946, 1; memo on Detroit, March 10, 1946, YIVO F: Misc., 1946, 1; *New York Times,* March 10, 1957.

61. TAF 1946, 260, 1144; Resolutions passed by the American Mothers, February 1, 1946, AJC F: Beatrice Knowles.

62. Meeting reports, Current Events Club, May 8 and 19, 1946, June 7, 1946, February 27, 1947, September 19, 1947, AJC F: Misc., 1946 and 1947; Memo, "National Blue Star Mothers," YIVO F: 1949, 1.

63. Meeting report, January 18, 1946, YIVO F: Misc., 1946; Meeting reports, January 24, March 14, March 21, March 28, April 24, and July 18, 1947, AJC F: National Blue Star Mothers.

64. Catherine V. Brown, "Wanted! Militant Christians to Fight Communism," 1, AJC F: National Blue Star Mothers; *New York Times,* May 8, 1949.

65. TAF 1946, 1072–3; Catherine P. Baldwin to Congress, March 4, 1946, AJC F: National Blue Star Mothers; Catherine Baldwin, *And Men Wept* (New York: Our Publications, 1954), 1–40.

66. See Felsenthal.
Women of the left sought new rights and preservation of rights already gained. Women of the left, like the mothers, were mainly interested in issues that did not relate specifically to gender. On the issues that divided women after the war and fueled the development of the New Christian Right, see Chafe, *The Paradox of Change,* 180–200; Eugenia Kaledin, *American Women in the 1950s: Mothers and More* (Boston: Twayne Publishers, 1984); Ferree and Hess, especially 23–7 and 115–39; Glenna Matthews, "Just a *Housewife": The Rise and Fall of Domesticity in the United States* (New York: Oxford University Press, 1987); and Gordon, *Woman's Body, Woman's Right: Birth Control in America,* rev. ed. (New York: Penguin Books, 1990).

Some leaders of the New Christian Right, among them Pat Robertson and Jerry Falwell, were strong supporters of Israel, yet there were anti-Semitic elements in their movement. Ferree and Hess also detect anti-Semitism within the feminist movement. See 109–10.

Chapter Thirteen

1. Among works that emphasize Roosevelt's caution in the face of opposition to war are Burns, *Roosevelt: The Soldier of Freedom, 1940–1945;* Dallek; Davis; and Cole, *Roosevelt and the Isolationists.*

2. Cole, *Roosevelt and the Isolationists,* does not portray the isolationists as villains but as persons clinging to the past. He examines the split between Roosevelt and some New Deal supporters over foreign policy. Also see Cole, *America First,* and Michele Flynn Stenehjem, *An American First: John T. Flynn and the America First Committee* (New Rochelle, N.Y.: Arlington House, 1976). Schneider, *Should America Go to War?,* is a useful study of isolationism in the Midwest, including excellent accounts of the *Chicago Tribune* and the America First Committee.

Coughlin's unifying influence on the far right and opposition to the New Deal are described in Brinkley. Coughlin's anti-Semitism and opposition to the war undermined the credibility of his movement. In *Gerald L. K. Smith,* I describe Smith's attempts to frustrate Roosevelt's foreign policies. In *Messiah of the Masses: Huey P. Long and the Great Depression* (New York: HarperCollins, 1993), I argue that although Long posed the most serious threat to Roosevelt, he would have been ineffective in a presidential campaign in which foreign policy was a major issue. Wolfskill and Hudson focus chiefly on right-wing opposition to Roosevelt, as does Geoffrey S. Smith, *To Save a Nation: American Countersubversives, the New Deal, and the Coming of World War II* (New York: Basic Books, 1973). The interaction of the mothers' movement and other ultraright opponents of war is described in McEnaney's article and thesis.

3. Ribuffo, *The Old Christian Right,* 178–228.

4. Mary Florence Sargant, Catherine Marshall, and C. K. Ogden, *Militarism versus Feminism: Writings on Women and War,* Margaret Kamester and Jo Vellacott, eds. (London: Virago Press, 1987; reprint of a 1915 work), 15.

5. Reardon asserts that sexism and war have common origins. "Misogyny is the core of both militarism and sexism," she writes (58). Alonso notes that "Frances Willard, the indomitable leader of the WCTU, wanted to make peace a women's issue because she felt that alcohol abuse and militarism were intrinsically linked" (49). Catt, who had supported American participation in World War I for the purpose of obtaining President Wilson's support for suffrage, wrote in 1921 that "war is in the blood of men; they can't help it. They have been fighting ever since the days of the cavemen. There is a sort of honor about it" (86). During the 1920s the Women's Peace Union led a campaign against the Boy Scouts of America, which it termed "a kindergarten for war" (97). Alonso elaborates on this theme in 63–125.

Also see Cott, *The Grounding of Modern Feminism.* Cott quotes Belle Case La Follette's statement that "great masses of women do feel that the conservation of life, that the saving of the race from destruction is a feminist movement" (70). See also Chafetz and Dworkin, *Female Revolt,* 28–30; Gertrude Bussey and Margaret Tims, *The Women's International League for Peace and Freedom* (London: Allen and Unwin, 1965); Anne Marie Pois, "The Politics of the Women's International League for Peace and Freedom," Ph.D. dissertation, University of Colorado, 1988; and Steven B. Burg, "The Program of the Woman's Peace Party," M.A. thesis, University of Wisconsin—Madison, 1991. On the mixture of disillusionment and idealism that contributed to isolationist sympathies, see Jeansonne, *Transformation and Reaction,* chapters 7 and 13.

6. Alonso, 17. On the decline of the isolationist movement as the world situation deteriorated, see John E. Wiltz, *From Isolation to War, 1931–1941* (New York: Thomas Y. Crowell, 1968); and Manfred Jonas, *Isolationism in America, 1935–1941* (Ithaca: Cornell University Press, 1966); and Cole, *Roosevelt and the Isolationists.*

7. Campbell, 216–8. Alonso agrees the women's peace movement was virtually dormant by the late 1930s (see chapters 4 and 5). Ware, *American Women in the 1930s,* 103–4, includes a brief account of Dilling. Hartmann, *The Home Front and Beyond,* does not discuss the mothers.

8. McEnaney, "Defending the Family Altar," 34–5.

9. Alonso, 202–22; Amy Swerdlow, "Ladies' Day at the Capitol: Women Strike for Peace Versus HUAC," *Feminist Studies* 8 (Fall 1982), 493–520. Two collections that survey women's peace politics are Daniela Gioseffi, ed., *Women on War: Essential Voices for the Nuclear Age* (New York: Simon & Schuster, 1988); and Adrienne Harris and Ynestra King, eds. *Rocking the Ship of State: Toward a Feminist Peace Politics* (Boulder, Colo.: Westview, 1989). Judith Porter Adams, *Peacework: Oral Histories of Women Peace Activists* (Boston: Twayne Publishers, 1991), includes interviews with women in peace and reform movements.

10. Alonso, 234–63; Chafetz and Dworkin, *Female Revolt,* 30–1. Other works that consider recent aspects of the racial and gender dimensions of United States foreign

relations include Carol Cohn, "Sex and Death in the Rational World of Defense Intellectuals," *Signs* 12 (Summer 1987), 687–718; John Dower, *War Without Mercy: Race and Power in the Pacific War* (New York, 1986); Michael H. Hunt, *Ideology and U.S. Foreign Policy* (New Haven: Yale University Press, 1987); Susan Jeffords, *The Remasculinization of America: Gender and the Vietnam War* (Bloomington: Indiana University Press, 1989); Elaine Tyler May, *Homeward Bound: American Families in the Cold War Era* (New York: Basic Books, 1988); and Geoffrey Smith, "National Security and Personal Isolation: Sex, Gender and Disease in the Cold-War United States," *International History Review* 14 (May 1992), 221–40. In general, the early women's peace movements have been treated in more detail than similar movements since World War II.

11. Nancy C. M. Hartsock, "Prologue to a Feminist Critique of War and Politics," in Judith Hicks Stiehm, ed., *Women's Views of the Political World of Men* (Dobbs Ferry, N.Y.: Transnational Publishers, Inc., 1984), 123.

12. Alonso, 243. For a recent discussion of gender and war, see Miriam Cooke and Angela Woolacott, *Gendering War Talk* (Princeton, N.J.: Princeton University Press, 1993).

13. Josephine Donovan, review of Karen Anderson, *Wartime Women: Sex Roles, Family Relations and the Status of Women During World War II,* in *Women's Studies International Forum,* 15:3–4 (1982), 381.

14. Elshtain, *Women and War* (New York: Basic Books, 1987), xi–xiii, 3–4, 140.

15. Ibid., quote from dust jacket.

16. Ibid., xi–32.

17. The idea that women suffer from war more than men was the principal theme of Sargant, Marshall, and Ogden, in *Militarism Versus Feminism.* Ogden, for example, writes, "Militarism has been the curse of women, as women, from the first dawn of social life" (56). Alonso continues the tradition of attributing wars to men and male domination. "For me, the main theme that defines this peace movement is the connection made between institutionalized violence and violence among women" (8). Going further, she argues that destruction of the natural environment is related to male aggression: "The violence to the planet is the larger manifestation of violence against women. It is all symptomatic of a sick world, one that needs to be remolded using a more female, nuturing approach to life" (10).

I do not wish to minimize the suffering of women in war. It was clear that the woman with whom I spoke had suffered for more than fifty years from the loss of one she loved. Yet the argument that those who live suffer more than those who die or are wounded is similar to the argument that life imprisonment is a more severe punishment than the death penalty. (Women also die in wars, as combatants and as civilians.)

Nancy Huston points out that men have enjoyed a near monopoly not only in deciding to go to war and in waging war but in recording the histories of war. Women writing about wars might provide a different perspective, she explains. See Huston, "Tales of War and Tears of Women," *Women's Studies International Forum* 5: 314 (1982), 271–82.

18. Elshtain, *Woman and War,* 47–60, 140–6, 207, 241; Ruddick, 151–4.

19. Ruddick, 153.

20. Ibid., 154.

21. Elshtain, *Women and War,* 9, 239–41. Hartmann observes that class, race, and

political orientation helped shape women's attitudes towards World War II, and that not all women experienced the same degree of loss or gain from wartime changes. For example, although many upper- and middle-class women disdained the military, impoverished women viewed it as a means of rising economically. See Hartmann, "Women's Organizations During World War II: The Interaction of Class, Race, and Feminism," in *Woman's Being, Woman's Place,* Mary Kelly, ed. (Boston: G. K. Hall and Co., 1979), 313–28.

22. Elshtain, *Women and War,* xi–32.

23. Lerner, *The Creation of Patriarchy,* 26; Dworkin, *Right-Wing Women,* 206; Elshtain, *Women and War,* 40.

Interestingly, in the 1940s Philip Wylie wrote a diatribe against motherhood that was considered reactionary at the time. But it is similar in some respects to the arguments of feminists who consider motherhood a burden. Wylie argued that society was being ruined by overprotective mothers who selfishly coddled their children to control them. This practice prevented them from developing independently. See Wylie, *Generation of Vipers* (New York: Rinehart and Company, Inc., 1946).

24. Eisenstein, 69. Eisenstein discusses many feminists' rejection of maternalism in 69–87.

25. Carol Gilligan, *In a Different Voice: Psychological Theory and Women's Development* (Cambridge: Harvard University Press, 1982), 65.

26. Alonso, 263. For an excellent general treatment of the evolution of the concept of motherhood, see Maxine L. Margolis, *Mothers and Such: Views of American Women and Why They Changed* (Berkeley: University of California Press, 1984). Margolis believes many of the duties of the modern homemaker are unnecessary and designed to foster self-worth. Margolis has useful insights into the roles women have played in society since colonial times and how they have been depicted in popular stereotypes.

A study of Mildred Scott Olmsted, a leader in the WILPF, discusses Olmsted's peace crusades in the context of her rather turbulent private life, including her effort to deal with her sexual identity. It would be intriguing to apply this type of analysis to the ultraright women of the 1930s, yet biographical information, particularly of a personal nature, is sorely lacking. See Margaret Hope Bacon, *One Woman's Passion for Peace and Freedom: The Life of Mildred Scott Olmsted* (Syracuse: Syracuse University Press, 1993).

27. Gilligan, 220. Other studies that relate politics to maternalism include Seth Koven and Sonya Michel, eds. *Mothers of a New World: Maternalist Politics and the Origins of Welfare States* (New York: Routledge, 1993); and Michel and Robyn Rosen, "The Paradox of Maternalism: Elizabeth Lowell Putnam and the American Welfare State," *Gender and History* 4 (autumn 1992), 364–86.

28. J. Echergray, "Severed Heart," quoted by Ruddick, 10.

29. Allport, *The Nature of Prejudice,* 25. On this point, the discussion of Chafe in chapter 1, n 37 also is relevant.

30. Ribuffo, "Why Is There So Much Conservatism in the United States and Why Do So Few Historians Know Anything About It?" *American Historical Review,* 99:2 (April 1994), 444–6.

Among studies helpful in understanding the right are Charles W. Dunn and J. David Woodard, *American Conservatism from Burke to Bush: An Introduction* (New York: Madison Books, 1991); Clinton Rossiter, *Conservatism in America: The Thank-*

less Persuasion, 2nd ed. (New York: Knopf, 1962); and Michael W. Miles, *The Odyssey of the American Right* (New York: Oxford University Press, 1980).

Some studies describing the Old Right are George Wolfskill, *The Revolt of the Conservatives: A History of the American Liberty League, 1934–1940* (Boston, 1962); and Justus D. Doenecke, ed., *In Danger Undaunted: The Anti-Interventionist Movement of 1940–1941 as Revealed in the Papers of the America First Committee* (Stanford, Calif.: Hoover Institution, 1980). The intellectual variety of the New Right is described in J. David Hoeveler, Jr., *Watch on the Right: Conservative Intellectuals in the Reagan Era* (Madison: University of Wisconsin Press, 1991).

Other analyses of the right include Ronald Radosh, *Prophets on the Right: Profiles of Conservative Critics of American Globalism* (New York: Simon and Schuster, 1975); Roy; and George Norris Green, "Some Aspects of the Far Right Wing in Texas Politics," in E. C. Barksdale, et al., eds., *Essays on Recent Southern Politics* (Austin: University of Texas Press, 1979).

31. Dworkin, *Right-Wing Women,* 52, 195. Dworkin is attempting to describe the women of the New Christian Right. Apparently she has no knowledge of the mothers' movement. Also see Lerner, *The Creation of Patriarchy,* 8, 217, 218, 234; Eisenstein, 8, 31; and Shirley Rogers Radl, *The Invisible Woman: Target of the Religious New Right* (New York: Delacorte Press, 1983), 2–9, 106.

32. Frederickson, 25. Also see Blee, *Women of the Klan;* and MacLean, *Behind the Mask of Chivalry.*

33. Chafe, *Women and Equality,* 133.

34. McEnaney, "Defending the Family Altar," 64. That bigots such as Dilling and Smith crusaded in the face of hostility and bad publicity supports the belief that they were not charlatans. Unlike Smith, who became fairly wealthy, none of the mothers' leaders profited from their activities. It was impossible to interview Smith at length, as I did, without perceiving the sincerity of his bigotry. Had he been motivated chiefly by money, he could easily have found ways to get rich with fewer side effects and less stress. Feminists and early women reformers demonstrated similar perseverance despite daunting opposition. See Jeansonne, *Gerald L. K. Smith,* chapters 6–7, 10, and the Epilogue.

For the factors that motivate extremists, especially those who lead movements, see Hoffer; Allport, *The Nature of Prejudice;* Arnold M. Rose, ed., *Race Prejudice and Discrimination: Readings in Intergroup Relations in the United States* (New York: Alfred A. Knopf, 1951); Ehrlich; Michael Parenti, *The Anti-Communist Impulse* (New York: Random House, 1969); and Jorstad.

The mentality of dogmatists is explored in Hofstadter, *Anti-Intellectualism in American Life* (New York: Vintage Books, 1963), and *The Paranoid Style;* Bell, *The Radical Right;* T. W. Adorno, et al., *The Authoritarian Personality* (New York: Harper & Bros., 1950); Hadley Cantril, *The Psychology of Mass Movements* (New York: John Wiley and Sons, 1941); Milton Rokeach, *The Open and Closed Mind* (New York: Basic Books, 1960); Fromm; and David Shapiro, *Neurotic Styles* (New York: Basic Books, 1965).

35. McEnaney, "Defending the Family Altar," 62–76, 80–100; Zwisler.

36. Dworkin, *Right-Wing Women,* 23.

37. Ibid., 22–3. For other feminist scholars who find organized religion inhibiting, see Cott, *The Grounding of Modern Feminism,* 42; and Lerner, *The Creation of Patriarchy,* 201.

Right-wing women have not been the only women to discover comfort in religion. As we saw in chapter 1, religious movements have been a major avenue for women attempting to effect political and social change. Women generally have been attracted to organized religion. In early America, the followers of Roger Williams and Anne Hutchinson included large numbers of women, and women were drawn particularly to the egalitarian and pacifist aspects of Quakerism. Evangelical Christian movements, from the nineteenth century to the New Christian Right, have found enthusiastic participants in women. Finally, in the United States, women attend church more frequently and in greater numbers than men. The twenty-three principal religious denominations have female-majority memberships, led by Christian Science (sixty-three percent)—a sect founded by Mary Baker Eddy. See Chafetz and Dworkin, *Female Revolt*, 3-4.

38. Dworkin, *Right-Wing Women*, 34. For another perspective, see Elly Bulkin, Minnie Bruce Pratt, and Barbara Smith, *Yours in Struggle: Three Feminist Perspectives on Anti-Semitism and Racism* (Ithaca, N.Y.: Firebrand Books, 1984).

39. One way of testing the logic of an ideological argument is to apply to other groups the implications of the reasoning. For example, could a woman who complained her ideas had been rejected because of her sex plausibly reject the ideas of a man because of his sex? That an argument is logically constructed does not make it objectively true; that it is logically inconsistent does not necessarily invalidate the argument entirely, yet it indicates an element of bias. It is neither possible nor necessary to eliminate all bias from debate, but we need to be self-conscious of what we are doing, to realize that our assumptions, like those of our opponents, arise partly from self-interest. Once we realize this, we can attribute good faith rather than moral turpitude to our ideological opponents. There is no point in opening a dialogue when both sides are equally dogmatic, unwilling to consider that the other side's arguments are valid.

It should be emphasized that Dworkin uses her logic to explain not the vicious Jew-baiting women of the 1930s, of whom she seems unaware, but the milder anti-Semitism of some contemporary Christian Fundamentalists.

There is limited research on the role of gender in personality disorders, including anti-Semitism, although this, too, is insufficient to explain the mothers. In *Gender and Disordered Behavior* (New York: Brunner/Mazel, Publishers, 1979), edited by Edith S. Gombery and Violet Franks, several scholars suggest that stress contributes to anxiety and frustration, influencing personality disorders; that limitations imposed by socially defined roles exacerbate women's stress; and that gender stereotypes inhibit women's ability to relieve their stress in a socially acceptable manner. Therefore, by imposing burdens on women, society makes them more prone to scapegoating.

Some social scientists would disagree, believing genetic factors, rather than gender roles, contribute to personality disorders. Moreover, many persons, female as well as male, respond to stress without blaming it on scapegoats. (Conversely, many persons cannot handle their stress without turning to scapegoats; Smith was a frustrated personality who blamed false enemies.) If society places undue stress on women, and longevity is related to reduced stress, why do women in the United States outlive men? Anxiety is central to prejudice, I believe, yet it would be wrong to attribute the mothers' frustrations solely, or even primarily, to their womanhood.

40. This echoes Ribuffo's argument in "Why is There So Much Conservatism in the United States and Why Do So Few Historians Know Anything About It?" Ribuffo

considers my condemnation of the far right excessively moralistic, yet he shares my view that the study of the right has been simplistic. We agree that a more sophisticated analysis of the right does not demand ideological agreement; it simply demands going beyond the superficial.

Epilogue

1. *Los Angeles Times,* May 2, 1992; *Facts on File Yearbook 1992,* 52 (New York: Facts on File, Inc., 1993), 329.

2. My biographies *Leander Perez: Boss of the Delta* (Baton Rouge: Louisiana State University, 1977) and *Gerald L. K. Smith* are largely the basis for these ideas. Also, I have written numerous articles dealing with Perez, Smith, and various aspects of racism and anti-Semitism. See, for example, "Combatting Anti-Semitism: The Case of Gerald L. K. Smith," in Gerber, ed. *Anti-Semitism in American History,* 152–66, and "What If There Had Been No Slavery?" in Herbert M. Levine, ed., *What If The American Political System Were Different?* (Armonk, N.Y.: M. E. Sharpe, Inc., 1992), 165–9.

In addition, some of my interests grew from several of my articles on race in Louisiana and Southern politics. In *Messiah of the Masses,* and especially in "Huey Long and Racism," *Louisiana History* 33: 3 (summer 1992), 265–82, I explore Long's views on race. Racism was not a major theme in Long's career, although his personality included some of the archetypical characteristics of dogmatic racists, among them repressed hostility, alienation, insecurity, and a need for scapegoats.

Anxiety played a role in Long's quest for power and in leading some of his lieutenants, such as Smith and Perez, into building careers of racism after his death. I try to establish personality traits common to Long, Smith, and Perez in "Huey P. Long, Gerald L. K. Smith and Leander Perez as Charismatic Leaders," *Louisiana History* 35: 1 (Winter 1994), 5–21.

Perhaps the work that has most influenced my studies is the somewhat-dated classic by Allport, *The Nature of Prejudice,* which I have used as a text in courses on prejudice. Allport synthesizes massive research in simple, eloquent prose, provides remarkable insight, and exhibits common sense.

Additionally, I have benefitted from the insights of my academic mentor, the late William Ivy Hair, who encouraged my interest in race, personality, and politics, and helped shape my views; of Paul Elovitz, former president of the International Psychohistorical Association; of Henry Lawton, secretary-treasurer of the association; and of Ribuffo, who has studied the far right, conservatism, and anti-Semitism, with emphasis on the 1930s.

3. See my analysis of Dilling in chapter 6, and my examination of Smith's bigotry and prejudices in chapters 6–7 of *Gerald L. K. Smith.*

4. See John Higham, *Strangers in the Land: Patterns of American Nativism, 1860–1925* (New Brunswick, N.J.: Rutgers University Press, 1955).

5. Remember that none of the mothers' leaders enjoyed prominence or replenished their followings after the war. Consider, too, that Smith declined after the war, even though he continued to publish *The Cross and the Flag* until his death in 1976 and built several religious shrines that attracted tourists to Eureka Springs, Arkansas. On Smith's decline, see *Gerald L. K. Smith,* chapters 6–12.

6. Smith never renounced anti-Semitism, and near the end of his life, he expressed

no regrets about his career. When I gently suggested some of his ideas were unrealistic and unprovable, he replied that his beliefs were no more irrational than those of Mormons. If I argued that *The Protocols* was a forgery, Smith said, he could argue with equal logic that the Book of Mormon was a forgery. Yet he was ostracized for his beliefs, Smith complained, whereas Mormons were accepted by many Americans, as well as by the organizations that fought him and his ideas. See Jeansonne, interview with Gerald L. K. Smith, January 21, 1975, Glendale, California (in author's possession).

7. The book I found most helpful in analyzing the mentality of Hitler is Robert G. L. Waite's psychobiography, *The Psychopathic God: Adolf Hitler* (New York: Basic Books, 1977).

8. Sen. Joseph R. McCarthy, for example, rose to national prominence by exploiting Americans' fears about communist infiltration into the government. The most complete biography of McCarthy is Thomas C. Reeves, *The Life and Times of Joe McCarthy* (New York: Stein and Day, 1982). Also see Richard H. Rovere, *Senator Joe McCarthy* (New York: Harper and Row, 1959); and Edwin R. Bayley, *Joe McCarthy and the Press* (New York: Pantheon Books, 1981). Helpful in understanding the Cold War mentality are M. J. Heale, *American Anticommunism: Combating the Enemy Within, 1830–1970* (Baltimore: The Johns Hopkins University Press, 1990); and Stephen J. Whitfield, *The Culture of the Cold War* (Baltimore: The Johns Hopkins University Press, 1990).

9. The segregationist leader Perez opposed school desegregation out of a fear of interracial sex: "You make a Negro believe he is equal to the white people and the first thing he wants is a white woman." See *Leander Perez,* 223. Regarding Long and miscegenation, Hair writes, "The Kingfish's ultimate way of identifying white enemies with blacks was to say, or at least insinuate, that they had African blood." See Hair, *The Kingfish and His Realm: The Life and Times of Huey P. Long* (Baton Rouge: Louisiana State University Press, 1991), 303. Furthermore, the propaganda of segregationist groups, including the White Citizens' Councils and the KKK, is replete with references to interracial sex, and miscegenation is a leading theme in the fiction of William Faulkner and other prominent southern authors.

10. To Smith, the militant demonstrations that Jews and liberals launched against him confirmed his fear that Jews were conspiring against him. After much debate within the Jewish community, the Anti-Defamation League of B'nai B'rith decided that demonstrations and subsequent newspaper coverage aided Smith by providing him with publicity. The organization then sought to minimize that publicity. See Jeansonne, "Combatting Anti-Semitism." It is also useful to remember that Smith, Perez and the mothers' leaders refused to believe evidence that contradicted their opinions.

11. Dinnerstein to *The Chronicle of Higher Education,* July 27, 1994, B2.

══ BIBLIOGRAPHICAL ESSAY ══

Primary Sources

The only leaders of the mothers' movement who left collections of papers were Elizabeth Dilling and Cathrine Curtis. Both collections are small, contain no photographs, and reveal little about the private lives of Dilling and Curtis. Dilling's papers, as well as her library, are at the School of Christian Liberty, Arlington Heights, Illinois. Curtis's papers, which offer little information about her postwar activities, are at the New York Public Library. By contrast, the Gerald L. K. Smith papers at the Bentley Historical Library, University of Michigan, Ann Arbor, are a lode of letters and publications from men and women of the far right. Many women discussed in this book wrote to Smith and sent him copies of their speeches, books, and pamphlets. Also, the Henry B. Joy papers at the Bentley Library have correspondence between Dilling and Joy, a Detroit businessman who provided Dilling with money and moral support.

Mothers' leaders and their organizations left publications, including books and newsletters. Dilling wrote *The Red Network* (Chicago: self-published, 1934); *The Roosevelt Red Record and Its Background* (Chicago: self-published, 1936); *The Octopus* (Omaha, Nebraska: self-published, 1940), under the pseudonym Rev. Frank Woodruff Johnson; and *The Plot Against Christianity* (Chicago: self-published, 1954). Agnes Waters's essays and speeches are collected in *The White Papers* (Washington, D.C.: self-published, 1940). Like *The White Papers,* Catherine Baldwin's account of her ideology, *And Men Wept* (New York: Our Publications, 1954), is at the Library of Congress. In addition, I read complete runs of Dilling's Patriotic Research Bureau *Bulletin* and Lyrl Clark Van Hyning's *Women's Voice* in libraries and in the University of Iowa collection of right-wing materials, published by University Microfilms.

The two largest collections of papers were at the Blaustein Library of the American Jewish Committee and the YIVO Institute for Jewish Research, both in New York City. These included news clippings, investigative reports, minutes of meetings, articles, and books. The Anti-Defamation League of B'nai B'rith in New York City also furnished such information. The Mothers of Minnesota Collection at the Minnesota Historical Society, St. Paul–Minneapolis, includes the papers of the Jewish Community Relations Council of Minnesota, which investigated the movement, including groups beyond Minnesota. The Pennsylvania Historical Society in Philadelphia has a small but valuable file on isolationist mothers in Philadelphia.

The Hoover Institution in Stanford, California, sent me documents and some excellent photographs. Other photos were obtained from the Library of Congress. Unfortunately, neither the Library of Congress nor the National Archives has collections on the mothers' groups or its leaders.

The Federal Bureau of Investigation (FBI) compiled dossiers on groups and leaders, which I obtained under the Freedom of Information Act. The FBI file on Dilling, the most voluminous, was about three thousand pages. Other sizable FBI files were on Curtis, Laura Ingalls, Beatrice Brown, Catherine V. Brown, Waters, Van Hyning, Mary Leach, Grace Keefe, Baldwin, Blanche Winters, Josephine Mahler, Ethel Groen, Lucinda Benge, Frieda Stanley, Ella Monreal, Opalma Montagne, Lillian Parks, Bessie Burchett, Maude DeLand, Ida Mae Cooper, Marguerite Morrison, Charlotte Aycrigg, Kathleen Norris, Francis Sherrill, Lois de Lafayette Washburn, and Leslie Fry. None of the files included much on the women's personal lives, and the FBI ceased tracking them after World War II. The FBI report on Father Charles E. Coughlin and the ten thousand-page file on Smith were useful, however. In addition, the State Department, Defense Department, Army Intelligence, and Navy Intelligence made available their collections on the mothers' movement.

Court documents were among the more useful primary sources. Transcripts of the sedition trial, *United States vs. McWilliams* (originally *United States vs. Winrod*), at the Washington National Records Center, Suitland, Maryland, are voluminous. For profiles of the judge who presided over the trial, see "Eicher, Edward Clayton," *Biographical Directory of the American Congress, 1774–1971* (Washington, D.C.: Government Printing Office, 1971); "Eicher, Edward Clayton," *Current Biography,* 1941, p. 256; and Eicher's obituary in the *New York Times,* December 1, 1944.

The transcripts of *Elizabeth Dilling vs. the Billboard Publishing Company, et al.,* found in the Dilling papers, have a biographical summary of Dilling's career. Transcripts of the lawsuits dealing with Dilling's divorce, also in the Dilling papers, lend insight into her personal life.

Articles about the mothers' movement appeared in the *Chicago Tribune,* the *New York Times,* and the *Washington Post.* The *Detroit Free Press,* the *Milwaukee Journal,* the *Los Angeles Times,* the *Los Angeles Herald-Express,* and the Cleveland *Plain Dealer* covered local organizations. The Washington *Times-Herald* and New York *PM* reported on the sedition trial. Contemporary magazine articles included Patricia Lochridge, "The Mother Racket," *Woman's Home Companion* 71 (July 1944), 20–1, 72–3; Russell Whelan and Thomas M. Johnson, "The Menace of the 'Mothers',", *Liberty* 1 (July 26, 1944), 18–9, 72–3; John Roy Carlson (pseudonym for Avedis Derounian), "They Praise the Lord and Pass the Poison Leaflets," *The Woman with Woman's Digest* (October 1944), 9–13; Carlson, "Daughters of Dissension and Defeat," *The Woman with Woman's Digest* (November 1944), 8–12; Lillian Greenwald, "Fascism in America: The Distaff Side," *Contemporary Jewish Record* 4 (1941), 616–24; Charles Dexter, "Wreckers of American Morale," *Magazine Digest* 24: 6 (July 1942), 37–44; Upton Sinclair, "Mrs. Dilling Entertains," *Common Sense* 5 (November 1936), 13–5; and H. K. Thompson, Jr., "A Survey of the Right Wing," *The Independent* 124 (August 1962), 1, 3–12.

Among investigative books that include the mothers' movement are the works of Derounian, a journalist who posed as a Nazi sympathizer to infiltrate far-right organizations: Carlson, *Under Cover* (New York: E. P. Dutton and Company, 1943), and *The Plotters* (New York: E. P. Dutton and Company, 1946). Derounian's books were sensationalized best-sellers. Other contemporary studies include George Seldes, *Witch Hunt: The Technique and Profits of Red-Baiting* (New York: Modern Age Books, 1940); Harold Lavine, *Fifth Column in America* (New York: Doubleday, Doran, and Company, Inc., 1940), primarily about the Communist Party; Michael Sayers and Albert E. Kahn, *Sabotage! The Secret War Against America* (New York: Harper and Brothers, 1942); Sayers and Kahn, *The Plot Against the Peace: A Warning to the Nation* (New York: Dial Press, 1945); E. A. Piller, *Time Bomb* (New York: Arco Publishing Company, 1945); and Henry Hoke, *It's a Secret* (New York: Reynal and Hitchcock, 1946). Hoke includes detailed information about the indictments leading to the mass sedition trial.

Maximilian St. George and Lawrence Dennis describe the trial from the defense viewpoint in *A Trial on Trial: The Great Sedition Trial of 1944* (N.p.: National Civil Rights Committee, 1946). Former Attorney General Francis Biddle gives his perspective in *In Brief Authority* (Garden City, N.Y.: Doubleday and Company, Inc. 1946). O. John Rogge gives his views in *The Official German Report: Nazi Penetration 1924–1942: Pan-Arabism 1939–Today* (New York: Thomas Yoseloff, 1961).

Unpublished Papers, Dissertations, and Theses

The most helpful unpublished source, and the only extended scholarly treatment of the mothers' movement, is Laura M. McEnaney, "Defending the Family Altar: Gender, Race, and Family Politics in the America First Movement, 1940–1945," M.A. thesis, University of Wisconsin—Madison, 1990. McEnaney emphasizes the connections between the isolationism of ultraright women and their religious, gender, and family values.

Two of my students wrote studies of Dilling and Curtis: Stasia Von Zwisler, "Elizabeth Dilling and the Rose-Colored Spy Glass," M.A. thesis, University of Wisconsin—Milwaukee, 1986; and Kari A. Frederickson, "Voices on the Right: Cathrine Curtis and the Women Against World War II," unpublished paper, December 1991.

Among the more useful Ph.D. dissertations are William Cecil Rogers, "Isolationist Propaganda, September 1, 1939 to December 7, 1941," University of Chicago, 1943; William C. Baum, "The Conspiracy Theory of the Radical Right in the United States," State University of Iowa, 1960; Ira Sherman Rohter, "Radical Rightists: An Empirical Study," Michigan State University, 1967; Gary Bernard Rush, "Status Crystallization and Right-Wing Extremist Attitudes," University of Oregon, 1965; Eckard Vance Troy, "Ideology and Conflict in American Ultraconservatism, 1945–1960," University of Oregon, 1965; Daniel James Klotz, "Freda Utley: From Communist to anti-Communist," Yale University, 1987; George Sirgiovanni, "An Undercurrent of Suspicion: Anti-Communist and Anti-Soviet Opinion in World War II America," Rutgers University, 1988; and Evelyn Rich, "Ku Klux Klan Ideology, 1954–1988" (2 vols.), Boston University, 1988.

Unpublished works on Jeannette Rankin include Ronald Schaffer, "Jeannette Rankin, Progressive Isolationist," Ph.D. dissertation, Princeton University, 1959; John C. Board, "The Lady From Montana: Jeannette Rankin," M.A. thesis, University of Wyoming, 1969; and Ted Carlton Harris, "Jeannette Rankin: Warring Pacifist," M.A. thesis, University of Georgia, 1969. A leading women's pacifist group is the subject of Anne Marie Pois, "The Politics and Process of Organizing for Peace: The United States Section of the Women's International League for Peace and Freedom," Ph.D. dissertation, University of Colorado, 1988.

Articles on the Mothers' Movement

McEnaney, "He-Men and Christian Mothers," *Diplomatic History,* 18:1 (winter 1994), 47–57, is one of the few scholarly articles on the mothers' movement. Also see Glen

Jeansonne, "Furies: Women Isolationists in the Era of FDR," *Journal of History and Politics*, 8 (1990), 67–96, and Jeansonne, "Gerald L. K. Smith's Shattered Alliances," ibid., 41–66. Several of my articles on aspects of the far right contain relevant material, including "Preacher, Populist, Propagandist: Gerald L. K. Smith," *Biography*, 2:4 (fall 1979), 303–27; "Huey P. Long, Leander H. Perez, and Gerald L. K. Smith as Charismatic Leaders," *Louisiana History*, 35:1 (winter 1994), 5–21; and "Personality, Biography and Psychobiography," *Biography*, 14:3 (summer 1991), 243–55.

Women

Many books about women and feminism were used to help place the mothers' movement in a variety of contexts. None included specific information on the ultraright women isolationists of the 1930s. Andrea Dworkin, *Right-Wing Women* (New York: G. P. Putnam's Sons, 1983); and Rebecca E. Klatch, *Women of the New Right* (Philadelphia: Temple University Press, 1987), discuss right-wing women of the 1970s and the 1980s. Shirley Rogers Radl, *The Invisible Woman: Target of the Religious New Right* (New York: Delacorte Press, 1983), attacks the religious right for its views on working women. The differences between feminists and partisans of the New Right over gender issues are examined in Pamela J. Conover and Virginia Gray, *Feminism and the New Right: Conflict Over the American Family* (New York: Praeger, 1984). Carol Felsenthal, *The Sweetheart of the Silent Majority: The Biography of Phyllis Schlafly* (Garden City, N.Y.: Doubleday and Company, 1981), is a sympathetic study of a leading conservative woman in the post–World War II era.

Kathleen Blee, *Women of the Klan: Racism and Gender in the 1920s* (Berkeley: University of California Press, 1991), and Nancy MacLean, *Behind the Mask of Chivalry: The Making of the Second Ku Klux Klan* (New York: Oxford University Press, 1994) are valuable for their discussions of women's participation in the Ku Klux Klan in the 1920s. It should be noted, however, that the Klan of that time has no direct relevance to my study of the mothers. Perhaps most important, there is no evidence that any of the women prominent in the mothers' movement belonged to the Klan in the 1920s. Moreover, there are significant differences between the groups. Women who joined the Klan became members of a gender-integrated, male-led (although some women operated as leaders under the KKK rubric), anti-Catholic organization; women who joined the mothers became members of a female-dominated movement that had large numbers of Catholics. Also, Klan women were not chiefly concerned with foreign policy and did not produce an outpouring of widely read books, pamphlets, and magazines—quite unlike the mothers. Nor was there a significant mass of women isolationists in the South, a region that was fertile Klan territory (as opposed to the Midwest, where the mothers and the KKK had a solid base). Finally, the Klan of the 1920s operated and flourished in a politically conservative environment, but the mothers lived in an America led by hated political liberals and New Dealers.

Books dealing with women during World War II include Philip Wylie, *Generation of Vipers* (New York: Rinehart and Company, 1942); Susan Ware, *Women in the New Deal* (Cambridge, Mass.: Harvard University Press, 1981); Ware, *Holding Their Own: American Women in the 1930s* (Boston: Twayne Publishers, 1982); Susan M. Hartmann, *American Women in the 1940s: The Home Front and Beyond* (Boston: Twayne Publishers, 1982); Lois Scharf and Joan M. Jensen, eds., *Decades of Discontent: The*

Women's Movement, 1920–1940 (Westport, Conn.: Greenwood Press, 1983); Maureen Honey, *Creating Rosie the Riveter: Class, Gender, and Propaganda During World War II* (Amherst: University of Massachusetts Press, 1984); Sherna Berger Gluck, *Rosie the Riveter Revisited* (New York: New American Library, 1987). D'Ann Campbell, *Women at War With America: Private Lives in a Patriotic Era* (Cambridge, Mass.: Harvard University Press, 1984), analyzes the contributions and the frustrations of women in the military and on the home front.

Other accounts of women in World War II are Doris Weatherford, *American Women and World War II* (New York: Facts On File, 1990); Russell Birdwell, *Women in Battle Dress* (New York: The Fine Editions Press, 1942); and Margaret Culkin Banning, *Women For Defense* (New York: Duell, Sloan, and Pearce, 1942). Judy Barrett Litoff and David C. Smith, *"Since You Went Away": World War II Letters From American Women on the Home Front,* (New York: Oxford University Press, 1991), is a compilation of letters from women whose husbands, sons, and friends were in the armed services. Studs Terkel, *"The Good War": An Oral History of World War Two* (New York: Pantheon Books, 1984), consists of interviews with men and women. Penny Summerfield, *Women Workers in the Second World War: Production and Patriarchy in Conflict* (London: Croom Helm, 1984), describes women workers in Britain.

Sketches of women in Congress during the period appear in Annabel Paxton, *Women in Congress* (Richmond, Va.: The Dietz Press, Inc., 1945); and Hope Chamberlin, *A Minority of Members: Women in the U.S. Congress* (New York: Praeger Publishers, 1973). Rudolf Engelbarts, *Women in the United States Congress, 1917–1972: Their Accomplishments; with Bibliographies* (Littleton, Colo.: Libraries Unlimited, Inc., 1974), is an excellent bibliographical source.

Rankin is the subject of Hannah Josephson, *Jeannette Rankin: First Lady in Congress* (New York: Bobbs-Merrill Company, Inc., 1974), and of Kevin S. Giles, *Flight of the Dove: The Story of Jeannette Rankin* (Beaverton, Ore.: The Touchstone Press, 1980). Articles on Rankin include Joan Hoff Wilson, " 'Peace is a Woman's Job . . . ' Jeannette Rankin and American Foreign Policy: The Origins of Her Pacifism," *Montana: The Magazine of Western History,* 30:1 (January 1980), 28–41; Hoff Wilson, " 'Peace is a Woman's Job . . . ' Jeannette Rankin and American Foreign Policy: Her Lifework as a Pacifist," *Montana: The Magazine of Western History,* 30:2 (April 1980), 39–53; and Ernestine Evans, "Woman Against War," *Scribner's Commentator,* 11:1 (November 1941), 27–30; and John C. Board, "Lady From Montana," *Montana: The Magazine of Western History,* 17:3 (summer 1967), 3–17.

Among studies dealing with the philosophical issue of women and war are Jean Bethke Elshtain, *Women and War* (New York: Basic Books, 1987); Betty A. Reardon, *Sexism and the War System* (New York: Teachers College, Columbia University, 1985); Leila Rupp, *Mobilizing Women for War: German and American Propaganda, 1939–1945* (Princeton N.J.: Princeton University Press, 1978); Carol R. Berkin and Clara M. Lovett, eds., *Women, War, and Revolution* (New York: Holmes and Meier, Publishers, Inc., 1980); Miriam Cooke and Angela Woollacott, *Gendering War Talk* (Princeton: Princeton University Press, 1993); and Pam McAllister, ed., *Reweaving the Web of Life: Feminism and Nonviolence* (Philadelphia: New Society Publishers, 1982). Catherine Marshall, C. K. Ogden, and Mary Sargant Florence, *Militarism Versus Feminism: Writing on Women and War,* ed. by Margaret Kamester and Jo Vellacott (London: Virago Press, 1987; originally published in 1915), is an attempt by British feminists who opposed

World War I to link war with the oppression of women. Shelley Saywell, *Women in War* (New York: Viking, 1985), describes the roles of women in several countries in World War II and later conflicts. For a comparative context, see Claudia Koonz, *Mothers in the Fatherland: Women, the Family and Nazi Politics* (New York: St. Martin's Press, 1987). The movement Koonz describes was quite different from the mothers' movement. First, Nazi women supported their government and its war-making, although the women isolationists in the United States were dissenters who opposed their own country's participation in the war. Second, the Nazi women were to some extent tools of the government, whereas the American women were hostile to their own government. Third, German women operated in a nation where reactionary ideology was the status quo, and the American isolationist women functioned in a nation dominated by liberalism. Further, the free-speech guarantee that permitted women such as Dilling to criticize Roosevelt did not exist in Germany.

Among useful articles on the issue of women and war are Judith Hicks Stiehm, "The Protected, the Protector, the Defender," *Women's Studies International Forum*, 5:3–4 (1982), 367–76; Nancy Huston, "Tales of War and Tears of Women," *Women's Studies International Forum*, 5:3–4 (1982), 271–82; Hartmann, "Women's Organizations During World War II: The Interaction of Class, Race, and Feminism," in *Woman's Being, Woman's Place*, ed. by Mary Kelly (Boston: G. K. Hall and Co., 1979), 313–28; and Berit As, "A Materialistic View of Men's and Women's Attitudes Towards War," *Women's Studies International Forum*, 5:3–4 (1982), 355–64.

Although right-wing women's peace movements are rare, several studies trace the development of women in pacifist organizations and liberal peace movements. The most complete is Harriet Hyman Alonso, *Peace as a Women's Issue: A History of the U.S. Movement for World Peace and Women's Rights* (Syracuse, N.Y.: Syracuse University Press, 1993). Alonso's earlier work, *The Women's Peace Union and the Outlawry of War, 1921–1942* (Knoxville: University of Tennessee Press, 1989), is also useful. Carrie Foster, *The Women and the Warriors: The U.S. Section of the Women's International League for Peace and Freedom, 1915–1946* (Syracuse: Syracuse University Press, 1995), is the study of an important women's peace organization. Simona Sharoni, *Gender and the Israeli-Palestinian Conflict: The Politics of Women's Resistance* (Syracuse: Syracuse University Press, 1994), is a pathbreaking work. Margaret Hope Bacon, *One Woman's Passion for Peace and Freedom: The Life of Mildred Scott Olmsted* (Syracuse: Syracuse University Press, 1993), is a profile of the public and private life of a leading peace reformer. Judith Porter Adams, *Peacework: Oral Histories of Women Peace Activists* (Boston: Twayne Publishers, 1991), includes interviews with peace activists. Edward P. Crapol, *Women and American Foreign Policy: Lobbyists, Critics, and Insiders* (2nd ed., Wilmington, Del.: Scholarly Resources, 1992), is of related interest.

Works in the growing field of peace studies, a field that includes women activists, include Charles DeBenedetti, *The Peace Reform in American History* (Bloomington: Indiana University Press, 1980); John Chambers, *The Eagle and the Dove: The American Peace Movement and U.S. Foreign Policy, 1900–1922* (Syracuse: Syracuse University Press, 1991); John Lofland, *Polite Protesters: The American Peace Movement of the 1980s* (Syracuse: Syracuse University Press, 1993); DeBenedetti, *An American Ordeal: The Antiwar Movement of the Vietnam Era* (Syracuse: Syracuse University Press, 1989); Melvin Small and William D. Hoover, eds., *Give Peace a Chance: Exploring the Vietnam Antiwar Movement* (Syracuse: Syracuse University Press, 1992); Mark Hussey, ed.,

Virginia Woolf and War: Fiction, Reality, and Myth (Syracuse: Syracuse University Press, 1991); Michael True, *An Energy Field More Intense Than War: The Nonviolent Tradition and American Literature* (Syracuse: Syracuse University Press, 1995).

Among studies that consider aspects of female distinctiveness in peace and reform movements are Sara Ruddick, *Maternal Thinking: Toward a Politics of Peace* (Boston: Beacon Press, 1987), a philosophical approach to war and maternalism; Seth Koven and Sonya Michel, eds., *Mothers of a New World: Maternalist Politics and the Origins of Welfare States* (New York: Routledge, 1993); and Robyn Muncy, *Creating a Female Dominion in American Reform: 1890–1935* (New York: Oxford University Press, 1991). Maxine L. Margolis, *Mothers and Such: Views of American Women and Why They Changed* (Berkeley: University of California Press, 1984), illustrates the evolution of views on motherhood and homemaking. Mary P. Ryan, *Womanhood in America: From Colonial Times to the Present* (New York: New Viewpoints, 1975), also traces changing roles for women. Women who worked at home and away from home, as well as the image of women's work, are described in Glenna Matthews, *"Just a Housewife": The Rise and Fall of Domesticity in America* (New York: Oxford University Press, 1987); and Alice Kessler-Harris, *Out to Work: A History of Wage-Earning Women in the United States* (New York: Oxford University Press, 1982).

Carol Gilligan, *In a Different Voice: Psychological Theory and Women's Development* (Cambridge: Harvard University Press, 1982), attributes to women an approach to conflict resolution derived from their experiences. Edith S. Gomberg and Violet Franks, *Gender and Disordered Behavior* (New York: Brunner/Mazel Publishers, 1979), analyzes gender differences in personality disorders. Research on such differences is tentative and preliminary. Jean Baker Miller, *Toward a New Psychology of Women* (Boston: Beacon Press, 1986), analyzes the effects of socially imposed gender roles. Janet Saltzman Chafetz and Anthony Dworkin, *Female Revolt: Women's Movements in Worldwide and Historical Perspective* (Totowa, N.J.: Littlefield, Adams, and Company, 1986), evaluates the conditions in which women's protest movements develop, traces the history of women in dissenting movements, and shows how a consciousness of gender oppression developed. It presents a theoretical framework for understanding women's movements. Gerda Lerner, *The Creation of Patriarchy* (New York: Oxford University Press, 1986), describes the worldwide development of patriarchy over many centuries. Nancy Cott, *The Grounding of Modern Feminism* (New Haven, Conn.: Yale University Press, 1987), shows how feminism emerged from women's reform movements in the early decades of the twentieth century.

Two classics that provide an intellectual framework for later feminists are Betty Friedan, *The Feminine Mystique* (New York: W. W. Norton & Company, 1963); and Simone de Beauvoir, *The Second Sex* (New York: Vintage Books, 1952). Also useful in understanding feminism are Caroline Bird, *Born Female* (New York: Pocket Books, 1975); Hester Eisenstein, *Contemporary Feminist Thought* (Boston: G. K. Hall and Co., 1983); Kate Millet, *Sexual Politics* (New York: Ballantine Books, 1970); Germaine Greer, *The Female Eunuch* (New York: McGraw-Hill Book Company, 1971); Greer, *Sex and Destiny: The Politics of Human Fertility* (New York: Harper & Row, 1984); Kirsten Amundsen, *The Silenced Majority* (Englewood Cliffs, N.J.: Prentice-Hall, Inc., 1971); Lerner's essay collection, *The Majority Finds Its Past: Placing Women in History* (New York: Oxford University Press, 1979); and Glenda Riley, *Inventing the American Woman: A Perspective on Women's History* (Arlington Heights, Ill.: Harlan Davidson,

Inc., 1986). Myra Marx Ferree and Beth B. Hess, *Controversy and Coalition: The New Feminist Movement* (Boston: Twayne Publishers, 1985), shows how the centrifugal forces of the 1910s and 1920s, which Cott describes, grew with the second wave of feminism. Linda Gordon, *Woman's Body, Woman's Right: Birth Control in America* (rev. ed., New York: Penguin Books, 1990), traces the history of a crucial issue in women's history and feminism.

Among general histories of women in the United States, most useful were Sara Evans, *Born for Liberty: A History of Women in America* (New York: The Free Press, 1989); William H. Chafe, *The Paradox of Change: American Women in the 20th Century* (New York: Oxford University Press, 1991); Chafe's book of essays, *Women and Equality: Changing Patterns in American Culture* (New York: Oxford University Press, 1977); and the readings in Ware, *Modern American Women: A Documentary History* (Chicago: The Dorsey Press, 1989).

For understanding the era from the awakening of feminist consciousness to the rise of the mothers' movement, some of the more useful works are Dorothy M. Brown, *American Women in the 1920s: Setting a Course* (Boston: Twayne Publishers, 1987); J. Stanley Lemons, *The Woman Citizen: Social Feminism in the 1920s* (Charlottesville: University Press of Virginia, 1973); and Scharf and Jensen, eds., *Decades of Discontent*. The best study of women in the New Deal is Ware, *Beyond Suffrage: Women in the New Deal* (Cambridge: Harvard University Press, 1981). The period of ferment before the second wave of feminism that followed publication of Friedan's *The Feminine Mystique* is analyzed in Eugenia Kaledin, *American Women in the 1950s: Mothers and More* (Boston: Twayne Publishers, 1984). The relationship of motherhood to the controversy over abortion, a more recent issue, is examined in Kristin Luker, *Abortion and the Politics of Motherhood* (Berkeley: University of California Press, 1987).

The Right

Many studies have been devoted to the far right. Smith's career is covered in Jeansonne, *Gerald L. K. Smith: Minister of Hate* (New Haven: Yale University Press, 1988), and Leo P. Ribuffo, *The Old Christian Right: The Protestant Far Right from the Great Depression to the Cold War* (Philadelphia: Temple University Press, 1983). Ribuffo also profiles the careers of ultrarightists Gerald B. Winrod and William Dudley Pelley, and has a chapter on the sedition trial. Studies on Coughlin include Alan Brinkley, *Voices of Protest: Huey Long, Father Coughlin, and the Great Depression* (New York: Alfred A. Knopf, 1982); Charles J. Tull, *Father Coughlin and the New Deal* (Syracuse: Syracuse University Press, 1965); and Sheldon Marcus, *Father Coughlin: The Tumultuous Life of the Priest of the Little Flower* (Boston: Little, Brown, 1973). Louisiana Sen. Huey P. Long, a major opponent of FDR, is described in Brinkley and in Jeansonne, *Messiah of the Masses: Huey P. Long and the Great Depression* (New York: HarperCollins, 1993); William Ivy Hair, *The Kingfish and His Realm: The Life and Times of Huey P. Long* (Baton Rouge: Louisiana State University Press, 1991); and T. Harry Williams, *Huey Long* (New York: Alfred A. Knopf, 1969). A contemporary who helped Long and later became a racist political boss with numerous allies on the far right is the subject of Jeansonne, *Leander Perez: Boss of the Delta* (Baton Rouge: Louisiana State University Press, 1977). Neil M. Johnson, *George Sylvester Viereck: German-American Propagan-*

dist (Urbana: University of Illinois Press, 1972), describes the career of another figure associated with the extreme right.

The German-American Bund and similar groups are described in Charles Higham, *American Swastika: The Shocking Story of Nazi Collaborators in Our Midst From 1933 to the Present Day* (Garden City, N.Y.: Doubleday and Company, Inc., 1985); Susan Canedy, *America's Nazis: A Democratic Dilemma; A History of the German-American Bund* (Menlo Park, Calif.: Markgraf Publications Group, 1990); and Curt Riess, *The Nazis Go Underground* (Garden City, N.Y.: Doubleday and Company, 1944).

Analyses of subversion and conspiracy theories are found in Nathaniel Weyl, *Treason: The Story of Disloyalty and Betrayal in American History* (Washington, D.C.: Public Affairs Press, 1950), which has data on Waters, Curtis, Dilling, Washburn, and Ingalls; Geoffrey S. Smith, *To Save a Nation: American Extremism, The New Deal, and the Coming of World War II* (rev. ed., Chicago: I. R. Dee, Publishers, 1992); Ralph Lord Roy, *Apostles of Discord: A Study of Organized Bigotry and Disruption on the Fringes of Protestantism* (Boston: Beacon Press, 1953); Ronald Radosh, *Prophets on the Right: Profiles of Conservative Critics of American Globalism* (New York: Simon and Schuster, 1975); David Brion Davis, ed., *The Fear of Conspiracy* (Ithaca, N.Y.: Cornell University Press, 1971); Morris Kominsky, *The Hoaxers: Plain Liars, Fancy Liars, and Damned Liars* (Boston: Brandon Press, 1970); George Johnson, *Architects of Fear: Conspiracy Theories and Paranoia in American Politics* (Los Angeles: Jeremy P. Tarcher, Inc., 1983); David H. Bennett, *The Party of Fear: From Nativist Movements to the New Right in American History* (Chapel Hill: University of North Carolina Press, 1988); and Seymour Martin Lipset and Earl Raab, *The Politics of Unreason: Right-Wing Extremism in America, 1790–1970* (New York: Harper and Row, 1970). George Thayer, *The Farther Shores of Politics: The American Political Fringe Today* (New York: Simon and Schuster, 1968), includes chapters analyzing groups on the far right and the far left.

Other books tracing the history of the far right include Arnold Forster and Benjamin R. Epstein, *The Trouble-Makers* (Garden City, N.Y.: Doubleday and Company, Inc., 1952); Forster and Epstein, *Cross-Currents* (Garden City, N.Y.: Doubleday and Company, Inc., 1956); and Forster and Epstein, *Danger on the Right* (New York: Random House, 1964). The studies by Forster and Epstein, who were employed by the Anti-Defamation League of B'nai B'rith, focus on extreme right groups that espoused anti-Semitism. Additional works include Harry Overstreet and Bonaro Overstreet, *The Strange Tactics of Extremism* (New York: Norton, 1964); Mike Newberry, *The Yahoos* (New York: Marzani and Munsell, 1964); Samuel Stouffer, *Communism, Conformity, and Civil Liberties* (New York: Doubleday, 1955); M. J. Heale, *American Anticommunism: Combating the Enemy Within, 1830–1970* (Baltimore: Johns Hopkins University Press, 1990); and Michael W. Miles, *The Odyssey of the American Right* (New York: Oxford University Press, 1980).

Useful in understanding the mentality of the ultraright are Richard Hofstadter, *Anti-Intellectualism in American Life* (New York: Vintage Books, 1963); Hofstadter, *The Paranoid Style in American Politics and Other Essays* (New York: Alfred A. Knopf, 1965); Daniel Bell, ed., *The Radical Right: The New American Right Expanded and Updated* (Garden City, N.Y.: Doubleday and Co., 1963); T. W. Adorno, et al., *The Authoritarian Personality* (New York: Harper & Bros., 1950); Hadley Cantril, *The Psychology of Mass Movements* (New York: John Wiley and Sons, 1941); Gustavus Myers, *History of Bigotry in the United States* (New York: Capricorn Books, 1960); Milton Rokeach, *The Open and Closed Mind* (New York: Basic Books, 1960); Erich Fromm, *Escape From Freedom* (New York: Avon Books, 1941); Harold D. Lasswell, *Power and Personality* (New York: W. W. Norton and Company, 1948); David Shapiro, *Neurotic Styles* (New York: Basic Books, 1965); Anthony Storr, *Human Aggression* (New York: Atheneum, 1968); and Eric Hoffer, *The True Believer* (New York: Harper & Row, 1966).

The *American Historical Review,* 99:2 (April 1994), has a forum on the history of American conservatism, including essays by Brinkley, Susan M. Yohn, and Ribuffo. The forum helps define the right in historical context and offers commentary on historians' treatment of the right. The footnotes offer a wealth of sources on the right.

Anti-Semitism

There is a large body of work on prejudice and anti-Semitism. Gordon Allport, *The Nature of Prejudice* (Reading, Mass.: Addison-Wesley Publishing Company, Inc., 25th anniversary edition, 1980), is a superb analysis. Useful, although dated, is Melvin M. Tumin, *An Inventory and Appraisal of Research on American Anti-Semitism,* (New York: Freedom Books, 1961). Older works that remain useful include Carey McWilliams, *A Mask for Privilege: Anti-Semitism in American Life* (Boston: Little, Brown, 1948); and Oscar Handlin, *Race and Nationality in American Life* (Boston: Little, Brown, 1957). The works of the influential racist writer Madison Grant offer insights into the development of anti-Semitism in the United States. These include *The Passing of the Great Race, or The Racial Basis of European History* (New York: Charles Scribner's Sons, 1923); and *The Expansion of Races in America* (New York: Charles Scribner's Sons, 1933).

Frederic Cople Jaher, *A Scapegoat in the New Wilderness:* The *Origins and Rise of Anti-Semitism in America* (Cambridge: Harvard University Press, 1994), traces anti-Semitism from its origins in the ancient world to its pronounced outbreaks in the United States during the Civil War. Leonard Dinnerstein, *Anti-Semitism in America* (New York: Oxford University Press, 1994), is a careful, thorough study.

Additional works on the Jewish experience in America, particularly anti-Semitism, are Stephen D. Isaacs, *Jews and American Politics* (Garden City, N.Y.: Doubleday and Company, Inc., 1974); John Higham, *Send These to Me: Jews and Other Immigrants in Urban America* (New York: Atheneum, 1975); Michael N. Dobrowski, *The Tarnished Dream: The Basis of American Anti-Semitism* (Westport: Greenwood Press, 1979); Ernest Volkman, *A Legacy of Hate: Anti-Semitism in America* (New York: Franklin Watts, 1982); Forster and Epstein, *The New Anti-Semitism* (New York: McGraw-Hill Book Company, 1974); Nathan Perlmutter and Ruth Ann Perlmutter, *The Real Anti-Semitism in America* (New York: Arbor House, 1982); Harold E. Quinley and Charles Y. Glock, *Anti-Semitism in America* (New York: The Free Press, 1979); Weyl, *The Jew in American Politics* (New Rochelle, N.Y.: Arlington House, 1968); Gertrude J. Selznick and Stephen Steinberg, *The Tenacity of Prejudice: Anti-Semitism in Contemporary America* (New York: Harper and Row, 1969); and David A. Gerber, ed., *Anti-Semitism in American History* (Urbana and Chicago: University of Illinois Press, 1986).

More general studies that deal with anti-Semitism include the analysis of the psychoanalyst Sigmund Freud, *Moses and Monotheism* (New York: Vintage Books, 1939). Other important works include Fred Gladstone Bratton, *The Crime of Christendom:*

The Theological Sources of Christian Anti-Semitism (Boston: Beacon Press, 1969); Norman Cohn, Warrant for Genocide: The Myth of the Jewish World-Conspiracy and the Protocols of Zion (New York: Harper and Row, 1967); Franklin H. Littel, The Crucifixion of the Jews (New York: Harper and Row, 1975); Jules Isaac, The Teaching of Contempt (New York: Holt, Rinehart and Winston, 1964); Dagobert D. Runes, The Jew and the Cross (New York: Philosophical Library, 1965); Rosemary Ruether, Faith and Fratricide: The Theological Roots of Anti-Semitism (New York: Seabury Press, 1974); Ernest A. Rappaport, Anti-Judaism: A Psychohistory (Chicago: Perspective Press, 1975); Paul E. Grosser and Edwin G. Halperin, The Causes and Effects of Anti-Semitism: The Dimensions of a Prejudice (New York: Philosophical Library, 1978); Malcolm Hay, The Roots of Christian Anti-Semitism (New York: Anti-Defamation League of B'nai B'rith, 1981); and Leon Poliakov, The History of Anti-Semitism (New York: Shocken Books, 1974).

Among the more recent studies that are helpful are Theodore Isaac Rubin, Anti-Semitism: A Disease of the Mind (New York: Continuum, 1990); Bernard Lewis, Semites and Anti-Semites (New York: W. W. Norton and Company, 1986); and Shmuel Almog, ed., Anti-Semitism Through the Ages (New York: Pergamon Press, 1988).

Solomon Andhil Fineberg, Overcoming Anti-Semitism (New York: Harper and Brothers, 1943), is an analysis by a rabbi who was a leader in fighting American anti-Semitism in the 1930s and early 1940s.

Isolationism

The most thorough study of isolationism during the World War II era is Wayne S. Cole, Roosevelt and the Isolationists, 1932–1945 (Lincoln: University of Nebraska Press, 1983). Cole's America First: The Battle Against Intervention, 1940–1941 (Madison: University of Wisconsin Press, 1953), is an account of the most prominent antiwar organization. Other works include James C. Schneider, Should America Go to War? The Debate Over Foreign Policy in Chicago, 1939–1941 (Chapel Hill: University of North Carolina Press, 1989); Warren F. Kimball, The Most Unsordid Act: Lend-Lease, 1939–1941 (Baltimore: Johns Hopkins University Press, 1969); Waldo Heinrichs, Threshold of War: Franklin D. Roosevelt and American Entry into World War II (New York: Oxford University Press, 1988); John E. Wiltz, From Isolation to War (New York: Thomas Y. Crowell, 1968); Manfred Jonas, Isolation in America: 1935–1941 (Ithaca, N.Y.: Cornell University Press, 1966); and Ernest C. Bolt Jr., Ballots Before Bullets: The War Referendum Approach to Peace in America, 1914–1941 (Charlottesville: University Press of Virginia, 1977). On pacifism, see Charles Chatfield, For Peace and Justice: Pacifism in America, 1914–1941 (Knoxville: University of Tennessee Press, 1971).

The Roosevelts

The leaders of the mothers' movement directed much of their propaganda against Franklin and Eleanor Roosevelt. Typical of the far-right attacks on the Roosevelts is Gerald L. K. Smith, Too Much and Too Many Roosevelts (St. Louis: Christian Nationalist Crusade, 1950).

Recent books that reexamine the Roosevelt legacy include Brinkley, The End of Reform: New Deal Liberalism in Recession and War (New York: Alfred A. Knopf, 1995), and David Fromkin, In the Time of the Americans: FDR, Truman, Eisenhower, Marshall, MacArthur—The Generation That Changed America's Role in the World (New York: Alfred A. Knopf, 1995).

Insights into the foreign policies of the administration during Cordell Hull's tenure as secretary of state can be gained from Irwin F. Gellman, *Secret Affairs: Franklin Roosevelt, Cordell Hull, and Sumner Welles* (Baltimore: Johns Hopkins University Press, 1995).

Shedding new light on the first family are Doris Kearns Goodwin, *No Ordinary Time: Franklin and Eleanor Roosevelt: The Home Front in World War II* (New York: Simon and Schuster, 1994); and Geoffrey C. Ward, ed., *Closest Companion* (Boston: Houghton Mifflin, 1995), a collection of diary entries and letters from Margaret Suckley, a neighbor and personal friend of FDR.

The best biography of Eleanor Roosevelt's life before becoming first lady is Blanche Wiesen Cook's *Eleanor Roosevelt:* Vol. 1, *1884–1933* (New York: Viking, 1992), which the author intends to continue in subsequent volumes. Still useful is Joseph P. Lash, *Eleanor and Franklin: The Story of Their Relationship, Based on Eleanor Roosevelt's Private Papers* (New York: The New American Library, 1971).

Among the better works on FDR are Frank Freidel, *Franklin D. Roosevelt: A Rendezvous with Destiny* (Boston: Little, Brown and Company, 1990); Nathan Miller, *F. D. R.: An Intimate History* (New York: New American Library, 1983); James MacGregor Burns, *Roosevelt: The Lion and the Fox* (New York: Harcourt, Brace, and World, 1956), and *Roosevelt: The Soldier of Freedom, 1940–1945* (New York: Harcourt, Brace, Jovanovich, 1970); and Kenneth S. Davis, *FDR: Into the Storm, 1937–1940* (New York: Random House, 1993). Arthur Schlesinger Jr.'s important three-volume work, The *Age of Roosevelt* (Boston: Houghton Mifflin, 1957–60), does not as yet cover the war years.

General Histories of the Period

The most detailed survey of the era is Page Smith, *Redeeming the Time: A People's History of the 1920s and the New Deal* (New York: McGraw-Hill Book Company, 1987). Jeansonne, *Transformation and Reaction: America 1921–1945* (New York: Harper-Collins, 1994), emphasizes the tension between change and resistance to change, which characterized society. Other studies are David A. Shannon, *Between the Wars: America, 1919–1941* (Boston: Houghton Mifflin Company, 1979); Sean Dennis Cashman, *America in the Twenties and Thirties: The Olympian Age of Franklin Delano Roosevelt* (New York: New York University Press, 1989); and Michael Kurtz, *The Challenging of America, 1920–1945* (Arlington Heights, Ill.: Harlan Davidson, Inc., 1986).

The Home Front During World War II

Although books on American society during the war do not include specific information on the mothers' movement, they help place the movement in context. These include John Morton Blum, *V Was for Victory: Politics and American Culture During World War II* (New York: Harcourt Brace Jovanovich, 1976); Geoffrey Perrett, *Days of Sadness, Years of Triumph: The American People, 1939–1945* (Baltimore: Penguin Books, 1973); and Richard Polenberg, *War and Society: The United States, 1941–1945* (Philadelphia: J. P. Lippincott Company, 1972). Michael C. C. Adams, *The Best War Ever: America and World War II* (Baltimore: John Hopkins University Press, 1994), which covers the military and home fronts, argues that World War II was a traumatic experience for Americans. Richard M. Ketchum, *The Borrowed Years, 1938–1941* (New York: Random House, 1989), helps establish the mood of the nation on the eve of war. In the same vein are Jeffrey Hart, *From This Moment On: America in 1940* (New York: Crown Publishers, Inc., 1987); and William K. Klingaman, *1941: Our Lives in a World on the Edge* (New York: Harper and Row, 1988).

≡ INDEX ≡